P9-DNR-025

Also by Wilmarth Sheldon Lewis

COLLECTOR'S PROGRESS 1951

This is a Borzoi Book published in New York by Alfred A. Knopf

ONE MAN'S EDUCATION

WILMARTH SHELDON LEWIS

ONE MAN'S EDUCATION

ALFRED A KNOPF NEW YORK 1968

THIS IS A BORZOI BOOK
PUBLISHED BY ALFRED A. KNOPF, INC.

PUBLISHED SEPTEMBER 24, 1967
SECOND PRINTING, JANUARY 1968

Distributed by Random House, Inc.
Published simultaneously in Toronto, Canada,
by Random House of Canada Limited.
Library of Congress Catalog Card Number: 67–18624
Manufactured in the United States of America

To

OUR AUDIENCE

Ben and Betty Holden, Fritz and Laura Liebert,

Andrew and Jane Ritchie, Carl and Margaret Rollins,

Isabel and Thornton Wilder, and Annie Burr Lewis,

who listened patiently for years and years

and helped me more than I can say.

CONTENTS

CONTENTS

ILLUSTRATIONS

FOLLOWING PAGE *178*

PREFACE

Years ago my wife urged me to write this book. I made a tentative start on it but did not take it seriously until she died. Then the memory of what she wanted helped me to surmount self-consciousness and the alarm caused by John Trusler, an eighteenth-century parson, who noted in his memoirs that "laying one's life before the public is certainly running the gauntlet and subjecting oneself to the censure not only of our friends, but of the world at large."

The difficulties of writing one's life are intimidating. No one can recall all that he has seen or heard; much of what we do remember is trivial or farcical or incorrect. And of what we recover how much should we tell? You mustn't libel; you mustn't praise yourself; you mustn't run yourself down. Trollope said, "That I, or any man, should tell everything of himself, I hold to be impossible. Who could endure to own the doing of a mean thing? Who is there that has done none?" questions that sound old-fashioned today when aging novelists fling away the last veils of reticence to describe their sexual initiations and confess that as children they lied, cheated, and pulled legs off flies.

I take it that a man's education begins in the cradle and continues to the grave and that an account of it should show the material and spiritual advantages that enriched his life, what injured it, and what he admired and did not admire in people. The reader of such a work, isolated in his own experience, shares with the author the universal human odyssey.

In running the gauntlet my intention has been to show Wilmarth Lewis's education that began in Alameda, California, in 1895, to give an account of the beginnings of various enterprises in which he had an initiating hand, to record certain convictions for what they may be worth, and to offer such entertainment as biography can provide. "To me, at any rate," Cicero said in *De Senectute,* "the composition of this book has been so delightful that it has not only wiped away all the annoyances of old age, but has even made it an easy and a happy state." If I cannot go quite that far I can say that writing this book has deepened my awareness of the many blessings I have received and helped me to appraise such education as I have been able to acquire.

In addition to those mentioned on the dedication page, the following have read or heard parts of this book: John Nicholas Brown, Lee Fierro, Jacqueline Kennedy, Charles L. Lewis, Joan Lewis, Edmund W. Nash, John and D. D. Ryan, Charles Ryskamp, Lee Stone, and Edward Weeks; all of it has been read by Howland and Priscilla Auchincloss, Stanhope and Nan Bayne-Jones, Corinne Alsop Cole, Bernhard and Mary Knollenberg. These friends have made suggestions that I have followed gratefully. My special thanks are due to my secretary, Ruth Tyrrell Day, who has patiently typed every page a dozen times and made the index.

ONE MAN'S EDUCATION

I

ALAMEDA I

Wilmarth's first exposure to formal education was a failure. In 1900 at the age of four and a half he was taken by his nurse, Anna Crowe, to Miss Alice's kindergarten, which was a block and a half from the Lewises' house in Alameda. He was welcomed warmly, too warmly, by Miss Alice herself who bent over him with a terrifying smile. Anna hurried him, screaming, away. Things went better six months later when he returned, but not brilliantly: he was incapable of weaving smooth paper mats and no amount of patting made them lie flat; even recess was a failure because he had to play prisoner's base with girls of six, seven, even eight, all as big as medicine balls, who bounced and rolled over him. Two of them introduced him to the subject of sex as they chaperoned him home, whispering and giggling about Miss Alice and the janitor and treating Wilmarth as an incredible innocent. After he reported these conversations to his mother she withdrew him from Miss Alice's influence and took him herself to Mastick Grammar School where the sexes were segregated. Instead of delivering him and departing, she sat on the platform with the teacher, a comfortable woman whose clothes were no match for Mrs. Lewis's. The latter nodded and smiled encouragement to Wilmarth at his little iron desk while the rest of the class stared at her. It was his introduction to embarrassment.

Grammar school studies in California at the turn of the century were restricted for the first five years to the three R's, drawing, and singing. Reading was Wilmarth's favorite study by a long way. He began it with the *Second Reader* and the boy who cried "Wolf!" once too often. Then came the trial of strength between the sun and wind. They looked down and saw a man walking on a plain in a cloak. The stronger would get the cloak off. The wind blew and blew, but the man only wrapped the cloak tighter. Then the sun came out and beamed and beamed until the man took off his cloak. What followed the *Second Reader* I cannot recall, but I do remember a pretty young teacher who told stories about Odin and Thor and Balder alive and dead. They were not spoiled by being made into lessons; you just enjoyed them. When Wilmarth thanked the teacher for her stories she was pleased and told him that the principal had reprimanded her for wasting time on something not required by the State Board of Education. This confirmed what Wilmarth suspected, that members of the older generation were not perfect, did not know everything, and quarreled among themselves like children.

Whatever he read at school was less interesting than his reading at home. He began each morning with the text over his washstand. It was written on simulated tanbark covered with used postage stamps: "Consider the postage stamp, my son. Its usefulness in life consists in its ability to stick to one thing until it gets there. Josh Billings." As a very little boy his father read him *Bible Stories for Children* and *Ben Hur;* Anna Crowe, *Alice in Wonderland* and *Through the Looking Glass;* but he pored over the pictures in these works by himself. Like all small boys he liked violence—Bill the Lizard being kicked up the chimney, Joshua watching the walls of Jericho fall to the sound of trumpets, and later the flags, bayonets, and floundering horses at Antietam and Shiloh in his family's bound volumes of *Harper's Weekly*. However, he cried over *Black Beauty* and *Beautiful Joe* and he loved *St. Nicholas, an Illustrated Magazine for Young Folks*. Besides his subscriber's copy to it he had his brothers' earlier bound volumes. He did not read "The Practical Boy" with its hints on how to make tents and water wheels, nor was he interested in "How Some Flowers got their Names." He preferred the accounts of kings and queens and, in time, the stories of derring-do in war and sport. He would have liked to compete in the St. Nicholas League against children from all over the country, not for the prizes in photography, drawing, verse, or puzzles, but in the prose sketches on assigned subjects such as "My Feathered Friends" and "Day Dreams." Gold badges, silver badges, honorable mentions were awarded to the successful whose names, addresses, and ages were published, but his mother discouraged him from trying to make the League. She wanted, she said, to keep Wilmarth a little boy and there was no one to tell her that this was unwise.

Singing at Mastick was taught by Miss Fisher who roved from class to class, flew, rather, for Miss Fisher was more bird than mammal. Her thin brown feathery face had a sharp beak; the movement with which she popped her pitch pipe into her mouth and flipped the index finger of her other hand skyward was birdlike and so was her bright expectant expression when she gave the down beat and the nod that launched the class into song. Wilmarth once imitated Miss Fisher at home to his father's great entertainment, but when Dr. Lewis asked for an encore Mrs. Lewis intervened: Wilmarth must not be encouraged to show off.

Miss Fisher was culture and ridiculous; Miss Figg who gave private piano lessons was likewise culture, but she was never ridiculous. Wilmarth went to her on Tuesdays and Fridays after school and on Saturday mornings as well, at which time he was instructed in "Composition." He would not of course write his compositions himself, but would put his head in his hands (under orders) and think and think and then sing a phrase that Miss Figg would transcribe. In this way he once produced a "theme" that Miss Figg, who did not praise lightly, said could have been expanded into a symphony. He practiced half an hour a day on the upright piano in the Lewises' living room, half of which time had to be devoted to scales and Czerny. To make this discipline bearable he was given an hourglass, or rather, a quarter-of-an-hour glass, which he would shake to stimulate the flow of red sand. He wanted to get on to his pieces, which he supplemented with forays into *The Family Book of Music*. Handel and Beethoven were his men: he had won Miss Figg's annual prize for her best boy pupil two years running and the prizes were a photograph of Beethoven and a life of the youthful Handel. Wilmarth's first public appearance was at an evening musicale given by Miss Figg in her house. He played "Träumerai" and "Consolation." When he finished there was a burst of applause and everyone said, "Wilmarth has a lovely touch."

Miss Figg subscribed to the Puritanical taboos and restraints that held Alamedans in check, but she did not submit to the iron laws that prescribed their patterns of living, dress, and speech. She was not precious or contemptuous; she did not carry the lamp of culture in Grecian robes; but she surmounted the fear that rules circumscribed communities, the fear of not being mediocre. Miss Figg was the first nonconformist Wilmarth knew. To be with her helped him to be on his own, which is what from the first he determined to be. She was like the recurrent dream in which you open a door in your house and find a superb room that you did not know was there. Miss

Figg's music room was not superb, but in it stirred the forces of dissent, which were symbolized by dried pods, puffballs, and grasses that she gathered in the Berkeley Hills. She inserted them one by one into tall jars that she stood by the doorway where they were blundered into by the unwary and destroyed. When Miss Figg took to the hills for a fresh supply she was enlisted in the same good cause that led her pupils to Bach instead of to Ethelbert Nevin, a view of the world more ample than the one that her pupils usually found at home. She did so firmly, with an occasional shortness of temper. Wilmarth was more afraid of her than of anyone else, but he loved her and she loved him. When things went well he would prevail on her to play "The Erl-king" at the end of his lesson. The father galloped through the night clinging to his little son in terror, the Erl-king in pursuit. Miss Figg would sing, "Mein fäder! mein fäder!" and the little boy would be snatched away forever from his distracted parent.

Wilmarth's dislike of arithmetic grew slowly. The multiplication table and even long division went all right; the trouble came with wallpaper and garden beds. Worse was to follow: at the age of eighteen plane geometry reduced him privately to tears. I have wondered why he was stupid about mathematics; perhaps it was a congenital deficiency of his brain, perhaps it was an obstacle buried in his unconscious that might have been removed by sympathetic probing. His marks in drawing were even lower than in arithmetic. Oranges and bananas and highlights eluded him altogether. But one day he produced three pictures with colored crayons that at the time he believed were masterpieces and which may well have been. Aldous Huxley assures us that "up to the age of ten (provided of course that his teachers don't interfere) practically every child paints like a genius." I recall after sixty years the exaltation that these drawings produced in Wilmarth and the subjects of two of them: a castle (very brown) and a tree (very green). They were on large sheets of paper that gave the artist all the room he needed to express himself. There was no nonsense about highlights or verisimilitude. Wilmarth simply launched out on his own and drew what he felt. The results for him were extraordinarily satisfactory. They were not, however, well received at home. When he showed them there his mother smiled and looked at Anna, who simply stared; even Mrs. Anthony, his favorite neighbor across the street, smiled. After Mrs. Anthony smiled Wilmarth gave up. The grown-ups thought his beloved drawings were funny. In later years when his creative efforts were rejected Wilmarth usually saw why and was grateful to those who saved him from public failure, but he felt it was the judgment of his critics that was at fault in this first rejection and not what he offered them.

When he asked why it was necessary to study arithmetic and drawing the answer was vague and confused. Education was mysterious. Although you apparently had to have it no one seemed to know what it was. Reading was "a good thing," but not too much of it: when Wilmarth was called a bookworm he did not feel that he was being flattered. Shakespeare was a respected name, yet the adult Shakespeare Club was "literary," and "literary" was a term of contempt in the Lewis family. Years later he read in the eighteenth-century Abbé Galiani that education is learning how to endure boredom and injustice. Schooling, Galiani said, is "like the *manège,* where the horses do not trot, gallop, or walk as it suits them, but as it suits their masters. So a young man is trained and disciplined and taught to fit into the social order." This saturnine pronouncement does not interfere with the *Oxford English Dictionary*'s definition of education: "to bring up children and animals . . . the systematic instruction, schooling, or training given to the young . . . in preparation for the work of life," but it ignores the Anglo-Saxon emphasis upon the formation of character in sport and the lessons taught by the opposite sex.

At the age of eight Wilmarth wrote a story, "What Happened to Jance," which appeared in *The Arrow,* the Mastick School paper. It was inspired by a postcard that his brothers sent Wilmarth from Holland on their European trip. Jance lived on the Island of Maarken, wore wooden shoes, and had a cat, which he put on flypaper, a misdemeanor that resulted in Jance having to take his meals off the mantelpiece. When Wilmarth wrote about the cat on the flypaper he couldn't hold his pencil for laughing. Wilmarth's pleasure in the cat's discomfiture, unlike Jance's, went unpunished, perhaps because his mother regarded the incident as "only a story," perhaps because since she disliked all animals she was pleased that the cat was discomfited. No one laughed at "What Happened to Jance" as they had at Wilmarth's drawings; they laughed with it. His success determined him on his future career. He would be a writer. So when a competition was held for the business managership of *The Arrow* he went out for it. The more he learned about magazines the better. He had no idea what the manager did, but he sounded important, and important was what Wilmarth intended to be. The office was to go to the boy who brought in the most advertisements in a month. Within twenty-four hours Wilmarth had wrung eleven of them from the tradesmen his family patronized. This proved to be ten more than any other competitor secured. Wilmarth stepped forward to assume his new duties only to be told that he was too young for them and that an older boy who had brought in no advertisements would be the manager. Wilmarth's family was indignant, but he took this reasonable injustice philosophically: he had won the competition with dazzling brilliance and he had none of the bother attendant upon success. Yet the experience made him wary of business in the future.

Life, it became increasingly clear, was not ordered for his special benefit outside his own home. Not even Church was safe. "Church" was Christ Church, the Episcopal Church. Other churches existed, notably the Unitarian and the Congregational, and a new one, the Christian Science. Miss Figg was a member of the last church and so were the Lewises' next-door neighbors, the Wellmans. Miss Loveland, Mr. Wellman's sister-in-law, gave an impressive demonstration of the power of this new faith: one day in the pouring rain she sat by the Wellman's cow that had gone dry and read it *Science and Health.* The cow was benefitted. Occasionally Anna would take Wilmarth to the Baptist Church where they sat in the front row of the balcony. She gave Wilmarth a pad and pencil in case his attention wandered, but there was little danger of that, the minister was so active and loud. He discovered still another Church, the Roman Catholic, one day when he and Marie Louise Michaels, who lived next door, were taken to it by her nurse. There for the first time he saw a Crucifix and frightening pictures and images of the suffering Jesus. Mrs. Lewis said that this must never happen again.

Christ Church was reassuring on the surface. It had an imposing steeple in the American Protestant Episcopal style and stained-glass windows. At Christmas and Easter the altar was smothered in lilies and climbing roses that had been collected in wheelbarrows by the Altar Guild. On Christmas Eve the Sunday School teachers paraded up and down the aisles at the head of their flocks, bearing anchors and other early Christian symbols picked out in white roses; their star pupils carried banners with the names of California bishops lettered in gold. It was the most beautiful sight of the whole year. Wilmarth was in a class that was addressed by the rector himself, but what he looked forward to was the conclusion of the half hour when he and the rest marched round the room singing, "Onward Christian Soldiers," and each put five cents in a plate on the teacher's desk.

In this room that was dedicated to the subjugation of the old Adam Wilmarth first encountered wanton and triumphant cruelty. One morning while he was sitting on the aisle looking brightly at the arriving rector, a fellow student, an ill-favored newcomer, jabbed him hard in the thigh with a long sharp thorn. Wilmarth's pain, which was intense and which he did not conceal, was heightened by the shock of discovering that strangers can be dangerous. "Fiend" was not yet in his vocabulary, but "fiend" was the image presented to Wilmarth by his assailant whose glee become even greater when he was expelled forthwith from the class. Neither this just and condign punishment nor "Onward Christian Soldiers" restored Wilmarth's confidence in so uncertain a Sunday School and he eagerly accepted an invitation to join the Church choir.

The choir, apart from the rector's long and noisy sermons, was delightful. Dressed in cassock and cotta, Wilmarth, consulting his hymnal from time to time before raising his head in replenished song, believed himself the center of attention as he moved up the aisle behind the crucifer. He was an initiate in divine mysteries, marked off from the laity by his vestments, by his participation in ancient rites, and by his pronouncing "and" "ond." It was pleasant passing the family pew and meeting the family's eyes without acknowledgment, especially just as he was singing "ond." The choir was a professional man's world since the choristers were paid for their services. Wilmarth, whose voice soared up almost beyond the range of human audition, became the second highest paid choirboy, received fifty cents a month, and wore a silver cross.

To this ampler and lucrative life he brought the activity to which from his earliest days he had given his passionate attention, collecting. His first venture in the science, made perhaps at the age of six, was a collection of house flies; his second was shells; his third insects, any insects. Then at the age of ten he settled on stamps, noting in his album, "Mar. 31, '06. Began 300." By Feb. 1, '07 the collection had grown to 1130 stamps and was worth $180.93. The brilliant growth was due to the gift of collections formed by his brothers Azro and Charles and by a friend. Wilmarth tipped the duplicates into oblong gray-green notebooks and took them to church on payday, writing below each stamp its price in "Scott," the catalogue of stamp prices, or, rather, half the price, since Scott was inflated. Wilmarth converted all the choir except the tenor, baritone, and bass, to stamp collecting. On paydays he would bring out his notebooks and come away, month after month, with most of the choir's money. Then Mrs. Lewis let him go across the Bay to San Francisco to buy a stamp in the Hawaiian Island Provisional Government, 1893, issue. Charles told him he should specialize and that the tigers of the Straits Settlements and the quetzals of Guatemala (favorites with the unsophisticated), were merely pretty. The best stamps, Charles said, were our own and those of our new dependencies. No one could say that the Hawaiians were pretty, but the men and women they honored were more grown up than the three-year-old Alphonso XIII who appeared on the earlier Philippine and Puerto Rican stamps. The Hawaiians became invested with a radiance so bright that Wilmarth was not put off by the San Francisco dealer who instead of making him his slave, which he could easily have done, merely asked, "How much have you got this time?" In good months Wilmarth might have three dollars and sixty-five cents. The dealer would take it and hand over another stamp in the series. When Wilmarth protested feebly that he was paying more than the price in Scott the dealer said Scott didn't know everything and Wilmarth could take it or leave it. He always took the stamp and peered at it in its little jacket a dozen times on the homeward journey.

His connection with the Church ended after the choirmaster gave him a solo in the *Te Deum,* "The Cherubim and Seraphim Continually Do Cry." Even the organ was silent during this testimony. The Lewis family, whose attendance at Church had become spotty owing in part to their dislike of the new rector who put candles on the altar and preached loud and disagreeable sermons and in part to the new automobile, returned to the family pew, but their nervous and prideful smiles faded when Wilmarth's solo was reached, for he also remained silent and the seraphic conduct went unrecorded that day in Alameda. Just before church the soloist read in the San Francisco *Chronicle* about prima donnas in general and Mme Tetrazzini in particular. When she sang at Lotta's Fountain in San Francisco her high D carried as far as Fifth and Market Streets. Prima donnas, he read, were privileged persons who got their own way; they sang if they felt like it and didn't sing if they didn't feel like it, and instead of being censured for their wilfulness they were called "divine." Wilmarth's silence placed him among the prima donnas, but it was held to have been misjudged; he lost his silver cross and had his salary cut to twenty-five cents a month. The full benefit of this disciplinary action was missed by his being allowed to carry out a further Tetrazzini gesture: he left the choir for good instead of being encouraged to acknowledge his mistake and sing his way back to the silver cross, and he still lacks the 2 c. vermilion (black surcharge), 12 c. red, and 1 d. of the Hawaiian Island Provisional Government, 1893, the only series in all of Scott that is apparently worth no more today than in 1906.

Wilmarth at this time was aged ten. At Mastick his teacher

was one of the best he was ever to have, Mrs. Blood in the Upper Fifth. Hers, she explained, was the responsibility for preparing pupils to enter the enlarged life of the Grammar Grades, which began in the Lower Sixth. She did this by enforcing her rules that regulated the smallest details of deportment; had she been the choirmaster at Christ Church Wilmarth would have sung his solo. Mrs. Blood introduced him to effective discipline and he loved it. The single resort to a hairbrush at home left everyone punished except Wilmarth. More successful was the invocation of the fictitious Belle. Belle was black and she would come and take him away if he didn't behave. Belle worked until the day when Wilmarth said to go ahead and get her. The front-door bell rang and Wilmarth was told she had arrived. He, who was then older, replied, "That isn't Belle. It's only Anna. You got her to ring the doorbell," and Belle was called upon no longer.

Mrs. Blood brought Wilmarth under control for the first time in his life. He obeyed her meticulous exactions with pleasure, and when one day she made him copy an exercise three times to get it on a single page her commendation of the third draft filled him with satisfaction. He became a model pupil and received his reward. "There is a boy in this room," Mrs. Blood said one morning, "who will be famous some day." Since it was what Wilmarth himself believed he would be he looked demurely at his desk under the impression that the class was gazing at him. That he was the boy was confirmed in the following term after Mrs. Blood arranged with Miss Frost of the Lower Sixth to send Wilmarth into her room with a written message. He opened and shut the door as Mrs. Blood taught her pupils to do, delivered the message, waited respectfully for the answer, bowed and left, opening and closing the door in the same flawless manner. At recess he was told by a boy who had witnessed this performance that after the door closed Mrs.

Blood said, "That boy will be famous some day." Wilmarth was pleased but not surprised.

Everything about Mrs. Blood commanded respect: her name, her size, her age, her features (very strong), her carriage (she was lame). Wilmarth became familiar with the concept of perfectability, which is implicit in all correction and reproof. He accepted it without question, unfortunately for him and for those in his life whose imperfections from time to time he exposed, but so great a woman was Mrs. Blood that she made allowance for failure to reach her high standards. Stern she was, yet flexible when charity invoked mercy. Perfection was less odious in the Upper Fifth because Mrs. Blood knew that one aim of education is to teach how to live with imperfection, your own and other people's. Wilmarth wrote her on his own initiative at the end of the term to thank her for what she had done for him. She replied that it had been a pleasure to have him in the class and that she would follow his future career with interest.

Arrived at the Lower Sixth, he was introduced to grammar, manual training, and geography. Of these advanced subjects he much preferred geography. Grammar was only diagrams with the subject, predicate, and object marked off from each other on a line with modifiers sliding away at an angle below them. Grammar stifled interest in reading. Grammar was a bore. The saws and hammers and chisels of manual training were worse than a bore, they were dangerous, as Wilmarth proved one day by sawing into his left thumb while trying to make a Turkish tabouret. He fainted away and the tabouret was finished by the carpenter-teacher. Wilmarth gave it as a birthday present to his father who after critical examination praised it. Wilmarth let it be believed that it had been entirely the work of his own hands, his sole venture, I think, in deceit. The tabouret has disappeared, but the scar on Wilmarth's thumb survives.

As opposed to these afflictions, geography was a pleasure. It came in an oversized green book that was evidence of growing educational maturity as one carried it conspicuously to and from school. Geography pointed out that Quito is right on the equator and that Lynn, Massachusetts, makes boots and shoes. It was so realistic about volcanoes and earthquakes that when at 5:13 a.m. on Wednesday, April 18, 1906, Wilmarth was awakened by the disturbance later known locally as The Fire he recognized it at once as an earthquake.

Like all California children he had been cradled in earthquakes and took the big one in his stride until pictures, plaster, and bric-à-brac began falling around him and a chimney crashed just over his head. Then he cried out in terror. His father, lurching from his room to reach him, was floored by a bookcase that left its wall and buried him under *Alice, Ben Hur,* and *St. Nicholas.* Breakfast was held, perforce, *al fresco,* after which the neighbors, who ordinarily seldom met, inspected the damage done to each other's property. Mr. Wellman of Wellman, Peck, wholesale grocers in San Francisco, had lost his greenhouses; Mr. Michaels of Langley & Michaels, wholesale druggists in San Francisco, had suffered a more exotic accident: his full-sized Venus de Milo that stood on a landing at the top of a long flight of stairs stepped from its corner, tottered down the stairs, and dived, all unbroken, through a window in the lower hall.

School was out of the question. At ten thirty came the report, "The City's on fire!" Some said it couldn't be, but the answer to them was smoke billowing high into the northern sky. "The water mains are broken," it was reported. "They are fighting the fire with wine." Refugees—a new word to Wilmarth—began drifting along Central Avenue pushing baby carriages that contained everything but babies. Wilmarth learned other new words, "martial law" and "looting." On the second night his father and George, one of Wilmarth's much older half-brothers, took him to the edge of Alameda nearest San Francisco, four or five miles across the Bay. The City was on fire from Telegraph Hill to the Mission several miles distant. While they gazed every window in the Merchant's Exchange stood out sharply, a flame shot into the sky, and the roar and heat came over the still water.

San Francisco burned three days and three nights. The Fire became a milestone, as the wars were to become milestones. Time was measured by it. San Franciscans dated events thereafter by saying, "Before the Fire" or "After the Fire." The young who saw it, even from a safe distance, were prepared for the later disasters that created refugees round the world; burned-out cities were to be no novelty to them. The Fire stood to Wilmarth for nature on a rampage running riot in nations and individuals, including on more than one occasion in Wilmarth himself.

II

ALAMEDA II

The drive to see San Francisco burn was one of the few excursions Wilmarth made with his father. When he was older he might join Dr. Lewis on the eight o'clock commuter's train if he had an errand in the city, but that was not an excursion. On those trips he learned what popularity is. His father, a short, stocky, amply mustached man with a friendly jaunty air greeted fellow-passengers cheerily; the conductors treated him respectfully, humbler functionaries were gratified by his nod and smile. Wilmarth following in the wake of this regard checked his pride in it because his mother would want him to check it. At home Dr. Lewis was subdued. His wife spoke to him rarely and then with cold formality. There were never scenes or shows of temper, only frigidity on the one side and rueful acceptance on the other. That this estrangement was long-standing is suggested by an early entry in Dr. Lewis's diary that came to light after his death: "Miranda was nice to me today." He imparted paternal wisdom to Wilmarth's brothers when they were small and they maintained a furtive loyalty to him, but he had few chances to instruct his youngest son. Two bits of advice that he did give him were followed later: learn how to make a speech and date everything you write.

Mrs. Lewis's chief contribution to Wilmarth's schooling was with his spelling. His brother Charles couldn't spell, and because Wilmarth wanted to be like Charles in every way he needed the corrective measures that his mother undertook with firmness and skill; yet although Wilmarth was lifted above illiteracy he was never to win a spelling bee. His mother also gave him a jigsaw puzzle of the United States that he put together on her bed in the mornings, an exercise that enabled him in later life to bound Colorado and even West Virginia to the disappointment of an impressed company. Her contributions to his education lay outside its formal curriculum. She was good at exorcising evil spirits, such as the one that for a while infested "The Rockery." This was a tiny garden with small palms on an oval-shaped mound two blocks from the Lewises' house. A cement walk ran round it, up a few steps to the top, and down the other side. At one end was a drinking fountain in a yellowish shell and a horse trough. The Rockery was designed for children to scamper over with cries of pleasure, but Wilmarth as a little boy was terrified of it, so terrified that he didn't dare tell his mother it was a horror to him. Then one day he did tell her. She led him to it, encouraged him up the steps and along the top, holding his hand as she walked on the pavement below, and after that he didn't mind the Rockery.

He loved the family's house, 1625 Central Avenue, which his parents built in 1900. It had classically severe lines; gone was Victorian frippery. A feature of the street elevation was a Palladian window on the second floor above a bay window in the living room beneath. A row of windows just above the ground let light into a billiard room and suggested that the house had sunk to its lower windows owing to some subterranean weakness. The front steps rose to a porch stiff with Ionic columns that would have given status to anybody. You entered a hall too large for the dining room on the right and the living room on the left. At one end of the latter was the upright piano, at the other, a fireplace. The walls of the living room were blue; the carpet, sofa, and chairs were blue; its tone in spite of the cheerful fire was blue. Up two "hardwood" steps, very treacherous, was the unvisited library. Wilmarth's imagination enlarged these rooms to the noble proportions suitable to his family's views of its own importance.

Wilmarth would explore the closets and cupboards and drawers in the bedrooms. His mother's dresser had sweet-smelling lavender; in her jewelbox were diamonds and one ruby instead of the trash that filled the jewelboxes of his male relatives. There was a desk in a corner at which Mrs. Lewis paid her bills and wrote in the course of a year perhaps six letters with a sharp pen in a silver penholder. Much of her life was spent lying down, for she had headaches that shattered her and the rest of the household as well. The outstanding feature of his father's room was a Victorian bed with an elaborate dashboard over which Dr. Lewis would occasionally dive to end a nightmare. Wilmarth never heard these nocturnal plunges, but their effects upon his father's broad brow were evident at breakfast. As a very little boy he used to get into the enormous bed on Sunday mornings to hear the story of the wreck of the *Bay City,* a ferryboat that one day collided with another ferryboat, the *Encinal,* in the fog. The story was told in the same words each time, Wilmarth saw to that, and when the climax approached his excitement became intense. After the collision several women were thrown down on the deck and one man said, "Darn!" But Mrs. Lewis discouraged these visits and they were given up when Wilmarth was six or seven.

His half-brother George's bedroom was filled with curiosities. George was a bachelor whose room was that of a man of the world in revolt against Victorian taste. Its woodwork was painted black, the walls were covered with green burlap, a green burlap spread covered the couch, not bed, on which George slept. Two pieces of furniture had been made expressly for the room at great expense, an oak stretcher table with hearts cut at the ends and a cabinet, both painted black. On the table were early pistols and daggers. There were reminders of George's trip abroad with Azro and Charles: two plaster gargoyles, one Imp of Lincoln, half a dozen German steins, a brass samovar, and Boechlin's "Sin," a lady with nothing on but a boa constrictor. Here in a house dedicated to three good meals a day and not a speck of dust anywhere were the Middle Ages, Old Heidelberg, Russia, and Sin. (The Orient was not represented; its silks and porcelains on sale in Chinatown were for tourists.) George's library was limited to a directory of college fraternity men, a book on night life in Paris, and a copy of *Hamlet* with photographs of Sothern and Marlowe in their recent production of the play in San Francisco. Wilmarth particularly liked Mr. Sothern gazing at Yorick's skull and Miss Marlowe wearing a daisy chain and goodness knows what-all in her hair.

George, who graduated from Amherst in 1893, two years before Wilmarth was born, worked across the Bay in a San Francisco bank. He was tall, handsome, urbane. His chief contribution to Wilmarth's education was the revelation of the glamorous world to be found outside Alameda. The bright names of society and finance fell readily from his lips. So did those of the theater. The 1900s were the great days of the Road when world-famous artists came to the City and Oakland. George made Caruso and Melba as much a part of Wilmarth's daily life as were Joshua and Jezebel. With his small brother's fascinated eye upon him George might volunteer a little lecture at the dinner table on *A Doll's House* or *Patience*. The rest of the family addressed themselves to their food with a mixture of annoyance and pride, but Wilmarth stopped eating when George talked. Then one morning he discovered that these appraisals were not the distillation of George's own judgment and learning, but that of the dramatic critic on the San Francisco *Chronicle*. Wilmarth was disappointed, yet the glitter of George's world remained untarnished. It was the world in which he, Wilmarth, must live when he grew up.

Wilmarth's other half-brother, Stanley, lived in a very different world. His room was on the third floor where Anna and the "second girl" also slept. He was slight, gentle, and "sensitive" and was accordingly looked down upon by the rest of the family, especially by George, whom he adored. His placating smile and speech brought out the worst in everybody. One bold step he did take when he determined to be called Ralph, his first name, instead of Stanley, his middle name. To be R. Stanley Lewis was to be different from other men and therefore conspicuous, and conspicuous was the last thing that Ralph Stanley wished to be. The change was made, but it was years before "Stanley" did not slip out by mistake; when it did he said promptly with an apolegetic smile, "Ralph." He had inherited a little money from his mother, enough to free him from work and to enable him to go away for long intervals, once to Phoenix, Arizona, where he collected Indian baskets and had inflammatory rheumatism, once to Hayward, fourteen miles away, where he had a chicken ranch of perhaps thirty chickens, all white. He made two contributions to Wilmarth's education: he showed that people will look down on you if you are too nice, but that they will like you if you give them presents. Ralph did not confine his presents to Christmas and birthdays. One day he surprised Wilmarth with a box of agate marbles such as no other boy in Alameda had and on the Fourth of July—thc day in Wilmarth's calendar second only to Christmas—he would give him extra firecrackers. Once he contrived to scatter over a dollar in change on the lawn when he knew that Wilmarth was coming by and would find it, one nickel and dime after another, and finally a quarter. He would take his small brother to the circus, dragging him past the Bearded Lady, Snake Charmer, and Boneless Wonder into the best seats in the main tent. No money was spent on indigestible peanuts, popcorn, or pink lemonade (Ralph was preoccupied with health), but full attention was given to the flying trapeze, the clowns, and, above all, to the chariot race, the climax of which impressed upon Wilmarth the value of timing.

George and Ralph were Dr. Lewis's sons by his first marriage; Azro, Charles, and Wilmarth by his second. Azro was sixteen, Charles fifteen, and Wilmarth four when the Lewises moved into the new house on Central Avenue. Azro, who had inherited his father's short square build as well as his name, had some of his humor and his mother's good looks and questioning taciturnity. He had as little to do with Wilmarth as possible. Not so Charles, who was the only member of the family who treated its youngest member naturally. Wilmarth admired Charles so much that he also refused to eat butter and longed to wear glasses. Charles accepted this worship as his due because he was older, bigger, wiser. On the other hand, these advantages imposed upon him an obligation: "thc kid," as he alone called Wilmarth, was a spoiled brat and he, Charles, should do something about him. Opportunities for correction were never lacking. When they occurred Charles would speak what he believed was needful. Whereupon Wilmarth, who had not yet learned that tale-bearing is odious, would report this instruction to their mother. There would be a rustle of crisp skirts and Charles would be led swiftly into the room he shared with Azro. The door was closed, but Wilmarth would wait until it reopened. The crisp skirts would rustle past, their wearer pale with anger, and then emerged the flushed and impotent victim whose condition taught Wilmarth the advantages of having an overpowering ally.

The library was rewarding, not its two or three hundred books of English and American classics behind glass doors, but its window seats, which lifted up and disclosed a collection of family memorabilia and photographs. Wilmarth found one of his mother in 1864 when a solemn child of four. She was dressed in a silk hoop skirt and lace pantalettes and was standing by a workbasket on the photographer's canvas terrace. A second photograph showed her as a young lady wearing an Empress Eugénie hat with ostrich feathers, a long sealskin coat, and holding a muff in her left hand. She was tall and dark, with large eyes in a beautiful sad face. These pictures of his mother as a child and young woman made Wilmarth love even more the mother in whose lap he would sit as a little boy and around whose neck he would fling his arms in gusts of affection. She never called him anything but Wilmarth—she was too New England for endearments and demonstrations of affection—but he delighted in showing his devotion to her.

Under the window seats was also a red-plush portfolio with a broad silk red ribbon across it. Inside were photographs of Uncle Charles Lux's San Francisco house at the northwest corner of Gough and Jackson Streets. Wilmarth's mother and her younger sister were moved there by Aunt Lux, their father's sister, after their father died at an early age leaving a large and inadequately provided-for family. Uncle Charles was a cattle king who, according to Mrs. Lewis, introduced eucalyptus to California from Australia and alfalfa from Brazil. His house had crystal chandeliers and frescoed walls; Leda and the Swan and other classical subjects in marble stood in corners. There was a music room with a parquet floor and a grand piano whose legs were discreetly covered by draperies. Beethoven and Mozart were painted on the ceiling; the Aubusson carpets and the ornaments had been bought in Europe by Aunt Lux. Wilmarth's mother was sent to the Friends' School in Providence. On her return an Episcopal clergyman wanted to marry her, but instead she married at the age of twenty-two a widower of forty who lived in Westerly, R.I., a dentist, Dr. Lewis, with two young boys, George and Ralph, and an older unmarried sister who made the bride's life unpleasant. Under the window seats in the library Wilmarth also found a sheaf of newspaper clippings about the prolonged lawsuit that reduced Aunt Lux's estate. There were photographs of his mother and mention of her as an "heiress." Wilmarth found this public talk about her disturbing.

All that was a far cry from Mastick, which Wilmarth liked except for some of its studies. He even enjoyed the half-mile walk to and from it four times a day. It was a dull walk by whatever streets he went, except after the livery stable burned down one night with the loss of nearly all the horses. Many of them were got out, but they broke away from their rescuers and fought back into their burning stalls. When Wilmarth asked why had they done that when they were safe he was told that was the way horses were. The horses were not buried for days, and Wilmarth, who had not known them when they were alive, became so familiar with their remains that I can recall clearly after sixty years what was left of one called "Lion" in the farthest right-hand stall and I think of Lion when I see people rush into situations that are the equivalent of a burning stable.

School began with the boys and girls lined up by classes in their respective yards. A bell rang, the band, dominated by a cornet and drum, crashed into its march, and the High Eighth led off up the stairs. Each class as it followed eyed its juniors with quiet superiority. Wilmarth's sense of well-being during this processional was enforced by the closed door to the schoolyard and the pitiful shoes of the tardy that were visible below it. They filled him with dismay, but he was secure: he had been on time; while the band played he swung upwards and onwards into the inflammable wooden halls from which the delinquents were temporarily barred. They would have to stay after school fifteen minutes while their punctual schoolmates rollicked homewards and to carry with them when released a yellow card for their parents to sign. The sight of the shoes below the outer gate made Wilmarth compulsively punctual and has caused him to waste hours of his life waiting for other people.

Mastick was a well-behaved school except for a lawless few who were sent for their misdemeanors to the principal's office to be "belted." The only insubordination that occurred was on the rare occasions when the teacher, never Mrs. Blood, had to leave the class suddenly. The moment the door closed behind her two or three boys, but not Wilmarth, raced to the blackboards, threw chalk wildly round the room, and hammered each other with erasers. The air was filled with shouts, screams, and chalk dust. When the teacher returned, red and self-conscious, punitive measures were not taken even upon the ringleaders, who were easily identifiable from the marks of erasers upon their persons. The class resumed its disciplined course amid the shambles, more tractable for the intoxicated interlude. Wilmarth's abstention from these outbursts of independence did not mean that the old Adam in him was buried. The boys who sprang up the moment the teacher left the room were two years older than he; hefty boys who ate heartily, which Wilmarth refused to do; in fact, he hardly ate at all. The older boys were not only bigger; they were farther along the road of rebellion against the older generation. Wilmarth's mother had made it clear to him that those who were not "good" (by which she meant submissive) went to state's prison. So while the chalk and erasers flew he stayed in his seat, aghast at the lawlessness about him and loving it. Dimly he sensed that the assault was against the grown-ups and their rule.

The girls at Mastick were too young to instruct the boys even if they hadn't been segregated, the boys on one side of the room the girls on the other. A high board fence divided their yards. Boosting each other up to look over the fence was a pleasure that the boys gave themselves from time to time, not to admire, but to jeer. "The sissies" were an alien, inferior lot who skipped rope and sat on the ground playing jacks.

The boys on their side of the fence had no organized sports, but during recess marbles were played—"for keeps" by the more reckless—and when Wilmarth produced Ralph's agates they were stared at with envy. Wilmarth would gaze with awe at an older boy who would stand in front of the long privy batting a baseball, left- or right-handed with equal ease. The universal regard in which he was held introduced Wilmarth to the eminence enjoyed by an outstanding athlete. Although he and this remarkable boy had the same surname, Wilmarth could not claim kinship with him. "Duffy" Lewis went on to achieve national fame as an outfielder for the Boston Red Sox.

Wilmarth's introduction to mass struggle was mysterious and disturbing. I see now that it had cosmic significance. Every once and so often word would get around that during recess there was going to be "a war." Wilmarth never knew who decreed these wars, he only knew that there was no escape from them. The boys would divide up at either end of the yard and then rush shouting at each other. When they met they would wrestle and fight. It was Matthew Arnold's darkling plain where ignorant armies clash by night, the universal aggression that surges from the molten depths of man's darker nature. Wilmarth dreaded this trial of strength for which he was ill-equipped: he was small and thin and alone of all the boys at Mastick he wore a shirtwaist and a Windsor tie.

These sissified clothes, like his first name, which was not only a fancy one but was spelled one way and pronounced another, "Wíl-muth," might have made him a legitimate target, especially since the teachers were impressed by his elegance, yet he managed to come through the wars intact. His strategy was to appear to be seeking out the battle where it was hottest rather than to be evading it. To offset an uneasy feeling of cowardice (the heroes in *St. Nicholas* were all brave), he thought of himself as leading from the rear where he could keep an eye on his troops, a difficulty since he did not know which they were. When the battle swirled his way he would hurry to another part of the field to lend his support there or would fall flat and be counted among the slain. Only once did he assume the offensive. Approaching a boy his own size he growled and gave him a tentative push. The boy, surprised and offended, walked away with dignity and Wilmarth felt foolish and ashamed.

Yet it was by physical combat that, at the age of ten, he achieved a notable success. One day as he was skipping lightheartedly away from school a burly German boy tripped him up. Wilmarth crashed to the sidewalk, tearing a hole in the stocking of his left knee. Leaping up, he rushed at his assailant and hit out wildly. By great good luck he landed on Karl's nose, which spouted blood instantaneously and gratifyingly. Karl yelled with pain and shock and started to slouch off to report, he said, Wilmarth to the principal. Wilmarth told him, truculently, to go ahead and do it. At that Karl turned and delivered a glancing blow off Wilmarth's forehead. Wilmarth flung out his puny right fist again and landed on the same point where he had landed before. Karl's nose gushed blood and, bawling loudly, he again started across the street to the principal's office, hesitated, and slunk away. David and Goliath. Wilmarth's stocking was torn and there was a strawberry-colored bruise on his knee, but his shirtwaist and Windsor tie had come through unruffled. The exploit brought him respect, a change that he enjoyed with becoming modesty. He had learned that bullies are cowards, that surprise can be an effective weapon, and he was never to forget the delicious feeling of his fist smashing into Karl's face. Karl treated him thereafter with a slavish regard that Wilmarth received with dignity and the hope that he was concealing his dread of a second encounter.

His family also looked on him with new eyes. George said, "This is the first time we've had a pugilist in the family." Mrs. Lewis viewed the episode with mixed feelings: pride that Wilmarth had punished an attack upon him by a lout, regret that he was growing up and fear that she would "lose" him. The Fire accelerated this emancipation. A refugee family rented the house opposite the Lewises. Their youngest son, Dode Wolff, introduced Wilmarth and the neighborhood to field hockey. They played it in Central Avenue, which was wide and seldom invaded by a vehicle. Wilmarth also played "one-o'-cat" and "numbers" (forms of baseball) in a nearby vacant lot and practiced high and broad jumping.

A social grace that was forced on the gently reared was Professor Rankin's Select Dancing Class, which was held in a musty wooden building called Harmony Hall. It had one large room and two small dressing rooms on either side of the front door, one for the boys, the other for the girls. At the end of the room was a stage with a piano. Around the walls were gilt chairs for the mothers of the dancers. Wilmarth found the girls inscrutable with one notable exception, Doris. In her presence he was assailed by unaccustomed humility. He did not presume to cultivate her friendship. It was enough to know that she was there. When Professor Rankin clapped his hands and called in his elegant voice, "Now, little gentlemen, take your partners for the lancers," Wilmarth did not dare to claim Doris, and his feeling for her might never have been known had he not once said to his mother, "I like Doris best in pink," a remark that gained wide circulation and inspired Doris's mother, who was "literary," to write a story about Doris and Wilmarth which was printed in *The Sunset* and ended all possibility of their becoming friends.

A smart set emerged in the class in accordance with society's laws that determine the selection and segregation of "the best." Wonderful these rules are and mysterious. Wilmarth was later to ponder upon them and to discriminate the qualities that assure and debar acceptance, but at the time he was only aware that he had failed to satisfy them. He envied and disliked the radiant elite as they glided effortlessly about apparently unaware of the outsiders even when they were bumped into by one of them, who was not infrequently Wilmarth. That he might have moved up the social ladder is suggested by his having been picked out once by Doris and once by another of her friends, when, in the spirit of leap year, the girls chose partners, but he was too embarrassed to seize these opportunities and they were wasted. Dancing, like arithmetic, was not for him.

One other girl entered Wilmarth's life briefly, so briefly that I've forgotten her name. She was for him a star that dwelt apart, but when he told his family about her, superior looks and smiles were exchanged and "puppy-love" was said with a smile. Wilmarth didn't care, he was living for the picnic, where he would see—Emily, could it have been? It was an evening picnic, and Emily came beautifully dressed, carrying a small fan with a mother-of-pearl handle. Wilmarth borrowed the fan and then to show how manly he was he slapped it on his knee and broke it. Emily wept. Wilmarth never saw her again, but is still ashamed when he recalls breaking her fan.

The back yard of the Lewises' house had a small garden and an "orchard" of one large plum tree and five feeble cherries. The flowers were in a border around a patch of lawn that had at its center a drying yard for the laundry. Occasionally a Frenchman came with a youthful assistant to put in or take out annuals and mow the small lawn in front of the house, but the garden managed pretty much by itself. Wilmarth was at the age to get the most out of flowers—the right height, an acute nose, eyes 20–20. He met lemon verbena, heliotrope, and cosmos head on; nothing today brings back his extreme youth more sharply than heliotrope and lemon verbena. He loved the garden and after repeated requests was given a package of radish seeds and one of carrots. However, as no one showed him how to put them into the ground or what to do thereafter nothing came up. It was thus established that Wilmarth did not have a green thumb.

One set of teachers, animals, made only a slight contribution to his education. Everyone in the house disliked animals, but he was allowed to keep a semi-greyhound that attached himself to the Lewises' garbage can. Don was not permitted in the house, and a despised dog is not much of a teacher. More instructive were the Michaelses' hens next door. Wilmarth collected the eggs for the Michaelses' cook and discriminated between the hens' personalities. Although he did not anticipate the studies that led to the recognition of a pecking-order, he did note that some hens were more aggressive and noisy than others and named them for the corresponding members of the Lewises' circle. Birds, mice, fish, and cats he could not have, but after much begging he was given three rabbits. They were his, he could give them carrots and lettuce and watch them nibble and wrinkle their noses, but not on the evening of their arrival because it was his bedtime. When he hurried to them early in the morning the thin chicken wire over their box had been pulled out and the rabbits had gone—stolen, Ralph said; eaten by cats, said George. In twelve hours Wilmarth learned what joy and grief are. The rabbits were not replaced: they cost fifty cents apiece and couldn't be protected. Rabbits were not "practical."

Dancing and animals were not for him, but what was to be for him, his mother kept assuring him, was illness. He was "delicate" and must not get too tired because she had given him "a poor constitution." A dark outlook, but she proved by her use of illness that it has its points. It makes you the center of solicitous attention; it enables you to avoid doing what you don't want to do; it gives you dominion and power over the healthy. Everyone waits on the sick. The only drawback to illness is that once it has been acquired it is unpleasant and hard to get rid of.

When his mother came down with one of her headaches a conference was held in low tones in the darkened room. Should Dr. Reynolds be summoned? After it was decided that he must come, there was the wait for his arrival, an interval that called upon the patient's reserves of fortitude. Dr. Reynolds's horse clop-clopping down Central Avenue announced that relief was at hand. Wilmarth at a living-room window would watch John, the veteran coachman, draw up to the curb. Dr. Reynolds, who was the image of William H. Taft, would heave himself up and walk heavily into the house where Wilmarth would greet him. The doctor had officiated at Wilmarth's birth, a circumstance that gave the pair a sense of professional alliance. The older man's clothes were redolent of therapeutic drugs and spicy essences that heightened the all but divine mystery of a profession that has been in practice since man first caught the common cold. Wilmarth gazed up at him with love and awe, received his admonition to drink soup and milk with steely resistance, and watched the dear man climb upstairs. Before leaving his patient he would solemnly produce a pad and stylographic pen and slowly write illegible prescriptions for fresh liquids, pills, and powders that he knew, his patient knew, and Wilmarth knew would have been of no avail even if Mrs. Lewis had taken them, which the three knew that she would not do. The cause of her illness was not discovered, but it is clear now, I think, that it came from hatred of her genial uncomplicated husband.

This early instruction in the uses of illness, the mysteries of medicine, the limitations of physicians, and the malignant effects of strong emotion was and has remained a major factor in Wilmarth's education.

III

ALAMEDA III

Majestic, romantic San Francisco overwhelmed flat, pedestrian Alameda. All glamorous cities have a suburb that serves as a foil to it. What Yonkers was to New York and Jefferson City to New Orleans, Alameda was to San Francisco. One would suppose that its being an island covered with oak and maple would have saved it from ridicule, but no. Visiting vaudevillians at the Orpheum in San Francisco and Oakland who asked the name of a nearby town that would bring a sure laugh were told Alameda. They were also told Milpitas and Petaluma, which meant that the Alamedans in the audience had to suffer only once in three weeks. When the joke fell on Milpitas and Petaluma their laughter was the loudest of all.

The municipal inferiority that oppressed Alamedans, including Wilmarth, came less, I think, from its suburban respectability than from its name, which was then pronounced "Alameeda." To escape from this comical sound the higher echelons of the local society began saying "Alamayda," and the town so pronounced was no longer comical but elegant. George alone of the Lewises took up the new pronunciation, which seemed affected to the rest of the family: it was new as well as fancy and little good came from change. Nevertheless, when someone in the Bay area asked where you lived if you said "Alamayda" confidently he did not smile. "Alamayda" evoked palm-lined avenidas along which trotted hidalgos with arrogant mustaches.

Our language lacks words to denote the first two decades of a century. We don't talk about the "noughts" or the "teens," and so social historians tend to jump from the nineties of one century to the twenties of the next and to give the intervening years a name like "The Regency" or "The Federal Period." Study of Alameda from 1901 to 1920, from the Gay Nineties to the Lawless Twenties, would repay the social historian. When were the streets and gutters paved? That innovation marked the end of the watering cart with its cascading sprays that turned the dust, briefly, into mud. The Chinese fruit and vegetable peddlers, when did they cut their pigtails and stop tottering along in felt slippers with large wicker baskets swaying from a yoke balanced across their shoulders? When were the ice wagons with their dripping contents and their rear step on which boys jumped while their friends yelled at the driver, "Nip behind!" unhitched for the last time? Such recollections enable a septuagenarian to breathe a second spring. Thrift, industry, sobriety ruled in Alameda; drink, divorce, and nervous breakdowns were unknown. (There *was* one suicide, but there was one at Grover's Corners also.) And frugal Alameda had the last laugh: the number of its citizens who became extremely rich is remarkable. They built up their businesses—lumber, fruit, groceries, drugs, shipping—and when they invested their money they did so wisely. It was as simple as that.

San Francisco, "the City," cast its spell on all Alamedans, including Wilmarth. The trip across the Bay to it was an adventure from the moment that he, dressed to the nines, left home. At the Morton Street Station he could see the train far down the track hurrying towards him with screams of excitement. When it paused to pick him up it sighed with relief, exhaling pent-up steam that enveloped him in warm metallic-smelling mist as he clambered up its iron steps, clutching the hand rail with tight-fitting gloves. In fifteen minutes he was at the Mole, where the ferry was waiting, either the *Bay City* or the *Encinal.* Men traveled on the lower deck; women and children on the upper where there was no smoking. Wilmarth used to gaze fearfully into the reeking maw of the lower deck (which had a bar) as he was whisked past it and up the steps to light and air and purity. The trip across the Bay took twenty minutes. Halfway you passed Goat Island, wooded and mysterious. Sea gulls wheeled about crying impatiently for the garbage that at any moment might be ejected from the lower deck. Before you, drawing nearer and nearer, was the Ferry Building, the sentinel guarding the hills and towers of the City. The ferry-boat glided into its slip at an angle, caromed off the tall piers that staggered back with irritated squawks and came to rest. Deck hands tossed great ropes to colleagues on the dock who whipped them around stanchions, a rattling winch brought down the apron with a plop on the deck, the most agile and impatient passengers leapt upon it, and the trip across the Bay was over.

Wilmarth's visits to San Francisco as a little boy were infrequent but memorable. One was to see President McKinley ride down Van Ness Avenue. When the President passed, Wilmarth, under direction, took off his sailor hat and shouted "Hooray!" shouted it so piercingly that a man in front whirled around and said, "Shut up!" a disconcerting response to a demonstration of loyalty. The calls on Santa Claus at the City of Paris were pleasanter. Best of all were visits to the Chutes with Anna. There was no question of shooting the chutes in the boat that slid wildly down from a vast height into a pool while its occupants clung together and shrieked; there was no question of the scenic railway with its similar clutchings and shriekings. What Anna and Wilmarth did, sometimes twice, was the Flume. Rides on it cost five cents and took perhaps five minutes. You got into a rowboat and floated past scenes on the right and left that lit up as the boat, squeaking round the corners, approached them. Towards the end of the ride you glided into a tunnel. Wilmarth disliked this interlude and was puzzled by the noises of pleasure that came from the couples crouching together in the stern. The tunnel led to Hell, very red, with devils and pitchforks, and then you emerged into the final bliss of Paradise, which might have been the Santa Clara Valley with the fruit trees in bloom. Wilmarth thought of the Flume years later when he read about the River of Life and when he was punted along the Backs at Cambridge where each foot's slow advance reveals new beauties and enchantments. After Anna left him in his ninth year he was taken across the Bay to see Buffalo Bill and Annie Oakley and matinees of *Robin Hood* and *Ben Hur,* entertainments that were wonderful in their way, but not up to the Flume.

The Lewises on both sides came from Rhode Island, which remained "home" even though Wilmarth's grandfather Sheldon had gone out to California in 1850. Wilmarth's mother was born ten years later in a mining camp at Sonora. The Sheldons, like so many thousand others, went back to Roger Williams himself, a glory that rested lightly on them like a blessing. Although the Lewises descended from one of the early settlers of Westerly in the 1660s they had no pretensions to blood or quality. Wilmarth never knew his grandfather Lewis, who was born in 1786. His father, born in 1842, was a leading citizen of Westerly, active in raising funds for the new public library and Episcopal Church. He and Miranda, who was eighteen years his junior, were married in San Francisco at the Luxes' house in 1882 while Uncle Charles Lux, so Mrs. Lewis once told Wilmarth, cried all through the service. The married pair returned to Westerly and remained there until a dozen years later when Dr. Lewis became executor of Aunt Lux's estate, a large one for 1894. The family then moved to California, where in the following year Wilmarth was born in Alameda. Dr. Lewis gave up his profession on leaving the East and thereafter engaged in mining speculations that, with two modest exceptions, turned out badly. The exceptions, together with Aunt Lux's bequest to her niece Miranda, enabled the Lewises to live in comfort, according to the quiet Alameda standards. This meant, besides Anna, a cook, and "a second girl" who got all of thirty dollars a month for waiting on the table, doing the bedrooms, and dusting the entire house. The cook was frequently a Chinese with a pigtail who made presents to the family on "Chinese New Year" of narcissus bulbs set among stones in a dish; he also gave lichee nuts, and stringy candy that Wilmarth was not allowed to eat. As for Mrs. Lewis herself, when the daily ordering by telephone was over she had little domestic employment except occasional genteel darning.

Clothes were taken solemnly by the family. Clothes made the man and woman. Anything wrong with them caused suffering. "I am being crucified in a velvet hat," Mrs. Lewis confided to Wilmarth one spring morning en route to San Francisco and a vernal hat. Wilmarth's father and his brothers had two suits made for them each year by the local Mr. Olsen. (Wilmarth's own clothes were bought in a store in Oakland.) He went once or twice on their visits to Mr. Olsen, but he did not enjoy it. His brothers apparently knew more about tailoring than Mr. Olsen and treated that mild and compliant man with authority. The only feature of the shop that Wilmarth enjoyed was the framed prints of gentlemen at the opera and fashionable assemblies, but when Wilmarth asked George if men in Society really looked like that, George smiled the quick smile that made Wilmarth realize he had asked something silly.

Thanksgiving and Christmas dinners were exchanged with Aunt Emma Hall and her family in the New England tradition, but otherwise the Lewises' social life was limited. Billiards was played occasionally in the Lewises' billiard room after dinner by a club of Dr. Lewis's friends, but their visits were not welcomed by Mrs. Lewis and they gradually ceased. A bridge whist club of a dozen ladies met fortnightly during the winter at their respective houses; the winner carried off a prize, a teacup that cost five dollars. Mrs. Lewis's youngest son would await her return with anxiety and would rejoice when, as frequently happened, she brought home the teacup, which was put in a cabinet and never used. Cards were played by the family at 1625 Central Avenue in the blue living room except on Sunday. Wilmarth became a cribbage enthusiast and played to win. There was no nonsense about the game for the game's sake. Dr. Lewis, it was true, would say, "It's a good game whether you win or whether you lose," but as George would point out he said it only when he had won. Mrs. Lewis did not take part in these family games, electing instead to knit baby blankets from afar, but her attention, with averted eyes, was on the players.

The self-sufficiency of the Lewises was indicated in 1905 when they acquired their first automobile, a two-cylinder Rambler that cost $1,500. Wilmarth's introduction to automobiles had taken place four years earlier when a one-cylinder, two-seater Knox went thrashing down Central Avenue. "Don't let Wilmarth see it!" Mrs. Lewis cried out to Anna, the only time he ever heard her raise her voice. He was safe indoors when the car first appeared, but when the alarm, "Here it comes again!" was sounded he was on the sidewalk before the house. Anna, appalled, tried to shield him as he clung, screaming, at her rear. The driver was a stranger, which added to the terror, but Dr.

Lewis liked talking to strangers and on the motorist's third appearance he stepped into the street, raised his hand, and introduced himself. Then with Wilmarth on his lap they drove wildly down the block and back. Mrs. Lewis and Anna looked on aghast, but Wilmarth at the center of the whirlwind was discovering that the terrible stranger and his terrible machine were delightful as well as harmless, and after that he liked automobiles.

The Lewises' purchase of the Rambler seems somewhat out of character: in 1905 conservative people echoed the Duke of Wellington when he said of railways, "I see no reason to suppose that these machines will ever force themselves into general use." The Rambler's license number, Cal. 3530, showed that it was only the 3530th car sold in California up to that time. It had, so its salesman said, "One million dollars' worth of class," a remark that introduced the family to lyric salesmanship. The Rambler had a great deal of brass and it was green instead of black. One got into the back seat, or "tonneau," through side doors, a marked advance upon the earlier models in which the middle of the back seat was also the door to the tonneau and might open inadvertently when the car was in motion. The new Rambler, furthermore, was stripped of non-essentials such as the wicker baskets for golf clubs and umbrellas that were formerly in the corners of the tonneau.

The Lewises became passionate motorists. The males wore goggles, gauntlets, leather caps; Mrs. Lewis, a thick veil; all were in linen dusters. So dressed they rode forth on Sunday mornings carrying with them a can of gasoline as well as the picnic lunch and picnic table. Ralph and Azro were the only acceptable drivers. Over the narrow, dusty roads five of the family (that always included Wilmarth and his parents) went, cheerfully accepting the blowouts and punctures, which were dealt with in under an hour each by the uncomplaining Ralph or

Azro. The pleasures of motoring far outweighed the attendant inconveniences, especially for those who did not have to change the tires: there was the bustle of departure, the speed so much in excess of the fastest pair of horses, and, best of all, the sense of superiority to the generality in whose eyes motorists were the new aristocracy. Your rank in the motor age was revealed by your radiator. At the top of the American hierarchy were the three P's, Pierce-Arrow, Packard, and Peerless; at the bottom was the Cadillac, a risible car with only one cylinder; the Rambler, like the Lewises, was in the middle, but all motorists were lifted above the common herd, socially as well as physically. The Lewis family driving forth on Sunday morning into the country rode like Tamerlane in triumph through Persepolis; chickens raced back and forth before their wheels, horses reared up at their approach, pedestrians stared with respect and envy. Perhaps a dozen times during a Sunday outing they would meet another motor car churning towards them in its dust cloud. Its radiator would be identified by Wilmarth and its occupants accorded the degree of respect to which they were entitled. The Lewises received a raking appraisal in return and were momentarily elevated or depressed by the encounter.

The Rambler made it clear why money was deeply respected in the Lewis household. Money was more important than education, which you needed chiefly to get more money, and more important than religion because without it you couldn't have a pew of your own in church. Money provided comfort, "position" (as "status" was then called), and happiness. Money must not be vulgarized. When Wilmarth reported to his mother that one of the girls at Mastick frequently had money for candy that she placed prominently on her desk telling how much it cost, he learned that her behavior was "common," the most damning epithet in the language. Money must be husbanded, not squandered (if you did not take care of it you ended up in the poorhouse), and then when you had saved enough over and above your daily needs you could have a nice trip. Wilmarth obeyed his mother in the matter of small economies and walked great distances rather than spend five cents on a streetcar, but he noted the satisfaction that she took in her occasional sprees of buying fine linen and when in time he went on similar book sprees remembrance of her extravagance sanctioned them.

The only money he had during the year from his parents was a five-dollar gold piece in the toe of his Christmas stocking and he felt the need of a steady income. Two days before his thirteenth birthday he wrote his father:

ALAMEDA, CAL.,
Nov. 12, '08.

Dear Dad,

My birthday will soon be here and perhaps you are wondering what I would like, and as there is nothing I would like as much as an allowance from you, say two and a half a month, I think that would be a fine present.

Out of that I would buy my shoes, collars, neckties, shirts, my club dues and other small [a word omitted on turning the page] that come up.

Your affectionate son,
Wilmarth S. Lewis.

This document, which gained its object, throws light on the cost of living in 1908. The club dues show that Wilmarth accepted clubs as a necessity of life at an early age.

With the sanctity of money established in his mind at home, he was unprepared for the sacrilegious view of it presented at school one morning by the principal, a tall, thin, rather wild man with a streak of white hair in a tawny mane, features that inspired his nicknames, "Hatchet Face" and "Cotton Top." The school marched past him three times a day when he stood at the junction of the steps from the two yards, but only the delinquent met him. So his appearance in Wilmarth's classroom would have been notable if he had merely walked in and had not come, as he did come, with dramatic suddenness. The door flew open and there he was, tall, ascetic, pale, in black clothes. He sprang on to the platform beside the startled teacher, whipped out a silver dollar, held it aloft, and said it was the root of all evil. Then he bowed elegantly and was gone as swiftly as he had come. Wilmarth's family was shocked when they heard about it. This was a sharper whiff of dissent than emanated from Miss Figg's puffballs. The principal, it was immediately recognized in Central Avenue, was a "crank," and Wilmarth heard for the first time the sinister remark, "Something should be done about him." Meanwhile, he was made to understand that he must reject the principal's heretical teaching. It was not hard for him to do. He accepted money as essential, but he did not want to hear it talked about either respectfully or disrespectfully and certainly not with the overtones of uncertainty that his family used from time to time. When the subject came up thereafter he left for his room, a withdrawal that led to the remark, "Wilmarth has no idea of the value of money." He was more pleased than offended by this stricture, which raised him above the common run. His position on money couldn't have been simpler; he didn't want to hear it talked about; he didn't want to earn it; he just wanted to have it. Years later Azro reminded him of the time when Wilmarth, aged perhaps eight, was surrounded by a circle of elders. The question was, "What work will Wilmarth do when he is a man?" By "work" was meant gainful employment. One of the elders said he would be a lawyer, another a doctor, a third a bishop; Mrs. Lewis said, "A nice businessman." The symposium was concluded by the object of it when he announced: "Wilmarth will never work," a prophecy that proved him to be more prescient than his appraisers.

A subject as venerated as money was San Francisco Society. George's references to it, light, casual, frequent, implied that membership in it was the greatest prize in life. People "in Society" were superior to other people. They lived in big houses with butlers and drank champagne at five dollars a bottle. You had to be rich to live in this paradise, but there was more to it than money. You had to "belong." Society had "old families" and "climbers." Wilmarth scorned the climbers and identified himself with the old families who were secure and "took up" or "dropped" newcomers. Society was magical when George talked about it, but not when Mrs. Lewis discussed it with Aunt Emma Hall, who was not a blood relation, but Mrs. Lewis's oldest friend and one of the very few who called her by her first name. He gathered that Aunt Emma and his mother had been in Society when they were young. They spoke of the comings and goings of their former friends and their families as recorded daily in the *Chronicle* in a wistful way that puzzled Wilmarth. "Why," he asked one day, "don't you see those people now?" but as with his question about education he was put off and with the same show of impatience.

The views of the Lewises and their friends on politics were as firm as about money and "position" and they believed that the three subjects were closely allied. The Party, the Republican Party, of course, stood for sound money and ordered ways; it was the bulwark of the Union. Democrats were impractical characters like William Jennings Bryan and dangerous ones like Samuel Gompers who stirred up the working people. Dr. Lewis, whose first vote had been cast for Lincoln, never voted for a Democrat in his life, nor did any of his sons except the youngest, who did not meet a Democrat until he was ten. This object of curiosity, a fraternity brother of Azro's and Charles's at Stanford, spent a weekend at 1625 Central Avenue. He came from Missouri, which explained his oddity; yet he might as well have been a Republican, so far as dress and manners went, and Wilmarth's horizon received another enlargement.

This young man introduced Wilmarth to the power of the mind over the body. He noticed that Wilmarth had an unsightly wart on his left hand. "You ought to get rid of that," he said, "and I'll tell you how you can. Go to the kitchen," he added in a low voice, "get a potato and a knife; cut the potato in half; rub it on the wart and throw it over your left shoulder. But don't tell anyone, and then forget all about it." Wilmarth stole out to the kitchen at once, got a potato and a knife, went into the garden, held the potato in his left hand and cut deep into his forefinger. When he recovered he repeated the experiment, this time placing the potato on a bit of wood before cutting it. He followed the rest of the directions carefully and the wart went away immediately, but to this day the scar on his finger is sensitive to the touch and is a reminder of the mysterious power of suggestion.

With the final settlement of Aunt Lux's estate some ten years after her death the lives of the Lewises expanded. The material benefits that stemmed from her were highlighted here and there in their house by the bronze of Admetus and his herdsman in the library, by the oil painting of a fawn (very large) on the lower landing of the stairs in the hall, by the enormous steel engraving of Bach playing for a company of ladies and cherubs that hung on the wall above the stairs. Mrs. Lewis was Aunt Lux's namesake, Miranda Wilmarth Sheldon, and in matrimony their initials, displayed on pieces of silver, were still united. Wilmarth, to his mother's disappointment, missed being Miranda, but the rest of his name brought him as close as could be managed to his mother and great aunt, whose influence did not stop with her bequest. Mrs. Lewis would say, "Whenever I am undecided I ask, 'What would Aunt Lux do?'" and then Aunt Lux would tell her. At the mention of that name an awed silence would fall. In Wilmarth's pantheon there were Mother, Aunt Lux, and God. The majesty of Aunt Lux's person, the infallibility of her judgment, the splendor of her houses, continued to shape the lives of the family at 1625 Central Avenue, Alameda, yet the suspicion that her influence on his mother had not been wholly beneficent increased in Wilmarth as he grew older. That Aunt Lux wished to improve the lot of working girls was proved by her founding a school for them in which they were taught useful trades—the first school of the kind in the country—but that he would have found her agreeable he questioned, a doubt strengthened years later when he saw a bust of her in the President's office at Lux College. The sculptor presented a woman with the habit of command:

She would have ta'en
Achilles by the hair and bent his neck;
Or with a finger stay'd Ixion's wheel.

The bust had been attacked by some sinister marmoreal disease that prevented Aunt Lux from looking her best. W. S. Lewis, gazing at her, was grateful for the comfort she left him and thankful that he was not under her domination. Aunt Lux had bequeathed harm as well as good; yet, he came to realize, it is foolish and unfair to blame one's family for our shortcomings and failures. I found this view confirmed recently before turning out the light. "To accuse others for one's own misfortunes," Epictetus said, "is a sign of want of education; to accuse oneself shows that one's education has begun; to accuse neither oneself nor others shows that one's education is complete," a truth I wish I had taken in years ago.

IV

ALAMEDA IV,
TRAVEL

Travel, "getting away," was an important feature of Mrs. Lewis's life and so of her youngest son's as well. The first journey that he was to remember was to Upper Soda Springs in Northern California. This was in 1900, his fifth summer. It was like the raising of a curtain. It went up when he descended from the sleeper and there was snow-capped Mt. Shasta, the most beautiful mountain in the world, 14,162 feet, at the head of the Sacramento Valley, alone except for its lady-in-waiting, Little Shasta. There was also the stripling Sacramento. Wilmarth loved its noise and gaiety, its eddies swirling every which way over the rocks and river grasses. The redwoods were tall and aromatic; the bark of the sugar pines came off in strange shapes when Wilmarth picked at it; the wild flowers were so brilliant and commanding that he wouldn't have been surprised if, like the flowers in the garden of Looking Glass House, they had begun to talk. Mariposa lilies and tiger lilies were his favorites, with honorable mention of the honeysuckle that covered the arbor leading to the privy. This last, which was built over a frisky tributary of the Sacramento, was a welcome novelty. Visits to it were almost too exciting.

Two incidents of the summer left lasting impressions on

Wilmarth. The first occurred in a baseball game when a young Englishman was hit on the jaw by a pitched ball. A great fuss was made about it and deep sympathy was extended to the injured. He explained that it would have been much worse had he not learned to clamp his teeth together when playing cricket. This incident implanted in Wilmarth the disastrous fear of a pitched ball that made him "step back from the plate" and so ruin his baseball in later years. The second occurred in the *tableaux vivants* that were directed by an Englishwoman who painted Mt. Shasta by moonlight and who was full of the rich mountain air. Wilmarth appeared twice as Little Boy Blue, first blowing his horn and then asleep in the hay. As the curtains parted upon him asleep in the hay there was a gasp from the audience and then tumultuous applause. In his fifth year he had heard the most seductive of all sounds.

Later trips contributed not only to his education, but also to what might be called his counter-education, an example of which was provided by Azro and Charles at Santa Cruz. Wilmarth's brothers loved the great booming breakers, but Wilmarth preferred to put sand into a pail and dump it out again well up the beach. Azro and Charles had read that the way to teach little boys to swim is to throw them into the water. Accordingly, they pounced upon Wilmarth one morning when he was engrossed with his spade and pail and raced him to the Pacific Ocean. Anna followed in pursuit, but her protests were lost in the wind and Wilmarth's shrieks. With nothing between him and Japan he was flung under a wave that haunted his dreams for years and that kept him from ever becoming a swimmer.

Mrs. Lewis and he were asked several times to Uncle Henry Miller's camp on Mt. Madonna. Uncle Henry was one of the last robber barons. He went to California in 1850 as a poor but daring immigrant from Germany; when he died in 1908 he left his daughter an estate of forty million dollars. His partner was Charles Lux, in whose house Wilmarth's mother, as already noted, was brought up. Not to be outdone by Charles Lux in any way, Henry Miller married Aunt Lux's sister and when she died, her niece. He was a legendary figure of whom fabulous stories were told such as the one about his being held up. It was his practice to ride over the Miller and Lux land alone (there was over a million acres of it) and it was known that he wore a belt lined with twenty-dollar gold pieces. When the bandit of the story relieved him of this valuable cincture the victim is said to have asked, How was he to pay his hotel bill at Bakersfield? Whereupon the bandit flipped him a twenty-dollar gold piece and rode off. Some months later when Uncle Henry was sitting in the lobby of the hotel at Stockton his assailant walked in. Uncle Henry went up to him, put his hand in his pocket, drew out a twenty-dollar gold piece, and said, "Here is the money I owe you." True or false, this sort of story made Henry Miller very popular.

Mt. Madonna is about eighty miles south of San Francisco. To get to it you went by train to Gilroy where you were met by a team of horses and a surrey and driven smartly away to Bloomfield, the smallest of the Miller and Lux ranches, six miles off. The ranch house was so large that Wilmarth mistook it for a hotel. In its parlors were plush chairs whose arms were steers' horns; lace curtains covered the windows; peacock feathers salvaged from the peacocks that stalked and screamed about the place were stuck into tall jars. There was a street lined with barns and stables, a blacksmith, and a saddlery. Wilmarth used to watch the ranch hands stampede into their dining room and stroll out again in a remarkably short time. Early in the morning he and his mother would be driven to the top of Mt. Madonna, a trip that took hours. The road wound up and up with many turns; the checkreins on the horses were unfastened so that they could bob their heads up and down; at the steepest pitches the coachman dismounted and walked to lighten the load. Little brown lizards scurried amid the red madrone trees and Indian paintbrush. At last the travelers reached the vineyard, heavy with red, white, and blue grapes, that stretched down the mountain from the camp. The Lewises stayed with Cousin Nellie Nickel, Uncle Henry's daughter, in a cottage built of sweet-smelling redwood. On arrival Wilmarth would be taken to pay his respects to Aunty Miller in her cottage next door. She never got out of her enormous bed, why not was a mystery since she was very red and jolly. Wilmarth did not enjoy calling on her because of her quills. He would be lifted up, tipped forward, and impaled upon them. Kissing Aunty Miller, he thought, was like kissing Anna Crowe's pincushion.

The camp swarmed with Wilmarth's cousins and their friends, nearly all of whom detested him. His training at home had led him to believe that he could do exactly as he pleased and have things exactly as he wanted them, a view not shared by his contemporaries at Mt. Madonna. Cousin Nellie, on the other hand, took to him at once. She was handsome, thin, short-tempered, and made cutting remarks with relish. Her words, few and deadly, were uttered in a clear low voice. They were never directed against Wilmarth, with whom she played old maid by the hour and whom she encouraged in his antisocial behavior. He missed what she said to her own children because it was in French, but when it was translated for him he was impressed, such as when she told the sorrowing Beatrice to "get out and water the flowers with your tears." It was Beatrice who sixty years later confirmed Wilmarth's impression of himself at this time. "You were dreadful, and your mother used to try to protect you from us." Yet it was at Mt. Madonna that he received his first compliment. It was paid at an evening barbecue. Uncle Henry, very small and old, sat to one side studying the excited children, the firelight flickering over his white beard. Suddenly he pointed at Wilmarth with his stick. "That boy," he said, "has very bright eyes." Wilmarth was disconcerted, but gathered that something agreeable had been said. The compliment made him more unpopular than ever.

During the summer of 1906 while staying with his mother at Miramar, "a cottage hotel," on the ocean below Santa Barbara, his horizon was widened by a slightly older boy named Courtenay. He was tall, handsome, and had a certain reserve. He was unlike any other boy Wilmarth had met. There was a special aura about him: he came from the East and combined manliness with good manners. Wilmarth had not realized that there were such boys and he wanted to be like him. Courtenay confirmed what his family had assured him, that Easterners, particularly New Englanders, and their ways were superior to all others, and so it was that when Wilmarth was taken East by his mother and Azro in the summer of 1907 he went in a receptive frame of mind.

At Duxbury, Mass., he won a doubles tennis tournament, or rather, it was won for him by his partner, a boy four years his senior who in time was to be on the Harvard tennis team. When this older boy was forced into the partnership by his uncle and aunt (Boston friends of Mrs. Lewis) he accepted the imposition with dignified resignation. Wilmarth was struck by the fifteen-year-old's self-possession: he was so popular that if he did not wish to gratify the clamor of friends for his society he remained quietly by himself. Ed Woods, like Courtenay at Miramar the previous summer, became a figure to be emulated. On the tennis court he was overwhelming. The only games the ill-matched team lost were those when, by the inexorable laws of tennis, Wilmarth had to serve. Once the ball was in play his partner sensibly took over. The prize was a copper stein, which Azro had gone to Boston to buy. Although Wilmarth's defeated opponents made it clear that he had won in spite of his playing he *did* have the copper stein and after the tennis tournament he was no longer a little boy. The victory, earned or not, moved him on a square.

Even more rewarding than the copper stein was the month spent with Miss Hattie Cottrell at Westerly in the house where the Lewises had lived and where all four of Wilmarth's brothers had been born. At Westerly he was introduced for the first time to a circle who had known his family forever and who welcomed the Lewises as natives. This feeling of "belonging" was different from anything he felt in Alameda. Thanks to the weekly edition of the *Westerly Sun* that his family discussed wistfully in Alameda, the names of the Westerly streets and families were familiar to him: Elm, School, Quarry Streets; Wilcox, Utter, Champlin. Fortunately for Wilmarth, he had learned something about how to get on with people since his Mt. Madonna days and the younger Cottrells accepted him. The boys had gone or were going to St. Mark's and Yale, the girls to Farmington, and they generously overlooked the shortcomings he retained. He was helped, as one of them told him only the other day, because "you always had a sense of humor." He had never been so happy. The early part of most mornings he spent in the printing plant "Works" owned by his hosts in the company of its future president, Charlie Cottrell, then aged eight, making "flasks" for modest parts of the big presses under the eye of a dear old workman who may have been all of forty. The two boys stood in line at the end of the week to receive their wages. The Works came back to W. S. Lewis years later when he saw the prints of Piranesi, the flaming furnaces and huge shadows with pigmy men dominating elemental forces in murk and smoke. At Westerly Wilmarth also became aware for the first time of a sense of obligation and responsibility to one's community. The Cottrells had been the great people there since its founding in 1660. The three brothers of the older generation quietly furthered the welfare of the town, its library, schools, park, hospital. Wilmarth was not to hear of *noblesse oblige* for some years, but when he did he thought of the Cottrells and Westerly.

Educational as the East was in its widening of Wilmarth's horizon, his trip abroad two years later in 1909 was even more so; in fact, it was the most instructive trip to Europe he ever made. He was taken by his mother and Azro, and they were gone five months. They went primarily in the hope that the waters at Carlsbad might cure Mrs. Lewis's headaches. A secondary purpose was to improve Wilmarth by travel. By way of preparation he was given *Beacon Lights of History* to read. When this proved to be impossible the second objective of the trip was abandoned even before the travelers set out.

Travel has an honored place in any system of education. "Home-keeping youth have ever homely wits," Valentine observes at the opening of *Two Gentlemen of Verona,* and France, Switzerland, Germany, Austria, and England had more to offer a thirteen-year-old boy than Alameda, California. I am not sure what in all the European panorama Wilmarth enjoyed most. At the time he might have said it was the Austrian officers strolling along the Ring in their many-colored uniforms, the German students with their slashed left cheeks, chocolate at Vevey, a shooting gallery at Carlsbad, the Iron Maiden at Nuremburg, London hansom cabs and Lily Elsie in *The Merry Widow,* or Blériot's monoplane.

One morning while the Lewises were at the Lord Warden Hotel at Dover sirens blew briefly; a small crowd gathered on the cliffs below; the hotel servants peeked through the lace curtains: Latham, the intrepid aviator, was flying from France. After he flew six miles his machine plunged into the Channel. When he was rescued he was sitting on a wing smoking a cigarette, which the papers pointed out was further proof of his daredevil spirit. The Lewises were in London when Blériot flew the Channel a few days later, but after his monoplane was put on public view in Selfridge's basement Wilmarth queued up and touched it as he moved past. This was a more normal impulse than the one that guided him when he was invited to meet Gentleman Jim Corbett in the foyer of the Russell Square Hotel, where the Lewises and Gentleman Jim were staying. "Want to meet Jim Corbett?" his manager asked. The former champion, no longer handsome, was hovering in the background. Wilmarth looked at him dubiously. The manager was incredulous: "You know, Jim Corbett, the champion fighter of the world." A pugilist. Wilmarth's mother would not approve. "No," he said and left.

Dr. Lewis joined his family. Azro met him at Plymouth and took him first to France, while Mrs. Lewis and Wilmarth went to Leamington for three weeks. Mrs. Lewis was nervous and irritable. Wilmarth became homesick for Alameda and went on a semi-hunger strike. There was nothing, apparently, for him to do except to take a tram to Warwick four miles away. After visits to the Castle, the Beauchamp Chapel, and Leicester's Hospital, Warwick began to pall. And then he found an antique shop with a collection of English coins. They were not expensive, but they were beyond his reach. There was a musty and mysterious atmosphere in the shop, the first antique shop he had ever been in, which worked powerfully upon his imagination. Relics of former ages stretched into the dim and cluttered distance out of which the proprietor would emerge with a wan face and narrow steel spectacles that might have been taken from the collection of spectacles, snuffboxes, and teaspoons in a glass case opposite the front door. A way to acquire the coins presented itself to Wilmarth, for in the solution of such problems lies a collector's peculiar skill: Mrs. Lewis was worried by his not eating; Wilmarth was worried by not being able to buy the coins. So he proposed that he be paid four shillings a week for eating. The proposal was accepted and went into effect with complete success. Wilmarth bought the coins one by one; time passed quickly and pleasantly as he rode back and forth to Warwick; he put on a little weight and lived to get back to California.

Memorable as these experiences were, more lasting have been the effects of the bound copies of *Punch* during our Civil War that Wilmarth discovered in the library of the Hotel Schweizerhof at Lucerne, the "Dance of Death" on the panels of the Mill Bridge there, the Art Gallery in Dresden, and German militarism.

He had played with toy soldiers rather longer than is usual. They were red and blue, the Tories and the Minutemen. The red of course always got the worst of it. Looking down one day at the carnage Charles said pityingly, "He doesn't realize that the English are our best friends"; a disconcerting remark. In Wilmarth's boys' books the redcoats were always the enemy, and when he went through the bound volumes of *Punch* at Lucerne they still seemed to be. *Punch* had been for the South. Week after week it printed hateful caricatures of the immortal Lincoln. Then, dramatically, Wilmarth came to Tenniel's drawing of Britannia placing a wreath on the fallen leader while Columbia and a freed slave mourned by his bier. Opposite were Tom Taylor's verses, "Abraham Lincoln. Foully Assassinated, April 14, 1865," that begin:

> You *lay a wreath on murdered Lincoln's bier,*
> You, *who with mocking pencil wont to trace*
> *Broad for self-complacent British sneer,*
> *His length of shambling limb, his furrowed face.*

Punch had apologized and Wilmarth thought better of the English. It was the first time that he had found something of historical significance on his own. His discovery showed him that "education" is not confined to the classroom; that, in fact, what one learns outside it is more rewarding. So great was the impression left on him by *Punch* that when forty-five years later he saw one of its caricatures of Lincoln again he recognized it at once and scored a success as dramatic as when the curtains parted at Upper Soda Springs and disclosed him as Little Boy Blue asleep in the hay. He and his wife had just finished lunch at Rapallo with Max Beerbohm and Elisabeth Jungman. They had been told by Thornton Wilder to be sure to see Max's library in the Villino above the Villa Chiara. Max, in dark glasses, a Panama hat, and with alpenstock in hand, led his visitors up to it after lunch. The first book that he showed them was Henry James's *Partial Portraits*. Just above James's name on the title page he had pasted, very neatly, a caricature of Lincoln. "You cut that out of your family's set of *Punch!*" Lewis cried. Max looked at him in astonishment.

"*How* did you know?" he asked.

The panels on the Mill Bridge at Lucerne were Wilmarth's second confrontation with death. The first was when Marie Louise Michaels's mother died and a window looking towards the Lewis house was covered with a violet sash. Wilmarth, aged seven, was aware of his mother's and Anna's absorption in what was going on next door and their concern that he should be protected from it. They did tell him that Marie Louise had asked for her mother not knowing that she had gone away forever and they said that this was very sad. The "Dance of Death" at Lucerne was not sad, it was alarming; all those skeletons with their ghastly grins summoning people from every walk of life. The panels did not depress Wilmarth, but they sobered him by calling to his attention that death is inescapable, a fact that he was never to lose sight of entirely.

Fortunately for Wilmarth in 1909, Azro had some interest in pictures and communicated it to him. He learned the names of the masters as he had learned the names and recognized the radiators of automobiles. Titian, Rembrandt, and Van Dyck took on the same interest as Reo, Stanley Steamer, and Lozier, and in no time he was able to recognize schools and even hands. This knowledge led to museum snobbery, which came to flower at Dresden. Each morning he walked across the Theaterplatz from the Bellevue Hotel to the Art Gallery, where he would hurry past the small room at the right of the entrance in which the most famous picture in the collection, the Sistine Madonna, hung alone before tourists with guidebooks in their hands, past Liotard's "Chocolate Girl," Van Dyck's "Charles I and His Family," and Correggio's "Magdalen," the other three pictures that the Joneses had to see, on and on and around until he reached a small remote room where no one ever was. There he would stand before "his" picture, the little van Eyck altarpiece. Why, I wonder now, did Wilmarth choose this, of all the pictures in the gallery, to be his? Doubtless it was partly because it is a triptych, which was then a novelty to him. Certainly color came into it, the Virgin's dark-blue dress and deep crimson mantle lined with gold, the brocaded cloth of honor behind her, the rich Turkey carpet that stretches before her throne, the Virgin's and St. Catherine's rubies, sapphires, and pearls, the donor's olive-green robe lined with fur, and St. Michael's azure wings and bronze armor. All four figures are serene and secure in their radiance and wealth. Wilmarth believed that the donor of the picture, kneeling reverently on the dexter shutter, is not about to touch his fingertips in adoration, but is clapping his hands in a pious pattycake. The delighted smile of the Child and the gently amused expression of the Virgin, both of whom are looking at him, give credence to this possibility. In any event, I am pleased that Wilmarth chose so celestial a picture from all the rest to be "his."

This discovery of how to see a gallery has led me in later life to choose one and only one picture in a collection as "mine," so as to be ready with my answer just in case the director of the gallery should come to me, bow, and say, "My Board has instructed me to give you any picture you want here." What I have selected with this prospect in mind have not been the most famous pictures, but those that I would most like to have on my own walls. In this way I have acquired the Mantegna "Circumcision" at the Uffizi; the smaller Houckgeest of the "Tomb of William I" at the Mauritshuis; Antonello da Messina's "St. Jerome in His Library" at the National Gallery, London; Constable's "Wivenove Park" in our own National Gallery; the Naroccio "Annunciation" at Yale; Gainsborough's "Heneage Lloyd Children" at the Fitzwilliam, and many others, but first from every point of view is the van Eyck at Dresden.

Wilmarth's third strong impression was of the forthcoming war between Germany and England. The papers were full of "The Arms Race," "Lebensraum," the growing German fleet. German officers with slashed cheeks strutted about glaring through their monocles. They were going to destroy England and rule the world. Wilmarth was not taken by surprise in 1914; nor in 1939, because on the *Europa* in 1936 after the Nazis had seized the Ruhr, barging irritably about were beefy Germans distinguishable from their predecessors of 1909 only by their brown shirts.

Wilmarth was glad to get home in 1909. Amid the excitements of his travels he had had bouts of homesickness. "How can you be homesick when you are with me?" his mother would ask, and he had no reply because it seemed disloyal to her to say that he missed his friends. Three months before the Lewises set out for Europe he had graduated from Mastick and proceeded to the Alameda High School. There he found a curriculum less constrained and an atmosphere of expanding social amenity. "Reading" became "English"; freshmen "had" *Ivanhoe* and

Gayley's *Classic Myths* and learned about dactyls and anapests. Wilmarth dissected a grasshopper. Algebra proved to be more tractable than Arithmetic, and there was Latin, and Ancient History. The teaching was better than at Mastick. When Mr. Agard taught *Ivanhoe* he saw to it that the class should learn its way about a twelfth-century castle from the moat to the keep, and by directing his pupils to make a list as long as they could of the customs and manners revealed in the book he introduced them to the pleasures of social history. (Wilmarth was particularly struck by the Normans, who had no napkins and dried their hands after a meal by waving them in the air.) There was also Waldemar Westergaard, fresh from graduate school, who was to go on to become an historian of international reputation and to return years later into Wilmarth's life.

Stimulating as were these opening vistas of learning they were less exhilarating than those revealed by the social life of the school. Progress from one classroom to another was an exercise in politeness and affability. When manners are new, as Booth Tarkington pointed out, they are elaborate. Behind and around and over these felicitous exchanges and determining one's place in society were the Greek-letter fraternities and sororities. Their rank was as fixed as the alphabet. To join the best of them was to become one of the elite, a serene and gilded figure raised to a heady height. Wilmarth achieved this eminence on arrival at the school, because Azro and Charles had preceded him in it. He was given a "pledge pin" which he wore on his coat lapel. To be the glass of fashion and received into a devoted sodality of superior beings was to know the joy of living. As a little boy he had been much affected by the story of the ugly duckling that was pecked and tormented by its fellows until one day it looked into the water and, lo! it had become a beautiful swan. When he confided to Anna Crowe that he was an ugly duckling, she told him to wait, that one day he, too, would become a beautiful swan. The metamorphosis occurred on his arrival at high school.

But what the mysteries of the fraternity were he was never to learn because on his return from Europe an unheard-of thing took place: he was unpledged. One of the boys who had been pledged with him and who had been particularly friendly had been initiated while Wilmarth was abroad. He had then persuaded his fraternity brothers that Wilmarth should be dropped. What caused this disaffection Wilmarth never discovered, but its results for him were far-reaching. From being one of the brightest and best of the stars of the morning he became an object of persecution and ridicule without Satan's compensation of knowing why he had fallen. The beautiful swan, contrary to the laws of nature, became again an ugly duckling. No longer did Wilmarth walk the mile to and from school four times a day with members of the fraternity on Alameda Avenue, but instead he hurried along Central Avenue by himself, concentrating on the cross streets as he neared and passed them—Grand, Union, Lafayette, Chestnut, Walnut, Willow—hoping as he came to the corners that the *jeunesse dorée* a short block away would not see him. No longer an aspirant for fame and glory, what he prayed for was to be unnoticed. He became afflicted with shyness so devastating that he would frame sentences which frequently came out not only wrong, but with words unknown in any language, to the delight of his auditors. Life, he learned, could be horrible. He confessed his misery to George, the adjusted to the world, and George said, "Just be yourself," but Wilmarth did not know what he himself was.

He found consolation in reading and in collecting butterflies and beetles. His mother could see nothing wrong with this latter activity. It took him out of doors, and the killing bottle that his teacher gave him was not lethal for human beings. Mrs.

Lewis was rather amused by the net, scalpel, forceps, black pins, glass slides, and cabinet that invested his collecting with the aura of science. "The killing bottle is cyanide of potassium," he would say importantly. When the family drove out into the country in their 1909 Stevens-Duryea the net and killing bottle went with them. Forty years later Wilmarth wrote: "I can still feel my hot anxiety as a 'new' butterfly sailed into view, darted off over the warm summer fields, and finally came to rest, opening and closing its wings. This is what collecting is—the all but unbearable excitement when the longed-for quarry appears, the fierce and crafty pursuit, the cyanide bottle, the black pins, the cabinet, and one additional factor, the admiring and (supreme felicity) envious visitors."

Wilmarth learned to adjust himself to his lowered social condition by finding companionship among others of the non-elected. Tennis came to his rescue. Two years had improved his game and he beat everyone he played with although a year or two junior to them. He also learned to bowl. The bowling alleys were at the Encinal Yacht Club that jutted out into the Bay. The pins were set up by a Japanese who was occasionally drunk and savage. The boys slid over the foul line far down the alley. Wilmarth became a good bowler even without sliding very far over the foul line. He was introduced to gambling, which he loved. As much as thirty cents might change hands, but Wilmarth won more often than not.

A further amelioration was the weekly walk with three of his tennis friends on Saturday evenings to the public library a mile away. There he would choose a "boy's book," which he would read and return the following Saturday. These books were looked upon with more favor at home than was *Hamlet* because, so his family said, he was not ready for grown-up books and premature reading of them would "spoil" them for him later. Oliver Optic and Horatio Alger had gone out of fashion;

Henty was going; the reigning authors were Kirke Monroe, Everett Titsworth Tomlinson, and Ralph Henry Barbour. The staple of these books was manliness tested by adventure and sport. They had only two sets of characters, the good and the bad and it was apparent to which set each character belonged on his first appearance. The good were all good, the bad were all bad until the final pages when the goodness of the good redeemed them.

Although his trips to the library were one of the chief solaces of Wilmarth's week, and although he enjoyed going to the stacks and picking out his next book, he found the library and its atmosphere uncomfortable. He loved books, but he disliked the rigmarole connected with them: the letters and numbers that defaced their spines, the tacky little envelopes on the inside covers, and the disagreeable rules and regulations printed on them. When he asked about the drawers of fumed oak to the left of the delivery desk he learned that they contained "library cards," which proved to be less interesting than playing cards or even calling cards. Wilmarth was told that he ought to use the library cards, but that he was still too young to do so; he would have to grow up before he could savor their joys. As for the librarian, she had as many eyes as Argus and pince-nez for every one of them. When she slapped her date stamp on the ink pad and ground it on the charge slip of the books he was daring to borrow she put Wilmarth on a probation that she hoped he would violate.

There was a non-library book that circulated widely among the older boys, to whose company he had been readmitted on inferior status. Although he never had the book in his hands, he heard all about it. I can't recall its title, but I remember Wilmarth's saying in effect that you could see the deterioration in the boys after the book had come among them. I find this interesting in view of the redefinition of pornography and society's satisfaction today in having Fanny Hill safely in the hands of every man, woman, and child in the Republic. Wilmarth did not tell his mother of the book, but he did tell her that he wanted to go to a private school. She was disturbed by his unhappiness and by the way his school marks had fallen off. At Miramar in 1906 she heard of the Thacher School in the nearby Ojai Valley and that it compared favorably with the best schools in New England. To send Wilmarth there would be a cruel separation, but it was four days nearer than New England and it would be equal proof of social superiority. And so with the approval of Dr. Reynolds he went to the Thacher School, aged fourteen, in the fall of 1910.

Had the boy who turned against him remained a friend Wilmarth would almost certainly have stayed in Alameda. If he had stayed there he would not have gone to Yale or settled in Farmington or met Annie Burr Auchincloss or collected and edited Horace Walpole. Purgatory with its salutary troubles proved to be Godsent. Wilmarth sensed this dimly at the time and has noticed since that he has usually been better off in the end for bitter disappointments.

V

THACHER I

The Thacher School is on the southeastern slope of the Ojai Valley, a dozen miles inland from the coast at Ventura. Azro took Wilmarth that far, an overnight railroad journey from San Francisco, to make sure that he got off at Ventura. Wilmarth, rising fifteen and a veteran of foreign travel, thought that he might be trusted to do so on his own, but his mother wouldn't hear of it. Actually, he was glad to have Azro go with him. Azro in 1910 was still more uncle than brother—twenty-six and fourteen could hardly be anything else—but the two were drawing closer all the time. Mystery surrounded Azro because he understood about money and worked for a private banker in San Francisco. Neither his mother nor youngest brother knew what his life there was; all that Mrs. Lewis wanted was to have him home every night being her son until she died, not "lost" in matrimony as Charles was. Since her welfare and that of the family was the chief concern of Azro's life, he was glad to start Wilmarth on his way to school and a better chance than he had had. He watched his young brother drive off in a buggy to the Ojai from the Ventura station and waited patiently several hours for the return train to San Francisco. The family took this compliance for granted, but the example of Azro's unselfishness was not wholly lost on Wilmarth.

While Azro waited in Ventura, Wilmarth was happily on his way with two of his new schoolmates to the School, a three-hour drive in the heat and dust of late September. The first view of the Valley is spectacular. Its floor is only seven miles long and less than two miles wide; to the north is Mt. Matilija, a beautiful mountain of the Sleeping Giant type, and Matilija Twin Peaks; to the east is the six-thousand-foot wall of Topa Topa. Pyramidal peaks with sage and wild lilac on their rugged sides tumbled down into the Valley. On the south and west the mountains—hills by California standards—are a mere 3,000 feet, but they are high enough to support the belief that "Ojai" means "nest" in the local Indian dialect. The final uphill mile to the School was and is through orange and lemon groves whose scent fills the air with celestial fragrance.

In 1910 Thacher was limited to forty boys who were housed in the Upper, Middle, and Lower Schools, two-story wooden structures. Each boy had a room to himself. It was what is known as "a family school." There was no hazing, no discrimination in dress; the denomination of the Lower Schoolers as "Smuts" was prompted as much by affection as by a desire to keep the young in order. The teachers, who were not called "masters" and were not addressed as "Sir" as in Eastern schools but by name, "Mr. Cooke," "Mr. Blake," were genial young men with the milk of Yale and Harvard still wet upon their lips; a different type from the average "Normal School" teacher in Alameda. Thacher followed one practice of Eastern schools: the new boys were cautioned by the Headmaster not to call the older boys by their first names until they were so addressed by the older boys themselves. Wilmarth did not receive this distinction from Upper Schoolers during his first year, but the formality helped to make him feel that his new world was superior to the one he had left.

The School was a New Haven colony. Sherman Day Thacher, its founder and Headmaster, was the son of the Professor Thacher who Clarence W. Mendell says in the *Dictionary of American Biography* "played a larger role in the building of modern Yale than that of any one of his contemporaries." Mr. Thacher's mother, "Madame Thacher" (a nonagenarian who lived at the School, wore little caps with cranberries on them, and dressed in mauve), was a grand-daughter of Roger Sherman. Mr. Thacher took an ailing brother out to the Ojai a few years after he graduated from Yale and began the School casually in 1889 with the son of a Yale professor as the first boy. It was natural that its earliest pupils should come from Connecticut and New York and that many should continue to come from the East. By 1910 half of the boys did so if you count Colorado East. This national aspect of the School was unknown elsewhere in California at the time. The contrast between most of the boys, East and West, with those in Alameda was marked. Wilmarth, or Lewie, as he soon became, found his Lower Schoolmates immature; even the Upper Schoolers had a freshness that had been lost by their Alameda contemporaries. Lewie was thankful he was at Thacher and wanted to do well there.

A unique feature of the School was the rule that every boy had to have a horse and take care of it himself. The educational gains that accrued from this association were clearer then than they are now when horses are restricted to racing, fox-hunting, and ancient ceremonial. "A boy and a horse" evoked a picture of health, manliness, command, but for Lewie horses were merely a means of transportation that was being superseded. He did not think of the reek of the barns that pervaded every corner of the School as an upper-class smell and although he overcame his finicky approach to manure he never learned to like it. However, horses at Thacher had to be accepted whether you liked them or not. They were ridden in the Western style: Mexican saddles; silver conchas on bridles. If Eastern boys on arrival spoke of "cantering" instead of "galloping" or attempted to "post" they were quickly put right. Chaps, leather vests, and ten-gallon hats were worn by some; by others, including Lewie, they seemed as affected as English riding clothes would have been. Lewie loved the School in spite of the horses.

As I have pointed out, he had been indoctrinated at home against animals in general, but I can dredge up only one unpleasant incident in his early life connected with riding. At the age of eight during a summer at Los Gatos he rented a solemn saddlehorse for a dollar an hour, a sum that must have taken most of his savings. It is hard to believe that he did so with the knowledge and consent of his mother, and I assume that this was a demonstration of independence. In any event, he and the horse walked slowly down the street and on to the railroad tracks just as the gates were descending. There they were, horse and boy, trapped on the tracks as the train came round the bend. Horror appeared on adult countenances; a lifesaver ran up the track waving his arms. The train, which was slowing down for the station nearby, stopped abruptly. The gates were raised, and Wilmarth and the horse walked sedately back up the street to the livery stable. Since he had hired the horse for an hour he was not expected back in five minutes, nor would the livery-stable keeper abate his charge below fifteen minutes. "We never rent horses for less than fifteen minutes," he said, a rule that seemed absurd to Wilmarth, as well as exorbitant. The episode made him wary of horses in the future, an unfair aspersion upon the Los Gatos horse, which had done only what it had been asked to do and was not responsible for its owner's attitude towards money.

At Thacher he proved that he was no horseman at once by falling off his Chiquito (who was elderly as well as small and did unwelcome tricks such as sitting down when you tapped his knees). He got a concussion and was the first patient of the new School Matron. This brought him the respectful notice given to those who have been injured by falling off a horse and fixed him in the pedestrian set. Chiquito was replaced after two years by Jim, a bigger and more stylish horse, but Lewie was not worthy of Jim and was glad to dispose of him his last year for Betty. Betty was white, an unfortunate color that exposed Lewie's indifferent care and reduced his marks from the Outdoor Committee even lower than they had been. When he left the School he sold Betty for sixteen dollars and everyone said that he had got a good price for her. He did not go into the gymkhanas or on camping trips to the Sespe; in fact, he kept his horses in the School pasture as much as he could. I see now that he was the loser by this; that the talk about the horse being a teacher is true; that dawn beyond the ranges in a dew-drenched sleeping bag with your horse snuffling your hair is a memory you would cherish, but these rewards and benefits he missed.

He came to the attention of the School on the evening of his arrival by falling into the Parlor fireplace. He was standing awkwardly before it, twisting around one of the large andirons in adolescent embarrassment, and then, there he was sprawled upon the logs and kindling wood. Because fires were unnecessary until later in the season, he was in no danger of cremation, which was not the case a few weeks later when the Upper School burned down in no time at all. An overheated stove placed too close to one of the flimsy wooden walls set off a roaring blaze one morning just before breakfast. When Lewie, in hastily donned khaki trousers and evening pumps, reached the fire he found boys and teachers rushing in and out of the furiously burning building and was much impressed by the strongest boy in the School, who in four years was to become Captain of the Yale Crew, wrenching up iron desks from the schoolroom floor. The fire was like the Mastick wars except that everyone was on the same side against an enemy that would certainly prevail. Lewie did his part. He rushed into the room of an Upper Schooler who had been friendly to him. The fire was very close. He grabbed up something and ran dropping, like Cinderella, one of his slippers as he fled. He was the last to leave the furnace and proudly turned over to his friend what he had rescued, an empty marshmallow tin.

A third public failure occurred in General Exercises, which introduced the boys to public speaking. Here was the chance for Lewie to take his father's advice, which had worked so powerfully on his mind that when he stood in the bathtub in Alameda he addressed vast audiences and held them spellbound. (In those visions his speeches had no subjects, only the spellbound audiences.) To be ready for his first speech at Thacher he wrote out a talk on the Iron Maiden of Nuremberg. When the awful moment came to deliver it he rose, spoke the first sentence briskly, and then stood in deathly silence until he sank, speechless, into his seat.

These gaucheries were offset somewhat by his being good even at algebra, because he was taking the same course he had at the Alameda High School, and the best tennis player in the Lower School. Tennis was the chief sport at Thacher owing to Mr. Thacher's younger brother, William, having been an intercollegiate champion at Yale in the eighties and a missionary of the game in Southern California. Since there was no outstanding player in the School, Lewie's last year his serve and forehand (both very slashing) made him Number One in the tennis ranking in spite of a weak backhand. On the way to winning the School championship he was tripped up by a boy during recess baseball, fell on a rock (the Thacher baseball fields were rugged), and hurt his thigh badly. Nothing was done about it (Thacher boys didn't need doctors), and he had to default. Nor was he able two weeks later to play in the Second Man Tournament, and so he failed to earn the coveted School letter. It was some consolation for him subsequently to win the local Ojai Valley Tournament in which he beat both the first and second man; but Mr. William Thacher, who disliked Lewie, instead of presenting the winner's cup to him before the School according to custom sent it to him after School was closed. This was administering the second of Abbé Galiani's essential points of education, injustice.

Sport has an honored place in education. Those who are bad at games must learn to live with their shortcoming. To cower back from the pitcher striking wildly into the void, to miss completely an easy smash, is to be ridiculous. How much better to run the length of the field in the last seconds of play or hit a fourbagger with the bases full in the last of the tenth. Yet the most memorable sporting feat I ever saw was performed on a tennis court by an uncommonly strong, awkward, and determined player. Whenever he could get at the ball he gave it a musclebound slash. He fell down, he got tangled in the net, a shoelace broke and forced him to play in his stocking feet, but no one laughed, no one got annoyed, because he was doing the best he could and that is what you are supposed to do. Had he showed a trace of embarrassment he would have been an object of contempt. Instead, his unself-consciousness commanded respect; the coordination of his spirit was as plain as the uncoordination of his body. Secure, earnest, insensible to the possibility of ridicule, when beaten at last he said, "Good game!" Lewis, whose partner he was, felt humbled by the example of such goodness and simplicity.

In contrast to the athletically inept how bright is he whose

Dexterity so obeying appetite
That what he will he does!

To the charms and graces of physical coordination are added the satisfactions of practice and the rewards of improvement; control of temper and dark unconscious forces brings an inner strength and awareness of superiority over those who have failed in such tests; yet this awareness has in it the germs of pride and defeat. No wonder that sport possesses men's minds and souls and is preferred to all other forms of education. Lewis's place in that world was between the extremes on either side of him; his mediocrity saved him from ridicule and overseriousness, but in later years he was to lose his adolescent balance and to find golf, which he never played well, merely frustrated aggression. He had an uneasy feeling that he should overcome this weakness and regard golf as a test of character, working at it until he could break ninety, then eighty, and that his unwillingness to submit to this discipline was a spiritual lapse. In the evening of life I have given up "exercise," but I still think of my small athletic triumphs and failures, more of the failures than of the triumphs, especially those failures where I was beaten, not by my opponents' skill, but by myself; failures that could have been changed to successes by care and resolution. I think less often of the time when twenty-odd years ago I had to make twenty-nine to win in the last frame of a game of duckpins, two strikes and nine, and got them than of the time, ten years earlier still, when I needed only one on a spare to win and threw the ball off the alley, but I look back with pride at Lewie's good behavior at Thacher while suffering a disappointment so great that even now, more than fifty years later, I am wistful when on returning there as a trustee I read the list of school tennis champions and do not find my name among them.

It does appear as an editor of the *Thacher School Notes* and *El Archivero.* The *Notes* filled a page in *The Ojai,* the local weekly; the *Archivero* was the School annual. Lewie, mindful that he was going to be a professional writer, took his membership on these boards as a matter of course. He was not elected to the committees that went to the most popular and respected, but no one questioned his place on the *Notes* and *Archivero.* As an editor of the latter his final year, he wrote biographical sketches of each Upper Schooler. These were read by the author at the Farewell Spanish Banquet. By way of preparation Lewie bought a notebook in which he reserved a page or two for his subjects and made notes on them throughout the year. This exercise introduced him to the biographer's power. The results rewarded the time and care spent on the sketches. Although personal idiosyncrasies were recorded, only one biography was considered too savage for the printed page. Lewie was sobered and flattered by the Commencement speaker, Amos P. Wilder, the father of Amos and Thornton, who warned him after the banquet that he had "the very dangerous gift of satire." This he had already demonstrated, not only in the *Notes,* but on Valentine's Day when valentines were written for each boy by a little group of bards, of whom Lewie was always one. In his second year he had a triumph that rivalled his appearance as Little Boy Blue. The valentines were read by Mr. Thacher in Evening Reading. Lewie had written several that were received well enough, but apparently Mr. Thacher had decided that the parody of "Abou Ben Adhem," in which Lewie had recounted an episode in the Middle School, should not be read. Then Mr. Thacher announced, "We now come to the last." It was the parody. At the first line the whole School burst into shouts of laughter. Mr. Thacher could hardly read for laughing himself. At the end Lewie, for the second time in his life, received tumultuous applause.

This extracurricular education was more effective than the formal lessons of the classroom. What was taught there was routine drill rarely stirred by the breath of life. Latin, French, German, and English became four dead languages; there was no Greek at all. Mr. Twichell did make his class memorize Cicero on the pleasures of reading, *Haec studia adulescentiam acuunt,* and Mr. William Thacher had his class record on the back flyleaves of their Virgils that nuts were thrown at Roman weddings, but these glimpses of ancient thought and manners were exceptional. No attempt was made to render the original into respectable English; it was enough for the boys to hack through their assignments and show that they recognized an ablative when they saw one. That the *Aeneid*—or *Macbeth,* for that matter—had any interest beyond the pending college exams was not suggested: you "had" the *Aeneid* and *Macbeth* as you had mumps and measles and then you were inoculated against them forever. Lewie's protection against *Lycidas* lasted until he had to look up a line in the poem thirty years later; whereupon

> *the high lawns appeared*
> *Under the opening eyelids of the morn,*

and he was safe from *Lycidas* no longer.

The informal teaching was much better. Of the faculty—Mr. S. D. Thacher apart—the one who influenced Lewie most was "Tully" Williamson. He was gayer and more amusing than anyone Lewie had ever met. He was hopeless at baseball and tennis and ridiculous on a horse; he was too staccato and flippant in the classroom; but his gaiety released Lewie's own exuberance. He sanctioned high spirits, even though they might be followed by low spirits. "I am mercurial," he would say, and no one talked like that in Alameda, not even Miss Figg. He encouraged Lewie's latent nonconformity and hostility to authority and he laughed at the snobbery of Alameda as it filtered unconsciously through Lewie's talk. Since Tully dropped the proud San Francisco names Lewie concluded that snobbery was condoned if the persons of its regard were exalted enough and that Alameda's were not. This implication was dismaying to Lewie and strengthened his dimly felt determination to live eventually on an ampler stage. I am much in Tully's debt, but I wish that in one of his outbursts of sarcasm he hadn't discouraged Lewie from keeping a diary and memorizing verse.

Forest Cooke was a gentle soul, small and cheerful, with a Brownie face on which good nature and humor were permanently reflected. He never lapsed into sarcasm; only once did he say anything to Lewie that was critical of anyone. This was a regret that a certain boy had a bad voice because, he observed, voices are "important," a fact then presented to Lewie for the first time. He was interesting on snobbery, which was apparently universal. "Everyone is a snob about something," he once said pleasantly. "I'm an intellectual snob and proud of it." This impressed Lewie who took up the remark and said it of himself. Forest taught physics Lewie's last year. It was the first time that either of them had met the science. By working hard at night while the class slept Forest tried to keep a page ahead of the brighter physicists in it, but with their eyes on him in the morning it was hard to recall just how the experiment went that he had practiced so conscientiously the night before. He fumbled and fooled, mist gathered on his glasses, he puckered his lips, and then gratefully accepted help from the class. Physics with Forest Cooke proved that it can be self-taught.

The School had one teacher who knew precisely what the

answers were and how they were reached, Mr. Dodge in math. He was older than his colleagues and was deaf, so deaf that he had to use a hearing machine, as it was then called. There was no possibility of concealing it nor any wish to conceal it, for Mr. Dodge made it an adjunct to his teaching. The machine was attached to a metal hoop that went over his head like a telephone operator's hoop; in one hand he held a battery, in the other a plug. Adjusting the earphone while he fixed a boy with his eye, he would repeat a proposition and ask sharply, "What did I say?" uniting the battery and plug as he spoke. Easy and friendly outside the classroom, inside it Mr. Dodge ruled by terror. Every eye was riveted upon him every second of the period, and when he stepped forward, made one of his frightening statements, plugged in his battery, and asked sharply, "*What* did I say?" the most gifted mathematician answered in a tense voice. The effect on the weaker pupils could be paralyzing, not only at the moment, but forever. A fellow trustee of mine on the Thacher Board cannot even today, when he is in his seventies, speak of Mr. Dodge in the classroom without showing traces of panic. Mr. Dodge did not paralyze Lewie, he hypnotized him: Lewie could speak, but not think. He did not know what the words meant that he parroted back, but he could repeat them and did so except once when he became paralyzed instead of hypnotized. To fix the lapsed words in Lewie's brain Mr. Dodge directed him to write them ten times on the blackboard after school, together with a very long equation that illustrated them. Mr. Dodge watched while Lewie carried out his sentence, for he was not one to spare himself. The tenth repetition, which was finished at the end of an hour, covered the last inch of black-board. The task was over, the punishment had been endured, and Lewie assumed that he and his taskmaster had reverted to their friendliness outside the classroom. He smiled (not, I think, impudently), raised his voice and asked, "And now shall I write it on the floor?" Mr. Dodge regarded him coldly. "You may erase what you have written and rewrite it ten times more on the board." When the last of the original ten examples had been rubbed out, Mr. Dodge retired to watch the tennis, knowing that Lewie when he had finished his task the second time would do the same. Did he, as he sat there on the bank looking down at the First Ten Court, wonder if he hadn't been a little severe? Had, perhaps, Lewie not been impudent? Had he, Avard Dodge, yielded to a spurt of anger of which he was ashamed? The question I am sure that he did not ask himself was, "Is this the best way to teach Wilmarth Lewis geometry?" His pupil reached the tennis court late that afternoon. "You wrote it out ten times again?" Mr. Dodge asked quietly. When Lewie said, truthfully, that he had it was as if there had been no awkwardness between them, but the episode was not forgotten. Twenty-five years afterwards on returning to speak for the alumni at the School's fiftieth anniversary W. S. Lewis found that about all that was remembered of him during his schooldays was that he had asked Mr. Dodge if he should write the equation on the floor.

Two aids to scholarly success were absorbed by Lewie in Thacher classrooms. The first was repeated over and over by Mr. Twichell while his class groped and gagged its way through Cicero. "Boys," Mr. Twichell would plead, "look for the verb!" Sometimes the stress would fall on *look,* sometimes on *verb,* but the tone of the exhortation was always that of a gallant man in the closing moments of a hopeless struggle: if only, if *only* boys would look for the verb! Whereas Mr. Twichell's plea was made daily, Mr. Trotter's advice was given but once. "This talk about dates being 'hard' and 'uninteresting,'" Mr. Trotter said, "is foolish. If you make a little extra effort to remember them they are yours forever as pegs on which you can hang facts." He also urged his students to underscore passages in their reading and to add marginalia. I am glad that years later I thanked him and Burt Twichell for their advice.

That the intellectual life of Thacher was no lower than at other good American schools of half a century ago is proved by its graduates' record at college, but the contrast with the best English schools was marked. William Johnson Cory, an Eton master, wrote that at a school of the first rank ". . . you are not engaged so much in acquiring knowledge as in making mental efforts under criticism. . . . A certain amount of knowledge you can indeed with average faculties acquire so as to retain. . . . But you go to a great school, not for knowledge so much as for arts and habits; for the habit of attention, for the art of expression, for the art of assuming at a moment's notice a new intellectual posture, for the art of entering quickly into another person's thoughts, for the habit of submitting to censure and refutation, for the art of indicating assent or dissent in graduated terms, for the habit of regarding minute points of accuracy, for the habit of working out what is possible in a given time, for taste, for discrimination, for mental courage and mental soberness. Above all, you go to a great school for self-knowledge." Deficient as Thacher was in teaching Cory's arts and habits it did encourage self-knowledge and, above all, self-control.

There were a few traditional schoolboy prizes, one for each English class and one for an essay, which Lewie won in his last year with an essay on Greek Architecture, an achievement less notable than might appear since only one other boy competed. There was also a prize for "outside" reading, which was supplemented one year by William Thacher who got his mother's permission to break up her set of the Arden Shakespeare and announced that he would distribute it to those who during the summer had read "good books" and submitted a list of them to him in the fall. Lewie liked competitions, especially those with prizes, and submitted his list. He would have read many books anyway—he had little to do in the summers except read—but since a prize was being offered he might as well try for it. His list proved to be longer than anyone else's and included such time-consuming works as *Lorna Doone* and *The Cloister and the Hearth.* Lewie was a slow reader and studied as he went along how the author expressed himself, noting and enjoying his felicities of phrasing and rhythm. He thought that his list was rather impressive and that it might be rewarded with *Lear* or *Macbeth,* but he was reckoning without the inveteracy of W. L. Thacher. What Lewie got as his reward was *All's Well That Ends Well,* a play lost on him at the time.

Mothers—the *bêtes noires* of headmasters—were not encouraged to visit their sons. When they did come Mr. Thacher knew how to discourage further visits: he invited them to supper. Following a modest but rapid meal, which was shoveled out by Chinese servants on a lazy Susan in the center of each table, the mothers adjourned with the entire School to the Parlor for Evening Reading. There they were seated under pitiless electricity (the only light in the room other than Mr. Thacher's reading lamp), beside Mrs. Sherman Thacher and the other faculty wives who worked away on little garments. Before them sat the Upper School, behind them the Middle School, on their flank was the Lower School; the faculty was hidden about in the rear. All eyes were upon the mothers whose ghastly smiles were riveted on the reader. Their sons agonized in the dark. Slight relief was afforded as the five-pound box of chocolates, which the victims had brought as an oblation, passed from hand to hand round the room. The little papers in which the chocolates rested rustled as their contents were removed; sixty-odd jaws worked silently and approvingly. The ordeal of his mother's annual visits made Lewie wonder if he might not, after all, be able to live without her.

VI

THACHER II

At a boarding school the boys teach themselves unconsciously. The winged words of correction and reproof that leap from adolescents like swords from scabbards hack away excrescences of personality. Boys in boarding schools cannot creep home to mom and dad for first aid, but must learn to bind up their wounds. Lewie received this instruction so well that it was conceded in Alameda on his first vacation that he had "improved." At Thacher he had lived for the first time under conditions where he had to respect the comfort of others if he wished to be comfortable himself and he liked it. This laudable change in his behavior was brought about by nothing more violent than the pressure of a well-ordered society. He was submitting, in Burke's phrase, to "the soft collar of social esteem . . . subdued by manners." How effective it can be was shown him one day by Crandall, one of the leaders of the School, who besides being a good athlete and student had pleasant manners and a quiet reserve that made allowance for others while protecting himself. Lewie saw him with a younger boy who was running around in circles, a demonstration of spirits that Crandall was regarding with quiet reservation. Lewie identified himself with the younger boy and realized that it was better to be like Crandall as the younger boy came to a self-conscious halt. I see the pair now by the pepper trees that shut off the light from the crude little laboratory, a candid snapshot with the background stored in my memory. Although the sublimated form of the Mastick War, football, was not played at Thacher, the struggle and flight of life occurred there as it does everywhere else. Lewie, sharp-tongued and with an eye for imperfections, gave and received spiritual wounds, but part of him longed to have the old Adam buried and the new man born and he accepted with a certain gratitude the instruction of the informal teachers, the boys themselves.

He was aware of how much the School meant to him during his vacations from it when, to make up for the months of separation, his mother enforced a rigid attendance upon herself. The only visits to San Francisco that Wilmarth could make readily were to the dentist, but once a summer he would spend a night with Appie Eyre and his family in their delightful rambling house at Atherton. Mr. and Mrs. Eyre were model hosts; treading the middle way between too much attention and too little. Lewie adopted Mr. Eyre as a fellow surrogate with Mr. Thacher for his father. Mr. Eyre, a genial, outgoing man, supplied the qualities that Mr. Thacher lacked—social ease and belief in a civilized life. Wilmarth had to secure his mother's permission to visit the Eyres in a circuitous way. The subject was led up to and introduced casually, perhaps as a tiresome necessity to avoid hurting his friends' feelings by a refusal. The proposal would be received with a smile of pain and a silence that might last for days and end up with one of the terrible headaches that brought Dr. Reynolds to the darkened room. Not only would his mother refuse to speak to Wilmarth, she would refuse to look at him. He knew what she was thinking because she said it often: "Wilmarth is selfish"; "Wilmarth must have a brass band every minute." He saw that the selfishness gambit is won by the person who gets the word in first, yet since he loved his mother so much he hated to have her miserable. He would wait for the transition to speech to begin and made it as easy as he could. In this way he gained ascendancy over her. The daily drives in the Pierce-Arrow limousine were resumed. Down to Hayward and back the reunited pair would go, a stretch of fourteen miles of unrelieved dullness. The chauffeur rolled along the virtually empty highway at precisely thirty-five miles an hour. Occasionally they heard a meadow lark, once they passed an Indian holy man walking with his right arm permanently stuck upright; but for the most part the rides were uneventful. The Abbé Galiani would have applauded these vacations, which were advanced courses in boredom and injustice. Wilmarth would return to school with relief.

Although education at Thacher flourished more outside the classroom than in it, the ostensible work of the place was not taken lightly. The marks of each boy were posted weekly and were pored over by all, a practice now given up to spare the boys who receive low marks. High marks brought special privileges, which were assumed with quiet ostentation. Marks were in everybody's mind, teachers' and boys'—marks, not the content of the studies themselves. (Tully was sardonic on this subject.) The School had to get its boys into the college of their choice, above all, into Yale. If they picked up some bright pebbles of culture along the way, well, there was no harm in it. Drawing and modeling were not taught at Thacher, but there was music, which came to a climax once a term in a school concert that was supervised by an Englishwoman who could be persuaded to play the "Moonlight Sonata" on the tinny grand piano in the Parlor. Mr. Twichell might sing "The Road to Mandalay" or a drinking song that made Mr. Thacher uncomfortable; Tully Williamson's mandolin supplied a spectacular finale; but the programs were chiefly in the hands of the boys, whose mandolins, guitars, and banjos tinkled and twanged galops, polkas, and schottisches with the aid of facial contortions. Lewie played Chopin's "Raindrop Prelude" his first year to the satisfaction of the audience, but the music teacher lacked the inspirational quality of Miss Figg: there was no talk of Bach preludes or other high achievements and she defaced his beloved Chopin with pencil marks. He persuaded his mother to let him "give up music," and so the pleasure in later years of being able to sit down at a piano and play whatever is open on it was not to be his.

Occasional speakers addressed the School at Evening Reading. The boys became used to hearing themselves addressed as leaders of the future in a world that was getting steadily better in every way, a world in which war was no longer possible and in which there would soon be no poverty. There were lectures on the stars, on Japan, on moths. It is the touching hope of all who talk to boys and girls in schools that they may say something that will enlarge the minds of their audience, and one visitor, Samuel McChord Crothers, did just this for Lewie. Dr. Crothers, a wise and witty Unitarian divine from Boston, avoided the familiar recommendation of noble conduct; he merely pointed out the pleasure of becoming as familiar with some past age as with our own. The seed that he dropped into Lewie's mind lay dormant for years, but when it finally sprouted it directed the course of his life.

Most of the cultural seeds that were scattered came from the hand of S. D. Thacher. The School had no library and little to read except the *Yale Alumni Weekly*, the *Yale Daily News*, and the *Yale Banner and Pot-Pourri*. These were left on the Parlor table. Nearby hung the long strips of the *Yale University Bulletin*. The lectures, concerts, and learned society meetings listed on it had taken place days before the *Bulletin* reached the Ojai;

yet only good could come from the constant reminder that Yale, across the mountains and great rivers, was awaiting two thirds of all Thacher boys. What reading there was outside that prescribed by the college entrance exams was done by Mr. Thacher himself in the morning at the Opening of School and at Evening Reading after supper.

The routine announcements that began the day concluded not with a prayer, but with a poem. (The only prayer offered during the week invoked the safety of the Republic and was sung in Latin after supper on Thursday evenings.) Except for one or two of Shakespeare's sonnets, Polonius's advice, Gray's "Elegy," and "A Man's a Man for a' That," no poet earlier than Wordsworth was read. Each year began with "The Chambered Nautilus" and its petition for more stately mansions, O my soul!; other hardy perennials were "Intimations of Immortality," "Rabbi Ben Ezra," and Longfellow's "Psalm of Life." The lines in this last,

Be not like dumb driven cattle!
Be a hero in the strife!

were followed by an effective pause. One out of every three poems was by Kipling with annual repetition of "Something Lost Behind the Ranges" and the Feet of the Young Men responding to the call of the Red Gods; virtuoso numbers were "Bury the Great Duke," "Bells," "The Song of the Shirt," and the water coming down at Lodore. Lewie used to watch Mr. Thacher hurry out of his office, plunge into the big red *Home Book of Verse* on the schoolroom table and hastily settle on the poem of the morning. Great as was his respect for S. D., Lewie couldn't help thinking that so important a decision deserved a little more thought and that it was unfortunate the absence of it should be quite so publicly revealed. These reflections were the dawn of the suspicion that perhaps even Mr. Thacher was not perfect. Where he was at his best was in Evening Reading, particularly during the winter term when he read Dickens. His shyness and habit of critical reserve relaxed as he cast himself into Quilp or Betsy Trotwood or Dick Swiveller. When the horse ran away with Mr. Tupman the School shouted with laughter, but Lewie had to read the death of Little Nell to himself after he got home because Mr. Thacher was unable to get through it. The books during the other two terms were seldom notable. I can recall only three that were: *Joseph Vance, Penrod,* and Charles Flandrau's *Diary of a Freshman.*

Saturday Evening Reading was usually taken by W. L. Thacher. The audience was reduced to the wives of teachers and a handful of boys who, like Lewie, preferred staying at home to camping beyond the ranges. W.L.'s selections were wider than his brother's—he even read the bit about the Happy Valley in *Rasselas*—but his voice was too soothing and his performance too long. The faculty ladies, sitting under the electric lights and stabbing away at the work in their hands, managed to stay awake; the boys, having no such employment, went to sleep. This was an evasion of the Abbé Galiani's first principle of education, the endurance of boredom, but since the boys went to sleep sitting bolt upright in their hard, straight chairs, they were at least decorous. On Sundays S.D. was again in charge. The reading began with a dutiful ten minutes from a bowdlerized Bible, after which came a play. One would have expected S.D. to shine in the plays, but he didn't, possibly because he was too fearful of coming upon something embarrassing. He knew he was safe with *The Blue Bird,* but a venture into an unbowdlerized Shakespeare was disastrous. By glancing warily ahead he could skip a word or phrase not to be spoken in the Parlor, yet there was the ever-present threat of a dubious passage not discernible from afar. Trapped in one, he raced through it or leapt down the page to safety. Most of the boys—with the exception of a few men of the world—were thankful for the murk in which they sat.

Mr. Thacher was so aware of the ever-present danger of suggestion that he cut the most familiar lines from *She Stoops to Conquer* when it was given under his admirable direction in Lewie's second year. Mr. Hardcastle was not permitted to say to Mrs. Hardcastle "I love everything that is old: old friends, old times, old manners, old books, old wines; and I believe, Dorothy (taking her hand), you will own I have been pretty fond of an old wife." When Lewie, who played Constance, made so bold as to ask why this speech had been cut, S.D. blushed and murmured something about boys should not be praising wine. Although he was an inveterate enemy of wine and tobacco, his blushes sprang from a stronger lure and Lewie concluded that on this occasion they were caused by Mr. Hardcastle taking his wife's hand. The School play was given before the social climax of the year, the School dance, the sole dance of the year. Mr. Thacher tolerated the dance only because a school has to have one sometime. In 1914 the waltz and two-step were being threatened by the turkey trot and bunny hug. The two latter were of course not permitted at the Thacher School, and when S.D. caught a visiting couple dancing one of them on a side porch he ordered them off the grounds, remarking afterwards that they now had nothing to do but get married.

The boys were encouraged to go to the one Protestant church in the Valley not so much to nourish their souls as to exercise their horses. It was a Presbyterian church with a Scots minister who mentioned John Knox every Sunday, a trying allusion for his namesake in the School. Mr. Thacher conscientiously praised Mr. MacPherson's sermons, but they were lost on Lewie, especially after he and Harrington Shortall discovered a Bible with a page torn in half. When the text of the mutilated half was put on the page beneath and read across it new words such as "snofuse" appeared that were even funnier than Newbold Rhinelander dropping the plate. Lewie was enough of a Puritan to believe that these hysterical delights were wicked, but he could resist them only by staying away from church altogether, a course he was allowed to follow in his last year.

His time at Thacher drew to a close. In the late spring Evening Reading was held on the pergola and the boys watched the sunset burn and face over Matilija. Lewie was eager to get on to the next square, but it was sobering to be leaving the beautiful place where he had made such close friends and to which he knew he owed so much. Two of his closest friends, Hy Shortall and Herb Allen, were going to Harvard, which was too bad, but they would visit back and forth between Cambridge and New Haven. Thacher would always be a bond between them. His career at the School could be summed up: at the bottom in its horse and camping activities, above the average in his studies, and at the top in tennis, writing, and dramatics. The sketches of him in the *Archivero* let him off easily. It seems that he sang loudly and continuously, "caterwauling" one biographer called it, and that he delighted in exposing the ignorance of his friends by asking quiz questions the answers to which he announced triumphantly on their failures. It is not surprising that he was not more popular.

Yale moved closer when S.D. summoned to his office all the boys who were going there to be instructed about its famous Society System. The two-hour talk began with the defunct Freshman and Sophomore Societies and the still active Junior Fraternities whose significance at Yale was that they were essential stepping-stones to the ultimate goal, the Senior Societies, Skull and Bones, Scroll and Key, and Wolf's Head. The Senior Societies were so secret it was said that a member of them would leave the room if his Society was mentioned in his presence by a nonmember. This supersecrecy was conducted with superpublicity. The Society Halls, or "tombs," had no windows; elections to them were printed in full in the New York papers, those who tapped as well as those who were tapped, and where they came from; the local press throughout the nation reported the elections of its local boys. On the second Thursday in May the entire Junior Class gathered under the "Tap Day Oak" on the campus at five in the afternoon. A few minutes before the hour the first of the Seniors worked their way through the crowd and stood at attention behind the Juniors whom they were going to tap. They wore derbies and dark suits; on the knots of their black ties were pinned the gold badge of their society. (This was the only time that it was revealed publicly; normally it was worn out of sight and in the mouth when bathing.) At the first stroke of five the expressionless Seniors banged the Juniors' shoulders shouting, "Go to your room!" The crowd burst into nervous applause. This went on for nearly an hour while the excitement grew as the three Societies filled up their number of fifteen each and it became evident that some prominent Juniors were going to miss out. S.D. had had to wait until fourteenth man for Bones, he said, but everyone knew that it was Bones or nothing for him.

It was all familiar to Lewie even before he left Alameda, but he listened spellbound as Mr. Thacher, who had been tapped and who had tapped another, told it again. In conclusion Mr. Thacher explained that membership in Bones had been one of the great experiences in his life and that anything one did to secure it—anything honorable, of course—was justified. He admitted that occasionally elections to it were declined for an election to Keys, some Thacher boys had made this mistake, but when it happened Keys had "packed" or pledged the Junior beforehand. Finally, one should not discuss the societies with anyone until one's own Tap Day was imminent. With this warning the group was dismissed into the California sunshine, but Lewie's instruction was not over. Outside Mr. Thacher's office was hovering Mr. Twichell, another Yale man. He came up to Lewie and said, "I think I know what you have been hearing in there. It's all true except that the great experience at Yale is not Bones, but Keys." Lewie was impressed because he knew that Mr. Twichell was not a member of either Society.

The period of cramming for the Yale exams, which followed Commencement, and the taking of the exams themselves was the climax of the year. The boys were trained and drilled as if they were athletes on the eve of the Olympics: their futures hung in the balance; what they were doing was much the most fateful thing they had yet done, as Lewie wrote sententiously to his mother. He had the exhilaration of learning under pressure; matters that he had not understood before suddenly became clear. The boys took an infinite number of the exams that had been given in earlier years; they learned to relax, to be confident, to sit with their heads bent over the desk, to drink a great deal of water. W. L. Thacher was at his best during this professional crisis, telling his pupils of uncommon uses of the dative that would impress the examiners in Latin Composition, and when Lewie contrived to work in one or two of these proofs of learning he was rewarded with a very respectable mark. This was not true of his plane geometry and physics papers, but thanks to divine intervention with them he entered Yale without a condition. A very few Thacher diplomas were given "with Commendation," "with High Commendation," or "with Highest Commendation," but Lewie's diploma had no such honorable addition.

Just before he left Mr. Thacher had him into his office for a valedictory talk. Lewie, he said, was too critical and too fastidious. Mr. Thacher confessed that he, too, was over-critical, as Mrs. Thacher had told him at Miramar during the summer when he had first seen Mrs. Lewis and Wilmarth there. He could sympathize with Lewie's tendency to point out the faults of others, yet it would make him unhappy in the long run unless curbed and would frustrate whatever he tried to do. But the greatest danger to his future lay—in his mother. "You are much too fond of her," Mr. Thacher told him. "Don't let her keep you at home. You should go to Yale. Go back to her in vacations, but don't let her lead your life for you." Mr. Thacher, the surrogate for Wilmarth's father and for God, had spoken. It was like the time when Wilmarth was rolled in the huge wave at Santa Cruz. Instead of his mother being his protecting angel on earth, to whom no sacrifice could be too great, her possessiveness was malign. The confirmation of what Lewie had suspected overwhelmed him, he broke down, but accepted the truth of what he had been told.

Why did we feel that S.D. was "a great man?" He stood for moral rectitude, high purpose, dedication to the general good. When two boys got tipsy on dago red Lewie's last year he expelled them that night. His concern for our personal welfare, which we felt really did mean much to him, was flattering. He never talked down to us, not even when he had us in his office and told us our faults; he was rarely sarcastic. The boys were not aware that he tended to turn them into prigs and prudes and would have resented anyone's saying so. He accepted as self-evident, as did all the leading schoolmasters of his generation, Herbert Spencer's dictum, "Education has for its object the formation of character." He sought to infuse in Thacher boys a desire to live a generous and useful life. When I think of him now it strikes me as odd that Wordsworth's "Happy Warrior" was not one of his hardy annuals at the Opening of School. He read it, I think, but it wasn't stressed as were "The

Chambered Nautilus" and "A Psalm of Life," yet I should say that it comes as near to expressing what he hoped for his charges as any poem in the language. He strove to make each boy become a man

> *Whose high endeavors are an inward light*
> *That makes the path before him always bright.*

Character employed in the tasks of life, that was the great thing. He could forgive a boy for being stupid about the ablative absolute, but he would not have one in the School who he knew smoked during vacation. A boy's studies were of less account than his enlistment in the forces of good, which were committed above all else to holding the demon of biology at bay. From the Opening of School until you said good night to him in the Parlor, there he was, a rather short, stocky, untidy man with a fine forehead and quizzical little eyes, running your world that was dedicated to the Highest Good and encouraging you to do as well as you could in it.

On one of his last nights at the School Lewie was initiated into a society which was so secret that none of the boys not in it knew of its existence. Mr. Thacher told him to go out to the Middle Barn after the last tomtom, a most unexpected command. When Lewie got there he was jumped on by members of the society. While he lay blindfolded upon the ground he was warned that he hurt people's feelings. The period of plain speech over, his blindfold was removed, he was comforted with grape juice, and welcomed into the stern brotherhood that secretly and nobly ran the School. There they were, the chosen band, drinking grape juice under the bright stars while the unchosen slept. Here at last was acceptance. After Lewie got home a spectacle case arrived that contained the society's gold pin. The newest member suspected that his tardy election was owing to the boy who tripped him up at recess baseball, a guess confirmed two years later by the boy himself who then regretted his repeated blackballs. (The reason for them, he said, was not so much that Lewie hurt people's feelings as that he did not chase his share of tennis balls.) Still, the gold pin was a comfort to Lewie, or Wilmarth as he remained in Alameda, even though he had earned the right to wear it only at the last possible moment. It represented an achievement of sorts and it helped him get through the summer. Mr. Thacher had said that he was too fond of his mother and that he must not let her spoil his life. The struggle between the generations, the oldest in the world, of authority against independence, had been placed squarely before him, with the unusual feature of the rebel having in his corner the strongest representative of authority in his life. "You are changed," Mrs. Lewis would say to him coldly, and he would feel guilty, but he knew that Mr. Thacher was right.

The heroes in *St. Nicholas* had as their enemies redcoats, bears, and wicked knights, not possessive mothers, nor were mother's-boys heroes. They were (and are) comic when effeminate, contemptible when weak. Less obvious versions of the type are the Lotharios and alcoholics. The result in every case is an individual who has been maimed to a greater or less extent. After Sidney Howard showed in *The Silver Cord* the deadly nature of their plight, they gained some sympathy and now the genesis of the mother's possessiveness, hatred of her husband and her unconscious wish to emasculate their son, is better understood. Wilmarth's situation in 1914 was made harder during the past year by his mother having had a major operation, following which she was nearly burned to death in an electric blanket, a horrible experience that made her a legitimate object of solicitude.

Wilmarth did one fortunate thing during that summer. He rented a typewriter, bought *Teach Yourself Typewriting by the*

Touch System, and practiced several hours daily in the billiard room. As he moved from lesson to lesson he had an agreeable sense of preparing himself for his future profession. By the time he left for Yale he was doing sixty words a minute with not too many mistakes. The summer of 1914 was memorable for him, as it was for so many others.

VII

YALE I, FRESHMAN YEAR

On his arrival in New Haven as a Freshman in September 1914 Lewie was dismayed by the prevailing ugliness of the city and the University. The handsomer past could be seen here and there: the three churches on the Green and the three eighteenth-century houses that had somehow survived there; eighteenth-century Connecticut Hall, and the neo-Gothic Library; but the Victorian dormitories and the cheap shops in the heart of the University were dispiriting. Lewie brushed this treasonous thought aside. Whatever Yale was, was right. Arching elms were all over the place; three statues of Yale worthies (including Nathan Hale, 1773) gave dignity and an air of well-being (since only the rich had statues); the winey air was redolent with roasted chestnuts and sweet cider; over all, beckoning, heavy with fate, were the windowless tombs of the secret societies.

Thanks to his roommate, Dunham Barney of Farmington, Connecticut, who had been at Thacher with him, Lewie lived in Wright Hall, the Freshman dormitory just built with contributions from alumni of whom Dunham's father had been one. The boasted "Yale Democracy" did not withhold from its benefactors' sons the dividends of generosity and so Dunham and his roommate were housed in Wright instead of in one of the bleak asylums reserved for the less fortunate on York Street. Wright Hall was the last word in collegiate comfort. Its suites for two consisted of two bedrooms and a sitting room with a fireplace over which was a panel carved with the name and class of the Yale graduate in whose memory the room was given. Dignified Irish ladies made the beds and cleaned the rooms and followed the careers of their young men. Before the year was over Mrs. Shea, who looked after 655 Wright, confided to Lewie that on the last Tap Day two of her young men had made Bones, two Keys, and three Wolf's Head. A fine record.

At the beginning of the year slightly sinister characters milled in and out of Wright selling contracts for newspapers and laundry, for pressing clothes and shining shoes; there were second-hand furniture men; there were tailors; there were up-per-classmen soliciting subscriptions to collegiate enterprises. It was all rather heady for Lewie, a stride towards independence away from the constant surveillance of Alameda and Thacher. For the first time in his life he had no one standing over him to see that he picked up his clothes. He found untidiness so intoxi-cating that he was never to give it up entirely.

Concern with clothes was a major difference between Yale and Thacher, where the Headmaster and his brother demon-strated that a marked disorder in one's dress goes with moral ascendancy. At Yale (as elsewhere, for that matter), it helped to have the right clothes and to know how to wear them; the strait jacket of accepted conventions in dress, speech, and manner was as tight as the strait jacket worn in Alameda, but it was better tailored. More important than clothes was the air of "belong-ing." The swift appraising eyes of adepts in the art of social intercourse recognized a fellow initiate on sight, the rest might as well not exist, but acquirement of an acceptable appearance was not in itself enough to ensure success. You had to prove your worth, a fact subsumed in the concept of "Yale Democracy." To the Western boys who came to Yale from Thacher without a year or two in a good Eastern prep school, the talk about Yale Democracy was ironical. Although it made no difference whether you had money or not (few knew who were rich unless they had famous names) and there was no Harvard Gold Coast into which the *jeunesse dorée* withdrew, by Western standards Yale was anything but "democratic." The word at Yale had a special meaning. When in 1902 the Public Orator presented Theodore Roosevelt for an honorary degree he explained that the President "is a Harvard man by nature; but in his democratic spirit, his breadth of national feeling, and his earnest pursuit of what is true and right, he possesses those qualities which represent the distinctive ideals of Yale." This was received not with gales of laughter, but with prolonged applause. By "democratic spirit" the Public Orator meant that Yale was a place where the highest undergraduate social honors were attainable by boys without money or "family," a refinement lost on some of the Western Thacher boys who found Yale so chilling that they clung together in obscurity, longing for the smell of wet sage on mountain sides and fishing in the Sespe. Lewie was fortunately among those who adapted themselves to their new environment.

The four-hundred-odd members of 1918 came from two thirds of the States in the Union; "over in Sheff," which joined with the College only in extra-curricular activities, were three hundred and fifty more in the entering class. Yale was a national institution, but hardly an international one: the only foreigners in 1918 were half a dozen Chinese. Three quarters of the class had been to preparatory schools, the best of which impressed a stamp on their graduates, as Lewie wrote to Mr. Thacher. Leaders in the big schools came to Yale with an advantage over their less successful schoolmates because the pecking-order established at them tended to survive at college to the disadvantage of those who developed slowly. Boys from small schools, on the other hand, once they got beyond the trying period of isolation, could make their way with greater ease than the boys who had been submerged in a big school. Lewie bolstered his confidence by wearing his Thacher secret-society pin out of sight as the Senior Society members wore their pins. He felt slightly silly doing it, but faith in the talisman strengthened him.

The Class met daily with the entire College at Morning Chapel, a breathless service that lasted from 8:10 to 8:20. It was conducted by a member of the faculty, President Hadley at his side. A preliminary chant was followed by a Lesson, a hymn, the Lord's Prayer, and a racing benediction after which President Hadley scurried down the central aisle. The Seniors bowed deferentially as he sped past and then crowded in upon his heels accelerating his naturally brisk gait and bringing the service to a rollicking close. Daily Chapel gave the College a sense of cousinhood. It was perfunctory, but morning after morning, year in, year out, one heard great passages of the King James Version. There was no nonsense about the young not understanding "a glass darkly" or "charity." Whether you were receptive, casual, or hostile the most beautiful book in our language insensibly furnished your mind.

During the winter a discreet religious revival was held. It was Lewie's introduction to organized evangelicalism and he liked it. (At Thacher Mr. MacPherson did not extend his pastorate beyond the pulpit.) Eminent preachers came from New York and preached; there were "group meetings" presided over by well-dressed and athletic young graduates who said with conviction "I *know!*" and urged the undergraduates to express their doubts and be fortified in Christian faith. Lewie learned for the first time that Jesus was an historic person. He bought a New Testament and for several mornings read Acts. This was the second time he read the Bible on his own. The first time was at Thacher. He reported the venture to Tully Williamson who discouraged its repetition by saying, "I thought you looked smug." No one talked like that during Religious Week at Yale; Lewie was doing what it was hoped he would do. The gift of tongues and the conversion of Saul took on a reality that they had lacked when reported in church. He felt grown-up as he read about them by himself; and here and there he had the pleasure of discovery, such as when he came upon Ananias and understood at last what Theodore Roosevelt meant when he talked about the Ananias Club. Acts was full of instruction as well as strength and comfort, but when he finished it Lewie did not go on to Romans.

It cannot be said that Religious Week changed the tone and atmosphere of Daily Chapel, the chief interest of which for ambitious Freshman gazing down from their gallery continued to be the Seniors of the Class of 1915 whose leaders were known from the *News* and *Banner and Pot-Pourri.* Those publications showed the successful looking the camera squarely in the eye. How did the "big men" differ from the lesser? They had an air of well-being, their walk was confident, they had prevailed, and life was good to them. Although four of the leading Seniors—Dean Acheson, Norman Donaldson, Archibald MacLeish, and Douglas Moore—were later to become his intimate friends, Lewie did not know them while they were in college. Freshmen might meet a Senior while competing, "heeling" in the Yale dialect, for a paper or other activity, but that was a professional, not a social, encounter. Yale College was a hierachy with ranks and procedures; it imposed its terms and reserved its rewards for those who dedicated themselves to its way of life. If you weren't willing—if you weren't eager—to accept Yale's guidance you had better go elsewhere. One Junior in two thousand would rebel with deeply felt words about "the Bitch Goddess Success" and refuse to offer himself for election on Tap Day.

Lewie's first class was in Freshman English. Arrived at the top of Phelps Hall he saw a striking figure sitting behind the desk on the platform. It was Chauncey Brewster Tinker, aged just thirty-eight, who was teaching his first class as a full professor. He sat motionless, gazing at the top of his desk, giving his new students time to accustom themselves to his appearance: hair *en brosse,* an artificial eye, a fearful swelling on one cheek. He was dressed in a carefully pressed green suit with Homeric lapels. The last Freshman arrived and still Tinker sat without moving. Then the Chapel clock struck the half hour. He scraped back his chair, bounded to the door, slammed it shut, and began as he returned to his desk, "Shakespeare dated this play in the first speech. Did anyone notice how?" The play was I *Henry IV,* and Lewie, who had read the assignment as if his life depended upon mastering it, remembered

> *Those blessed feet*
> *Which, fourteen hundred years ago, were nail'd*
> *For our advantage, on the bitter cross,*

but he was too frightened to raise his hand. Nor did anyone else raise a hand. Tinker then quoted the passage and went on to elucidate and illuminate the text, occasionally asking a carefully prepared question, which the class soon found courage to answer caught up by the urgency of his manner and the skill of his direction. When Lewie walked down the stairs of Phelps Hall after his first class he thought, "No wonder Yale is what it is when you find such a teacher in the first class you go to." Now fifty years and more later I can still feel the excitement of Freshman English, the fear that Tink aroused, the wish to satisfy him who could be so alarming, revealing, and confidential.

He left with his thousands of students enlightenments that lasted their lives. One among many such for Lewie was his elucidation of a passage in Tennyson's "Ulysses":

> *. . . experience is an arch wherethro'*
> *Gleams that untravell'd world, whose margin fades*
> *For ever and for ever when I move.*

Although Mr. Thacher had read the poem often, this figure had been lost on Lewie. To understand it, Tink said, one should walk through Phelps Gateway, a tunnel-like passage beneath Phelps Hall, with one's eyes on the further end, and when Lewie did so the fading margin became clear. Years later he was to repeat this walk annually at Commencement as a member of the Yale Corporation. The procession winds up from Center Church on the Green. At the College Street entrance to the Gateway the vigorous military band is left and the procession moves into the tunnel-like passage. The honorand on W. S. Lewis's right, no matter how old a hand he was at Commencements, would fall silent. It is always a little intimidating to enter a tunnel—what is at the other end?—but as the cortège proceeds, dignified and stately, even the most behooded and bemedalled are impressed. The view through the Gateway gets wider and wider as the procession nears the Old Campus. Trumpets sound, the chimes of Harkness Tower dingdong madly, flags flutter, ten thousand parents and loved ones rise and stare with curiosity and respect at the advancing dignitaries. Tink made me realize that education is a similar enlargement.

What would have happened to the undergraduates of 1914 if all instructors had been Tinkers? Alas, they were not. The next class that Lewie went to on that first morning in 1914 and the classes that followed it—Latin (Livy, Tacitus, the satires of Horace), Elementary Chemistry, Advanced French (which was conducted in English), and History (from the fall of Rome to Woodrow Wilson)—were pedestrian or worse. The instructor in Latin discouraged further study of it and so Lewie missed the learned and humane men who instructed the upper-classmen. All I remember of Freshman Chemistry is the effect of boiling sulfuric acid on a pongee shirt. Lewie was diddling his test tube up and down over a Bunsen burner in the way the professor diddled his test tubes. The bubbling sulfuric acid suddenly leapt out on to his neighbor, Robert A. Lovett. I can see now the burnt spots that appeared instantaneously on his beautiful shirt and the imperturbability of the future Secretary of Defense who instead of emptying the test tube of his wrath in retaliation accepted the accident calmly as a consequence of having W. S. Lewis as a neighbor in the chemistry laboratory. No doubt the latter got more out of his formal Yale education than he realized at the time or than I realize now. Spanish in Sophomore and Junior years taught him to speak and understand that language temporarily, a weekly lecture for Juniors by Roy Angier gave him insight into the psychological origin of certain illnesses, "Daily Themes" with John Berdan helped his writing; and then there was Sophomore Physics. This was the same course, from simple machines to light, that Lewie had at Thacher with Forest Cooke. He remained baffled by the simple machines, but learned that the end of the long arm of the lever is the most effective place to exert force, a fact demonstrated to him in later years by the heads of undertakings, who are in a better position to accomplish what they want to do than are those nearer the fulcrum.

Of the three repositories of learning, the University Library, Art Gallery, and Peabody Museum of Natural History, the undergraduates knew little and cared less. Although Lewie liked museums and sightseeing, so indifferently were Yale's collections housed and so forlorn were their aspect that he was repelled by one visit to each. Most undergraduates never set foot in them throughout their entire college course. Only once did Lewie withdraw a book from the Library and that was under compulsion. His Freshman History instructor actually led the class into the building, showed it how the catalogue worked, and made each student take out at least one book and use it in an essay. The class agreed that this was going too far. The undergraduates had a library of their own, Linonia and Brothers, the descendant of two eighteenth-century debating societies, which was occasionally sought out by those who wished to escape from visitors in their own rooms, but it was presided over by a little man who talked at the top of his lungs above a sign on his desk labeled "SILENCE." "L and B" was a disturbed refuge.

The melancholy state of the Yale Library and museums reflected the prevailing attitude towards them of the faculty and administration. This ranged from the gently interested to the openly hostile. Mr. Hadley once quoted a remark made to him by a leading Yale Professor that "the chief educational use of a university library is to lend an occasional book to a professor who does not happen to have that book on his own shelves." Yale rested on the mines of Ophir, but the miners were few. Tinker, it is true, while teaching Carlyle in Freshman English drove home the point that "The true university of these days is a collection of books" and when the class reached Ruskin, he made it go over to the Gallery and write a note on Titian's "Circumcision," but Tinker was a law unto himself.

As for the Graduate Schools, the undergraduates hardly knew that they existed, even though their two grim dormitories were in the middle of the University. Their inmates fell far short of the social standards acceptable in Yale College. The University itself made it clear that whereas "outsiders" might come to Yale to do graduate work and teach lower-classmen, they were, inevitably, second-class citizens. Anson Stokes, the very able Secretary of the University, wrote in the 1917 *Banner and Pot-Pourri:* "It is a matter of vital importance to the future of the University that we should always have a strong nucleus on our Faculty of men born and bred in the spirit of Yale who can help to hand down . . . its traditions of work, democracy, and Christian faith and service," a statement that did not make the graduates of other universities feel more at home.

Learning was not fashionable at Yale. What Yale had to give, which was much, it gave outside its classrooms. A few courses were "hard" and their instructors were respected accordingly, but the average student like Lewie quickly sized up how much time was required to "get by" in the others. There was little of the rapport between students and instructors that Lewie had enjoyed at Thacher. Although now and then members of the faculty made little speeches on the desirability of study, no one, not even the speakers, took them seriously. What Yale really believed was painted on the proscenium over the stage in Lampson Lyceum: *Non Scholae sed Vitae Discimus.* At Yale we learned life, not studies. "Life" was primarily finding out how to get on with one's fellows and to advance in the never-to-be-relaxed struggle for the first prize, which was not in the minds of most undergraduates the acquirement of bookish knowledge, but an election to a Senior Society.

This was accomplished in various ways. Anson Stokes in a sermon preached before the College in the winter of 1915 said that "the iron doors of mystery may be opened by work and prayer"; that is, you could make a Society by working hard in one of the innumerable competitions, so hard that you prayed to be successful. Certain successes were, however, more esteemed than others, and it was part of your testing that you should discover which they were. Football and crew ranked above baseball and track, hockey above basketball, golf above tennis, the *News* and *Lit.* above the *Courant* or *Record.* The important managerships made election to a Society virtually automatic; so did the Presidency of Dwight Hall, the Christian Association. Membership in Phi Beta Kappa counted for little unless it was buttressed by success in some other activity that was universally respected; nothing was so fatal as earning the reputation of being "a greasy grind." A marked divergence from the narrow norm was not acceptable. I can think of one promising youth who fell by the way because he hung curtains in his room; I can think of nobody who went so far as to keep birds or hyacinths. Yale scorned mediocrity, but the excellence that it rewarded was conventional.

The excitement of the place was found outside the classroom. "What are you going out for?" was the question Freshmen asked each other most frequently. Lewie's answer after three months was "The *Lit.*," the oldest literary magazine in America, of which it was said with awe that the British Museum had a complete run. Although the *Lit.* was read by few except its five editors and its "heelers," a very small band, election to its board was an undergraduate prize. Unlike the *News* competitions, of which there were three of four months each and which required hours daily of their heelers' time on and off bicycles, the *Lit.* competition drifted quietly along until the middle of Junior year when the five who led it were elected by vote of the entire class. The heeler with the most contributions became the Chairman and a marked man; at Yale to be "literary" was not to be blighted so long as one was not *too* literary. Lewie took the competition with utmost seriousness. He denied himself even the movies—foul-smelling firetraps, but centers of social life and so of education—and he worked

Saturday nights. Wilmarth had chosen writing as his vocation at the age of eight and the time had come to get on with it. He repeated to himself:

The heights by great men reached and kept
Were not attained by sudden flight,
But they, while their companions slept,
Were toiling upward in the night.

When his first two contributions to the *Lit.* were rejected he worked harder still and became more dependent upon the poets:

Then welcome each rebuff
That turns earth's smoothness rough,
Each sting that bids nor sit nor stand but go!

Longfellow and Browning, in S. D. Thacher's well-remembered voice, were needed to combat the sound of fellow collegians singing on their way home at night.

The *Lit.* was conducted with ritual, as were all the most respected activities at Yale. Make-up nights were on the first Wednesday of the month. The five editors met in the *Lit.* office on the ground floor of Osborn Hall. After they made up the next number they wrote out its table of contents on a sheet and hung it, face out, in the northwest window. They then departed noisily and self-consciously, and the heelers, who had been hiding in the cold and dark, hurried forward and struck matches to see if their contributions were accepted. The first great moment of illumination for Lewie came in February 1915. His contribution was a sketch in the modest section of the magazine called "Portfolio." The hero of the sketch was a newsboy who suffered in soul and body from a bully. Then one day the hero struck out (very much as Wilmarth had struck out at Karl), was brilliantly successful, was restored to a position of respect among his fellows—and then resumed his former arrogant ways with them. The faculty reviewer praised "Mr. Lewis's spirited sketch." The change of attitude towards the author was immediate. Elegant youths who had ignored him nodded affably; his instructors regarded him with new interest. Other sketches followed rapidly: the next proved that Mrs. Shea was Mistress Quickly in *Henry IV,* there was a Leacockian extravaganza about a spring suit, an afternoon tea party, and an essay on Lewis Carroll. These pieces were easier to read than the Tennyson-Browning verses and the Matthew Arnold prose elsewhere in the magazine and brought Lewie the reputation of being a wag, "human" as well as "literary," the acceptable Yale mixture. By the end of Freshman year he had won the gold *Lit.* triangle, which was awarded on the publication of five contributions and which thereafter dangled conspicuously on the winner's watchchain. Lewie's election to the board two years off was assured.

As I try now half a century later to recall Lewie in Freshman year and how he sought to get the most out of Yale I keep thinking of one morning that had nothing to do with people or the better life when he was waked by a strange scraping noise in Wright Hall Court. He got up and saw for the first time falling snow. The scraping was made by men shoveling it. He had seen snow on Mt. Shasta and other distant mountains, but all California children long to see it fall as it does on Christmas cards and here it was falling and it was as beautiful as he expected it to be. Before the day was over he learned what becomes of it in city streets and the need for galoshes, which he soon learned not to link up but to let their clamps click back and forth as he walked in conformity with the prevailing fashion.

Fifty years ago the University paid little attention to the health of its students. There was a casual physical examination at the beginning of Freshman year, after which each youth was given a card that recorded his age, height, weight, and physical excellences and defects. Lewie was six feet tall, weighed 145 pounds, and had a hyperlordosis, which on inquiry he learned was something wrong with his spine. However, nothing was done about it; Bob Kiphuth's corrective exercises, which have become a model for the entire country, had not yet been devised, and the present admirable University Department of Health was still in the future. When you became ill, as Lewie did several times under stress, you either stayed in your room or got yourself out to the Yale Infirmary where you were a private patient, but not so private that the matron might not drag you out of bed to dance to her raging phonograph. Illness at Yale had rough and ready treatment, softened by unexpected solicitude, from which Lewie once benefitted. At the end of his Sophomore year he had a mild case of diphtheria. Not to alarm his mother, he omitted his weekly letter to her. A mistake. Back in his room, when he was packing hurriedly to leave for the summer, there was a tap at the door and in stepped the President of the University, a letter of inquiry from Mrs. Lewis in his hand.

Exercise, apart from the University teams, was also left to the individual. There were half a dozen tennis-courts; two squash courts and two lanes of bowling alleys were built while Lewie was in college. He was quite good at these innovations, which became his winter sports. The University golf course had not yet been laid out; such walking as was done (which was a good deal) took place in the streets of New Haven. The attitude towards intercollegiate sports was not what it had been in the days when half the all-American football team was composed of Yale men. Lewie was shocked at his first game to see how bored two prominent Seniors were with the proceedings on the field. As the season wore on the cheering section did fill up, the cheer leaders labored mightily, the band blew and thumped; Lewie was not the only one who brayed himself into a laryngitis, but such excess of enthusiasm was regarded as slightly juvenile. Yale was withdrawing from the football hullabaloo it had started.

Where did the undergraduates eat? The extremes were the University Commons and the University Club, the least and the most exclusive of choices. In between were the "eating joints," noisome places in cellars run as cheaply as possible by undergraduate entrepreneurs. Lewie stayed in one until he established friendly relations with its members and then moved to another. Amiability, he discovered, makes life easier. He was helped by the murder of Rosenthal, the New York gambler whose end introduced the American public to the existence of gangsters who, for a fee, would kill anybody you wished. Among those employed to kill Rosenthal was "Lefty Louie." "Lewie," a commonplace diminutive, disappeared as swiftly as had Rosenthal, and was replaced by "Lefty," the name I shall carry to my grave. I am much in Lefty Louie's debt because the possession of a nickname is a gift beyond rubies.

Freshman English ended with a merited reproof. Flushed with his success in it Lefty did not review the last term's reading carefully and did badly on the final exam. Tink reduced his mark from a high A to a low B for the entire year. This was severe but just and Lefty was to recall it the rest of his life whenever he was assailed by overconfidence before a test.

VIII

YALE II, 1915–1917

Early in his Sophomore year Lefty was elected to a Junior Fraternity and the Elizabethan Club. Thanks to the *Lit.* and his discovery that things go better if one is agreeable he had won a certain position. (Tinker looked at him sternly one day and said, "Don't ever lose your gaiety." Lefty was startled but pleased and encouraged.) He had begun to bask in the sunshine of Yale.

He did not need his brothers' and Mr. Thacher's endorsement of fraternities because he had the normal American undergraduate's feeling for them, their comradeship, exclusiveness, and secrecy. He was impressed by the pen-and-ink sketches that preceded their sections in the *Stanford Quad* and the *Yale Banner and Pot-Pourri:* a monk or Death in a cowl, tripods, windowless temples, ravens, basilisks, bats. The initiated had learned the meaning of these symbols and mysteries and were bound together in a brotherhood that lifted them above the uninitiated. The Junior Fraternities at Yale were stepping-stones to the Senior Societies, but that did not mean they lacked virtues of their own. These included the loyalty that springs from selection and acceptance and the sense of sodality that helps to make the world a pleasant place.

The first fraternity elections came in the fall of Sophomore year. Those ahead in the race at that point might fall back, those behind might move forward, positions shifted constantly, but the first elections furnished a public assessment of one's position at that time. The agitation of the collective Juniors was as great as that of the individual Sophomores: the quality of the new delegation would be a public judgment on their own quality; without appearing to do so, they had to make themselves attractive to those Sophomores who could get whichever fraternity they wanted. The lyre-bird dance, "Calling," went on for two weeks and was followed by Hold Offs and Bottle Night. After the elections had been given and accepted there came Running Week when each elected candidate had to carry before breakfast a carnation of the fraternity's color to the member for whom he was running and be prepared to deliver cigarettes and chocolate buds on demand by any of its members. The public climax came with Calcium Light Night. Lefty watching it in his Freshman year thought it one of the most beautiful sights he had ever seen. The members of the five fraternities—Alpha Delta Phi, Psi Upsilon, Delta Kappa Epsilon, Zeta Psi, and Beta Theta Pi—marched and countermarched in their colored robes along the paths of the Campus singing their songs with gusto and gaiety while their leaders beat time with flaming torches. The songs rose and fell and mingled in the frosty night as the groups passed and repassed, now close, now distant. Within an hour the torches burnt out and the voices died away as the five groups marched off to their tombs.

In the fall of '15, an unusual circumstance occurred in the fraternity elections. The last fraternity established at Yale, Beta Theta Pi, had so much difficulty in getting members the year before that Dean Jones, in the belief that Yale should have five thriving fraternities, persuaded Charlie Taft and four other leading members of 1918 to join it and allowed them to "pack" the rest of their delegation openly. The Beta tomb was antiquated; to give the fraternity a cause it was decided that the new house should be "open," not a tomb at all. Lefty was lukewarm about the cause—he liked mumbo-jumbo—but when his roommate, Dunham Barney, joined he was delighted to go along. He found himself with a very congenial group who dined together twice a week on dubious fare without even beer to wash it down. Dinner was followed by a meeting at which the prescribed ritual was performed to the despair of the visiting national officers who came to see how the Yale Chapter was behaving. It gave Lefty friendships that have lasted a lifetime. Looking back, I don't see how the Junior Fraternities of fifty years ago could have been bettered.

They introduced one to the accidents and vagaries of elections, the luck that enters into acceptance and rejection. This was brought home to Lefty on the occasion when he almost got a candidate through after several frustrated attempts. Just as the vote was to be taken one of the brethren turned to him and asked: "Is he that *thing* in those *glasses?*" and Lefty had to admit that he was. The nonconformity proclaimed by pince-nez and a black ribbon was emphasized by a mincing walk and a small mouth both prim and contemptuous. Lefty regretted these imperfections as much as the scornful brother, yet he felt that it was trivial as well as unjust to let them outweigh the candidate's good qualities and proved talent. No use; his candidate disappeared under a rain of blackballs. Lefty was to learn that tribunals of older persons often make decisions on similar grounds, although the objectionable mannerism is seldom mentioned. An ill-timed laugh or grimace is noticed and recorded unfavorably in the mind of one who may later decide the grimacer's fate. I know of one man who almost missed a major post because he wore two rings and another who was passed over because he carried a comb in his pocket. "A man's attire and excessive laughter and gait," we read in Ecclesiasticus, "show what he is."

Although blackballs rolled at the Elizabethan Club there was nothing secret about it once you got in. You could even take guests to it provided they were not ladies. The early nineteenth-century clubhouse in the heart of the University had six pleasant rooms. There were fireplaces; there were portraits of Garrick by Robert Edge Pine, of Charles James Fox by Opie, and Queen Elizabeth herself by Zucchero—at least that is what it said on the frames; there was Jacobean furniture; there was a garden where bowls were played in the spring. There were no dues, everything was free: tea dispensed with bustle and importance by Sims, the Negro steward; tobacco and church-warden pipes on which you wrote your name. Once a year the Club gave a play. On Club Nights visiting luminaries such as Yeats, Masefield, and Chesterton dined with the Entertainment Committee at the Taft or Mory's and talked to the Club afterwards. The world-famous library was in a vault, but the books were either in slipcases or had been rebound in expensive modern bindings. Lefty did not know (nor did any other undergraduate know) which were the most important books bibliographically—the Shakespeare folios and quartos and certain other sixteenth- and seventeenth-century books of the greatest rarity. When he took a visitor into the vault he always showed off a copy of the first edition of *Paradise Lost* in modern green morocco with cypress trees on its covers. He would exclaim with admiration, his visitor would exclaim, and they did not know that they were exclaiming over the ugliest book in the collection. The joys of the Elizabethan Club were social, not bibliophilic.

The Club was only four years old in 1915, but it was already an established success. It had been given and endowed by Alexander Cochran on the encouragement of Professor William Lyon Phelps. The latter believed that Yale undergraduates interested in writing and the arts should have a place to congregate under civilized conditions and to meet members of the faculty. There were those who had doubts about the need for such an institution at Yale, which had got on very well for over two hundred years without it. Was it really desirable to have Yale men drinking tea? Yale took pride in the story of the visiting English don who asked at Cambridge, Mass., how far Yale was from Harvard and was told, "As far as Sparta from Athens," yet Yale was not a cultural desert. All the theatrical and musical stars came to New Haven. Bernhardt played at the Shubert; the Ballet Russe came with Nijinsky; Pavlova and Ruth Draper came on their own. In Woolsey Hall there were concerts by Schumann-Heink, Paderewski, Albert Spalding, the New York Philharmonic, and the Boston Symphony. They played to full houses, but the sophistication of their audiences may be gauged by Billy Phelps's letter to the *News* before the first of the New Haven Symphony's five concerts in 1915. "This is one of the opportunities of university life—to acquire a love and understanding of music. The Orchestra will play Beethoven's Fifth Symphony, one of the greatest masterpieces of all time."

The Elizabethan Club was founded and was an immediate success. That a high proportion of its initial members were also in Senior Societies did not go unnoticed. By good luck there happened to be in college during the Club's first decade the group of undergraduates now spoken of as "The Yale Renaissance," among whom were Monty Woolley, Cole Porter, Archibald MacLeish, Charles Merz, Douglas S. Moore, John Farrar, Phillip Barry, Stephen Vincent Benét, Henry R. Luce, Reginald Marsh, Walter Millis, Thornton Wilder. The club changed the tone and atmosphere of modern Yale more decisively than any other innovation up to the founding of its residential colleges. Monty Woolley dominated it during Lefty's undergraduate years. As coach of the Dramat he put on wonderful performances of *Lear, Troilus and Cressida, Coriolanus, Tamburlaine,* and even Tennyson's *Harold,* productions for which its members and heelers did everything except make the costumes. To Lefty, Monty was Tully Williamson with plumes. He was an impresario who lived in noise and agitation and comic situations of his creation and invention. He made up "draymas" of world-champion chess players, of habitués of the Comédie-Française, of the Judgment Day. His ebullience was unflagging and loud; his tone and manner were infectious. When twenty years later he created "The Man Who Came to Dinner" he was merely playing himself except that he was never malicious. If the founders of the Club had hoped that its members would be stimulated to discuss the profundities of life or acquire a taste for Elizabethan literature they were disappointed, but as a place to sow one's wild oats of preciosity under Monty Woolley's direction it was all one could desire.

Another emollient was the Brick Row Book Shop, which was opened in Lefty's Sophomore year. It was established by a few friends of the University in the belief that Yale undergraduates should be given a chance to handle early books and start their own libraries. Oxford and Cambridge had many such shops and Yale should have one, too. The *News,* always ready to promote a good cause, wrote that the Brick Row "will undoubtedly become an interesting and valuable asset to Yale's literary world. It is to offer at remarkably low prices good editions of the standard authors beside a large assortment of interesting old books of all descriptions, with special emphasis upon first editions. . . . The shop will be an influence at Yale that will undoubtedly become a very important factor," a prophecy that proved uncommonly accurate in the light of the collectors whom it nourished and whose books were eventually given to the Yale Library. The Brick Row's first consignment from England was only a few hundred volumes of the eighteenth- and nineteenth-century English classics that cost on the average perhaps five dollars a copy, but they seemed very wonderful to Lefty. He could not have said why the sight of a row of books in contemporary calf filled him with excitement, but he learned that it was one thing to be told in class, "The assignment for next Monday is Gay's *Fables,*" and another to find an early edition of it for himself. The assignment was a chore, the discovery of the little thin book with its fleurons and prints, a pleasure. Here at last was the real thing, not textbooks, which chill and repel, but the books that the authors of them might have owned. The only purchase that he felt he could make for himself was a copy of *Through the Looking Glass,* New York, 1872, for which he paid five dollars. He bought it under the delusion that it was the first edition. When on his next vacation he showed it proudly to John Howell in San Francisco the veteran bookseller disabused him: the first edition had been published in England. Lefty sold his copy to him at once. This disillusionment did not keep him from sending out a letter to the graduates of Beta Theta Pi soliciting funds for the new library. About a hundred dollars was given and Lefty spent it slowly and carefully in the Brick Row. His hours there were a valuable preliminary for the more advanced education he was to give himself later in bookshops.

The only college dances were at the time of the Big Game in the fall and the Junior Prom in the winter; each fraternity also had an annual winter dance in New York. Lefty went to the Beta dance and the Prom his Junior year. Chaperones, white ties, white gloves, dance cards were still the rule. Professor Rankin's alumnus found that his dancing had not improved, and his enjoyment of dances was further curtailed by the knowledge that his mother, sitting silently in her chair in Alameda, did not approve of his going to them. "The time for play is over," she would say, "the time for work is here." Girls hardly entered into college life. Biology was kept down to a degree that undergraduates of today cannot believe was possible. Sex was sublimated in the furious extracurricular activity; probably not ten per cent of a class had had "experience" when it graduated. It will be interesting in fifty years to compare the results of the present order with those produced by the celibate life of fifty years ago.

Lefty had the good fortune to be invited out often for Sunday lunch in New Haven—to the William C. Daggetts (Mrs. Daggett came from Alameda), the Frederick Williamses, and the Hadleys. To escape from college food and atmosphere into a delightful family circle was a blessed diversion. Lefty made the most of a discovery of Wilmarth's: older people are flattered by the attentions of thc young especially when their advice is asked. He further sensed that the older generation can go only so far in soliciting these attentions because they cannot afford to be snubbed, a secret shared by few of the young.

One of his sketches in the *Lit.* was "A W. S. Gilbert Quartette," Bunthorne, the Lord Chancellor, Lady Jane, and Katisha. Gilbert and Sullivan were (and have remained) one of the joys of Lefty's life. Wayland Williams, a charter member of the Elizabethan Club, liked the sketch, pointed out gently that the quartette had two second tenors and two contraltos (which Lefty hadn't thought of), and asked him to Sunday lunch. Wayland was as ardent a Savoyard as Lefty and played the scores of the operas well. Hours were spent by him, his sister Betty, and Lefty singing all of them except *Pinafore,* which they considered banal. Their singing was borne patiently by Professor and Mrs. Williams until one night, all patience spent, the master of the house denounced what they had believed had been a particularly fine performance of *Ruddigore* as "intolerable caterwauling." Monty Woolley and Lawrason Riggs were also frequently at the Williamses. Lawrason, who was then an instructor in English, had bought the little Victorian Gothic house on the Williamses' property and had just written *See America First* with Cole Porter, perhaps as witty a musical comedy as ever failed on Broadway. Numbers 135 and 155 Whitney Avenue were a long way from 1625 Central Avenue, Alameda.

Lefty's intimacy with the Hadley family began in Freshman English, which he had with the President's younger son, Hamilton. The two would go up to Tink after the hour was over to discuss the day's assignment and so became his close friends. Early in Sophomore year they formed with him one of the ephemeral little clubs that sprang up in every class. The father of one of the members, Sid Mitchell, had a property in Grace, Idaho, whither Sid was sent to work during the summer following Freshman year. Its inhabitants were Mormons who wore underwear on which strings were substituted for buttons. Sid bought one of these garments, a Mormon Bible and hymnal, and when he visited Lefty in Alameda (one of the very few friends who ever visited him there) later in the summer he and Lefty picked up tracts and other printed material from the Mormon booth at the San Francisco Exposition. A club was the natural outcome of such a collection. Tink consented to be the Angel Moroni of it; gold watch charms in the form of the Deseret, the honey bee that is the symbol of the Mormon faith, were worn as watch charms, additional relics were acquired at Woolworth's; special Mormon names were assumed to mark the members off from the rest of mankind. The Club dined at the Hadleys' house, from which Mr. and Mrs. Hadley absented themselves on club nights. A ritual was evolved assisted by John, the Hadleys' West Indian butler.

Most of Lefty's walks were with H. Hadley. The friends went out Whitney Avenue and off to the east through melancholy streets that contrasted with the freshness of H.'s latest absorption whatever it was—heraldry, geology, Leibnitz. On and on H. talked, block after block, day after day, while Lefty listened, marveling at flory-counter-flory, gneiss, the monad. These green pastures were alluring when H. pointed them out, but when Lefty took the introductory course in Philosophy he found it a morass. Each philosophical system from Thales to William James was proved false or inadequate by the system that followed it; the end of the whole matter was bewildered exasperation. The philosophers on the faculty were little help. One, befogged in thought, peered near-sightedly and unsmilingly at an incomprehensible and alien world. The 8:30 a.m. lectures of another suffered from the professor's subscription to the gayer creeds of antiquity. The class did not see him crowned with vine leaves the night before, Lalage on one knee, Phyllida on the other; all the class saw was the professor the following morning. A third man skipped about clipping and clapping dialectical castanets until he sank into a depression, had an attack of asthma, and missed half his classes. When H. himself became ill over the Problem of Original Sin Lefty realized that philosophy was nothing to fool with and accepted his awkwardness with the dialectical castanets.

The Alamedan spent a Christmas and Easter vacation with the Hadleys. The Easter vacation was interrupted by his coming down with German measles, the discovery of which filled his host with dismay since Mr. Hadley was not certain whether he had had the illness himself. When in the hall Lefty said good-bye en route to the Infirmary Mr. Hadley, whose eccentricity of manner delighted his family as much as it did the undergraduates, was caught in a conflict of emotion: the instinct to be courteous to a departing guest, eagerness to have the guest depart, concern for his illness, and the hope that he, Mr. Hadley, had not caught it. The result was a demonstration of the alternating attraction and repulsion that Forest Cooke strove to impart in his electrical experiments at Thacher.

Mrs. Hadley was the model president's wife, serene, perceptive, wise, the beloved leader of Town and Gown. Her low clear voice spoke with a gentle confidence that made her occasional dismissals of the unworthy devastatingly effective. Lefty was impressed by the protocol of the academic hierarchy, which Mrs. Hadley illustrated by the story of an assistant professor's wife whose husband was never going to be promoted. Did this mean that his wife must accept inferior social rank? Not without a struggle, and she boldly called upon the wife of a full professor. On leaving she hoped her hostess would return the call. "Thank you," said the senior lady. "Is it 'Thank you, yes?' or 'Thank you, no?' " the junior asked. "Since you insist, it is 'Thank you, no.' " New Haven's high priestesses were steeped in the histories of families. When one day Mrs. Hadley asked Lefty what sort of person a New Haven classmate of his was and Lefty replied guardedly that he was "rather political," Mrs. Hadley was not surprised. "They have always had to make their way," she explained, "There is illegitimacy in that family." "There is?" "Yes, they descend from an illegitimate brother of Jonathan Edwards," and Lefty realized that every family has its shadow. Lefty only half understood many of the things that Mrs. Hadley told him, but some of them came back to him years later when he was shown their truth. "In every marriage," she said one day, "both sides reach a point where they realize that they can't go on the way they're going and then they make concessions if they are wise." Another day she said, "The bitterest enmities in academic life spring up between sponsors and sponsored." Mrs. Hadley opened the widest vistas and the brightest prospects; she encouraged one to try for the highest prizes in the light of her own composed achievement. She and Tinker were Lefty's two most influential teachers at Yale.

The summers went somewhat better than the earlier ones, especially the summer of '16, when Mrs. Lewis took a sorority house at Stanford. Lefty discovered the heavens. He bought a fieldbook of the stars with diagrams of the constellations and on moonless nights lay on the lawn with a flashlight and opera-glasses to study the diagrams and verify them aloft. Vega, Fomalhaut, and Antares sparkled in the clear dry air, their beauties enhanced for him by his learning their names, remarking their colors, and fitting them into their constellations. Such words as "colure" and "occultation" he brushed aside, but he became aware of the shifting skyscape, the bustle of the heavens, "the stars that still sojourn, yet still move onward." Scorpio set and Cassiopeia rose; the biggest and most beautiful stars declined and disappeared, even Arcturus finally sank from sight.

Similar reflections occurred to him when he crossed the continent on the homeward journey. The twenty-four hours between New Haven and Chicago went with a rattle and bang, and Chicago, when he visited Hy Shortall for a night or two, was a delight, but the seventy-two hours and two thousand miles between it and the Coast seemed unending. A whole day was spent crawling across the dullest part of the trip, Western Nebraska. Lefty would read until he could read no more and then he held the timetable and watched for the tiny towns: Hershey, Ogallala, Lodge Pole, Sidney, Kimball, each with its identical saloon-lined street along the railroad tracks and its cross street that ended abruptly in the prairie which might have been a crude backdrop in a theater. Only twice did anything interesting occur. The first time was when William Jennings Bryan got on at Grand Island and rode to North Platte. There he was, Bryan in Nebraska, with the Indian face of a man on a cigarband, but tired and with little to say to the henchmen about him; more melting snowman than Great Commoner. The other memorable incident was a big man's stand on education. Since he was in the last section of the car and faced his interlocutor his remarks reached the entire car; indeed, they were so loud they might have reached the entire nation. His boy, it appeared, had gone to State where he was being forced to waste his time on books. As the train neared the big man's station he got up and roared out, "I don't give a good goddam if Jim don't open a book so long as he makes the football team," and Lefty felt that a gust of honesty had blown across the prairie. Ogden, when it was finally reached, offered the relief of a half hour's walk up and down the main street, and then after one more night he was home. The trip across the continent was like the passage through life: the East was youthful excitement and hope, Western Nebraska was middle age, and the arrival at San Francisco Bay was death. Life while it was dragging on seemed interminable, and then it was over and had been very short after all.

G. M. Young said that in assessing a man's character he asked, "What was happening in the world when he was twenty?" Lefty celebrated his twenty-first birthday on November 14, 1916, in the back room of the Bishop Hotel with his three closest Thacher friends at Yale, Dunham Barney, Appie Eyre, and John Knox. Wilson had just been re-elected President on the slogan "He Kept Us out of War," and the war news was not on the front page of the *Yale News.* The four friends without a thought of what was hanging over them got quite gay on a bottle of claret (Mr. Thacher would have been sorry to hear it), and then Lefty went to Beta Theta Pi to rehearse the initiation play, Shaw's *Gazogene.* But the war did come to Yale on the next Good Friday.

A dozen of Lefty's classmates, under the leadership of Trubee Davison, had already left for Florida where they were training to become naval aviators (their commissions were among the first hundred issued in that branch of the service). Soon the rest of the Class who had passed their twenty-first birthdays would be in the Army or Navy. Tap Day was moved up a month (which showed how grave the situation had become), and Lefty walked off the campus for Keys. A special Tap Day was held in Florida for the Yale Unit and its members who were chosen were brought to New Haven by private train (a leave granted by Secretary of the Navy Daniels). Since one of the Keys men was killed in the war it was the only time that the fifteen of Lefty's year were all together. Nineteen Eighteen missed its Senior year, a loss that is still for most of its survivors a major disappointment of their lives. When he took leave of Mr. Hadley to go to the Officers' Training Camp in San Francisco, Lefty said something to the effect that it would be easier to die for Yale than for the country because Yale was so intimate and close-knit and the country was so vast and diversified. This sounds rather dramatic now, but Mr. Hadley was impressed by its sincerity and quoted it later in a speech. Most undergraduates and graduates had a quasi-religious feeling about Yale.

Why did we—why do we still—care so deeply for it? Mr. Stimson in the introduction to *On Active Service in Peace and War* after confessing Yale's scholastic shortcomings in his day wrote: "The chief fruits of my four years at Yale came from the potent democratic class spirit then existing on the Yale campus; and that experience was most important to my life, both in the character developed and in the friendships formed." Yale's *forte* was not training the intellect, but, in the *Oxford English Dictionary*'s definition of education, "development of powers, formation of character." The small world of Yale prepared you for the world of fierce competition into which you graduated. It stimulated, bruised, rewarded, and punished you; it was a toughening experience that gave you friends and the opportunity to be worthy of them. Yale men sang *"Amici usque ad aras"* generation after generation with honest emotion. As undergraduates they gave themselves to a life that called for their best efforts, not merely to serve their own ends, but to share in the grace of the beloved community.

Today we may shake our heads over the feebleness of Yale's intellectual training half a century ago, yet if education is a preparation for the work of life the Yale College of that day must be ranked high. What it did for its young men struck Lefty with the force of revelation one day in his Sophomore year as he was walking to his room in Durfee Hall. "What Yale does is to produce gentlemen," a word that did not then make people angry. He had in mind, I think, not only the acceptance of high standards and values, the too-frequent statement of which tended to weaken the message, but an appreciation of what George Gordon called "the little arts of life so painfully evolved, which make us tolerable to one another and even to ourselves." The Society "System" (Mr. Stimson's "potent democratic class spirit") not only inspired useful activity and gratified the egos of those who were "recognized," but it enforced the simple "painfully evolved" rules of conduct and so disciplined the young men exposed to it. The spirit of those who were not elected was shown by an editorial in the May 1916 number of the *Courant:* "Tap Day. On the eighteenth of May eighty men at most were vitally worried as to whether they were to have the fateful, 'Go to your room!' Yet the event was a class affair, the most important in its history. Forty-five men were made happy; painfully bitter was the disappointment of a few; and the rest? Were they witnesses merely? No, it was a great thing in the lives of all; it was good discipline even for the least;

it was better for most than if they had been tapped. For who was there that did not feel the least thrill and experience the smallest introspection, who did not leave the campus with a smile on his face, but 'I'll show them sometime!' in his heart?" Of course mistakes were made each year, mistakes of election and omission as the latter history of every Class proves (the writer of the editorial became one of the outstanding men in his Class), yet Yale College produced national leaders in the professions, industry, government, and the arts, in a number out of all proportion to its comparatively small size, and the System, ridiculous or heartless as it has seemed to those who have not known it at first hand, had much to do with shaping the careers of those who experienced it.

IX

THE ARMY

When war was declared Officers' Training Camps were established throughout the country. Lefty applied to the one at the Presidio, San Francisco, not because he was eager to fight, but because all his friends who were twenty-one and over were hurrying off to the camps nearest their homes. The Army had become the thing. Flushed with success at Yale and supported by letters of recommendation from President Hadley, Billy Phelps, and Lawrason Riggs, Lefty took his acceptance in the training camp for granted. He chose the field artillery: Yale had a field artillery unit; a field artilleryman was what he would be in spite of the warning that a little mathematics was advisable for a useful career as one. The battery to which he was assigned was disciplined, but Candidate Lewis, encouraged by one or two gay dogs from Yale refused to take it seriously. They dined every night in San Francisco and never studied at all.

Lefty had gone into the Army against his mother's frightened remonstrances, and once in she urged him to get out. Couldn't he resign? No. Whether she suggested that he might get out by not working hard I cannot now be certain, but that stratagem was implied. It fell in with the young man's aversion to the Army, which was strengthened by the constant complaints of his more entertaining friends. When the course was over he got what he wanted.

It was years before he could mention his failure, but how foolish he had been was soon plain to him: he had thrown away the chance that he should have made the most of; he had let down his sponsors and his friends; his swelled head and frivolity had been deservedly punished. His prayer to get out of the Army had been granted, but the granting of it had not been most expedient for him. Every recruiting poster—"Uncle Sam wants YOU!" reminded him of his stupidity, and when he saw on a cover of the old *Life* a G.A.R. veteran in uniform putting his hand on the shoulder of his newly recruited grandson Lefty made up his mind to ignore his mother and enlist. This he did in a National Guard regiment of field artillery that was being raised by volunteers. The 144th F.A., the "Grizzlies" as it called itself, had a nucleus of officers who belonged to a smart San Francisco cavalry troop. They knew even less about the Army than Lefty did, which meant that in the prevailing ignorance he was something of a professional. On reaching the Grizzlies' camp he became at once a sergeant in Battery C and did his best to be a good one.

He was helped by a tough fellow sergeant named Casey who had been in the National Guard for years. One night when Lewis was Sergeant of the Guard Casey confided to him that, against orders, he was going up to San Francisco and that Sarge Lewis would be a good guy and overlook it. Connivance in lawbreaking was not admitted in the code of honor laid down by *St. Nicholas,* Thacher, and Yale, and Sergeant Lewis replied that if Casey went to San Francisco he would report him. Casey went and was reported. When on his return, drunk, he learned from his tent mates of Sergeant Lewis's action he announced in a voice loud enough to reach Sergeant Lewis on his rounds what he was going to do to him on the morrow. Immediately after reveille Sergeant Lewis, fortified by the brave boys in Kirke Monroe and Edward Titsworth Tomlinson, walked up to Casey glowering among his friends. "I hear you've something to say to me," Sergeant Lewis said, heroically removing his spectacles. Fortunately, Casey, though tough, was short and Lefty, though thin, was tall. With or without his spectacles he was ready for death, but Casey dropped his eyes and muttered, "O.K., Sarge," and slunk away.

The Grizzlies were sent before long to Camp Kearney, a dozen miles inland from San Diego, where they became part of the 40th Division. Sergeant Lewis was promoted to a second lieutenancy, a rank in which he was frozen for the duration. Although a commission had become essential to his happiness, Sergeant Lewis was happier than Lieutenant Lewis. The latter liked being saluted (even though he still had to salute as much as had Sergeant Lewis), and the sense of elevation to superior status, but a sergeant's standing among his fellows is higher than a second lieutenant's among his. Such respect as Lieutenant Lewis had among his fellow officers was owing to their assumption that because he had been to Yale he was a sound mathematician. This error was strongly held by the captain of his battery, Stewart Edward White, and displayed the imagination that made him a successful novelist. That Lieutenant Lewis retained the regard of the enlisted men is suggested by a birthday present he received from Private Marble. Marble had been a cowboy on one of the Miller and Lux ranches and was rumored to have killed a man. He might have been a star in a Western; he was dark, strong, and handsome except on the day when he presented himself at Lieutenant Lewis's tent. Then his face was swollen almost beyond recognition. "*What* has happened to you?" the lieutenant asked. "I heard it was your birthday," Marble said, thrusting forward a squashy mess of something in a newspaper and leaving abruptly. The newspaper contained a comb of honey freshly stolen from its hive.

Lefty had little time to himself during the day. Such of it as he could find he spent, homesick for Yale and grieving for his lost senior year, in poring over the Keys directory, an exercise that bolstered his ego in its lowly state. He learned the names and classes of a great many men, a store of knowledge that was helpful to him later in memorizing telephone numbers: 1591 could be remembered by Dean Acheson, '15, and Harvey Cushing, '91; 1013, by Lawrason Riggs, '10, and Arnold Whitridge '13. He varied this reading with Shakespeare, a set of which he gave, feeling like a patron of learning, to the post library, which had perhaps two hundred volumes and was presided over by a Thacher friend too tall and thin to get into the Army. Lieutenant Lewis borrowed the plays in his benefaction and read them in his tent secretly.

The two duties of his professional life that he liked best were firing on the range and close-order drill. His fellow officers were only too pleased to let him have the latter. Authority went with shouting orders and it was gratifying to see the men obeying smartly. After the battery mastered the evolutions of the smaller units Lieutenant Lewis moved on to battalion, regimental, and even brigade drill, until finally each squad represented a whole battery. The climax came one day when Lieutenant Lewis, self-promoted to a brigadier general, his sergeants to colonels, and his corporals to majors, conducted brigade drill on the parade ground. Marching backward he became aware of alarm on the faces of his disciplined troops who were gazing over his head as they marched sturdily forward. He turned and saw bearing down on him a real brigadier general on a real horse followed by a real brigade in a real parade. Battery C was quickly reactivated and retired at the double to the obscurity of its battery street, and Lieutenant

Lewis knew how Cinderella felt when she went back to the ashes.

After months of marching and countermarching on the Camp Kearney parade ground it was decided by the brigade commander that his three regiments should hold a competition in the conduct of a creeping barrage. The phrase brought everyone closer to the Western Front (where this mystery was performed with a minimum of fuss). A six weeks' course in "ballistics" was set up under the 144th's lieutenant colonel, a pleasant regular Army coast artilleryman who had spent the past several years at the fort on Point Conception undisturbed by serious military exercises. The most mathematically gifted young men in the brigade, one from each battery, were ordered to attend the ballistics school. Among them was Lieutenant Lewis. He fortified himself with a slide rule (which he did not know how to use) and went, deeply concerned, to his first class. As he feared, his fellow students all loved mathematics and seemed to know what they were doing. This, however, could not be said of the colonel. His sole support was the standard Coast Artillery Manual, "Ingalls," from which he copied formulas on the blackboard. The class transcribed them knowingly in their notebooks. At the final session the colonel outdid himself with a formula that covered all the blackboards in the room and himself with chalk. This accomplished he took another long look at "Ingalls" and, clearing his throat, said in a military manner, "This, gentlemen, concludes our course. I have enjoyed meeting with you, but I'm afraid we have wasted this last hour. The formula I have just given you is for the tide." The class was then dismissed to instruct its respective batteries in ballistics.

Lefty's previous experience as a teacher was limited to two lectures, or rather to one, because as no one came to the second there was no need to deliver it. He and a few of his Yale classmates in the short interval between the declaration of war and the exodus to their training camps were asked to give a series of talks to workmen in New Haven factories on the importance of good physical condition in the trial ahead of them. The undergraduates were coached by medical instructors who showed them how to draw the alimentary canal. When Lefty reached his factory he was startled to find posters asking, "ARE YOU PHYSICALLY FIT?" and announcing that Mr. Wilmarth Lewis of Yale was arriving at noon to discuss physiology with them. A group of operatives surveyed the speaker dubiously over their lunch pails. Lefty drew his diagram and faltered to the end. The silence was broken only by the closing of lunch pails. On the lecturer's second appearance, prepared to talk on hernia, the operatives were eating elsewhere.

Lieutenant Lewis was helped as much by a Virgilian tag as by a textbook on gunnery that had the answers to the problems in the back, *Possunt quia posse videntur,* "They get away with it because they put up a good front." The men who were not studying with him were out on the firing range digging emplacements and command stations for the forthcoming creeping barrage. The enemy positions were simulated by large billboards; our infantry by picket fences. The problem was to fire over friends and creep on to the enemy, leaving not a stick of them standing. Lieutenant Lewis, in charge of Battery C, had often fired on the range and did not need weeks of preparation to see that the first object was about 2,500 yards distant. He told the gun crews to set their sights at 2,500 (forgetting that the picket fences represented friends, not foes), and to advance the range 100 yards after each round. Then he went down into the Command Station, which had been finished that morning. On a table were four buzzers, one for each gun in the battery. Zero hour was to be announced by a rocket, after the firing of which Lieutenant Lewis would press the buzzers according to a schedule: zero hour plus ten seconds, Gun Number 1, Fire! plus twenty-two seconds, Gun Number 4, Fire! and so on, until the problem was over. Lieutenant Lewis stationed a man on the ground above to shout "Rocket!" down the dugout's sole vent when the signal was fired. Just before zero hour the watchman above ground was asked what he was doing there? The only word to reach the dugout was "Rocket!" Lieutenant Lewis pressed his stop-watch. In ten seconds he buzzed Gun Number 2. No sound. Twelve seconds later Gun Number 4 was ordered to fire. No sound. All four guns were silent, which was fortunate because the General of the Division and the Admiral of the Pacific Fleet, with their aides in capes and *fourragères,* were galloping over the range examining the targets before the problem began. Each of the four corporals of Battery C just hadn't pulled their lanyards. Had one of them done so . . . When the problem was finally fired Battery C lost it for the regiment: the stakes representing the supporting infantry were mowed down, the billboards representing the enemy were untouched, but the blame fell on Lieutenant Lewis's immediate superior who had not been to Yale.

In order that the regiment might put its best foot forward, Lieutenant Lewis was sent to the School of Fire at Fort Sill, Oklahoma, to take its ten weeks' course. "Sill" had acquired a frightening reputation. The Army saw that something had to be done about its regular officers in the field artillery who had rusted in peace. When they failed at "Sill" they were "benzened" and the Army knew them no more. To weed out the hopelessly unfit at the start a simple examination was given the candidates on their arrival. With his failure at the Presidio painfully in mind, Lieutenant Lewis approached the exam with extreme trepidation. Seated in the front row he was given the papers to distribute and so started after everyone else. He looked at the first question and could not answer it. This wouldn't do. He recalled the advice he had been given at Thacher—to relax, to let his arms hang by his sides, to drink water. The last palliative was denied him, but he relaxed and let his arms dangle. Then he looked at the first question again. It was, "What is your name?"

Another crisis occurred at the end of the fifth week when the lieutenant was faced with an exam in gunnery that he was afraid of. He came down with violent hay fever and went into the hospital. This was his first attack of an illness from which thereafter he suffered annually for thirty years. Hay fever was unknown to Wilmarth in California except for Mrs. Dodge at Thacher, a lady from Boston of whom Lewis had been particularly fond; hay fever was Eastern and aristocratic. In later years when the causes of it had been traced to allergies it was discovered that he reacted to grass and mink coats, but his first allergy was an exam that Lieutenant Lewis was afraid of flunking. Tension was relaxed when the Command at Sill abandoned the Civil War methods of warfare still being taught there for those used on the Western Front. This was in May 1918. Since the instructors at Sill, apart from a few frantic Frenchmen, were as ignorant of modern warfare as their students, everybody was passed, and Lieutenant Lewis returned to Battery C with an even solider reputation for mathematical and mechanical skill than before. This made him an obvious choice for the Advanced School Detachment that preceded the Regiment to France in midsummer 1918.

His career in the A.E.F. was marked by an accident and illness. The accident occurred when he rolled out of his upper berth on the train going East. In the all-male Pullman there was no need for curtains; the train lurched around a curve and out went the lieutenant head first. He was not killed because the porter was shining his boots directly underneath. It would not have been a gallant "killed in action at Cantigny" or wherever, but "killed by falling out of an upper berth," a ludicrous death that would have made people smile in spite of themselves. W. S. Lewis's debt to the anonymous porter so fortunately placed has been lifelong.

His first illness was mumps, a joke disease to those who are not having it. He came down with it the third night out from New York. Since by then the mumps bay (the empty swimming pool) of the *Aquitania* was filled, he had to stay in his inside second-class cabin, which he shared with three others. There he was visited twice daily by John Masefield, whom he had met at the Elizabethan Club before the war and who had recently spent a day with him at San Diego. Masefield had been on the circuit that provided speakers and "entertainers" (an unflattering reflection on the speakers) at the service Y.M.C.A. huts. His mission was to prepare the troops for England and to efface the unfavorable impression left on Americans by George III and the redcoats. (George III, Masefield explained, was really a German and so a natural enemy.) The author of *The Everlasting Mercy,* who had tended bar in New York, was an obvious choice for this task. He was glad to see anyone from Yale where he had just been given an honorary degree. Who, he asked Lefty, was his favorite poet? Lefty was as surprised as was Masefield when, with "Frost at Midnight" in mind, he heard himself answering "Coleridge." "At his best," the future Laureate pronounced after a pause, "he is very good," and went on to say how much Matthew Arnold meant to him, above all "The Scholar-Gipsy" and "Thyrsis," a remark that came back to Lefty years later and helped him through a trying time. During the two days on the *Aquitania* before the mumps separated them, he and Masefield, who was the first Englishman he had spent any time with, had their meals together and walked on deck. The poet unconsciously showed the young man how ignorant he was and inspired him with a desire to be less so; he was a casual acquaintance who taught Lefty more than most of his formal teachers. The mumps ended the instructive walks and talks, but the older man would extend comfort from the doorway of Lefty's stateroom where he surveyed the patient's three roommates nervously and hoped that he was not taking the mumps back to his family. He brought books from the ship's library. "Here is *The Four Georges,*" he said one day; "rather sad stuff." Lefty then read for the first time about Horace Walpole's letters and the fiddles that Thackeray heard singing all through his "jigging, smirking, Vanity Fair."

The ride from the dock at Liverpool to the American camp at Knotty Ash through the gray streets contrasted with the flags and bands that sent the *Aquitania* off down New York harbor. In Liverpool the only color, apart from a Union Jack wrapped around its pole, was in the blue hospital uniforms of the wounded out for an airing. At Knotty Ash Lieutenant Lewis was told that it was too bad he wasn't "a measles officer"; if he had been he could have had the company of two others; being the sole "mumps" he would have to live alone. He was put in a big tent and segregated from the enlisted men by a canvas partition. On the other side of it he could hear Southern soldiers talking in low and troubled voices. They had no idea where they were or why they were there, they found August in the strange country bitterly cold and they were unhappy. Lieutenant Lewis doesn't seem to have been, even though this was the first time he had been ill on his own without a hovering mother or nurse. The very modest hospital library produced *The Last Days of Pompeii, Under the Greenwood Tree,* and *Carnival;* an orderly with his solitary meals was a mild diversion; the departure of an American troop train from the nearby Rest Camp was livelier. The station was near enough for the patients to see and hear the troops being sent off by a small English band of ancient musicians who played "Tipperary" and "Over There" as bravely as their velvet-lined instruments permitted. When the train began to move they gave their all to "Dixie." "Yesterday," Wilmarth wrote his mother, "when a local train went by and all the occupants of 3rd class carriages leaned out and waved and threw kisses at us, I was glad to see a very dignified old gentleman in a first class carriage after carefully viewing us with his pince-nez and without it get up and wave his newspaper at us and sit down and get up and wave again, all the time being very determined about it. So the whole train waved, and that is the way England receives us."

A septuagenarian rereading letters that he wrote at the age of twenty-two is a subject for Max Beerbohm. Since the boy is father to the man, the latter cannot treat the boy as if he were an ordinary grandson. I began Lieutenant Lewis's letters to his mother with trepidation, but was not as embarrassed by them as I feared I would be. They are full of incident. One passage contains a declaration of independence: "I hope," he wrote, "I may marry and spend my life in the East. . . . It is funny, but I have never done very well in California, while everything seems just right for me in New England."

Participation in the life of the hospital camp was offered the lieutenant by a sergeant. To pass the time the mumps enlisted men held a mock court-martial when they could think up one. Would the lieutenant care to join them? He accepted eagerly although he had never been in a law court of any kind. Unlike the lieutenant, the judge and prosecuting attorney, who had been Los Angeles police court reporters, knew the rules of the game. The newcomer was assigned the role of attorney for the defense. When he made an impassioned plea for a client the prosecuting attorney would object on the ground that the plea was immaterial and irrelevant and the judge would answer promptly, "Objection sustained." Then everybody stared at the lieutenant, savoring his confusion and helplessness. He lost every case and came to dread the game as much as his clients, one of whom, a burly Georgian, on learning that he was to be defended by the lieutenant produced a Bible and knelt by his bed in prayer. When the Grizzlies reached Knotty Ash the lieutenant proceeded with them, convalescent but relieved, to France.

There after a month of rest near Poitiers and a school at Bordeaux he entered Base Hospital 6 nearby with what was called variously a sacroiliac strain, lumbago, rheumatism, and—twenty-odd years later—a form of arthritis. We are told now that arthritis (by any name) is one of the most frequent forms of psychosomatic illness, the nature of which was not generally understood in 1918. Lieutenant Lewis had done something to his lower spine at Camp Kearney months before, but had apparently got over it. I think his illness came through fear of failure at the new schools he had to attend, but whatever its origin the illness was extremely painful.

Base 6 had an excellent staff from the Massachusetts General Hospital in Boston except for the director. His chief concern was his own promotion to a full colonelcy, a goal he reached by having the largest and most economically run American hospital in France. Although American warehouses in Bordeaux were bursting with drugs and supplies Base 6 had acute shortages of all essentials. The daily sixty grains of aspirin that Lieutenant Lewis was ordered to take was drastically reduced (which was perhaps just as well) and the sodium salicylates given up entirely. The nurses were kept in such close sleeping quarters that they were mowed down by "the Spanish influenza." Lefty had to do what he could for his roommate, Conyngham Gifford, who had been with him at Yale and who had lost a leg. Lefty unrolled and rerolled the bandages so that they might be used again, dirty bandages were not to be thrown away. Since the stump was suppurating he was lucky not to lose a hand. Giff's and Lefty's room was next to "the Death Chamber" into which the men were put who were dying of the flu. They became delirious during the night, tried to struggle out of bed, and were cursed and thrown back into it by the orderly in attendance who hated officers. Our two young men reported this treatment, but were told in effect to mind their own business. Indecorous death continued to be their nightly companion until dawn when the room next door became quiet.

Lieutenant Lewis was put into a plaster cast that went from his hips to his chest. He was proud of being a good patient, uncomplaining, sunny, no trouble at all; like Paul, he took pleasure in infirmities, although he did not learn why until years later. At the time he rejoiced that he was removed from the war. Hospitals mercifully dull the mind and senses; everyone in them grows callous to unpleasant sights and sounds and smells. Convalescents normally enjoy the recurring phases of hospital routine, the arrival of meals, the new shifts fresh for their eight-hour tour of duty, and, above all, their doctor's visits when they become the object of scientific examination, must talk about themselves, and receive solicitude and encouragement. Lieutenant Lewis did not repeat the mistake of omitting his weekly letter to his mother, but even so she wished to have reassurance. One day a young man appeared at Base 6 from the American Red Cross on a visit that was reminiscent of President Hadley's two years earlier: Mrs. Lewis had written to Mr. H. P. Davison, the head of the Red Cross and father of Lefty's classmate, Trubee, enquiring about the health and situation of her son. Alameda was never far away.

Base 6 had its plus side. For Lefty, there was Giff himself, who bore his misfortune, which had become complicated by pleurisy, with such cheerfulness and character. There were also the frequent visits of the hospital chaplain, Henry Knox Sherrill, Yale '11, who, Wilmarth reported to Alameda, "comes up every few days with magazines, the *Alumni Weekly,* or to play some bridge. I like him immensely." Years hence he was to be the Presiding Bishop of the Episcopal Church, a beloved colleague of Lefty's on the Yale Corporation, and with his family was to supply a special niche in the slightly younger man's life. In 1962 when I read his autobiography, *Among Friends,* I learned without surprise that the young chaplain represented the patients' just complaints to the hospital authorities with the forthrightness that furthered his causes in later life. Henry helped the young Yale patients as he was to help the army of people who needed him throughout his ministry, and it was he, I think, who introduced Lefty to Trollope by bringing *The Last Chronicle of Barset* to him from the hospital library. Three days after the Armistice Lefty celebrated his twenty-third birthday with a dinner sent in from an excellent restaurant outside the hospital gates and with Henry Sherrill (who provided the orderlies to bring the food) as the principal guest.

Lieutenant Lewis was sent home on the *Tenadores* the end of November. She was very small and old (she sank, I understand, on her next voyage), but Lefty being the only "non-ambulatory" patient on board had the largest stateroom to himself in pleasing contrast to his situation going east. The *Tenadores* ran into the storm that was delaying President Wilson on his way to the Peace Conference and took two weeks to make the crossing, Lieutenant Lewis in his big double bed enjoyed the view of mountainous seas heaving and rushing past his portholes. He started to write a book of his experience in the A.E.F. that he called *Cushioned Campaigns.* New York gave the *Tenadores* a hero's reception, which patient Lewis, feeling something of a fraud, enjoyed. He got away from Staten Island hospital to spend several days over Christmas with the Davisons in New York. Other friends took him to New Haven to Keys and to see the Hadleys and Williamses. Lefty felt reprieved. When he reached California in January the doctors in the Letterman General Hospital at the Presidio were as mystified by his illness as the doctors at Base 6 had been. As soon as he could, he signed a waiver of all disability benefits and was at last free to go home. Anything was preferable to life in a hospital.

The following six months tested the character that the young man's teachers had striven to develop. Painful physical disability, the brooding silences of his watchful mother to whom he was still bound by infantile emotion, the similar silences of Azro, who dimly resented his own subjugation by her, the thought of Yale friends returning to New Haven or embarking confidently on their careers brought him as close to despair as he has ever been. A dear old osteopath came from Oakland every Sunday evening to treat him. Each week the patient walked a little farther on his crutches. His mother permitted him to take the older Pierce-Arrow to play golf, which he usually did by himself, throwing his crutches down to make a shot and retrieving them to walk the short distance to his ball. His ability to use a typewriter was a godsend. He finished *Cushioned Campaigns* and sent it to John Berdan for his criticism, but John's letter returning it began, "I hate to write what you will be sorry to read." On looking at *Cushioned Campaigns* now I am grateful to him for his candid criticism of a hasty and self-conscious performance.

Barsetshire was an escape. Lefty began with *The Warden* and went straight through to the *Last Chronicle.* I have reread all the Barsetshire novels recently and see why he enjoyed them so much: the well-to-do and highly placed members of the county and clerical hierarchy are the sort of people that he wanted to live with. Their stories are told with urbanity seasoned with satire and softened with sentiment. The good things of life remain with or are restored to the possession of the good, but only after they have been sorely tried by the bad. On rereading Trollope recently I recalled how in 1919 Lefty rejoiced when Mr. Harding was offered the deanship, laughed out loud when Bertie Stanhope pushed the sofa on to Mrs. Proudie's train, and enjoyed the social rivalry of Mrs. Lookaloft and Mrs. Greenacre at the Ullathorne sports. Whether he sensed that Barsetshire is a matriarchy where all the women are stronger than their men I am not certain, but I do recall how glad he was when Frank Gresham and Lord Lufton finally escaped from their mothers. Trollope gave him more pleasure and instruction than all other novelists that he had yet read.

Three authors that he read in rather than through were Marcus Aurelius, Thomas à Kempis, and Schopenhauer. It cannot be said that he took in very much, but glancing at them again for the first time since 1919 I recognize certain meditations that dusted off like pollen on the young man's mind such as, "It is in the power of the soul to preserve her own peace and tranquility and not to suppose that pain is evil" (Marcus Aurelius); "Blessed is the man who keeps the hour of his death always in mind, and daily prepares himself to die" (à Kempis); "Suicide is not the end; death is not absolute annihilation" (Schopenhauer).

In May he went down to the Ojai for several days to stay at Thacher where he enjoyed an outdoor performance of *Rhesus* in which the hero, aged five, became fed up with the play and sat down on what proved to be a nest of red ants. A second incident was Lieutenant Lewis's delivery of the Tuesday Morning Sermon, an ordeal normally endured in turn by the faculty. "Sermon" was a misnomer. What was given was a talk or, on one occasion, a demonstration, when Mr. William Thacher produced a dead wildcat and tried to find its vital organs, a demonstration frustrated by the disintegration of the cadaver.

The Old Boy's sermon was his first appearance before an audience as a speaker; a milestone. Most Old Boys would like to go back to their old school and address it, some to say how much they loved it, some to edify, some to shock. Lewie, going back with affection and gratitude in his heart, wanted to edify, but he also wanted to entertain. His success was mixed: he heard the athletic coach say afterwards, "He knows how to tell a story," but the effect upon Mr. Thacher of the subject he chose, the unwisdom of being too critical, was merely one of surprise.

The only man he saw in Alameda other than Azro and Charles (who lived there with his wife) was the new young rector at Christ Church. Lefty became confirmed and thought of going into the ministry, a solution of his life that was acceptable to his mother, who hoped that he would wear gray clericals. His own attitude towards the church was more emotional, but hardly more intellectual: since Jesus was the Son of God how could one be better employed than in entering His service? When he told Mr. Thacher on his trip to the Ojai what he was contemplating his former mentor asked, "Which church?" and when he was told answered, "Well that's the best one for you." Tinker, an ardent High Churchman, wrote that he was pleased Lefty had been confirmed, but regretted that he was a Low Churchman. However, that was better than becoming a Presbyterian. "In that case I should have regarded you as lost." A more serious check to his enthusiasm came when the young rector told him that he must learn Hebrew as well as Greek and that he should begin at once to file away bits and pieces of his reading for use in future sermons. The end came one day on the golf course after Lefty had made a bad shot and said "Damn!" There was a silence and then his clerical friend behind him said firmly, "Tut, tut, *tut!*"

He went back to New Haven in June for ten days at Commencement, and stayed with the Hadleys. It was a Commencement of rejoicing and hope for the future, a reunion in which old and young thankfully joined. Lefty realized then that his place was among the laity and determined that he would be well enough in the fall to return and get his degree.

What had Lieutenant Lewis learned in the Army besides how to behave in a false position? That, for one thing, Mrs. Blood of Mastick was right in her enforcement of apparently trivial rules in the interests of discipline. There was also the lesson about knowing your job and behaving well with your associates. He discovered that soldiers see their superiors with clarity; the simpler the man the more unclouded his discernment of phoniness, honesty, meanness, fairness, insecurity, confidence. He noticed that good sergeants may undergo an undesirable afflatus on becoming second lieutenants, and he reflected upon the dangers of success. His illness and long convalescence taught him to endure boredom, to accommodate himself to a curtailed life, and to substitute agreeable interests for those denied him, a lesson I find useful now in old age. A final lesson was given by a letter from the War Department after he returned to Yale in the fall. Where, it asked, were the ninety-six horse blankets that he had signed for at Camp Kearney in the winter of 1917? He showed the letter to his roommate, H. Hadley, who said, "Let me take care of it. I used to send out letters like that when I was in Washington." His answer silenced further inquiry and demonstrated the wisdom of mastering the language of one's profession, no matter how graceless it may be.

X

THE YALE UNIVERSITY PRESS

The Yale that Lefty returned to in the fall of 1919 was stirring with change. The first two Harkness dormitories were being built in the "Collegiate Gothic style" with a wealth of detail and antiquarian eclecticism that made the colleges of Oxford and Cambridge appear unadorned. There was a Wrexham Tower, a Boston Stump, little courts and cloisters, moats, oriel windows, bosses of Yale worthies, tablets preserving the names of earlier buildings formerly on their sites. The Magdalen Towers on other American campuses hung their diminished heads. The new buildings were Olde Worlde, but comfortable; there was no overcrowding; college servants were still in full supply. The amenities were not lost until the next war.

Equally striking changes were occurring in the University. With the appointment of three deans—Wilbur Cross of the Graduate School, Thomas W. Swan of the Law School, and Milton Winternitz of the Medical School—Yale became almost overnight a university in fact as well as in name. Furthermore, John W. Sterling on his death in 1918 left Yale a bequest that would eventually amount to over $40,000,000, a sum eight times as large as the University's total endowment at the turn of the century. Yale, like Alice, was opening out like a telescope.

Lefty went back resolved to make the most of the scholastic opportunities he slighted before the war. Academic credit was given to the returning veterans for their war service, an allowance hardly justified in Lieutenant Lewis's case. He took Tinker's "Age of Johnson" and led the class (his intimacy with the instructor would have made a lower grade embarrassing). Tink's virtuosity as a lecturer interested him more than the eighteenth century itself. Contemporary Drama with Billy Phelps introduced him to Ibsen and Strindberg. He was impressed by the slamming of the door behind Nora; he was haunted by the father in *The Father* being put into a strait jacket by his old nurse, hurling the lamp at his wife, and crying "Omphale!" (the princess whom Hercules had to serve as a slave, spinning wool by her side while she wore his lion's skin: even the strongest of men was subjugated by a woman). All I recall of a short-story course with Henry Seidel Canby is the first sketch by Thornton Wilder of what became his *Cabala,* which the author read, having secured the permission of the class, holding the lobe of his left ear. The returned veteran worked hard for fully six weeks, but extracurricular Yale was still too much fun for studies to be taken seriously. A member of Keys two years older than the Seniors, Lefty had a certain prestige that was new and agreeable to him, an elder statesman given to light after-dinner speaking. With his roommates, H. Hadley and Alfred Bellinger, and with the collusion of and favorable editorial comment by its Chairman, Brit Hadden, he wrote pseudonymous letters to the *News* that were intended to mold undergraduate opinion and behavior. He recalled Crandall by the pepper trees at Thacher calmly regarding the overexuberance of the younger boy. Things went better when one was composed as well as amiable. Lefty basked in the sunshine of Yale, which was so healing that he soon discarded the crutches on which he had returned along with his good resolves to improve his mind.

He spent much time in the Brick Row Book Shop. Masefield was now his man, partly because he liked his sonnets, partly because Masefield was an acquaintance, partly because Byrne Hackett, the manager of the Brick Row, was "pushing" him. The Masefield section of the shop was on the second floor. Lefty would climb the stairs several times a week to see if an addition had been made to it that he lacked. He would have been surprised if there had been; yet it was a joy just to look at the Masefields on which glowed the light that only collectors see.

With the coming of Prohibition in January 1920 Yale College, like the country at large, became less innocent and sober. The abominable and unenforceable law encouraged revolt against other laws and proprieties. The returned veterans showed little of the seriousness of their successors in 1946; the veterans of 1919 were chiefly concerned with salvaging what they could from their missed undergraduate life. A few of them planned to go into the law, almost none into medicine, the ministry, or teaching. Banks and brokerage houses were to draw the majority. Nearly everyone wanted to get rich as quickly as possible.

The University with its low salaries faced a shortage of teachers and did a little genteel recruiting. Lefty was invited to join the English Department and was told that he could start teaching at once. "Wouldn't I have to go through the Graduate School and get a Ph.D.?" he asked Tinker. "Well, yes, sooner or later, but there would be no hurry about it." Recognition of English as a respectable subject was of fairly recent date; its professors, mindful of the rigors of classical studies, buttressed it with philology and linguistics. To Lefty the Graduate School meant Old Norse and Old Frisian; it meant grubbing around in the Library with dreary people and writing a dissertation on a subject so dull that it had escaped notice, and he wanted none of it.

So he thanked Tink; he would like to teach, he said, but he knew that he could never be interested in research, a belief that proved to be mistaken. Yet I do not regret Lefty's decision. Had he gone through the Graduate School he would have had immediate professional status and the benefits of guild membership, but he would have been constrained by its discipline and would probably have escaped into illness. He was wise on graduating from Yale College in February 1920 to join not the Yale faculty, but the Yale University Press, an institution that he knew nothing about except that it had been started by a Keys man, George Parmly Day, the treasurer of the University, and that the Society supported it generously. Lefty had the common delusion that it is possible to be both a publisher and a writer.

His decision to join the Press was received with resignation in Alameda. There were no reproaches; Mrs. Lewis had always known, she said, that Wilmarth would remain in the East. He had moved out into the world. Azro would stay at home and look after her. Wilmarth recalled S. D. Thacher's injunction to cross the continent to spend his vacations with her and did so, but she died before his third visit.

In New Haven Dunham Barney, Ganson Depew (who were in the Yale Law School), and he rented Lawrason Riggs's Gothic 1840 house, 135 Whitney Avenue, while its owner was at a seminary becoming a Roman Catholic priest. With it went Lawrason's butler, Silk, a cook, and a chambermaid-waitress. There were usually Law School classmates of Dunham's and Gans's at dinner. Afterwards Gans and Lefty gave their vaudeville show. It is incredible, but they gave it every night. Gans was tall and urbane with a somewhat European manner (he had lived much abroad as a boy) that marked him off from his contemporaries, but it was not the disadvantage that it might have been because behind it were simplicity, good nature, and civilized humor. He spoke and acted uncommonly well; he had an interest in politics then unusual at Yale. After graduating from the Law School he became an Assistant District Attorney of Buffalo under William J. Donovan, but what all believed would have been an outstanding career was cut short by an early death.

When the law students retired to their books as soon as the vaudeville show was over, Lefty would wander next door for Gilbert and Sullivan and other innocent pleasures at the Williamses'. He contrasted the purposeful studies of his friends with his own rather brittle existence. Where was he heading? What should he do? On a weekend at Farmington he turned to Dunham Barney's father for advice. Mr. Barney listened to the young man's embarrassed and rambling statement of his situation and then asked slowly, "What do you *want* to do?" The question sank into Lefty's mind until in time he was able to answer it. Meanwhile, his belief that the Press was of vital importance to Yale gave him some support. George Day founded it in 1908 while he was still a broker in his early thirties in Wall Street. The University Presses of Oxford and Cambridge date from the sixteenth century; it was high time that Yale had one, too. Suspicion of graduates who wished to take an active part in American university affairs was normal then, but George and his wife refused to be discouraged. Yale finally permitted the Press to come into existence, properly insisting that it pass on all its books. In his last President's Report in 1921 Mr. Hadley cited the Press as the place in the University where might be found "the exemplification of its intellectual influence."

When Lefty joined the Press in 1920 it had acquired, thanks

to George Day's tireless solicitations, a handsome Greek Revival house on the Green and a dedicated staff of a dozen men, women, and boys. "Nig" Donaldson, Keys '15, who had preceded Lefty at the Press by six months, was chiefly responsible for his move. Nig was the advertising manager with a budget so small that there was little likelihood of his selling many books. Lefty had no title beyond "Nig's friend." He wrote circulars in glowing words extracted from the readers' reports on such books as *Dynamic Symmetry* by Jay Hambidge, and *Arms and Armour in Modern Warfare* by Bashford Dean, but his only direct contact with the book-buying public was limited to one icy February day when he left for Middletown by train at six in the morning carrying a suitcase heavy with samples to show at a meeting of the Connecticut Library Association. He called on a professor of English to propose that he use the Yale Shakespeare in his class. The professor looked at him with alarmed disgust. "It's unexpurgated! Do you think I would ask my boys to read *filth?*" Lefty did better at the meeting of the Association where he sold two fifty-cent books at the ten per cent discount allowed to libraries, netting the Press ninety cents. Since the trip cost over three dollars the Press lost money on it, but the Days and Nig generously charged off the loss to "public relations." The spirit of the Press could not have been bettered.

In the fall on his return from six weeks with his mother in Alameda he became editor of the Press, a post less important than it sounds, for he was little more than a postmaster, returning volumes of illiterate verse to their authors with polite notes and sending the more eligible works to Anson Phelps Stokes, who was Secretary of the Committee on Publications as well as of the University. Whereas George Day was often harassed and short-tempered, Anson Stokes was invariably courteous and efficient. Lefty was impressed by his knowing who should read any given manuscript, no matter what its subject or in what country the prospective reader lived. Anson Stokes, bearded, tall, humorless, was a figure of fun to the undergraduates, but Lefty was impressed by his energy and vision and thirty years later when writing the citation for his Yale Medal he called him "the architect of modern Yale."

When he joined the Press Lefty naïvely supposed that authors were one of the most interesting features of the publishing business, but Nig, the veteran of six months, assured him that they were its biggest headache. Authors, he explained, were touchy, dilatory, and vain. Each one thought that his book was of earth-shaking importance and "had to be in every library." They knew nothing of the complexities of book production and bookselling; worse still, academic authors didn't know how to write books that would sell. It was disillusioning. Nig and Lefty subscribed in general to the high purposes of the Press, but they longed for salable books and would ask each other at their daily lunches how they could inject the Press into the blood stream of American publishing. An opportunity seemed to be offered by the 1921 American Booksellers' Association meeting at Atlantic City. Conventions were no doubt comic, but there must be some reason for them. Arrived at the Traymore, they registered, received badges with their names and "Yale University Press" on them, and sallied forth. They knew only one bookseller, but since he did not introduce them to anybody and they felt that they shouldn't speak to strangers, the injection of the Press into the blood stream of publishing went slowly. Its representatives resisted the temptation to leave since retreat would not have been showing the Yale spirit. Instead of running away, they decided to separate, each to go out on his own for an hour or two; perhaps a veteran bookseller or publisher would stop and say, "I've noticed you and your friend. Won't you join a few of us in my suite upstairs for a drink before dinner?" After the experiment Lefty had to report total failure; Nig, on the other hand, had been spoken to by one of the outstanding figures at the convention. It had been quite a moment for him, but the man who stopped him did not invite him to join the innermost circle of the publishing world. What he asked was, "Where is the men's room?" And Nig didn't know.

In spite of being little more than a postmaster, Lefty did initiate the publication of two agreeable books, Henry Augustin Beers's *Connecticut Wits* and his *Poems.* Mr. Beers, of the class of '69, had recently retired from the English Department. His drooping gray moustache and the solemn expression of an elderly sealyham enhanced his quietly quizzical remarks. Memories of Emerson, Lowell, and Bronson Alcott clustered about him, but he was on easy terms with all literature and wrote about it with casual wit and confidence. I have recently come upon a passage in his essay "The English Lyric" that illustrates the turn his conversation might take. Speaking of the English pseudo-pindaric ode he concluded, "It is like a deaf man dancing to the motions of the orchestra, and not hearing the notes." Lefty would watch the dear little old man tacking down Elm Street and into the Press. His business there was of the simplest: it was merely selecting the verses and essays that he was willing to have reprinted from his *Ways of Yale, The Thankless Muse,* and other books, all as diminutive in size as himself, but it was conducted in the leisurely way appropriate to their style and content. Lefty particularly liked the verse in which humor, little classical allusions, the beauty of an unspoiled New Haven mingled with love for Yale. When Mr. Beers dined with Lefty and his friends a glass or two of wine worked the gentle change in their guest that is called "mellowing," and they felt that they had found a place among his acquaintance.

The Press gradually opened Lefty's eyes to the side of the University that he had only dimly sensed before, its adult side, the world of theory and research in which professional reputations must be made if advancement is to follow, a world that undergraduates did not know existed. His respect for it came slowly, but titles of the Press' books that at first seemed to him funny—*A Geographical Dictionary of Milton, The Maturation of the Eggs of the White Mouse*—began to seem less funny, and when he was called upon by the hopeful authors of similar works and was warmed at the fires of their enthusiasm, the narrowness of his own vision became increasingly evident to him.

He heard for the first time the names of the scientists who had made Yale outstanding in the nineteenth century, the Benjamin Sillimans, father and son, James Dwight Dana, Addison Verrill, Othniel Marsh, and above all, Willard Gibbs. There were also, it appeared, scholars of international reputation at Yale in 1920, Ernest Brown, the mathematician; Harrison in biology; Torrey in Arabic; Edgerton, Bloomfield, and Sapir in linguistics; Rostovtzeff and Charles Andrews in history; Albert T. Clay in Assyriology; and others in the renovated Law and Medical Schools. When Billy Phelps asked Lefty to show visiting English lecturers about the University he ended the tour at the Press, producing Ernest Brown's recently published *Tables of the Moon* as the climax. After Chesterton, very large in an Inverness cape and breathing heavily, peered through his pince-nez at the pages of, to him and Lefty, meaningless figures in this great work he roared with laughter and said, "One would want to read the funnier parts out loud, wouldn't one?" Lefty laughed promptly in return, but he felt disloyal.

How possessive research may be was brought home to him on the afternoon in 1920 when Galsworthy gave the first Bergen Lecture. Professor Clay was in Lefty's office telling him of the thrilling new light that had been thrown on the Hyksos, or Shepherd Kings, and their rule in Egypt. The hour for the lecture drew near; Lefty did not wish to interrupt, but was Mr. Clay going to hear Mr. Galsworthy? Mr. Clay said with a start that he was. While they hurried to Sprague Hall Mr. Clay continued with his story. Nor did he pause when Sprague Hall was reached. It was already so crowded that the pair could no longer walk abreast; Mr Clay had to raise his voice as they fought their way to the balcony. Soon the aisles were choked and the windows were filling up. Cries rose for "Woolsey, Woolsey! Let's go to Woolsey!" a demand so swelling and reasonable that at last it was heard: word came that the audience was, indeed, to move to Woolsey Hall. Since speed and initiative were called for if good seats were to be secured there, Lefty began climbing over the backs of the Sprague Hall seats as the nearest route to the stairs. Mr. Clay, his narrative uninterrupted, followed on the course as easily as the Hyksos had overrun Egypt. Down the stairs they clattered, across Wall Street, into Woolsey Hall, over the backs of more seats, while the Hyksos galloped with them. Mr. Clay showed Lefty how absorbing "research" can be. It offered a more engrossing life than that led by the nineteenth-century survivals who read Horace by their firesides and wrote urbane papers for their dining clubs. For these last "teaching" was a vocation rather than a profession; they hoped to make life pleasanter for the young by introducing them to culture, which was "to know the best that has been said and thought in the world." Mr. Clay and his eminent colleagues lived more exciting lives.

Among the cheerful amateurs at the Press while Lefty was there were two professionals, Carl Purington Rollins and Wilson Follett. Carl was one of the outstanding printers in the country. The door to his inadequate office opened only for him to issue forth rapidly to the University Library where he sought out woodcuts and typographical ornaments suitable to books he was laying out or, with even greater celerity, when there was a fire. Forty-five years ago New Haven had more fires than it has today and they all seemed to be in the Press' neighborhood. At the sound of the alarm the staff hurried to its windows to enjoy the dash and glitter of the fire department and its new motorized equipment with pompiers in red steel hats, waterproof coats, and rubber boots. First came the fire engine, then the hook and ladder, and then Carl Rollins.

Gradually his attitude towards Lefty began to thaw as that green young man became more and more aware of the skill and learning needed to produce a good book: application of the artistic principles of proportion and balance to the printed page; the choice of type and size that conformed to the subject and nature of the work being "laid out." These for Lefty were heretofore unimagined subtleties of an applied art that he slowly learned has a rich and varied history. He began to see what Carl Rollins meant when he talked of one type as "strong" and another as "effeminate"; he learned to recognize "Caslon Old Style," "Bodoni," and "Scotch Roman." Each book that Carl designed received his careful—at times it seemed maddeningly careful—consideration. Unlike the other outstanding contemporary printers of the day, he had to design most of his books to sell at as low a figure as possible, since the precarious finances of the Press forced him into economies the other "fine" printers could ignore.

As Lefty's awareness of Carl's skill and learning grew he became increasingly eager to win his good opinion. A chance was offered one day after a fire. On Carl's brisk but rather self-conscious return to his room, Lefty strolled in to get the details. When he had them he said casually, "I saw San Francisco burn."

Carl stared at him. "What did you say?"

Lefty repeated, as modestly as he could, "I saw San Francisco burn," and then he described the flames raging from

Telegraph Hill to the Mission across the Bay from Alameda. His friendship with Carl Rollins began at that moment and lasted until Carl's death forty years later. He designed *The Yale Edition of Horace Walpole's Correspondence,* the details of which occupied us for six months. We were both pleased when it won the highest typographical recognition and kept up the joke that I had been his collaborator. It is pleasant to record that on his retirement as Printer to the University Yale made him a Doctor of Humane Letters. I had the privilege of walking with him in the Commencement procession (I was by then a member of the Corporation), and of presiding at his seventy-fifth birthday dinner to which three hundred of his friends (all the ballroom at the Lawn Club in New Haven holds) came in a cruel sleet storm to do him honor as the dean of American printers and a beloved friend. For several years longer he continued, although totally blind, to produce books with the aid of his devoted wife. His last one was my *Horace Walpole* and I am not alone in thinking that it is one of the most beautiful books of his entire career.

Wilson Follett was brought to the Press to add a professional editor to its staff. He was only nine years senior to Lefty, but seemed years older. After Harvard he had taught at various colleges and written *The Modern Novel, A Study of the Purpose and the Meaning of Fiction,* which the preface explains is "a statement of some critical and aesthetic principles in terms of their historical evolution in and from the English novel." He had also written a few excellent stories. He was six feet one or two, had a neat precise manner, and a slow sententious way of speaking. He was an artist, an idealist, imprisoned in a pessimism that saw the world as an arena of hate and torment. "Curse God and die!" he cried one day, and, again, "The world owes me a living!" Lefty was disconcerted by these imprecations and pronouncements; he felt that there was something wrong with Wilson's attitude, but didn't see what he could do about it. So when such outbursts came he would contrive to say something that caused a wintry smile to break out on the ravaged face. Helen Follett was also a writer, a generous person, who at heart liked people. She loved her husband, gloried in his gifts, and bore his ferocious moods cheerfully.

Lefty often spent the evening with them in their large dilapidated Victorian house, especially after he began writing *Tutors' Lane,* which is a short novel about life in a small New England college. It was odd that no one had written about such a place. The loves and hates of people in a dedicated profession, their struggles for recognition and power, could be entertaining and illuminating, as Trollope had proved in a not dissimilar milieu. *Tutors' Lane* owes much to Trollope and something to *Cranford.* The title was suggested to the author by Mr. Beers who told him that Tutors' Lane was the original name for Prospect Street in New Haven. Lefty called his college Woodbridge. He had Farmington in mind when he described its main street; Dunham's mother, Mrs. Barney, Mr. Beers, Tully Williamson came into the story, and the Williamses' library. He enjoyed working on his book, writing anywhere and at any time including office hours. He was entering upon the profession that Wilmarth had chosen at the age of eight. The story trotted along without plan or plot from one episode to the next and when the author could think of no more episodes he stopped. The Folletts liked it more and more and when it was finished Wilson suggested that Lefty let him send it to Alfred Knopf for whom he had been a reader and who had shown an interest in the Yale Press. To become a Knopf author was to join a new club that was both select and lively. "*Tutors' Lane,*" Wilson wrote in his report "is pure drollery and diversion—the method of Little Mary Mix-up applied, with inimitable deftness, to another medium of communication and to those aspects of life in a small college town which hover between high comedy and the most delicate sort of farce." The typescript went to Knopf, and Lefty composed himself to await the verdict.

The contrast between Dunham and Gans, guided and disciplined, training for their professional futures, and himself bothered him more and more. What did he really want to do? Life after graduation was not clearly marked as it was in Yale College. If he didn't look out he would end up among the disappointed. Opportunities for employment outside the Press were offered him, including one to join the founders of *Time.* Brit Hadden and Harry Luce came up from New York one day to see him about it. Walter Millis, the third of the original triumvirate, had decided to stay with the Baltimore *News.* Wouldn't Lefty take his place? But Lefty was certain that journalism was not for him. Thanks to the good offices of John Farrar, who was making a great success of *The Bookman,* he was approached by the owners of the failing *Ainslee's Magazine,* but had the wit not to consider it. John also introduced him to Ellery Sedgwick, who was looking for a young assistant in the *Atlantic.* They met at the Century, the first time Lefty was in what was to be his favorite club in after years, but the two men did not become friends until thirty-odd years later when they wrote each other about such questions as, What became of Barsabas? and other biblical puzzles. Lefty had a brief connection with the old *Life* while still at the Press. Langhorne Gibson, then a Senior in Keys, persuaded his father Charles Dana Gibson, the owner of *Life,* to give Lefty a chance to do its book page. Mr. Gibson arranged for him to meet the editors, Louis Shipman and Oliver Herford, who reluctantly allowed him a month's trial, explaining frostily that the job was promised to Sidney Howard. Lefty tried it anyway, did quite well, I think, and then after the month was up wondered what he would do next.

He consulted Alfred Knopf who said, "If you really want to be a publisher, come down to our office for a few months to see how it works, then go to a London and Paris and Leipzig firm. I can arrange it for you. Regard it as a graduate school course in publishing. No one will have had such a training." George Day acquiescing (he was not unwilling to have the discontented young man out of the way), Lefty began this course in the fall of 1921, while the decision on *Tutors' Lane* was pending. In its six years of existence Alfred A. Knopf, Inc., had become a force in American publishing owing to its innovations in book design, the introduction of important foreign authors who were virtually unknown in this country, and the discovery of young American writers whose reputations the Knopfs established. Enterprise, imagination, and ideal relations with authors and booksellers were bringing their reward. The Knopfs and their half-dozen assistants in the small office at 220 West 42nd Street could not have been kinder to the visitor or more conscientious about his training. He was moved about, even to the two accountants with whom he stayed until nine one night until he found a missing item, a considerable feat for one who was unable to balance his own checkbook and an outcome more satisfactory than his first attempt to make an index. When it appeared Lefty furtively tested his work and found that in no instance did it refer to the right page. Then one day Alfred leaned over his desk and said, "Blanche and I have decided to do your book," and in that apocalyptic hour the publishing world of London, Paris, and Leipzig vanished swiftly away.

During the ten weeks he was in New York he had a glimpse of its literary life. The Knopfs included him in one or two of their evening parties where were Hergesheimer, Mencken, George Jean Nathan, Carl Van Vechten, Ernest Boyd, and Zona Gale. Very crowded were these parties with people sitting on the floor drinking bootleg gin. John Farrar asked him to a

Bookman lunch at which were F.P.A., Heywood Broun, Alexander Woollcott, and other luminaries. Of these F.P.A. was easily first in Lefty's regard. "The Conning Tower," witty, intimate, tense, was the first thing he read every morning in the *World.* When he later "made" the "Tower" two or three times he was very pleased with himself; when his contributions were not printed he knew that their rejection was deserved. He sat next to F.P.A. at the *Bookman* lunch, but was too self-conscious to make anything of his opportunity.

The writer he did feel at home with was George Day's brother, Clarence. He lived on Riverside Drive, was bedridden with arthritis, and saw only a few visitors late in the afternoon; that is, he was inaccessible except to those whom he wanted to see and who were ready to put themselves out for him. Knopf had recently published *This Simian World,* which introduced Clarence to the public, but Lefty knew his earlier *'96 Half-way Book,* "Printed for the friends and members of the Class of 1896, Yale College," a work that the *Tribune* was to call on Clarence's death, "a routine task transmuted into a volume of extraordinary portraits." When in 1921 Lefty told the author how much he admired it Clarence got him a copy and it is now behind Lefty's sofa at Farmington on the three-foot shelf of books that mean most to him. After apologizing in his preface for the sketchiness of his biographies, Clarence added, "Still, if scientists can re-build extinct animals, all complete, from mere shin-bones perhaps we can size each other up fairly well from these glimpses," and he spoke of the average man's fear of betraying himself unconsciously to his companions. "Don't you pity," he asked, "the classmate who walks about wearing a mask, knowing he's really one kind of a person within, yet determined to seem quite a different person without? Think of him holding it warily always in place, as preoccupied as a man with a high hat in a gale. Hard work! and so futile!" He spent four years on the book, badgering his classmates to reveal themselves, adding sketches and verses. He was sympathetic with the oddities in the Class, but pulled the masks off the prominent if they wore them, and they had not liked it.

I can recall little of Lefty's conversations with the invalid except his encouragement to write about the comedy of academic life, but I remember his disconcerting way of merely smiling when Lefty became too ebullient and how this silent commentary slowed his young visitor down. Clarence's silences were salutary, but his demonstration of the uses and advantages of illness was not. Like Mrs. Lewis, he had arranged his life so that he did nothing that he did not want to do.

Lefty's course with the Knopfs ended sooner than had been planned because the hard chair at his desk hurt his coccyx. He carried a rubber ring about with him for a while and then returned to his doctor in New Haven. From the tyranny of unwelcome routine he was always rescued by illness.

XI

GRAND TOUR

Lefty's father died in 1913 swiftly, mercifully, of a heart attack, the one and only illness of his life. The funeral was held in the Lewises' library, which was the sole time the family ever gathered there. Wilmarth stole in to take a terrified look at his father from whom he had been so alienated that it was years before he could think of him as a kindly human being who bore the affliction of a loveless marriage with cheerfulness and dignity. Mrs. Lewis's death on the eve of her sixty-second birthday in March 1922 was from pernicious anemia, a disease that was soon to be conquered, but from which death was the only escape in 1922. Wilmarth did not grieve for her; he had done that in Mr. Thacher's office eight years earlier. He went back to Alameda and helped Azro dispose of the contents of the house, taking little for himself, a chair or two, a few of Wilmarth's books, his stamp collection, the scrapbook he kept while at Thacher, the photographs of Aunt Lux's house, the "Wilmarth teapot"—an early nineteenth-century American teapot that belonged to a Wilmarth-Aldrich great-grandmother—and the enormous steel engraving of Bach playing for ladies and cherubs, which he never hung and eventually, incredibly, lost.

He wore a mourning band for some months, a custom

that was going out except among the conservative. His mother had not allowed him to wear one for his father, to the surprise of his Thacher friends. She wore mourning herself for a year, discarding a new red hat of which she was particularly fond, but Wilmarth was not permitted to wear even a black tie and felt rather cheated. When as a little boy he asked why people wore mourning he was told that it was a mark of respect for the deceased and he noticed that some of the respect rubbed off on the mourner and ensured his being treated with a certain deference. After his mother's death he assumed this distinction for six months, reminding himself conscientiously from time to time how much he owed to her whose death he was advertising. Yet he was not comfortable about it. He had adored his mother, but she had turned out to be malign. She was dead and he was relieved. Was he being hypocritical and cold-hearted? He had done what Mr. Thacher told him to do, he had crossed the continent to visit her during his vacations and had conducted their altered relationship so that she accepted his living in the East without rancor or resentment. He knew that he would have a better chance in life without her and not only because he now had enough money to live comfortably and did not need a paid job—Azro said he had a thousand a month not counting certain showers of manna that Azro would invest as they fell. He was free to do as he pleased, but his mother still had a hold on him.

On his return to New Haven he became even more disenchanted with the routine of the Press and with what he felt was the futility of his existence inside and outside it. Much as he enjoyed Keys he saw that being a perennial undergraduate would not satisfy him as his friends married and moved into their adult lives. There was, he believed, no future for him in publishing or in any other business. Like Mr. Barney, he would have no boss. Sir William Osler in *A Way of Life,* which Mr.

Thacher read to the School, advised living in the day without imposing upon oneself the burdens of the past and future. This is what he, Lefty Lewis, would do. His novel would be published in September by the most exciting firm in the country. Lawrason Riggs was going abroad in July and urged him to come along. He would resign from the Press, spend the summer in Europe, and see what happened.

The move from Alameda made a second move easier. Americans are migratory by instinct. "Something lost behind the ranges." Kipling and S. D. Thacher approved the questing spirit. Lefty learned that life is movement and change when Anna Crowe read to him how the Red Queen showed Alice from the hilltop the course that she, a pawn, would have to follow through the squares to become a queen. It was the first Commencement Address that he ever heard. When his turn came years later to give Commencement Addresses he used it, adding that one's native aptitudes and shortcomings affected one's performance in the differcnt squares: the ability to play football is more useful in the school square than in the middle-aged square and a sense of humor is less so; success or failure is not necessarily repeated in the next square. Lefty realized in 1922 that he was not at his best in the early squares, but he believed that he would improve later on since he sensed that in his cradle he had received the gift of perpetual middle age. Meanwhile, he was finished with the college square and would move into the next one, whatever it was.

In June he resigned from the Press and sailed for England with Lawrason Riggs and half a dozen other friends on the *Ryndam,* an old ten-day boat. By good luck he was placed at the same table with Owen Wister, the author of *The Virginian,* the first immensely popular Western. Wister was a man of the world of great charm and wide reading. Lefty found him more agreeable than the successful younger writers whom he had met in New York. One could not picture Owen Wister sitting on the floor drinking raw gin and ridiculing the American "booboisie." The "freshness and discovery" that critics born since 1930 find in the twenties was not evident in him; his was the freshness and discovery of the eighties. How composed he could be he showed one day when Lefty thoughtlessly repeated the stale remark about the author of *Lorna Doone* being a "one-book man." The author of *The Virginian* looked at him blandly. Lefty tried to recover himself by saying how much he enjoyed *Philosophy 4* and *The Pentecost of Calamity.* The perfection of Wister's manner was unruffled. He was surprised that Lewis had read those little books and was pleased that *Philosophy 4* was recommended by the bibulous professor who taught the equivalent course at Yale. *Philosophy 4* is about two Harvard Sophomores, ruddy and rich, who as a result of getting drunk the night before the final exam outshine the greasy grind classmate who tutored them for it. The Yale professor smiling boozily did not of course recommend that his class get drunk before the coming exam, but . . .

The *Ryndam* was so small that it sailed close in to the Cornish coast. Lefty was as excited as he had been thirteen years earlier when the *Nieuw Amsterdam* crept into Boulogne. The ordered fields and little villages straggling down to the sea under the chaperonage of their square-towered churches awoke in him awareness of kinship to the mother country, "sensations sweet felt in the blood and felt along the heart." At Exeter, where he and Lawrason motored after landing at Plymouth, he went to early Communion in the Cathedral the following morning, a week-day, and made his way, guidebook in hand, reverently up the nave, with its "Minstrels' Gallery (probably 14th cent.) on the N. side, with angels playing on various musical instruments" and around the choir with its *"Bishop's Throne* and stone *Sedalia,* exquisite works of the early 14th century" to the Lady Chapel where the service was to be held. At length a young cleric appeared who regarded him, the sole communicant, as an unappetizing intruder. Lefty's sentimental loyalties garnished with literary allusions were chilled; instead of being welcomed in the Mother Church as one who spoke the language Shakespeare spoke and held the faith and morals Milton held he was an ex-colonial in wrong clothes. Early-morning Communion in Exeter Cathedral was for him a failure.

London proved to be even worse. He and Lawrason stayed at Carter's Hotel in Albemarle Street opposite Brown's Hotel. It was a small establishment where they were the only Americans. That they were unwelcome was made plain by the way they were moved higher and higher until they ended up in the garret. Lefty loved the theaters, but he found London on the whole intolerable. It was still so smart, still so aware of being the capital of the greatest Empire in history. The way the natives pronounced "American" was particularly hard to bear. "Hev you *enny* conventions in America?" a not at all dear old lady asked Lefty with the expression of one smelling a bad smell. He escaped to Oxford where American tourists were accepted as a necessity of life. There he was bowled over by the colleges, which he visited one by one, their chapels, halls, libraries, and gardens. He lost his head in the men's shops, buying ties and socks and handkerchiefs recklessly. For the first time in his life he felt completely on his own. At the Mitre he had a little table in the dining room to himself. Two young waiters flew about the room saying, " 'kew!" whenever they offered a dish. At other tables were British visitors discreetly talking in low voices and occasionally eyeing the more exuberant American guests. After several days he was admitted cautiously into conversation by an elderly and clerical don at the next table who wore a straw hat (not in the dining room), the alternate diamonds of which were black; a hat that opened new vistas in dress. When he learned that Lefty had not been to Cambridge he shook his head, and lowering his voice confided with a meaningful glance, "It is not quite the same thing." It might have been Harvard speaking of Yale.

Masefield kindly arranged for him to have the privileges of the Radcliffe Camera, the undergraduate library, but Lefty used them only once because he did not know what to look for or how to do it and so felt clumsy as well as stupid. Masefield also asked him to Boar's Hill to a tea party where he was very much an alien in spite of the generous attempt of the daughter of the house to put him at his ease. When he began the four-mile return walk to the Mitre the cars of the other guests passed him by without stopping. He didn't think he should flag a ride, but by limping badly he hoped that someone might stop and volunteer a lift. In this he was disappointed. The drivers doubtless assumed that he *wanted* to walk. He had still to learn that the English really are shy, respect people's privacy, and that most of them would have been pleased if he had asked them to help him get home.

He did the honors of Oxford to visiting Yale friends who dropped in on him. "You must see the gardens at Worcester and St. John's," he would say, or, "Now we'll go down to Magdalen." It was at the latter college that he wandered one day through an open gate into a little walled garden that he had not seen before. The borders were filled with midsummer flowers. Not a soul was in sight. He strolled to the farther end where up a stone step or two was a seat on which he sat. Deer were grazing over the wall. The beauty of the place and day were suddenly almost overwhelming. That was over forty years ago. As I try to bring back this experience now I see the garden as a nearsighted person sees the distance. I am aware of hollyhocks, and probably delphiniums and larkspur as well. As for the mood that the day and scene inspired, the phrase "cosmic consciousness" comes into my mind to describe what Lefty felt, but I am not quite sure what it means. Exhalations from the poets rise such as:

> *With an eye made quiet by the power*
> *Of harmony, and the deep power of joy,*
> *To see into the life of things.*

At the time Lefty was brought back abruptly to earth by the sound of voices. A party was going on in the house to which the garden apparently belonged. The voices were coming closer. Lefty fled just in time to avoid, as he learned years later, the guests of the President of Magdalen in whose private garden he had been trespassing.

Oxford had half a dozen bookshops, all more crowded and untidy than the Brick Row and with a more professional atmosphere. They had few costly books, their antiquarian business was on a modest scale by West End of London standards, but it was active. Dons and undergraduates came to look at books on their special interests—mountaineering, constitutional law, Baudelaire, or what not—perhaps spending seven and six at the end of their stay. There was nothing of the esoteric about these shops, they would not have irritated the most anti-rare-book American professor, but Lefty did not feel at home in them until his shyness was overcome by an adventure that a Thacher-Yale classmate, Buell Hammett, provided. While spending the past year at Balliol Buell had found a shop at Newbury twenty miles away that had "a lot of old books in old leather bindings" which he thought must be valuable. They were upstairs, he reported, in a draper's shop that was run by the widow of the late proprietor and collector of the books, lots and lots of old books from the floor to the ceiling and all over the floor as well. They certainly sounded valuable. The draper's widow, he said, was a nice old thing who had no idea what the books were worth. It really was a chance to build up one's library. He, Lefty, and two other Elis hurried off to this cache and, sure enough, even while walking up the stairs to the treasure room Lefty picked off the shelves what he took to be the first edition of the *Idylls of the King*. The large upper room was just as Buell had described it, the shelves crammed and books all over the floor. They *must* be worth a lot of money. Each of the four took a quarter of the room as his particular claim. Soon they began to specialize; one in nineteenth-century poetry, another in nineteenth-century fiction; Lefty with Tink in mind appropriated the eighteenth century. They generously gave up nuggets from their claims that "belonged" to another. This went on for nearly four hours and they got very, very, dirty.

They returned the following day. There were four things that they learned to look for: the author, the title, the date, and the bookplate or autographs of earlier owners. Their knowledge of dates was sketchy; their ignorance of bibliography was total—they had not yet heard the word. Lefty did not hesitate to include in his pile a set of Fielding that lacked three volumes. Nor did they understand the importance of "condition." The sun filtered through the windows, motes rose in the shafts of light, dust from the great books that were passing into their possession.

After it was all over, the four had to face the delicate question of what they owed their hostess. When they raised it earlier she waved it aside, urging them to go ahead and take what they wanted; it would be time enough to talk about the price later on. After they washed off the grime under a cold tap for the last time she asked if tenpence a volume would be satisfactory? Lefty bought some two hundred and fifty volumes for about ten pounds. All four had twinges of conscience, but tenpence a volume was what they'd been asked. Arrangements to ship the books to America were made with surprising speed and before the summer was out Lefty suspected they had paid just about what the books were worth. Yet I still look back on those hours at Newbury as intoxicating: the discovery of early editions of English authors, the luck in getting to them ahead of the great dealers of New York and London, the bloom of enthusiasm unbrushed by knowledge or experience, all this still hangs about my copies of Bruce's *Travels,* 1790, and the fourth edition of *Robinson Crusoe*—which alone remain of Lefty's great Newbury find.

Henceforth Lefty regarded himself as an initiated book collector. What a first engagement is to a fighting man Newbury was to him. He was now "blooded." Thereafter he did not hesitate before a bookshop, but went boldly in. All, whether large or small, tidy or untidy, had the same feeling of expectancy, even urgency, for him and all had the same delicious smell. The shopkeepers bore a common stamp. Lean men they were, pale, detached. When Lefty on entering the premises, perhaps to the tinkle of a bell, asked, "May I look around?" they said, "Certainly, sir," and left him to drift about by himself as long as he pleased. The most fruitful phase of his education had begun.

In the course of the summer he handled thousands of books. He was still of an age when one can learn quickly whatever one is eager to learn, and this now included for him much that had been an effort earlier. It was the reading—or, rather, the skimming—just as inclination prompts that Johnson recommended to Boswell, the only kind that does one any good. This grazing on the slopes of literature provides the education that can be acquired so much more readily and pleasantly in a bookshop than in a classroom. Lefty was learning to be "at ease," as Trollope says, "among the creations of other minds." The books he bought made a miscellaneous collection. From the heights of Shakespeare and Milton it descended to Gray and Cowper, down to Douglas Jerrold and Praed, down, down, to Mrs. Hemans and Montgomery. He wandered from the highways and byways of English literature to Voyages and Travel, the Fine Arts, and the lush colored-plate books, buying on sudden impulse. He became aware of the standard works that were in every country-house library: Strickland's *Queens of England,* Bewick's *Birds,* Horace Walpole's *Royal and Noble Authors,* and dozens more that were new to him. Each day raced by until, a little before six, the proprietor began putting up the shutters. Lefty would pay his small bill and reluctantly depart.

He began to notice the changing styles in sizes, bindings, type, and illustrations, and to sense that they threw light on the times when they appeared. He was never to become a bibliographer with technical knowledge of book production, but thanks to Carl Rollins and his own instinct he grew aware of how books reflect in their formats the periods in which they are produced, just as buildings and songs and pictures do. The first editions of the *Alice* books made this clear to him. There was only a generation between them and his own beloved edition with the Peter Newell illustrations that Aunty Miller had given Wilmarth in 1900 and that had been first read to him by Anna Crowe, and yet the two editions were totally different in tone and quality. The first editions were modest in size and cheerfull in color, the product of an era serene in its security and respectability; Wilmarth's edition with its larger page, decorated margins, and opulent renderings of Tenniel's neat and precise drawings was pretentious and rather vulgar. It was the difference between the Mid-Victorians and the Edwardians. Years later he was unable to convince scholars who maintained that microfilms of books are "as good as" the books themselves that they were wrong; yet the hours he spent handling books in shops taught him what all the photostats and microfilm in the world could not have taught him.

He traveled south and west, north and east, without much thought or plan, sometimes with Yale friends, sometimes alone. His solitary excursions were also in the nature of peripatetic retreats. They were good for him he knew, not merely as practice in enduring boredom, but to touch base, so to say, with the fundamentals of which he was dimly and intermittently aware. Cathedrals were obvious places to visit on these retirements, and he went to Durham, York, Lichfield, Peterborough, trying in vain to recall from Freshman English what he had read in Ruskin. Their West Fronts filled his mind with a vague exaltation that cooled when he entered them: they were beautiful shells from which a living body had been extracted. However, educators agree that it is a good thing merely to walk in and out of great buildings and it heightens self-esteem to be able to say, "I have been there." The cathedral close was more vital to Lefty, who peopled it with a Trollopian dean in his gaiters and well-fed prebendaries, each knowing to a penny everyone's income and the income of his wife. No doubt there was a current crisis in which the Chapter was sharply divided with the opposing forces evenly matched. It was one thing to read about a cathedral close in Alameda and another to see the reality. Lefty found the reality rather depressing.

Tully Williamson once said to Lewie, "I am a spectator," and that was the role Lefty tried to assume on his travels, an easy task in England where hobnobbing with strangers was discouraged. It was the role for one whose first of doubtless many novels was shortly to appear, but he was not very good at it and could not enjoy fully what he saw unless he had someone with whom to share it. There was the melancholy day he spent going from York to Lichfield in pious pilgrimage to Dr. Johnson's birthplace, a gesture that he hoped would please Tink. The trip required three changes of trains with breaks of several hours each at the "way stations." The spectator made the most of the stationmasters and their gardens, he read the notices on the bulletin boards, he compared the Bovril and Oxo advertisements, but the solitude of that day was one of the most unrelieved lessons in boredom the spectator was ever taught. He learned a lesson of a different kind at North Berwick when playing in a foursome with Ben Sayres its famous professional. It proved to be Sayres's last round. His final stroke was a six-foot putt and he missed it. In the silence that followed he looked noncommittally at the sky. "Somebody moved," he said. The dignity of it, the justness of the reproof, held Lefty transfixed on greens the rest of his golfing life because he was the somebody who had moved. Ben Sayres imparted instruction to the end.

The climax of Lefty's book buying in 1922 came when he completed his Masefield collection with the purchase of *Salt Water Ballads,* 1902. The price he paid for it was much more than its value today: he had collected one of the few authors whose works have gone down in the book market during the past forty years. The Paris bookshops had little for him, but the quays on the Left Bank contributed his first rather grubby prints. He spent the day sightseeing with fellow Yalensians and dining with them before going to the Comédie or Opera afterwards; his summer ended with a three weeks' trip to Switzerland and Italy—Vevey, Zermatt, Stresa, Bellagio, Milan, and Venice—in the company of four of them. This, the 1922 version of the eighteenth-century Grand Tour, was such a success that the surviving travelers still exhaust their auditors' patience with reminiscences of it. They were at an age when the inconveniences and misadventures of travel—bad plumbing, lost baggage, mosquitoes inside the net instead of outside it—are funny, when impressions are sharp and the mind retains something of what has been seen. The five young men were model tourists, taking churches, galleries, and places of entertainment in their stride, observing with amused detachment the manners of the natives, and, most commendably, coming home even better friends than when they set out.

Lefty sailed to New York alone, with no clear idea of what he was going to do next. *Tutors' Lane* was about to be published: perhaps something would come of it. As a boy he had been impressed by Byron's waking to find himself famous; perhaps the time had come for the fulfillment of Mrs. Blood's prophecy: *Tutors' Lane* would reveal a new talent in American letters; money would pour in. Drudgery, routine, subordination, were not to be for him. What he had to live on was modest in the eyes of his friends who were working to be rich and it would be nice to have lots and lots and *lots* of money. Meanwhile, he had persuaded Azro, who on their mother's death was cast adrift, to come East for a visit.

At the age of nineteen while spending a weekend with the Barneys at Farmington Lefty decided that he would move there when, as, and if he could live where he pleased. It was love at first sight. Colonial houses were so attractive to him that he would wake up early on the last morning of his trip East to catch glimpses of those visible from the train as it crawled through the Berkshires to Springfield. The main street of Farmington was lined with colonial houses. Why they had such a hold on him I do not know. Perhaps it was his unconscious appreciation of their perfect proportions; more probably it was the charm of the past enhanced by the opulent present. He delighted in the Farmington residents he met, above all in Mrs. Barney. Azro and he went there in the fall of 1922 for a visit and there Lefty remained the rest of his life. Twenty-six is young to retire, but I do not regret the step that he took.

XII

FARMINGTON

Farmington is thirty miles north of New Haven and ten miles southwest of Hartford. It was the tenth largest township in the Colonies in 1774 when it had a flourishing trade with the West Indies in rum, indigo, and sugar. The local merchants, the Cowles family chiefly, built beautiful frame houses that still stand. When Farmington's peace and dignity were threatened in the 1840's by the new railroad, Miss Sarah Porter, the founder of the School that gives the community its chief celebrity, is said to have told the Connecticut Legislature, "You can't bring that thing near *my* girls," and secured the passage of a bill that kept the would-be intruder away forever. Seven of the original villages in the township broke off and became, some of them, cities, but unlike most American communities Farmington fought to remain small. In 1922 it still had a sleepy main street and little else.

Farmington has seemed a place of enchantment to many, including Henry James. "When," he wrote in the *American Scene,* "the great elm-gallery happens to be garnished with old houses [as at Farmington], and the old houses happen to show style and form and proportion, and the hand of time, further, has been so good as to rest on them with all the pressure of protection and none of that of interference, then it is that the New England village may placidly await any comer." In addition to these felicities, "the note of the aristocratic in the air" at Farmington secured for him "a positively thrilled attention. . . . Not only, moreover, are the best houses so 'good'—the good ones are so surprisingly numerous. That is all they seem together to say, 'We are good, yes—we are excellent; though, if we know it very well, we make no vulgar noise about it.' " When Lefty went to Farmington a few years later the people who impressed James so favorably were still there and were to introduce the young man to what was still called "the great world."

James had not the good fortune to meet Mrs. Barney nor did Lefty see her on his first visit in 1914 because she was having one of her headaches, but her lovely voice floated down to him from the upper hall to report that "The Wallabies are upon me." He remembered her at Thacher where she made a sensational contribution to Sunday Evening Reading. Mr. Thacher was in the midst of the *Blue Bird.* Mrs. Barney, sitting in the ladies' row, listened with such evident pleasure that Lewie found her total lack of self-consciousness as interesting as the play itself and so got the most out of her interruption when a laugh halted Mr. Thacher's reading. Before he could go on Mrs. Barney took over, announced that she had just seen the play in New York and described how amusing the actor was when he did that particular bit. Such an interruption had never occurred before in the history of the School. Mr. Thacher was thrown off his stride; there was an awkward silence after Mrs. Barney finished; Dunham was overwhelmed. When Lefty met her on his second visit to Farmington their friendship began. In 1922 she arranged for him to rent the small furnished house that belonged to a cousin, Robert Brandegee, the painter, who had studied in Paris and whose best work makes one realize that he rubbed shoulders with the great impressionists.

He had assembled the house rather than built it; a little schoolhouse had become the studio, a barn was divided up for the other rooms. On the walls of the large sitting room he painted a fresco that told, dimly, the story of a knight, dragon, and maiden; on the grand piano he painted white cyclamen; in the garden was a tiny wading pool in the shape of a bidet, or, if one preferred, a cello, an instrument that his wife played. These features helped to offset the discomforts of the house and gave it character. The furniture was nondescript, but you couldn't have everything for seventy-five dollars a month. Mrs. Barney let Lefty work out his domestic problems for himself, which he did with the help of a Negro couple named Adam and Martha. Although he was ready to accept Mrs. Barney *in loco matris,* she wisely maintained a perfectly balanced intimacy instead.

She had the air of what used to be called "a great lady," but it was often at variance with her costume, which might combine such incongruities as a lace mantilla and moccasins. The depth of her affections was concealed by New England reserve and fear of showing emotion; equally strong was her fear of being "cut and dried." The presence of a guest in the house whom she suspected of this tendency would stimulate her to acts of defiance such as shredding codfish in the living room or smoking a cigarette. She was, she said, "a Proudhon anarchist," but what she meant by it Lefty never discovered. The high-ceilinged 1830 house reflected her love of beautiful things and her opposition to conformity. The sitting room was originally a hallway that connected the dining room and the ample front porch. Behind Mrs. Barney's purple velvet sofa in it were banked etchings by Meryon and Whistler. There was a library on one side of the hall sitting room and a music room on the other side of it, but only Mr. Barney sat in the library and no one sat in the music room. The dining room opened on to another porch that looked down on a formal garden and a gazebo; beyond were greenhouses and woods. Lawns extended to the south and west, in which direction could be seen the Burlington Hills and the Farmington golf course in the middle distance.

The good that Mrs. Barney did was carried on so surreptitiously that only the local doctor and Congregational minister knew about it and they I am sure did not know all of it. She gave most of the books in the Village Library (which her husband had built and endowed); she rescued the finest seventeenth-century house in Farmington and turned it into a museum of local antiquities; and one evening, with gales of silvery laughter, she announced to her less amused family that she had just given a very large sum to the Hartford morgue. Her much-quoted irrelevancies were delivered with flawless timing. They were particularly effective at the bridge table where she might pause on the verge of a finesse that would make or lose the hand and say with a faraway look and the most distant of voices something like, "When the Revolution comes I shall march to the wall with my friends, but my sympathies will be with the firing squad," or, "If I could have had a son like Charles James Fox I would have been *anybody's* mistress."

On the Sunday of Lefty's first visit to Farmington, Dunham took him to tea with, as he said, "an old lady who lives down the street," an inadequate preparation for Mrs. William S. Cowles, the elder sister of Theodore Roosevelt. The door of "Oldgate" was opened by Hopkinson, the butler, and William his brother, the second man, both of whom were delighted to see Dunham. Hopkinson led him and his friend through a beautiful late eighteenth-century hall to the "den," a large low-ceilinged 1660 room with an enormous fireplace, where he announced the young men. It was Wilmarth Lewis's introduction to a roomful of people chattering away with what he was later to call "social sprightly." (How astonished he would have been had he known that in that room nine years hence he was to meet Annie Burr Auchincloss, his wife of thirty-one years.) Mrs. Cowles, an arthritic, was seated by a table to the left of the fireplace. Beside her was a chair in which, one by one, the guests sat for a few minutes of conversation with her. Who were there that first day I cannot now recall other than Mrs. Cowles's sister, Mrs. Douglas Robinson and her daughter, Corinne Alsop, who lived nearby. The Yale freshmen did not add to the gaiety of the occasion.

When at length it was Lefty's turn to talk to Mrs. Cowles, he reached a milestone in his career. He had never met anyone at once so formidable and so easy. She had a genius for drawing people out without seeming to do it and for arriving swiftly on ground where they appeared at their best. How in that first brief meeting *Alice in Wonderland* was reached I have no recollection, but *Alice* was reached and it became the point from which Lefty and Mrs. Cowles started on his next session by her chair. After he moved to Farmington in 1922 he became a regular caller at Oldgate, having tea there several times a week and often Sunday lunch as well. By then Mrs. Cowles had become more and more crippled. She was, furthermore, increasingly deaf, yet it was as if these handicaps did not exist, so gallantly did she carry on. Her husband, the Admiral, died in 1923, but her son, Sheff, and daughter-in-law, Bobbie, were living next door, and there were still many relations, Hyde Park as well as Oyster Bay, and old friends, English and American, who stopped off to see her. "Everybody" came to Farmington sooner or later.

Owen Wister came, William Amory Gardner of Groton came. The latter was known to Lefty from his Groton friends. He was one of the three founders of the school, had given the Chapel, and taught Greek and Latin. His eccentricities were not so marked nor his interest in literature and the arts so oppressive that he put the boys off; quite the contrary, most of them were devoted to him. When Lefty met him he recognized the source of some of his friends' intellectual attitudes and interests and guessed that Mr. Gardner's success was owing to his finding out what the boys were interested in and being quietly and amusingly helpful about it. Perhaps, too, his ease with them was furthered by his not having children of his own, a lack that meant he was less scarred in the struggle between authority and aspiring independence. Certainly his influence derived in part from his expecting the young to have the good manners required of their elders. Lefty introduced him to the first crossword-puzzle book, which had just come out. He was delighted with it, rapidly finishing a puzzle that had stumped the young man. The missing words derived from Greek, and as he wrote them in, pointing out casually that Greek was not a dead language after all, Lefty was for the first time ashamed of the serious gap in his formal education. I wish he had filled it then. When he tried to years later it was too late.

Mrs. Cowles carried on with her Sunday luncheons until she died in 1931. A memorable one occurred on the day after Lindbergh's flight to Paris. The den was full of rejoicing people. Among them was a lady from a very large house nearby that served her as a spring and fall waystation between Palm Beach and Bar Harbor. Suddenly amid one of those strange silences that occur sometimes in a company of voluble people the transient lady was heard chiming loudly at Mrs. Cowles, "Yes, but *is* he a GENTLEMAN?" Lefty wondered then if the word "gentleman" had perhaps not had its day.

Although Mrs. Cowles had lived much in the great world of New York, London, and Washington, where Jusserand in his memoirs says she maintained the only salon during his ambassadorship, she did not dwell on the past. Once she did call attention to a diamond sunburst that she often wore and explained that it was a wedding present from dear Mrs. Cornelius Vanderbilt in gratitude for Mrs. Cowles's mother being the first to ask the Vanderbilts to dinner; another time she mentioned that her father took her to the White House during the Civil War, that the President sat her on his knee, and that her father told her afterwards that she must never forget it; but such glimpses of the past usually came as a result of a question, "What was Henry Adams like?" (Malicious and affected.) "Did Edward VII really have a German accent?" (Yes.) Sitting in her chair, dressed always in white after the Admiral's death, she maintained the tone and manner of the age of assurance until she died. She might still at any moment incinerate Lord Aberdeen or Mrs. McKinley in a casual reminiscence, but they were dead long since and she concentrated on the lives of her little circle over which she had an inordinate influence. The ritual of the tea-table demanded that the conversation should never flag. To perform his part in it Lefty went to Oldgate as carefully prepared as he had gone to one of Tinker's classes and with the same sense of discipline. Fluency was essential to success; you spoke distinctly into the big box that now stood on the table beside your hostess. Long stories were not encouraged; you said what you had to say as pointedly as possible and then let someone else talk. Mrs. Cowles was not herself a storyteller, her forte was in maintaining a flow of conversation and a wit that might leave its object dismembered, but she was assiduous in practising what Horace Walpole called "the delicacies and attentions of friendship." Until she died in 1931 Oldgate remained an Edwardian redoubt, where one was taught "the little arts of life, so painfully evolved" and made to believe that their mastery was essential to the conduct of a pleasant existence.

Hill-Stead was described by Henry James on his first visit to Farmington. It was, he wrote, "a great new house on a hilltop

Mastick Grammar School

Christ Church, Alameda

Miranda Wilmarth Sheldon Lewis, 1882

Chiquito, 1911

WSL's Lower School Room, 1910–1911.
The Iron Maiden of Nuremberg stands on
the shelf below Dürer's house.

The School, 1912. WSL is standing with Mr. Dodge under the pepper tree.

Evening Reading, 1911. Tully Williamson is the second from the left behind Mr. Thacher.

H. Hadley and WSL, 1916

Yale 1918 at Farmington, 1958

2d Lieut Lewis, 1918, San Diego, California

Carl Rollins at his Birthday Dinner, 1955.
Reading from left to right: Mrs. George Parmly Day, August Heckscher, CPR, WSL.

View of the House from Main Street. The fence, designed by Richard A. Kimball, was added in 1935.

The Front Hall, 1966

Horace Walpole by Rosalba Carriera, 1741

At Cork with Father Leonard
in the garden of the late Richard Simcox, 1953

The Long Hall, 1966

The New Library, 1966

that over-looked the most composed of communities; a house . . . in which an array of modern 'impressionistic' pictures, mainly French, wondrous examples of Manet, of Degas, of Claude Monet, of Whistler, of other rare recent hands, treated us to the momentary effect of a slippery sweet inserted, without a warning, between the compressed lips of half-conscious inanition." At Hill-Stead "no proof of the sovereign power of art could have been, for the moment sharper . . . it was like the sudden trill of a nightingale, lord of the hushed evening." James was to make subsequent visits to Hill-Stead and to correspond with its owner, Theodate Pope Riddle, the wife of a former Ambassador to Russia, John Wallace Riddle, and daughter of Alfred Pope, an iron manufacturer of Cleveland who had collected the pictures. Mrs. Riddle, an only child, fell in love with Farmington when there at Miss Porter's School and later she moved her parents to it from Ohio. She took up spiritualism and kept a medium and his wife in residence, a connection that was broken in 1915 when Miss Pope, as she then was, and the medium embarked for a spiritualistic conference in London on the *Lusitania*'s last voyage. Miss Pope was miraculously saved, the medium was lost. When he failed to establish communication with her she gave up spiritualism for architecture, designing and building a boy's school in the Cotswold cottage style just north of Farmington at a cost, ultimately, of ten million dollars.

She told stories that illustrated her solution of vexatious problems, such as the one presented by her father's portrait, which hung in the house of his partner. The two families exchanged visits on Thanksgiving and Christmas. The portrait of Mr. Pope, so Mrs. Riddle would tell you, made him look like a satyr. Since this could not be tolerated, one Christmas morning while the herald angels sang Theodate tripped down stairs before anyone else was up, climbed upon a chair, and cut her father's head out of the canvas. "I can see the wallpaper now through the hole," she would conclude, gazing serenely at it in her mind's eye, "and the odd thing is that it looked more like father than the portrait had."

One evening at Hill-Stead she gave Lefty a lesson in the handling of a vexatious problem. As there was an odd number for bridge, he and his hostess were sitting in a little room with a Monet haystack over the fireplace. Mrs. Riddle was at her best, genial, warm; childlike laughter and little cries of delight rippled forth; a sparkling day on a summer sea. Then she remembered Babba, the Persian cat that had recently been added to the household. He was a beautiful cat but had a weakness: he preferred the back of the house to the front. The problem was to reverse the order. "I am meeting Babba more than half way," Mrs. Riddle explained as thunder clouds gathered on the summer horizon. "I'll show you how. Just ring the bell." Ernest, the dignified and gentle mulatto butler who had been in the family fifty years, appeared. "We'll have Babba," Mrs. Riddle said quietly in the voice that prepared the initiated for lightning close at hand. There entered a procession with measured tread: Alexis, the tall second man, an émigré Russian, carried a wicker basket lined with pink satin and filled with catnip; Ernest followed holding Babba whose legs stuck out stiff and whose tail swayed back and forth. Mrs. Riddle indicated with a nod where the basket was to be placed. The basket was put there; Babba was dropped gently into it; the servants withdrew. Babba nibbled the catnip and stretched in ecstasy. Mrs. Riddle beamed. "You see, it's working!" Her attention drifted to less pressing matters until Babba, the catnip eaten, was seen stalking, tail erect as an interrogation point, through a crack in the door to the dining room and the kitchen. Mrs. Riddle turned very red. Then she announced quietly, "I know what I shall do with Babba. I'll chloroform him." And she did.

Many of the educational novelties that Mrs. Riddle introduced in her school were admirable, others were farcical, and she was as determined to enforce the one set as the other. She drew up a Deed of Trust that contained Thirty-nine Articles, each one of which was to be obeyed without question by the Provost, as she called the headmaster. Disobedience meant going the way of Babba. Three Provosts were chloroformed. Three times the faculty was disbanded. Three times the boys were returned to their angry parents. Although the Deed of Trust was handsomely printed by Carl Rollins and its Articles were the law of the school, copies of it were retained by the Foundress and were produced only in times of stress. When after many years Lefty rose to the dangerous eminence of favorite trustee and asked for a sight of this document the Hill-Stead chauffeur brought him a copy, but returned almost at once to take it away. I can recall now only that the teaching of instrumental music was forbidden, that the "head shepherd" had to be of Nordic descent, and that attention was drawn to the virtues of the turtle, an Article with a footnote which added that it had been written "automatically." There was a Board of Trustees and a Board of Regents, but no such Boards were ever less of a problem to a school. The Deed of Trust in providing for the Regents added that they should have no responsibility whatever, which was not quite true: they were expected to meet once a year on the Foundress's Day and march in procession behind her and the Trustees to the High Table in the Refectory for lunch. Since Mrs. Riddle did not endow the school and since she paid the very large annual deficit out of her own pocket—often, alas, by selling a Manet, Renoir, or Mary Cassatt—and since, furthermore, she never required of the Trustees anything more than confirmation of actions that she had already taken their responsibilities were almost as light as those of the Regents. Directors of educational institutions may have cause to deplore the dead hands of benefactors, but Avon's history during its foundress's lifetime illustrates how even heavier the living hand may be. Not long before Mrs. Riddle died Lefty told her that she must choose between having a school or the Deed of Trust. She was much hurt, but she did modify the latter to the extent of making its more farcical exactions permissive rather than mandatory. After her death a bank acted as sole trustee. It was able to modify them still further and the school is now flourishing.

Feminine ascendancy at Farmington was strengthened by the frequent visits of other great ladies, three of whom contributed to Lefty's education in varying measure. The three were Mrs. Theodore Roosevelt, Sr., Mrs. Douglas Robinson, and Miss Annie Burr Jennings.

When Mrs. Cowles introduced the name of her sister-in-law "Darling Edith Roosevelt, my sister-in-law, Mrs. Theodore Roosevelt," one could expect a story illustrative of that lady's wit and independence. Between the two there existed a watchful, respectful, and not very affectionate regard. Mrs. Cowles had the advantage of being on her home ground, of being an invalid who suffered her afflictions with stoical fortitude, and the elder sister to whom the dynamic brother had turned for advice. Mrs. Roosevelt had the advantage of being lovely looking, of having a beautiful soft voice, and above all, of being the great man's widow, a fact kept in view by her wearing mourning for him until she died. Their contest for supremacy, Lefty decided, was a tie. Although Lefty saw Mrs. Roosevelt seldom, he was indebted to her for showing that strength may lie beneath a sweet exterior and that one may do just what one wants to do. She was a great traveler, going to remote places alone with casual intrepidity under the surveillance that accompanies a President's widow. Mrs. Cowles viewed these expeditions with amusement. "Darling Edith Roosevelt, my sister-in-law, Mrs.

Theodore Roosevelt," she said one day sentimentally, "is going to the Iguassu Falls." Pause. "I always send her a bunch of violets the day she sets out"; pause, followed by the look of one thrusting a rapier home, "so she can *throw* it overboard as she goes up the gangplank!"

There was no question who was number one in the relationship between Mrs. Cowles and Mrs. Robinson. In it the younger sister was kept in her place. Mrs. Robinson accepted her subordinate role with humor untinged by rancor. To the world her place was an enviable one entirely apart from the aura of royalty that still hovered over the Roosevelts; she was gay, generous, and talented: *My Brother* was well received and so was her collected *Poems*. April was her month, sun and showers, the swift alteration of which her friends accepted affectionately; only Mrs. Cowles would say, "She cries so!" Mrs. Robinson proved to Lefty that older people may be companionable without loss of dignity. Not to him did she speak of her brother as if he were the founder of a religion. I recall only one reference to him. " 'Singleness of Purpose,' that is what Theodore used to say," she volunteered one day, contriving to look like her brother as she said it. The framed admonition of Josh Billings to consider the postage stamp in Wilmarth's room at Alameda came back to him.

During the summer Lefty would spend a week or two with her at Henderson House in the Mohawk Valley, a large property that had been granted by Queen Anne to the first of her husband's family in this country. Mrs. Robinson presided over a houseful of guests who spent the days playing tennis and golf and swimming in the pool and the evenings at the bridge table. The weekend concluded with prayers in the big hall, the servants attending. A granddaughter played hymns on a harmonium that another grandchild assiduously pumped. The service was conducted by one of the two Robinson sons who read from a battered book long used in the Sabbatical exercises a little homily selected by his mother. The homily might be on helping lame dogs over stiles or keeping a smiling face before the world. When the visit was over and the guests got into their cars to leave, Mary, the waitress, stood at the top of the steps and blew into a large conch like a female Triton. When she was successful it produced a low, bleating, note; when unsuccessful, a great deal of wasted breath, fluster, and spit. Some weeks after Lefty's first visit to Henderson Mrs. Robinson sent him her *Poems* with the inscription:

a Thanksgiving—Nov. 28th 1924

For

Wilmarth Lewis who whether he knows it or not has brought me happy hours such as I knew with my Stewart [*who died as an undergraduate at Harvard*], *who laughs with me as Stewart laughed, and for whom I have warm affection and the wish that life shall give of its best to him—*

His friend

Corinne Roosevelt Robinson.

Lefty first met Miss Jennings in 1919 at one of her standing engagements, lunch with the Hadleys on the day of the Commencement baseball game. It was immediately evident that she was a person of consequence. In her crowded calendar the Princeton or Harvard football game in New Haven was an annual fixture. To it she would repair with a fleet of cars filled with elderly ladies and gentlemen. If it was raining she was dressed in rubber from head to foot, blue rubber. Her eyesight was not of the best, she had little comprehension of the game, yet she was as certain to be in the seats reserved for her by the University as were the goalposts to be on the field. She was, she said, "A Yale woman." She was also a Farmington woman, having gone there to Miss Porter's School and having saved it when on Miss Porter's death its future was imperiled. Other of her major interests were Mount Vernon, of which she was the Vice-Regent for Connecticut, the Republican Party, the State of Connecticut, and France. To all of these she gave her unswerving loyalty, which was the connecting word that explains her life. When in 1928 Lefty married her niece, namesake, and goddaughter he joined her family, her first loyalty of all.

A large woman, she moved through life with the power of elemental force. Clear-headed, direct, resolute, she was accustomed to having her side win, but if it lost she wasted no time in useless repining. Her houses at Fairfield and in New York were filled with objects that she had collected, many of which, the books and pictures and colonial furniture, were of importance; others, such as her collection of owls, were not. The explanation of the owls was found in the Yale Sophomore Society that her brothers had joined and that had an owl as its totem. Humor would have inhibited her *obiter dicta,* which were uttered with authority. Lefty used to try to remember them as they came, one after another, but while he was fastening one in his mind he would jettison it for another even more quotable and he ended up with few. One that he kept concluded his report to her on a cause in which they were both engaged, the building of a bypass around Farmington that would reduce traffic on its Main Street. (Aunt Annie had accomplished a similar deflection single-handed at Fairfield.) To stimulate the Highway Commission, a large subscription was raised by Farmington residents and friends, among whom of course Aunt Annie was one. Lefty in his report to her explained that there was another side to the problem: the proposed road went through the house of a woman who objected. At this point Aunt Annie interrupted. "Stop, Lefty, stop right there. *Never* listen to the other side. No good ever comes of *that.*"

Although Farmington, like Cranford, was in the possession

of the Amazons, it was not without men of consequence. Two of them, D. Newton Barney, Dunham's father, and Winchell Smith, contributed to Lefty's education.

Mr. Barney was an independent man in every sense of the word. He was on numerous boards such as the New Haven Railroad and the Hartford Electric Light Co., of which his father-in-law had been the founder, but "a man of business" relieved him of the details of managing his and his wife's affairs and left him free to play golf at Farmington, in Maine, or Florida. He spoke seldom except after dinner when he talked slowly and quietly without stopping. Lefty was impressed by his devotion to Farmington. He built and endowed its library; he bought up the land behind it and gave it to the adjacent public school as a playground and to forestall the day, which he alone anticipated, when that land would otherwise be divided up for small houses; he repaired the gravestones in the early cemetery and provided for their future care; he had the town records from the seventeenth century on repaired and bound; he had the church's famous spire drawn in case it should be burned; he reprinted the only antiquarian papers that had been written on the village's life and history. Mr. Barney's concern for local antiquities was unusual then in this country. It seemed to Lefty a good deal of a to-do about the past, but his example sank into the young man's mind and came back to him years later as one to follow.

While Mrs. Whitelaw Reid and the Esme Howards were staying at Oldgate, the Barrymores, Mary Pickford, and Douglas Fairbankses might have been staying with the Winchell Smiths. Bill Smith was said to be the most successful "play-doctor" this country had yet had. Beginning with *Brewster's Millions* he collaborated in hit after hit—*The Fortune Hunter, Officer 666, Lightnin'*, and others down to *The Wisdom Tooth, Waterloo Bridge,* and *The Vinegar Tree.* His final play was *The Tadpole,* which he wrote with Lefty in 1931 and 1932. It was the latter's only play and Bill Smith's only failure. We shall come to it in due course.

One other man who had a lasting influence on Lefty and on many others was John Alsop, the uncle of Joe, Stewart, and John, upon whom he lavished an affection that included unflagging attention to manners. He lived in the family's large 1840 house in Middletown that was filled with family possessions, but he was hampered by an inadequate income. During Lefty's first year at Farmington he rented a cottage there to economize and to run a small antique shop that he and Marie Bissell had just opened. Both had excellent taste—they were among the first to rediscover Victorian ornaments—but the Bissells were building a new house, John couldn't be bothered with routine, and the shop languished after the first buying sprees. He never "did" anything in the usual meaning of the word, yet although he died forty years ago his effect upon Lefty was so profound that even now I may ask myself, "What would John Alsop do?" and then I try to do it. Gerald Murphy once told how he asked John if he thought a certain man was "happy." "Yes," said John promptly. "How do you know?" "Because," John replied, "he's unselfish."

In 1926 Lefty bought a 1784 house on the Main Street next door to Oldgate that was said to have the best woodwork of the period in Connecticut, an opinion endorsed by the Metropolitan Museum, which offered to buy two of the rooms for its recently opened American Wing. The offer was reassuring to the new owner, but was not taken. Henry James would have found Lefty's new old house "good."

XIII

THE BEGINNING OF A COLLECTION

Lefty's nominal employment was writing a second novel. *Tutors' Lane,* dedicated to the Folletts, appeared in the fall of 1922, but it did not make him famous overnight, or, indeed, famous at all. "Caviar with paprika to the sophisticated and yet meringue glacé to the lover of a good sentimental tale," the *World* summed up indigestibly. Masefield wrote, "It has atmosphere and flavour, and what is better still it *goes on growing* all the way along." Owen Wister's encomium ended "Go on! and next time fly higher. You can do it. A nose against the grindstone is indicated." Wilson Follett also urged Lefty to higher flight, adding the almost fatal advice to steep himself in Henry James. *Tutors' Lane,* he said, was a lighthearted, incidental stunt by an amateur; Lefty must settle down and become a professional.

During the next ten years he wrote three short novels and several sketches. One called *Mrs. Jones and Son* has a son (an instructor in Woodbridge College), a girl (an attractive newcomer to the community), and a mother that seem to me life-like and a story that is kept up with suspense and invention. It is too Henry Jamesy, but I find the young people likeable as well as pitiable, and the mother, who triumphs in the end, a nightmare woman. I had not realized that Lefty saw his own plight so clearly. When the novels were turned down politely—even tenderly—by Knopf and Harper's and the Katherine Mansfield sketches by the *Atlantic* he accepted the unanimous rejection philosophically, hardened himself to disappointment, and put his fictions out of his mind so completely that until I looked at them just now I had forgotten even their titles. The mother-boy business is not an appealing subject even when handled with Sidney Howard's skill in *The Silver Cord.* It leads to "the great unpardonable sin," which John Gabriel Bjorkman said "is to murder the love-life in a human soul," but only a master hand can make its tragedy intelligible or sympathetic. When Lefty forced himself to work on his stories he did not feel that what he was doing was of life-and-death concern for him or anyone else; it was the ostensible reason for his existence, not a need that he was driven to express or the means of livelihood. It would be nice to be "a famous author," yet other things were more important to him, such as the life of Farmington.

The twenties have acquired the bloom of the past, but at the time Al Capone, Loeb and Leopold, and the Scopes trial were as remote from Farmington as the Wars of the Roses; nor was anyone there bothered by the scandals of President Harding's Administration. Tammany was scandalous but not Teapot Dome. All in Farmington were ritual Republicans, even though the great man of the Roosevelt family had divided the Party in 1912 and let in Wilson. In Farmington you would not have known that the world was in social and political upheaval. John Riddle offered examples of change in Russia when he showed the menus of dinners in St. Petersburg during his Ambassadorship there and told how this archduke carried a kitten in a pocket of his greatcoat when he went to the firing squad and how that countess had her legs blown off by a bomb, but that was Russia. Lefty was more interested in entertaining, an art that he studied, each minute detail that has been slowly and carefully evolved through the generations.

A bread-and-butter letter that he wrote to Mrs. Douglas Robinson after a visit to Henderson shows how he filled his time. "Yesterday," he reported, "I spent a tense Alsopian day. First of all I went with the entire family, except Joe *père,* to an auction at Canton. En route we all agreed that we should not bid against each other. Arrived at the auction we found among the most hideous trash in the yard a few possible bits of glass. I modestly selected one little thing and had it put up. To my horror Joe started the bidding. 'But,' I protested, 'our agreement!' At that John, who was gripping a dollar bill, bid 65¢. 'Don't you understand, John, you aren't to bid against me?' At that, with feverish eyes, Stewart bid 75¢. Corinne, who I'm sorry to say was leaning up against a refrigerator dissolved in laughter, at this point bid $1.00. 'It's *my* gasoline that brought you all here,' I flung out, too hurt for more, but Joe had already gone to $1.50. On the ride back I, unworthily, drove so rapidly over the bumps that certain of the purchases failed to hold water when put to the test.

"After lunch we went over to Middletown for tennis and to leave the two eldest who took the most extravagant farewells of their mother. Beth Dodge was with us, and, rather unwillingly, had to bring back a pair of bantams. They became rather hot and bothered on the homeward journey—much to Beth's urban surprise—and she was on the verge of tears at the thought of carrying them out to Detroit. . . .

"I simply can't realize that the visit to which I had been looking forward so long is over. Now you have succeeded to the comparative calm of Mr. Paris, but his cup is being filled with the same generous measure, I know—even though the raspberries may have refused to rise from the dead a fifth time. How I love every minute at Henderson! There is no place in the world where one laughs as much or eats as much or plays as much or *confers* as much! And where can one hear such discussions—Biblical, metaphysical or amorous?"

Lefty's life was not as futile as this may sound; he was learning how to get on with people, and all the time his library was growing, the form of collecting he had settled on. In *Collector's Progress* he was to describe Wilmarth's earlier collections—houseflies, shells, stamps, insects—but he was persuaded by Wilson Follett to cut out mention of one other collection that I think of more often today. At the age of perhaps eight Wilmarth was permitted, as I have said, to collect the eggs laid by the Michaelses' hens next door. He approached the coops

> *as an evening dragon came,*
> *Assailant on the perched roosts*
> *And nests in order ranged*
> *Of tame villatic fowl.*

Raising the lids of the coops was like opening Portia's caskets, but the chances were better than one in three that a gleaming miracle lay within. Purists can object that this isn't "collecting" in the sense of forming "a set of collected specimens," since the specimens were not kept together in a set, but were handed over to the cook and eaten, yet this ephemeral exercise in the art is what comes back to me now on finding a much desired book or manuscript or picture in a place that I hoped might contain it.

What, I have often wondered, gives collecting its motive power? Seymour de Ricci, a great authority on the subject, says "vanity"; others say "aggression," "escape," "infantilism." Collectors like to think that nobler motives are involved in their own cases, such as love of learning and salvaging civilization, but when the instinct to collect is as strong as it was in Lefty it is nourished by surges from the unconscious. He loved books for what was in them and for what they could do for him, but he also loved books as books, as objects, and he wanted to own them: a library of his own would lead him, somehow, into a fuller life and even, who knew? might help him fulfill Mrs. Blood's prophecy. A library of his own became as essential to him as a house of his own.

Wilmarth was introduced to rare books by Charles who took him to John Howell's shop in San Francisco. Charles was not a book collector, but he communicated his respect for rare books to Wilmarth. Mr. Howell heightened it by showing the books in his safe. Books in a safe! Lefty was prepared for the Brick Row when it appeared at Yale and on his return there after the war he haunted it, as I have said. His trip to England in '22 was such a success that he went back the following summer to stock a small section of Valentine Mitchell's bookshop in Hartford with rare books as well as to add to his own library. He found that spending money does wonders for the ego.

Lefty was met at Plymouth in 1923 by friends with whom he motored for ten days through the west of England. When they left for France urging Lefty to go with them he was tempted to do so. As they pointed out, Birmingham and Leeds over Bank Holiday compare unfavorably with Paris as places of entertainment, but he had committed himself to exploring the bookshops of the Midlands and the North and to them he went. Awaiting him at York was the book that directed the future course of his life, Jesse's *George Selwyn and His Contemporaries,* 1843, a work he had never heard of. It seemed to be a dull book of eighteenth-century letters, but the bookseller, Mr. Godfrey, assured him that Jesse's *Selwyn* should be in every gentleman's library and pointed out that this copy has over thirty pages of notes by Lady Louisa Stuart (another new name to Lefty) who knew the correspondents well. "You should have this in your library, sir," Mr. Godfrey said putting the notes tenderly back in the first volume, and so Lefty bought it—for thirty-five shillings.

The night after his return to Farmington Mrs. Douglas Robinson and the Alsops dined with him. While waiting for them he sat before the eight or nine hundred volumes of his growing library. "Here is all English literature spread out before me," he thought with considerable exaggeration, "and the truth is I don't want to collect any of it, but if I got really interested in one man I could go far with him." Before settling down at the bridge table after dinner Mrs. Robinson asked to see some of the books bought during the summer. What Lefty showed her I cannot recall. He put in Joe's lap a Dutch atlas of 1700 and gave Corinne Jesse's *Selwyn,* pulling out Lady Louisa's notes. "I think you may find them entertaining," he said, "but I haven't read them." Presently she began laughing and exclaiming. "Why, this," she said, "is just like Aunty Bye," her aunt, Mrs. Cowles. Then she began to read:

Poor Miss Pelham had always been fond of play, at which the impatience of her disposition made her always sure to lose. As she grew old, all other passions merged in that of gaming, carried to a height equal to what it ever was in any man. She ruined herself and would have ruined her sister, if the mild and excellent Miss Mary's friends had not risen in a body, and almost forced the latter to leave the house where they lived together, and withdraw to one of her own; which the other never forgave. Poor, poor, Miss Pelham! She was a person one could not help pitying with all her faults. I have myself seen her at that villainous faro-table, putting the guinea she had perhaps borrowed on a card—with the tears running down her face—the wreck of what had been high-minded and generous.

Mr. Fox.

Lord Holland's education of him will account for many of his faults but also for some of his virtues. It was a system of the most unlimited indulgence of every passion, whim and caprice. A great dinner was given at Holland House to all the foreign ministers. The children came in at the dessert, Charles, then in petticoats, spying a large bowl of cream in the middle of the table, had a desire to get into it. Lord Holland insisted he should be gratified and in spite of Lady Holland's remonstrances had it placed on the floor for the child to jump in and splash about at his pleasure.

Lefty's guests went home without bridge. After they left he stood before his little collection. Who was this Lady Louisa Stuart? He had few books on the eighteenth century, but he did have Austin Dobson's *Vignettes.* Taking down the Second Series, he opened it at random and read: "Lady Louisa Stuart was one of those writers whose silence is a positive misfortune to the literature of the *Memoir.* Living to a great age, for she died in 1851, at ninety-four, she had accumulated a store of memories, and she had inspected life with the keenest perceptions and with unusual advantages of position" as Lord Bute's daughter. "It was she," Dobson continued, "who contributed many of the more interesting notes to the Selwyn Correspondence [the notes that had kept us from the bridge table]"; and in conclusion he added that "in some respects, Lady Louisa could give points even to that inimitable gossip Horace Walpole himself."

The following day Lefty hurried down to New Haven to report his find to Tinker, who had also become a book collector. He was impressed by Lady Louisa's notes and so was Andrew Keogh, the Yale Librarian, who arranged for Lefty to have the run of the Library's stacks; yet it took Lefty months to discover that the bookplate in his copy of *Selwyn* was Lord

Home's and that a member of the family had published some of Lady Louisa's notes. This blundering around in the eighteenth century brought Lefty again and again to Selwyn's intimate friend, Horace Walpole.

In February 1924 Lefty went to London to buy books for a shop in New York, Laurence Gomme, Inc., that he and a few others had started. It was on that trip that he met a dealer who taught him more about life than about books. When Lefty walked into his shop he found himself in a defile that led through a canyon of books to the little office where Mr. X sat waiting and taking Lefty's measure. He was in no hurry to get up until Lefty murmured that Kermit Roosevelt suggested that he should call. Then X rose, levitated, rather, with the swimming grace of heavy bodies shimmering to the surface and bestowed upon Lefty a smile compounded of respect, shrewdness, and *bonhomie*. His soft voice began the caressing incantation that was to be the young man's undoing.

"Come upstairs, sir," he said quietly as a high priest might welcome a novice committed to the ultimate mysteries. He led the way up the narrow stairs that were lighted only by a naked bulb whose lowly candlepower was reduced by grime. Books crowded round and above the staircase; books, Lefty sensed, clustered about his feet; books were certainly piled on the landings. By contrast with this murky and dangerous ascent, the upper room was a haven of light and order. Windows overlooking the street revealed that the clutter here was under control. Drawings by Leech, Edward Lear, and Thackeray were plainly visible on the walls. One section of books that was protected by glass doors implied rarities within and, indeed, contained them—first editions of nineteenth-century poets and novelists "in parts." The manuscript of Trollope's *Miss MacKenzie* was lying casually on a lower shelf to be picked up for two hundred pounds. But it was hard to look at anything, for Mr.

X's flow of reminiscence demanded respectful attention. "Excuse me, sir," he interrupted with his appraising eye upon Lefty, "but that chair you're sitting in—many's the time I've seen Mr. Swinburne sitting in it, or his friend Captain Burton. They would come here after a rather wild night out, I'm afraid. Mr. Meredith used to pop in and out, and Mr. Watts-Dunton came looking for Mr. Swinburne."

Lefty succumbed completely to X's magic and spells. He had quite a lot of money to spend, his own and the shop's, as he confided to his grandfatherly friend. Would Mr. X care to help him? Mr. X would do what he could; any friend of Mr. Kermit Roosevelt's was a friend of his. On Lefty's confiding to him that he had already spent four hundred pounds with another bookseller X was shocked. "Oh, my dear sir, that was a lot of money! You could have done far better—but I mustn't say anything." The world of books, it transpired, was not as golden as it looked; in fact, it was filled with men who must bear watching. "I hesitate to say this to you sir, I do indeed, but since you have done me the honor to consult me . . ." Lefty consulted him every day. Mr. X confided to him the translation of his code name, the letters of which booksellers use to disguise the cost of the book or the price they are asking for it: if the name is Farmington, for example, with an X substituted for the second n, AX represents 20.

Lefty's faith in his new friend was justified by X's handling of his commissions at the Milnes Gaskell sale at Hodgson's. Lefty discovered the sale the day before it while walking casually down Chancery Lane. When he came to Hodgson's he hesitated but fortunately for him he went in. After an hour of looking at the books he hurried to X's shop and told its proprietor the books he would like to buy. X was surprised and rather annoyed because he was planning to buy many of them himself for stock. In addition, there were six letters from Horace Walpole and other Walpoliana, including the copy of his *Mysterious Mother* with William Mason's proposed alterations to it, which Mason had the effrontery to think improved the play. Mr. X regarded Lefty from a great distance before speaking and then spoke with the dignity of the law. It was well that Mr. Lewis should understand certain customs of the London trade—"no doubt very old-fashioned, sir, to one from your great country, but private gentlemen like yourself, sir, should not bid in the rooms themselves. To do so is not"—if Mr. Lewis would forgive the expression—"well, not quite cricket. Gentlemen give their bids to a member of the trade to execute for them, and it is just as well to keep the matter private."

On the day of the sale Mr. X and Lefty went to Chancery Lane in separate conveyances and took no notice of each other while they were there. Lefty felt that he had become an initiate in a trade whose dubieties were hidden behind an innocent mask. Mr. X bought all Lefty's lots except one for almost exactly what he said they would fetch. The lot they lost was Mason's copy of Walpole's *Mysterious Mother*. "Too bad, sir," Mr. X conceded gaily, "but we had to let Maggs have something!" and it was twenty-seven years before Lefty secured it. Mr. X would not take the usual ten per cent commission; acquiring such treasures for Mr. Lewis was its own reward: but he did like cigars. Lefty was not to be outdone: Mr. X was entitled to an eight-pound commission on the books he had bought for him at the sale. Accordingly, Lefty was back in his shop the next morning with a box of cigars that cost eight pounds.

The climax of Lefty's friendship with X was reached when Lefty asked him about some furniture on the top floor of the shop. "Oh, that, sir, is not ordinary furniture. Those Sheraton chairs, that pair, belonged to Dr. Johnson."

"Dr. Johnson!" Lefty looked at them with veneration.

"And that easel, that was Gainsborough's. This tea caddy was Charles Lamb's, and this sofa pillow was worked by Mrs. Blake for Blake." Lefty could have the lot for two hundred pounds.

He was staggered, but tried not to lose his head. "I confess, Mr. X," he managed to say, "my head is reeling. I don't want to sound extravagant, yet everything in me is crying out: 'get this furniture.' "

Mr. X was naturally pleased, and his pleasure added to Lefty's eagerness to own the furniture. Still, Lefty knew that he must have proof of authenticity. "I haven't the slightest doubt about these things," he went on, "but you know how people are. What is their history?"

"Well," Mr. X replied roguishly, "I never saw Dr. Johnson sitting in those chairs."

"No, of course not," Lefty laughed, "but where did they come from?"

Mr. X was serious again. "They belonged to a very distinguished gentleman, Professor Jackson, a great authority. When he died, the contents of his house were sold on the premises. They would have gone for nothing if I hadn't been there. I felt I should rescue what I could," and he told Lefty again of his fondness for the treasures of the past.

Professor Jackson, the friend of Pater and authority on Lamb, as X volunteered further, carried conviction, but Lefty felt that he should get another opinion, just to be sensible. A Johnsonian lady whom he consulted thought that the chairs must be all right. He didn't know where to turn for reassurance about the easel, tea caddy, and pillow. However, why hesitate further? He streaked back to X's shop.

"I'll take everything!" he announced.

"There is just one small thing," Mr. X added lowering his voice after the congratulations were over. "I'm a little short at the moment. If it wouldn't be too much trouble—"

"You mean money? Why of course—"

"And one other thing, if you don't mind, sir. It's very old-fashioned of me, I suppose—" He paused and viewed Lefty searchingly, "But why do I say this? Excuse me, sir."

"Go ahead, please!"

"Well, sir, I must tell you, I have enemies."

"Oh, no!"

"Yes, I have, sir. Excuse me for contradicting you, sir, but I have."

"What queer people they must be!"

"Thank you, sir. Thank you very much. It's American gentlemen like you, sir, who can understand how a person feels. . . . But I mustn't trouble you with my private affairs."

"Please, Mr. X won't you—"

"I was on the point of suggesting to you, sir, a moment back when I interrupted myself, in a manner of speaking." He chuckled. "I am getting on—oh, yes, I am sir. I know it very well." At last the point was reached. Would Mr. Lewis pay him in cash rather than by check?

Lefty did so at once, two hundred pounds in notes and then he asked himself just what he had got for his thousand dollars? He went to Arundell Esdaile, the Secretary of the British Museum, to whom Tinker had given him a letter of introduction.

"Oh, my dear boy!" Esdaile said when Lefty faltered out his tale. He gave Lefty the name of a man at the Victoria and Albert Muscum who would certainly know about the chairs, and then, to make him feel better, he added: "The tea caddy *might* be all right. Jackson knew a lot about Lamb. But Jackson at the end was on the optimistic side in such matters; in fact"—Esdaile paused to let Lefty have the full force of his next remark—"he was absolutely mad!"

"Dr. Johnson? Sheraton?" The pince-nez of the furniture man at the Victoria and Albert glittered. "But Sheraton didn't make chairs before 1790." And Dr. Johnson had died in 1784.

Lefty screwed up his courage and returned to X. "About those chairs, Mr. X." The first hint of coolness appeared in the gray eyes. "I've decided not to take them, after all." He continued to regard Lefty fixedly. "I believe that they were Dr. Johnson's, absolutely, but"—Lefty didn't find it easy—"as you said, you never saw him sitting in them."

"Just as you say, sir, of course. I told you you could return anything at any time."

"It's very generous of you. I am also returning Gainsborough's easel and Mrs. Blake's pillow. But," Lefty added brightly, "I am keeping Lamb's tea caddy."

"Of course, sir, you are not expecting me to return your money?"

"Oh, no! I'll take something else."

This proved to be difficult. Either the prices of the books Lefty looked at lacked the initials of Mr. X's book code or its initials no longer applied. Everything had trebled and quadrupled. There was a marked drop in the atmosphere of the upper room. Reminiscence ceased altogether. Lefty was made to realize that he had become that bane of shopkeepers, the weak-minded customer who returns the things he has bought. It was therefore with relief that he stumbled over a large gray box and was told that it had belonged to Lewis Carroll. It contained forty-two books and forty-four photographs of little girls, a box of wooden draughtsmen, two dice boxes, four dice, a small inlaid trick box, two matchboxes, and one side of a matchbox. Lefty gratefully took it in exchange for what was left from the chairs, the easel, and the pillow. Of all the instructors in Lefty's life none drove lessons home more expensively than Mr. X.

XIV

HORACE WALPOLE ARRIVES

When, months after his return to Farmington, Lefty looked at the six Walpole letters to John Pinkerton, the Scottish historian, that he bought in the Milnes Gaskell sale one stood out:

STRAWBERRY HILL,

July 31, at night, 1789.

Dear Sir:

Having had my house full of relations till this evening, I could not answer the favour of your letter sooner; and now I am ashamed of not being able to tell you that I have finished reading your Essay on the Ancient History of Scotland. *I am so totally unversed in the story of original nations, and I own always find myself so little interested in savage manners, unassisted by individual characters, that though* you *lead me with a firmer hand than any historian through the dark tracks, the clouds close round me the moment I have passed them, and I retain no memory of the ground I have trod. I greatly admire your penetration, and read with wonder your clear discovery of the kingdom of Stratclyde—but though I bow to you as I would to the founder of an empire, I confess I do not care a straw about your subjects, with whom I am no more acquainted than with the ancient inhabitants of Otaheite. Your origin of the Piks is most able; but then I cannot remember them with any precise discrimination from any other hyperborean nation: and all the barbarous names at the end of the first volume and the gibberish in the Appendix was to me as unintelligible as if I repeated abracadabra, and made no impression on me but to raise respect of your patience, and admire a sagacity that could extract meaning and* suite *from what seemed to me the most indigestible of all materials. You rise in my estimation in proportion to the disagreeable mass of your ingredients. . . .*

and so on for another page and a half. As I reread this letter now I feel again Lefty's surprise and delight forty years ago. Walpole had been to him merely the "Prince of Letter-writers," just another waxwork in the long gallery of dead authors. The letter brought him to life.

Lefty bought Mrs. Paget Toynbee's edition of his letters and read the seventeen volumes then published straight through. Walpole, he learned, was born in 1717, the son of Sir Robert Walpole, the great Prime Minister, who for more than twenty years kept England at peace and gave it (and his family) great prosperity. Horace was sent to Eton at ten, proceeded to King's College, Cambridge, spent two years on the Grand Tour in France, Switzerland, and Italy with Thomas Gray, the poet, and returned to London where he enjoyed the life of a rich young man about town. His father had him elected to Parliament from a family borough while he was still abroad. At thirty he acquired a cottage at Twickenham, ten miles from London. This was Strawberry Hill, which he remodeled in a Gothic style of his own invention and which was so admired that its influence spread throughout the English-speaking world, yielding only after a hundred and fifty years to the more informed pastiche of the early twentieth century. As a young man he wrote political tracts, essays, and verses and made a catalogue of his father's collection of pictures, the finest in England. In 1757 he set up at Strawberry Hill the first private printing press in England; during the next thirty-two years he issued several books by himself and his friends—including Gray's *Odes*. The most important book of his own that he printed there was *Anecdotes of Painting in England,* a work that is still respected. He wrote other books that were printed in London, among which were *The Castle of Otranto,* the romance that launched the Gothic novel on its grisly career, and *Historic Doubts of the Life and Reign of Richard III,* a defense that is still discussed. These many books, which were novel, instructive, and entertaining, established him as an influential writer in his own day. During his twenty-six years in Parliament his main concern was to further not his own career but that of his cousin and closest friend, Henry Conway. From 1746 to 1791 he wrote political memoirs; for sixty years, the letters on which his fame principally rests. He died unmarried in his eightieth year.

Lefty discovered that Walpole set out early to record as accurately as he could the history and manners of his time for us, posterity. He continued to do it until he died. Lefty was warmed by his desire to improve as well as to inform and amuse and by his sponsorship of underdogs. Walpole took up the causes of Admiral John Byng sentenced to death for cowardice at Minorca, of Henry Conway unjustly deprived of his regiment, of King Theodore of Corsica in a debtor's prison; he supported the Americans in 1776 and was among the first to inveigh against the slave trade. He printed one book at the Strawberry Hill Press for the benefit of a learned and indigent tailor and another to allay the misfortunes of a clergyman whose declining body and mind prevented him from accepting a comfortable living in South Carolina. These were examples of sensitive and imaginative philanthropy. Lefty found it significant that Walpole did not become attached to his father until he fell from power and that thereafter he was his fierce apologist and the unforgiving enemy of his father's opponents. One of Sir Robert's natural daughters, Lady Mary Churchill, was Horace's favorite close relation. He stood godfather to her children and left them all generous bequests. When he discovered another of his father's illegitimate daughters, a Mrs. Daye, he took her to Strawberry Hill where she lived until she died. A friend described her as being of a "squab, short, gummy appearance" and with scarcely more agreeable qualities of mind. She could not have been an attractive addition to Walpole's dinner table. Still another resident of Strawberry Hill was an elderly gentlewoman who had been a governess in his father's household.

The people in his letters were as varied as the events they caused: politicians, bluestockings, clerical antiquaries, great ladies, murderers, royalties. Lefty discovered that beneath their wigs and fancy dress they were very human people, loving and hating, absurd, heroic, or false. It was like seeing the portraits in *Ruddigore* step down from their frames. For Lefty the transition from Gilbert and Sullivan to Horace Walpole was easy. The latter might have been someone he knew, another Tully Williamson or Monty Woolley or Tink, someone who looked at familiar things in a delightful new way. As Lefty read volume after volume the panorama of the eighteenth century unrolled before him, the sweep of great events, the rise and fall of reputations; the lilacs and nightingales at Strawberry Hill and the mob loose in the streets of London; balls, entertainments, the theater. On nearly every page was something novel, instructive, and amusing reported by an original literary artist who lived at the center of affairs. Walpole made him think of Trollope. He does not give us the life of a cathedral close or a government office, but with him we have the arts and letters as well as prime ministers and dukes. Both writers describe unforgettable characters in unforgettable scenes. We see the Duke of Newcastle standing on the Duke of Cumberland's train at George II's funeral to keep out the chill of the marble as clearly as we see Planty Pal standing behind Lady Dumbello's sofa in the drawing room at Courcy Castle. Trollope's characters have the reality of historical people; Walpole's, the vividness of fiction. In both authors one encounters kindness and nobility, folly and weakness, the accords and antipathies, in Willa Cather's phrase, that lie beneath the surface in everyday life. Both sets of characters have flesh and blood, but it is the Duke of Newcastle's papers that are in the British Museum, not Planty Pal's, and if you want to study Newcastle you will find hundreds of volumes of his correspondence there; the history of Plantagenet Palliser, Duke of Omnium, is finished. Walpole and his time had more to offer Lefty, but he wondered if he was up to it, a question that was put tacitly to him one afternoon in New Haven when he and Tink were strolling along Hillhouse Avenue talking about the eighteenth century. Tink gave his former student a sidelong look and said that it wasn't easy to know another age as well as one's own. "Have you," he seemed to be wondering, "the will and perseverance to try?" Lefty was reminded of Dr. Crother's talk at Thacher a dozen years earlier. Horace Walpole and the eighteenth century became a test of character for the young man, as well as a life line by which he could pull himself to a better and more fruitful existence.

He took on Walpole so thoroughly that he identified himself with him. Walpole loved Eton as Lewie loved Thacher; the light of early morning shone on both. Walpole formed a little club at Eton with Thomas Gray and two others. To mark themselves off from the outside world they took private names—it might have been the Mormons at Yale. The Grand

Tour with Gray and the accounts of romantic prospects, foreign manners, and amusing accidents of travel might have been Lefty's own Grand Tour in '22. Walpole and Lefty in their late twenties moved to a fashionable neighborhood filled with witty old ladies. Walpole's first book appeared the year he settled at Twickenham, just as *Tutors' Lane* appeared the year Lefty settled at Farmington. Both young men were to assert their independence; there was to be no one standing over them saying what they must do. Lefty found still other parallels in Walpole's life and his own: Walpole's parents were unhappily married and he was brought up by an over-fond mother; Walpole was devoted to his friends and the companionship of older women; both men shared a taste for pictures, collecting, reading, writing, and conversation; both had recurring attacks of mysterious illness; when Lefty moved to the country he was also a bachelor. He swept aside the conspicuous dissimilarities—that Walpole's father was the most powerful man in his country for years and was very rich, that Walpole was absorbed in politics all his life, that a childhood spent in 10 Downing Street and Orford House was quite different from one spent in 1625 Central Avenue, Alameda, California. This identification made Lefty a less discerning student of his subject. He slid over Walpole's fear of ridicule, his aggressiveness, and pride, weaknesses that are as apparent in him as are his confidence, loyalty, and humility, and it was long before Lefty would acknowledge them, although they were pointed out by Walpole himself. For thirty years and more he felt that anyone who criticized Walpole was criticizing him.

Why, he wondered at the outset, wasn't Walpole better known? What did the critics and professors say about him? Macaulay, aged thirty-three, presented him as a foppish, malicious, little dilettante who was also something of a genius, the "inimitable gossip." "No man who has written so much is so seldom tiresome," Macaulay conceded, but went on to say that Walpole "sneered at everybody," and that "the conformation of his mind was such that whatever was little seemed to him great, and whatever was great seemed to him little." Lefty, who had read many more of Walpole's letters than Macaulay had when he wrote his essay knew that both these statements were untrue. Macaulay was blind to Walpole's merits as well as unsympathetic to him as a man. He was pleased to find that Byron said that Walpole was a greater writer than any man living in Byron's day "be he who he may," and that Carlyle saw him as a light shining in darkness. Croker and Liverpool, on the other hand, enraged by Walpole's partiality to the Whigs, agreed that his *Memoirs* poisoned history at its source. Thackeray's admiration for Walpole's "jigging, smirking, Vanity Fair" seemed to Lefty as superficial as Macaulay's caricature. Two generations later Lytton Strachey admired Walpole wholeheartedly and Saintsbury dismissed Macaulay's "cock-sure dexterity." In Walpole's letters, Saintsbury said, "You have the key to society" and "one continuous, curious, not too obviously intelligible life-panorama. . . . If the old game of selecting a thirdsman for the Bible and Shakespeare in a library of three were resuscitated Horace Walpole's letters might be, by no means in mere joke, put forward as a candidate."

This was reassuring, but before Lefty committed himself to Walpole he wanted to feel sure that certain charges against him were untrue. The charge that he quarrelled with all his friends was disproved by his lifelong attachments to them; no trouble was too great for him to take with them; his endurance of casualness and lack of consideration was remarkable in a touchy man. A second charge was that he was unkind to blind old Mme du Deffand, who, twenty years his senior, had fallen in love with him when she was sixty-eight. As only her side of their immense correspondence exists, the reader has little to go on except the complaints of an *exigeante* and passionate woman distraught with boredom and insomnia. Walpole made four trips to visit her, a racking, four-day journey for one who at any time might be tortured by gout; he stood by her with fierce loyalty after many of her old friends ridiculed and dropped her; when her income was cut he offered to make up its loss out of his own pocket. The final charge, that he was responsible for Chatterton's death, was the wildest of all. After Lefty became convinced that Walpole was no more guilty of it than President Coolidge he went down to New Haven to consult Tinker.

"Isn't Horace Walpole one of the major figures of the eighteenth century?" he asked.

"Yes."

"And he is greatly undervalued?"

"Yes," said Tink.

So Walpole, the friend and champion of underdogs, was himself in need of a champion, someone with the time, energy, and will to do him justice; someone, of course, who liked and respected him. Lefty believed that he was that person. He had what in the sacred profession is recognized as "a call," a compulsion to dedicate himself to a cause. He would rehabilitate Horace Walpole, give him his rightful place in history and in the regard of posterity, but to succeed he would have to collect him on the widest possible scale.

Lefty had arrived at the fork in the road, the choice between general and specialized collecting that he made at the age of ten when, with his stamp album ranging from Abyssinia to Zululand before him, he decided to stick to the Hawaiian Island Provisional Government, 1893. Now he left the broad highway of English literature and turned off on the narrow weed-grown road that led to Horace Walpole and as often happens when the time is ripe for decision fate gave a helpful push. At just this moment, December 1924, the Beverly Chew sale took place in New York. In it was Walpole's annotated copy of Gray's *Odes,* the first book printed at the Strawberry Hill Press. With it was Garrick's "Ode to Mr. Gray," which was also printed at the Press, one, the catalogue said, of six copies. There was also Walpole's annotated set of Pope. These were items a prospective collector of Horace Walpole could not ignore. Lefty went down from Farmington to see them.

On the way to the Anderson Gallery he encountered Annie Burr Auchincloss, whom he had met at Farmington the year before. She was walking two Scotties, Ginger and Jamie, and all four went to look at the Walpoliana. Lefty asked at the office what it was thought Walpole's copy of Gray's *Odes* would bring and was told four thousand dollars. This meant that Walpole was not to be for him. His future wife and her Scotties went uptown and Lefty strolled disappointedly down Fifth Avenue. At Scribner's he paused, debated going in, and started on until arrested by the occult force that all collectors possess. It led him back and into the shop and up the stairs to the mezzanine floor where the old books were then kept. Had they any Strawberry Hill Press imprints? Yes, they had ten of the "detached pieces," including Gray's *Odes* and the rare Garrick ode, one, they said, of six copies. The price? One hundred and fifteen dollars for the lot. Lefty promised to think about it and walked back to the University Club where he was lunching with Azro. "There is no point in my buying that lot," he said, "and stopping there. If I buy it I'll go on until I have the finest collection of Walpole in the world."

This was the valor of ignorance: he had no idea of how large the output of the Strawberry Hill Press was and how rare some of its publications are; he did not know how many books, tracts, verses, essays, and catalogues Walpole wrote, or how many of his manuscripts existed or where they were; the contents of Strawberry Hill, the books in its libraries, the prints, pictures, curiosities, and objects of art that crowded its walls and rooms were equally unknown to him. This ignorance was fortunate because had Lefty known the vastness of the subject he would not have attempted it. As it was, his talk about the greatest collection of Walpole in the world made Azro look grave. "Well," he replied, "it's your money, but I hope you won't do this." So, as soon as lunch was over Lefty went back to Scribner's and bought the lot. He had reached the "critical point, at that moment when a man's real concern begins to separate itself from his pretended, and almost to become independent of himself."

The first step taken, the second was easy. This was to search the bookshops of New York for Walpoliana. When he asked, "Have you any Horace Walpole?" the bookseller would look blank. "Horace Walpole. No, I'm afraid not." The same surprise greeted Lefty in London when he got there two months after his lunch with Azro, but in London Walpoliana were everywhere, lying about unwanted, the books that Walpole wrote and printed, and unique items, which Lefty later called "Bits of the True Cross": presentation copies of the Strawberry Hill Press and books from Walpole's library. The harvest was ready and Lefty reaped and gathered it in. He bought everything that had any connection with Walpole, no matter how remote—mention of his name in a book justified its purchase—everything except his letters because Lefty assumed, wrongly, that the Toynbees' edition made collecting them unnecessary. Many of the books that he bought so cheaply have become very scarce and his wide-angled approach was to pay dividends in ways he could not foresee. Such a book was the copy of Cooke's *Hesiod,* 1728, that he bought because Walpole's mother subscribed to it. Forty years later when he collected Hogarth as well he found in it a Hogarth print of great rarity.

Mr. X's shop proved to be relatively disappointing. Lefty's reception there was cool. Lewis Carroll's box had preceded him. "Certainly, sir," X said, "I told you you could return anything at any time. You will remember that, sir. What will you have now?"

He was now, Lefty explained, a collector of Horace Walpole. Since X kept out of the eighteenth century he received this news as the ultimate annoyance. "Come back in a week," he said more in anger than in sorrow, "and I'll have something to show you." When Lefty went back he found a handful of books with only one item in it that he wanted, Walpole's copy of a book that was worth, perhaps, a pound at that time. Mr. X's price, recently written in his code, was sixty pounds. "But," Lefty protested, "I have just bought a large paper copy of the King of Poland's *Works* with Walpole's arms on the sides for four pounds ten!"

"Very well," Mr. X was not friendly at all, "thirty pounds! *That's* the kind of man I am!"

Dr. Johnson's chairs, Gainsborough's easel, and Mrs. Blake's pillow were ultimately transmuted into a few books at prices that are exorbitant even today. The breach that followed was bridged in time. Mr. Lewis, grown older, returned to X's shop and was richly rewarded by unique Walpoliana reduced to fair prices. When he said good-bye for the last time to his restored friend X held his hand a moment and said with a smile, "Oh, Mr. Lewis, if I could only get you on to another man!" but his teaching did not go that far.

The lessons taught by A. W. Evans were painless. He was a retired clergyman who wrote about books in the *Observer* under the pseudonym "Penguin." With two young partners he had recently revived the firm of Elkin Mathews. They were amateurs, bookmen turned booksellers, and they helped to revolutionize the rare-book business. Evans was a man with a mission, which was to rescue eighteenth-century authors from oblivion. Until the 1920s the Manchus of learning had looked down upon them. A. E. Newton and Tinker in America, Austin Dobson, Saintsbury, and Nichol Smith in England, were pioneers in the work of reappraising and reclaiming it; Evans was its bookseller. "Any book printed in the eighteenth century," he would say with dignity, "is a good book." He raised innumerable authors from the dead by including their forgotten works in his catalogues at prices that were then sensational—some were as high as two guineas. Lefty, whose arrival coincided with the appearance of his famous first catalogue, bought many of them. This pleased Evans because he took a good bookseller's satisfaction in getting his books "into the right hands." Fortunately for Lefty, he decided that Walpole should go to the young American who came to his shop most afternoons for tea. Evans disliked Walpole, who had called Johnson a "saucy Caliban," but in the world where Shenstone and Mason were notable Walpole was a colossus, whether you liked him or not. Since he had been for the Americans in their War of Independence, it was right for Lefty to be keen about him. "You must have," Evans said with solemn emphasis, "the finest collection of Horace Walpole that has ever been made and I mean to help you get it."

When Lefty arrived for tea he would find the table in the back room littered with the books that had been bought by "runners" for sixpence in shops remote from the West End—the works perhaps of Warburton, William Hayley, and Stephen Duck. Evans would make room among them for the tea things and then would ask earnestly, "Well, what have you found today?" Lefty had always found something and needed no urging to talk about it. Evans would listen gravely, occasionally saying in his low pleasant voice, "Good, very good!" Outside the windows of 4A Cork Street the world was concerned with

Locarno and naval agreements, but all that mattered in the back room with its smell of books and tobacco was Horace Walpole and the eighteenth century.

Older collectors formed another set of his teachers, and of these Edward Clark Streeter was first. Lefty met him when returning on the *Olympic* in 1925. Ned, who had been twenty years ahead of him in Keys, had given up the practice of medicine to collect its history. He was one of the leading medical humanists of the time, the friend of Osler, Welch, and Cushing. When Lefty met him he had embarked upon a new field, weights and measures, going back to the Egyptian and Greek. It was immediately plain to the younger man that compared to Ned Streeter he was still a beginner in the art of collecting. Ned knew all the great booksellers of Europe as well as of London, but he listened patiently to Lefty's bubbling recital of his Walpolian finds until one day he asked with a certain sternness, "But what about the Marvelous Boy?" After Lefty had convinced him that Walpole was not responsible for Chatterton's death, Ned asked him down to his stateroom to see an object that he had waited long to acquire. This was the only known Anglo-Saxon weight outside the British Museum. King Alfred might have handled it. Ned had learned some years before that it was in the possession of a clergyman in the south of England. An introduction was managed; friendship was established; yet Ned forbore, with immense self-control, to explore the possibility of the weight's passing into his own keeping. Then the rector's lady developed signs of illness. What did Dr. Streeter recommend? It was plain to him, a surgeon, that what she needed was a warmer climate. Alas, there was no money in the rectory for such a trip. When the weight was shown Lefty in the *Olympic,* the lady and her husband were in Italy. Ned and his Anglo-Saxon weight indicated extra-stellar spaces for the exercise of the collecting spirit.

The following year the two collectors went to England together. They would go their several ways during the day. In the evening Ned listened patiently to the details of Lefty's finds, even though they were only of books printed in the eighteenth century. Ned belonged to the elite of the book world as well as of the weight world. He had Caxtons and Wynkyn de Wordes, books from Grolier's library, incunabula by the yard. He took an indulgent view of Lefty's collecting; better the eighteenth century than the nineteenth or twentieth, but why not go back to the real books? When one day Lefty produced Walpole's copy of Blount's *Art of Making Devises,* 1650, he was encouraged. "Ah!" he said, "that's better!" Although it was ten years too late for the book aristocracy, which ends abruptly at 1640, it was a respectable book, only a year older, Ned pointed out, than Jean Pacquet's *Experimenta Nova Anatomica.* "I have been trying to think," he went on, "of someone for you to collect, and now I've got him, Philip Melanchthon!" To Lefty this formidable name was merely one among many dimly remembered from Freshman History at Yale and he could only stare. Ned launched into a gentle disquisition upon Melanchthon that made it clear he was a tempting morsel for a young bibliophile, not only because of his historical importance, but because he could still be collected for a song. Lefty, however, was not to be moved. He wanted to collect Horace Walpole and the eighteenth century.

Ned was disappointed, but continued to talk quietly about Willibald Pirkheimer, Ambroise Paré, and Gui Patin and the copies of their works that he had bought in Paris and Bologna and Frankfurt. He was informative on the subject of bloodletting and the use of leeches; he was quietly possessive about Canano of Ferrara, whose marvelous work on the bones and muscles of the arm and forearm he and Harvey Cushing had just reproduced at Florence in facsimile. Lefty was struck by his writing about what he collected. At the moment Ned was concerned with a paper on the French barber-surgeons and their influence in spreading the use of the vernacular in medical works. Lefty was like Desdemona hearing of

> *The Anthropophagi, and men whose heads*
> *Do grow beneath their shoulders.*

The talks took place in the Brown's Hotel smoking room, which the two friends had to themselves after dinner. They sat in semi-darkness, deep in leather chairs that crackled when they moved. The pantry door would swish open suddenly and the smoking-room waiter would hurry past with two brandies for the drawing room. The door sighed discreetly behind him as he glanced at the strange American pair who bought books and *weights* all day and talked about them half the night. What he did not know was that the younger of the two was being encouraged along the road that he was to follow the rest of his life by the latest substitute for his father, since Ned Streeter made it plain to him that a life dedicated to collecting was a good life.

XV

1924–1927

Three months after Lefty began his new collection, Tinker invited him to lecture on Walpole to the Age of Johnson. This was a conspicuous endorsement because only once before had Tink had a guest lecturer and he was a member of the English Department. Lefty accepted the invitation fearlessly. "I never go out the night before I lecture," Tink volunteered significantly, "and I go to bed early." The guest presented himself as instructed at Tink's rooms at 8:10 a.m. on the appointed morning and the pair set out for A. I. Osborn Hall, a three-minute walk, at 8:11. "It will be better if we don't talk," Tink said. Arrived at the large lecture hall he asked where would Lefty like him to sit? On the right? On the left? Which row and which seat? Lefty decided that Tink should sit in the second seat in the third row on the right. Tink was the more nervous of the two.

The lecturer took his place in the chair on the platform, a swivel chair that tipped back. The two-hundred-odd members of the class filed in and Tink gave out the subjects for their ten-minute papers. When he had collected them he stood in front of the platform and in a few carefully conned words introduced his former student, concluding with a Miltonic gesture toward him where he sat exalted, "by merit raised to this bad eminence." All went well, a youthful imitation of the master, except for one treacherous dip of the swivel chair.

Tink also asked Lefty to make a selection of Walpole's letters for the Age of Johnson and similar courses in other universities. The young man read straight through the 3,000-odd letters in Mrs. Toynbee's edition again and picked out 149 of them for his book. He explained in his Introduction that "the letters have been chosen from the whole range of Walpole's life, from his nineteenth year to his eightieth." He was guided, he said, "by various motives: the desire to show a few great moments in the century and a few of its most characteristic people through the eyes of its wittiest chronicler." He was, above all, "anxious to show the character and personality of Horace Walpole." *A Selection of the Letters of Horace Walpole* was dedicated to Tink. On Henry Canby's recommendation it was published by Harper's in a one-volume textbook and a two-volume illustrated edition. The following year, 1927, the Oxford University Press brought out the illustrated edition. It has sixty photographs that really illustrate the text and are nearly all of unique items: the frontispiece is from Walpole's own copy of his print by McArdell after Reynolds, the sixtieth plate shows the draft of his famous last letter to Lady Ossory; in between are manuscripts, drawings, books, and prints that he owned. Fifty-three of the objects had been acquired by the editor during the first year and a half of his collecting. I am pleased today if I get three pieces in a year as important as those illustrated in the *Selection.*

So far as I know, only one other college course "adopted" the book, but English and American reviewers used it as an excuse to write an essay on Walpole. Encouraged by this reception the editor cast about for another publication. Dr. Rosenbach had just bought for him at auction a pocket notebook in which Walpole recorded from 1780 to 1783 fugitive thoughts, verses, and epigrams. It would make, Lefty thought, an admirable third Number of the Strawberry Hill *Miscellaneous Antiquities,* which Walpole started in 1772 "to indulge the taste for anecdotes and historic papers, for ancient letters that record affairs of state, illustrate characters of remarkable persons, or preserve the memory of former manners and customs." He gave it up after two Numbers because only 130 copies out of the 500 he printed for the public were sold. Although Harper's did not believe that the time had come to revive *Miscellaneous Antiquities* William E. Rudge did and published the third Number in 1927. Walpole's notebook was reproduced in facsimile with Lefty's transcription and annotation of the text. The latter is not exhaustive, but it shows how Walpole used the book in his letters and works and it foreshadows the more ambitious editorial undertaking that was to come. Where Walpole wrote, "A home brewed river—water in a garden to look like a river," the editor quoted from Walpole's letter to Lady Ossory of August 31, 1782: "The Thames gives itself Rhone airs, and almost foams; it is not one of your home-brewed rivers that Mr. Brown makes with a spade and a water-pot," and from the letter written to Lord Harcourt a week later, "Your Lordship's Thames must be brimful. I never saw it such a Ganges at this time of year; it is none of your home-brewed rivers that people make with a drain, half a bridge, and a clump of evergreens, and then overlay with the model of a ship." The fleeting idea of a home-brewed river had been saved, embellished, and used. Rudge published 500 copies, but as in 1772 only 130 copies were sold. Rudge's loss was fortunately reduced by a fire that burned up the insured remainder.

Numbers Four and Five were published by the Oxford University Press, American Branch, *Lady Louisa Stuart's Notes on Jesse's George Selwyn and His Contemporaries,* 1928, and

Horace Walpole's Fugitive Verses, 1931. The former was designed and printed by D. B. Updike at the Merrymount Press; the latter was printed at Oxford. Since these also sold only about 130 copies and the remainder were not burned up, public appearances of the *Miscellaneous Antiquities* ceased again. Thereafter for the next eleven years the editor engaged Edmund Thompson of the Hawthorn Press, Windham, Conn., to bring out a Number in 50 or 100 copies that the editor gave away as Christmas presents. They were little books of "anecdotes . . . that . . . illustrate the characters of remarkable persons, or preserve the memory of former manners and customs" and were drawn with one exception (the 3d Lord Chesterfield on letter writing) from Walpole's own papers. Among them were his notes on the Duchess of Portland's Museum, his notes on Shakespeare, and "Anecdotes told me by Lady Denbigh," scraps worth preserving that kept the editor's memory green in England between his annual visits. Edmund Thompson took great pains with them; the editor, alas, did not. He postponed putting them together until the fall and collated them carefully only after they were printed. Then he would write an errata slip that at the time he thought was funny, but that I now find embarrassing. Copies of the Numbers find buyers on their infrequent appearances in the market because they are the work of skilled printers and because they are rare.

These amateur publications were encouraged by Paget Toynbee. After his wife's death Toynbee gave up his own work on Dante to continue hers on Walpole and he did it much better. Lefty sent him copies of Walpole's six letters to Pinkerton that he bought in the Milnes Gaskell sale and which showed that the printed text was inaccurate. Thereafter he gave Toynbee copies of any "new" letters that he found for his Fourth (never published) Supplement and went down to Burnham Beeches to call, carrying with him whatever outstanding books he had just bought in London, such as Bentley's original drawings for the early rooms at Strawberry Hill and Walpole's copy of his *Description* of it inlaid to magna folio and extra-illustrated with prints and watercolor drawings. "Fiveways" had no electricity, central heating, or running water, but on Lefty's afternoon visits the sulky coal in the library fireplace was lit as a gesture of hospitality. More effective in combating the chill was whisky. Walpole's editors, present and future, talked only about the complicated and entertaining man who brought them together. By way of a breather they walked up and down the narrow paths of the rose garden, single file, while Toynbee's cape danced wildly in the cutting wind and had to be disengaged from the thorns.

His later years (he was seventy when Lefty first met him) were brightened by a robin that each spring attached itself to him, literally when it perched on his thumb and pecked oatmeal out of his hand. One year the robin brought its wife who also took up Toynbee and was the subject of a letter to the *Times.* A bell was sent it from Farmington; in return came Walpole's copy of Lucan's *Pharsalia,* 1750. However, towards the end Lefty grew aware of a certain uneasiness on the part of his friend who said that the young American's books had taken the bloom off his own recent Walpolian publications. Lefty couldn't believe it and went on reporting his latest finds and plans for still other little books, especially for his more ambitious *Walpole's Fugitive Verses.* As a youth Walpole hoped to be a poet, but in his twentieth year he recognized that "my cold soil nips the buds with snow" and thereafter wrote his verses mainly for his correspondents who found them graceful and clever and handed them about until they got into print. Toynbee agreed they should be assembled, edited, and published for their own merit and for the light they throw on Walpole as a person. He told Lefty that he had transcribed many more of them from one of Walpole's unpublished volumes of juvenilia, but instead of offering the copies to the editor he nodded with a roguish glance at a cabinet in the corner of the library and said, "Wouldn't you like to have a look in *there!*" Years later when Lefty acquired the originals he learned how much had been withheld from him and realized that he had been regarded as the younger generation knock, knock, knocking at the door. Yet in the end Toynbee gave all the help he could, for he left his and his wife's correspondence about Walpole and some fifty new letters for his Fourth Supplement to the Clarendon Press and the next editor of Walpole's letters, whoever he might be. After the Yale edition of them was begun R. W. Chapman, the Secretary to the Delegates of the Clarendon Press, sent this invaluable archive to Farmington.

Chapman came into Lefty's life in 1927. The Clarendon Press is that part of Oxford's publishing on which the University imposes its most rigorous standards. Chapman, a leading Johnsonian, was immediately aware of a new eighteenth-century collector when he appeared. He wrote to Lefty in 1926 to inquire about a bibliographical problem in Walpole's *Anecdotes of Painting in England.* Lefty confessed he had no idea what the answer was, but Chapman took him out to lunch at Oxford in 1927 and they arranged to sail to New York on the *Adriatic,* a crossing that cemented their friendship. Chapman, who had taken a Double First at Oxford, was tall and donnish and loved the classics, etymology, and the eighteenth century. Among the Janeites, or Austenians as he said they should be called, he was supreme. Lefty was forgiven for not joining that sect because he was an ardent Trollopian. Like Austenians, Trollopians can and do talk by the hour about the characters and incidents in their master's novels, a form of reminiscence that is asphyxiating to outsiders.

After Chapman discovered on one of his early visits to

Farmington that his host kept all letters and so automatically became posterity—since a collection of letters if kept long enough will eventually be read by somebody—he began sending what was virtually a diary that might begin with the first cup of tea at 5:30 a.m., give the temperature, and proceed with news of his children (Primus, Secundus, Tertia, and Quartus), and of friends, meetings, journeys, dinners, visits, all reported in the fewest possible syllables. There are nearly 1300 of these laconic but lively communications (in a very difficult hand). The paper on which they were written is a study in itself. There is Chapman's own very thin paper, the elegant paper he found in guest rooms, the backs of wedding invitations and Quartus's school exercises, calls to meetings and, later, galley proof of the Yale Walpole (which he read carefully and on which he made helpful suggestions). From time to time Lefty's attention would be directed to a verso that was of special interest. Before he died he returned some 600 of Lefty's letters with the note:

"Lefty Lewis"

When I am gone I think Lefty might like to have his letters to me (which no one else could ever decipher); he has kept all of mine. [Recently his widow returned dozens more in which is an extract from a collection of lucubrations that Chapman called Omniana, *'42.* Calligraphy.] *Wilmarth ("Lefty") Lewis . . . has a hand almost as illegible as any known to me—and I have been familiar with Andrew Lang's, George Saintsbury's, A. J. Carlyle's, and my own. I said to him once—we are regular correspondents—"Lefty, we are giving each other a great deal of needless trouble. We must study legibility." He agreed, and the pact was for some months observed on both sides, tho' he did not give up allusiveness nor his practice of abbreviating most long words. At last he told me he couldn't keep it up. "I shall not try to be legible; it seems to me to be unfriendly." I thought this was acute; for* any *conscious effort cramps a man's style.*

When you reread your own old letters you feel like an eavesdropper. It is saddening to find how little you have remembered and how muddled the residue is in your memory. Forgotten occasions, hopes and fears, the entertainment and boredom of life, return. You regard the young writer with mixed feelings—embarrassment for his mistakes and foolish remarks, pleasure in his successes, regret for his failure to make the most of himself, envy of his ardor and eagerness. Old letters bring back one's correspondents, the sound of their long-dead voices and laughter, their appearance and mannerisms, and you long to see them again at their best. My correspondence with Chapman reminds me (I knew it at the time) of how much I owe him for his interest in Lefty's welfare.

That young man became almost as much at home in England as in his own country thanks to a letter in 1924 from Mrs. Cowles to Hector Munro Ferguson with whose family she was intimate thirty years earlier. Ferguson laid himself out for her young neighbor, had him made an honorary member of Brooks's, carried him about to see Van Dycks in friends' houses, and proved that Englishmen can be the most hospitable people in the world if they wish to be. When Lefty showed him Lady Louisa Stuart's notes on Charles James Fox and Holland House, Ferguson wrote Lord Ilchester about them. He, who owned Holland House and whose ancestors were Foxes, came to Lefty's hotel to read them and so began a friendship that lasted until the older man's death nearly forty years later. He opened the doors of owners of Walpole's letters, answered questions from the collection of eighteenth-century papers at Holland House, and entertained Lefty when he was in England. A scholar in search of material in England is at a disadvantage without such friends. Descendants of the eighteenth-century oligarchy have usually been at school and Oxbridge together, they belong to the same clubs, they are connected in the great web of English consanguinity and "pass you on" to friends who they think can be of help to you. Lefty's debt to Hector Ferguson—and to Mrs. Cowles—was great.

Wayland Williams's aunt, Lady Gray, asked the young man often to her lovely Regency house in Chelsea. She welcomed him on two counts: he was the same age that her son (her only child) would have been had he not been killed in the war and he came as a close friend of her family in America to which, like most expatriated American women, she preserved a deep attachment. Her first husband was a peer's son, her second was Sir Albert Gray, Counsel to the Chairman of Committees of the House of Lords. Lady Gray demonstrated the American woman's power of adaptation to her husband's country: she looked, thought, and talked like an upper-class Englishwoman; to hear her on the Empire was to hold dominion over palm and pine. She was of the same vintage and school as Mrs. Cowles—whom she remembered in London in the nineties—and so had a gift for entertaining. References to her earlier and more fashionable days came with a slight nostalgia but no ostentation. Lefty was impressed when on Lord Curzon's being made a marquess she said, "Poor man! I don't suppose he will be happy until he's a duke," and he was sorry to hear how at the Chelsea Flower Show Queen Mary had recently been rude to her, she who had been a friend of Queen Mary's mother.

Lefty stayed at Brown's Hotel where the housekeeper still wore a net collar up to her chin, a black skirt to the floor, and an expression that would have commended her to Boadicea. Holmes was in the dining room; Turner was the hall porter on the Albemarle Street side; Nice at the Dover Street entrance.

Although bookshops were Lefty's chief concern, the men's shops contributed to his euphoria. His Hanover Street tailor, the apotheosis of Mr. Olsen in Alameda, produced with a maximum of fuss and bustle suits that gave him great pleasure to wear; equally beautiful shirts and shoes were made for him in the Royal Arcade and St. James's Street. He wore a bowler hat and spats and carried gloves and a rolled umbrella. Mr. Thacher would have shaken his head, but a newsboy seeing the glass of fashion emerge from a shop shouted promptly, "New York *Herald,* sir?"

The outward man was making a confident and uncommon life for himself. The "status" as it is now called that he along with the rest of mankind wanted to have became steadily more secure, yet periodic illnesses showed that all was not well within. They came at the end of a summer of visiting and entertainment and took the form of aches and pains. The young man felt brittle and meretricious. He recalled Clarence Day's remark about men who wore masks in a vain and underbred effort to bolster their egos. He grew more aware of masks on others: the "mucker pose" to disguise a gentle and protected upbringing; preciousness to disguise a sense of inferiority; the debonair to conquer; the profound to impress. Had he assumed a mask? His writing was disappointing because he was living in aspic. A classmate's remark was repeated to him, "Too bad Lefty has money." He was dropping back in the race. In the fall he would become ill.

His illnesses excused him from the mêlée of life and forced him to concentrate upon his physical condition. He had the habit of going to doctors and now moved on to specialists. When you go to a specialist you are promoted to the higher ranks of medicine. In the waiting rooms of famous specialists the carpets are thicker, the lights are softer, the magazines are current and glossy. Your fellow patients are fellow members of a small expensive club. The examinations and tests and ensuing diets and treatments make one feel important. When this fashionable therapy failed with Lefty he would sense that his illnesses were a form of expiation and of semi-suicide.

The Hartford doctor he went to in 1926 lived in a large Victorian house. The waiting room was in a high-ceilinged parlor that still had its original furniture. Hygeia and Old Hartford were enshrined in it. The patients were not kept waiting. When the hour of their appointment arrived the doctor slid back the folding doors, bowed gravely, and asked, "Will you come in?" With his fine face and noble head he was the medical humanist rather than the family physician and Lefty thought of the learned men that Ned Streeter had introduced him to, Vesalius, Willibald Pirkheimer, Gui Patin. At the end of Lefty's one interview with him he prescribed bicarbonate of soda and Dubois's *Influence of the Mind over the Body.* Lefty read and reread it, marking and pondering many passages that illuminated the interaction of the mind, soul, and body, and that reminded him of how he had cured his wart in the backyard at Alameda. He had long suspected that his illnesses were generated in his unconscious and that the conflict with his mother and the example of her illnesses lay at the root of his own. How could he rid himself of them for ever?

The last thing conservative people in 1926 wanted to see was "that hideous sight—a naked human heart," especially their own. "Nervous prostration" was treated by a change of scene and the recommendation of pleasant thoughts, but for the more venturesome psychoanalysis was being tried. Conservatives regarded it with fear and loathing; they believed it was conducted largely by foreigners who battened on sexual perversions, insanity, suicide, who used words like "complexes," "libido," "fixation," and who charged exorbitant fees. The thesis that dreams were significant the uninitiated dismissed as nonsensical; the idea that we may be possessed of a Pandora's box filled with horrors was "morbid"; the prospect of its contents being known by another, disgusting. "Neurasthenics" was giving way in the vocabulary of contempt to "neurotics," horrid words whatever they meant, but Lefty had reached the point where he wanted to be well, come what might. Corinne Alsop encouraged him to go to Dr. Beatrice Hinkle, Jung's chief disciple in this country, whom he had met at Hill-Stead, and he did go to her in the fall of 1926 after a summer of increasing pain and self-concern.

Since he had no business or family to distract him his analysis proceeded with unusual speed. He filled notebooks relating to his early history. Physical relief came at once. In two months his unconscious presented his mother one night as a vampire returned to destroy him. He drove her away, filled with pity for her, and the dream was a turning point in his life. Nearly forty years later he was startled to read in Coleridge's "Christabel,"

> *"Off, wandering mother! Peak and pine!*
> *I have power to make thee flee."*

These lines describe his dream precisely. He read "Christabel" as a Junior at Yale, but had no recollection of reading it between then and January 4, 1927, the night of his dream. In the spring of '27 he went to California and spent a day in Alameda. The first glimpse of his family's house confirmed what he suspected: it was his mother to him. He went over it with its friendly new owners, into every room from top to bottom, a visit that made him excited and ill. The trip helped him to disengage himself from the lethal aspects of his boyhood; he began to understand what is meant by being "reborn." It may be impossible to carry out the command, "Know thyself!" but Dr. Hinkle showed him the wisdom of trying to do so. He found himself closer to people and able to talk with them about their personal problems when they wanted to do so. These increased intimacies gave him a sense of wider participation in life. On a visit to an older couple he was struck by their companionability and devotion to each other: a happy marriage was possible and it brought strength and security to both. He became less afraid of emotion and gained insight into his own motives, good and bad, and those of others. He was struck by the truth of the copybook maxims.

He took Azro to England in the summer of 1927 to buy furniture for his brother's new house in San Francisco and for his own new house at Farmington. Antique shops acquired for him temporarily the magic and spell of bookshops. Coming home without Azro on the *Adriatic* he sat at the same table with Sidney Howard (also an ex-Californian), his mother, and three other American friends. Sid was returning after the opening of *The Silver Cord* in London, the play in which he dramatized his conflict with his mother and whose New York production moved Lefty more than any play he had ever seen. Sid and he talked freely about their problem, which was embodied in the ominous presence of Mrs. Howard who one day to Sid's delight unconsciously quoted the mother in the play.

As I have said, Lefty chose the *Adriatic* on Chapman's urging. With Chapman were Humphrey Milford, head of the Oxford University Press, and G. F. J. Cumberlege, the recently appointed director of the Press' New York branch. The three, depressed by the weather and homesick (Cumberlege had just become engaged), sat unsmiling and silent in the smoking room. A second set of Englishmen, very different from the first, included George Grossmith (to whom Lord Ilchester had given Lefty a letter of introduction) and his son, P. G. Wodehouse and his daughter, and Lord Dunsford. With this group Lefty played bridge and laughed a great deal. The *Adriatic* was a slow boat, the Oxonians recovered their spirits, and by the end of the voyage Lefty had the two British sets and the American playing bridge together quite happily. Three weeks later Chapman and Milford paid their first visit to Farmington. It was Chapman's fifty-sixth birthday. His health was drunk, and then Lefty took the wind out of his sails by announcing that he was engaged to be married.

XVI

MARRIAGE

Lefty met Annie Burr Auchincloss first in the winter of '23, as I have said, when she was visiting the Sheffield Cowleses at Farmington. She was twenty, Lefty twenty-seven. She was sitting by the tea table in the den at Oldgate; Lefty's entrance, she often told him later, was very gay. On his side he was struck by her special air of quiet separateness, a mixture of composure and shyness. No one ever met her without feeling that they were meeting somebody memorable. She was not in the least stuffy or prim, but was reserved, protected from the world in which she was not yet wholly at ease, much as she longed to be. She had a beautiful low speaking voice; her laugh was infrequent, spontaneous when it came, and infectious. One day after they were engaged Lefty saw her effect on strangers as she walked across Grand Central to meet him at the gate of the train they were taking. People turned to look at her as she passed, tall, very smart, and still another Virgilian tag came into his mind. "Truly, a goddess by her walk." Theirs had not been the usual courtship because both of them were emotionally constrained, yet they liked playing tennis and golf and going to the theater together, they took books for granted—

Annie Burr had not the faintest trace of bluestockingism—and they had many friends in common. She had gone to Farmington where her success in the school plays was so outstanding it was believed that she could have succeeded on the professional stage, but such a career was not to be thought of for young ladies in 1920, nor, with few exceptions, was college. Annie Burr, no rebel, stayed at home and regretted it ever after. In 1920 when she came out there was little for a girl in her situation to do except to travel and "have a good time" until she married, an inadequate existence for one with a fine mind. After 1923 she, Lefty, Lee Dodge, and Skinny Lawrence became a quartet that dined together in New York and spent weekends at Mrs. Auchincloss's houses in Fairfield and Newport. Annie Burr's Aunt Annie Jennings showed her approval of the slowly developing match by giving her niece, goddaughter, and namesake the Toynbee *Letters of Horace Walpole* in its de luxe edition.

Annie Burr and Lefty were married in January 1928 at the Madison Avenue Presbyterian Church in New York; Azro came East to be his brother's best man. While the Lewises were engaged they asked William Adams Delano to build an extensive addition to Lefty's house in Farmington. He urged them to stay away as long as possible on their wedding trip to avoid the trying transition. They went first to Brazil and then to Italy, France, and England, a honeymoon of three months. A wedding trip provides accelerated education: the achievement of marital compromise, the carrying out of the promise to love and to cherish after missing a train or losing a bag or during the first streaming head cold, tests that prepare for those that come later when, passion cooled, the partners' weaknesses expose their marriage to an infinite variety of challenges. The Lewises shared the same tastes and interests, they had complete confidence in each other and were able to talk freely and frankly about what bothered them. Of all the teachers Lefty had in and out of classrooms none could compare with Annie Burr.

She assisted at a lesson the first time they went into the sea at Rio. Lefty must get over his fear of waves; Annie Burr would help him repair the damage done by Azro and Charles at Santa Cruz. The sea was merciful after the heat of the land; the waves were high, but once you got beyond the breakers, not too high. Lefty, reassured, demonstrated Beatrice Lillie doing the breast stroke, unaware of the approach of a wave of mammoth proportions. It lifted him up, swept him forward, and turned him upside down. He struck out wildly, seized something firm, and was spewed out upon the beach with it, blind, gasping, and choking. "It" proved to be a large black woman much flattered by his submarine attention. From then on he was no longer afraid of waves, the higher the better, and dove through them like a dolphin. As with the rockery at Alameda and that first terrifying automobile, his fear was conquered with the help of a protecting and encouraging relation.

The Lewises' sixteen days in Rio were memorable because of Edwin Morgan, the American Ambassador of twenty years' residence, to whom they were given letters of introduction. He had them up to his house at Petropolis both weekends, on the first of which he introduced them to diplomatic colleagues and on the second to the members of an American naval mission. Instead of being friendless tourists in a strange land the Lewises found themselves welcomed by a delightful community. Annie Burr had her first experience as a chaperone—it may have been the last time there ever was a chaperone—when the Lewises rode in the corso of the Carnival with a young secretary of the Italian Embassy and the daughter of the British Ambassador. They did not appear to such advantage on the following day at Petropolis when Mr. Morgan took them to the annual "intrudo," which is held in a private swimming pool. The American trio stood with their hostess on a balcony overlooking a garden filled with bananas and brilliant birds that tried to outshriek the guests who were throwing each other, clothes and all, into the pool. Annie Burr and Lefty viewed these high spirits with dismay. *Must* they jump in with their best clothes on? Lefty asked Mr. Morgan anxiously. "Do just what you feel like," a reply that suggested he was a little disappointed in them. Suddenly their hostess could stand the strain of abstention no longer; screaming louder than any of the macaws or guests she raced to the pool and leapt, all chiffon and pearls, into it. I see now that the failure of the Lewises to follow her was a count against them.

Mr. Morgan sent the Lewises off to Genoa with an introduction to a Spanish colleague and his wife who were returning home on the same ship. The friendly Spaniard formed a little group that included an Argentine polo player and the wife and daughter of the Argentine Ambassador to France. The last evening of the voyage he arranged a game of poker in a private room off the bridge. When Lefty said that he and Annie Burr hardly played the game he was met with a knowing laugh, "Ah, you Americans, you understand the poker *very* well!" a belief endorsed by the quiet smiles of the other players. A box of chips made of jade, chalcedony, and chrysoprase appeared. When a jade object as big as a football was won, it was explained, the game was over. Lefty couldn't remember whether a full house counts more than a straight or where a flush comes in, but it didn't matter; he couldn't lose. He won the football and the game was over, and he hoped that the evening would help out with the expenses of the wedding trip. "I shall now announce the stake," said the manager of the evening. "We were playing for half a milreis"—a cent. Lefty had won almost three dollars. This would doubtless have been the stake if he had lost since the Spaniard was an honest man, but the evening impressed upon him the wisdom of finding out what the stake is before the game begins.

At Genoa the Lewises were met by Annie Burr's cousin Dunie Coe and her husband, Henry, both of whom had been in their wedding party. Henry and Lefty visited bookshops wherever they went and made a great point of restaurants. Life was very entertaining, particularly when Henry let his bath water overflow in Florence and they waited for it to come down through the ceiling of the main dining room, a different order of pleasure from the later Sunday afternoon in London when the Lewises went to see the tablet that Horace Walpole put up on the west front of St. Anne's, Soho, to the memory of King Theodore of Corsica who died in Soho, a debtor. After paying their respects to the tablet they sat on a bench in the churchyard that had been converted to a recreation ground. They had it to themselves except for one or two elders sitting vacantly on the benches and two or three little girls playing a game in which they hopped discreetly over chalk lines drawn on the pavement. There was nothing like the brouhaha that went on in the park before Notre Dame on an earlier Sunday when voices were shrill, conversation animated, and where every once and so often a mama held a very small child in the general direction of a grill in the graveled walk. What were animated and numerous in the park before St. Anne's were pigeons. They strutted around the visitors' feet, pecking savagely here and there and being as free with the walks as French children. Without any reason that Annie Burr and Lefty could see they would suddenly whirr away in a body across Wardour Street up to the roof of a warehouse where they strutted and cocked their heads about until, after a few minutes, they swooped back down to the little park. In that idyllic afternoon Lefty knew the happiness the older couple showed him not long before he became engaged.

The Lewises met Father Leonard who moved into a niche all his own in their lives. He was then Vice-Principal of St. Mary's, the Vincentian college that had recently bought Strawberry Hill. When the college's architect pointed out that Strawberry would be a costly building to maintain and urged that it be pulled down, Father Leonard intervened, "We must not destroy a landmark of English taste," and so he earned an immortal name in the annals of Walpoleshire. Towards the end of the Lewises' first visit to Strawberry Hill, which took three hours he pointed out regretfully that they had not been up to the roof of the Round Tower, "But, Madame," he said, "is tired." "Not at all!" Lefty assured him, thinking only of self, and up the Round Tower the three went. It was then that Father Leonard gave Annie Burr the name "Griselda" by which he always called her thereafter. Visits to Strawberry became a fixture whenever the Lewises were in England and Father Leonard would come up to London to take them out to a dinner planned with great care. In 1939 he returned to All Hallows College, Dublin, where after the war the Lewises went regularly to see him and became members of his closest circle, Mr. John Costello and his family, the Hugh Kennedys, Mrs. Leigh Doyle and her family, and Paddy, Mr. Costello's chauffeur, who was always put at the Lewises' disposal in Dublin. They sent him friends they knew he would enjoy, Jackie Bouvier among them. She asked him to marry her and Jack Kennedy and, later, to christen Caroline, but he was not well enough to make either journey.

On the Lewises' wedding trip Lefty went to Mallett's in Bond Street and bought his wife an antique diamond necklace. Then the pair went to Westminster Abbey and wept, quite quietly, in the Cloisters.

They drove down the Farmington Main Street on their return in 1928 eager for the first glimpse of the new addition, but the glimpse revealed that the ground had not yet been broken, and another year was to pass before the addition was finished, an interval that taught the Lewises that building takes longer than is anticipated before it begins. The most striking features of the new addition were a library, the hall to it from the old house, and a squash court. For the Lewises, who were to have no children, the house and its collections became something more than a habitation.

Whatever Annie Burr did she did very well, including housekeeping. Lefty's Negro couple, Adam and Martha, retired and were replaced by Hugh and Agnes Ross. Agnes had "begun service" in the house of Annie Burr's Coats relations in Scotland; Ross had been with another Coats cousin and spent a summer with a Jennings uncle and aunt who had taken a moor. So the Lewises benefitted by the Ross's sense of family ties. They were members of a now all but extinct profession that lived by rigid rules and iron discipline in the great English houses. The Lewises' house seemed very modest to Ross after Balmoral and Drumlanrig Castle, and it is possible that he would have moved on had not one evening a great lady remarked while he was serving her, "I don't like to talk about my money, but at that time my income *was* a million dollars a year."

Bessie Ross, Ross's sister, came over to join the ménage, but was lost to it in a few years by matrimony. Her brother and sister-in-law stayed for twenty-six years before moving back to Scotland. Ross taught himself to make violins by studying the article on them in the *Encyclopaedia Britannica.* It was easier for him to make a violin than to play one, but finally "Maxwelton braes are bonnie . . ." rose mournfully from the workshop that was built for him off the kitchen. He also made model yachts and won prizes racing them in reflecting pools at Hartford, Albany, Providence, and Washington, a success owing in part to the blueprints of the America Cup Defenders that

Starling Burgess, an occasional guest at Farmington, had designed and that he gave Ross. These satisfactions were equalled by the arrival of a new book from Walpole's library ("Another bit of the all right, Sir," Ross would announce, beaming), but the greatest pleasure of all was showing the house to visitors while the Lewises were away. He would begin at the top of the long hall: "These, madam, are watercolor drawings of Mr. Walpole's house, Strawberry Hill, at Twickenham, ten miles from Hyde Park Corner, and in this one you can see the vase in which Mr. Walpole's cat was drowned, immortalized by Mr. Gray." Agnes was one of those people who by some divine endowment knows what is right and does it. (She was also a wonderful cook.) Annie Burr and Lefty used to talk about this quality of goodness in her and certain others, the Horatios, Kents, and Peggottys of the world. Devotion and loyalty are bred in them; they suffer long and are kind, are not easily provoked, do not behave unseemly.

The Lewises spent the summer of 1928 and the two following it with Annie Burr's mother at Hammersmith Farm in Newport, a big shingled 1890 house that was later to be used occasionally as a summer White House by the Kennedys. (Jackie Kennedy is Hughdie Auchincloss's stepdaughter.) Annie Burr loved the house (where she was born) and its gardens and the rocks and sea of Newport itself, but her early friends were no longer there and her husband failed to adapt himself to the life of the summer colony, which he found fundamentally the same as Professor Rankin's dancing school in Alameda. Although Mrs. Auchincloss possessed a virtue admired by the young, noninterference in their lives, she said that "one should play one's part in the community," which at Newport meant following a rigid routine: tennis in the morning, Bailey's Beach (where news photographers lurked) at noon, lunch at one thirty, golf or sailing at three, dinner at eight or eight thirty. Hard work, often rewarded, alas, with the malice and unkindness that flourish in an endowed society committed to compulsory pleasure "under," as Henry James said of Newport, "the permanent pressure of luxury and idleness." At the end of the summer the wounded and exhausted might have to go to White Sulphur or Hot Springs to recuperate, a codicil not suspected by the occupants of the sightseeing busses that crept along Bellevue Avenue and the Ocean Drive while their guides identified the big houses and their owners. These were the houses that Henry James after the long interval between his first "infatuated" and his last disenchanted visit called "white elephants . . . all house and no garden," whose "averted owners, roused from a witless dream, wonder what in the world is to be done with them." Newport, the peak and summit of all social striving, was not Paradise, after all.

As at Alameda, there were sets ranging from the very smart to the very dull, and as at Alameda the lines between them were never crossed. The Lewises' set, a small and self-sufficient one, played tennis and golf and went to the beach the same as everyone else; however, since they also played an elaborate form of twenty questions they were looked at askance as highbrows. Bodies, not minds, were exercised at Newport. Lefty tried to get on with a novel because he had to say he was doing something, but his heart was not in it. A room on the third floor of the house was reserved for him and to it he climbed every morning with the solemnity of one engaged in creative activity. He began the day writing long, sometimes farcical, letters to Chapman or Moreau Delano or Ned Streeter and these exhausted such creative energy as he had on tap. Then he would stray to the windows of his eyrie that gave a wide-angled view of the passage from the ocean two miles south to far up Narragansett Bay on the north. A field bordered the water's edge in front of the house; a mile or so across the water was Jamestown, an island. The passage between was animated with little sailboats fluttering about like white butterflies; yachts with famous names steamed past; there were trawlers after mackerel and bass; there were oil tankers and barges plying to Providence and Fall River. Looking to the north over the woods that separated the garden from the water Lefty could see ferryboats bustling to and from Jamestown. Up the Bay gray destroyers and submarine chasers browsed at their moorings until they broke away and glided past Hammersmith Farm to take their exercise in open water. After they passed, the buoys nodded back and forth and rang their melodious bells. Lefty, feeling he was the sole unbusy thing in the entire panorama, would force himself back to his yellow pad and pencils.

Sometimes he took them down to the garden. You got to it by a walk through a little wood at the end of which it burst into view. In front was a wide semi-circular lawn; to the east, a formal garden beyond which was a rose garden, picking and vegetable gardens, and greenhouses in which were peaches, nectarines, and grapes. But the most notable garden was the rock garden to the west between the central lawn and the entrance to the harbor. Annie Burr's parents (Mr. Auchincloss died when she was a child) filled it with plants from Japan, Switzerland, and Kew. A path tunneled through the rocks wound along from one end to the other. Lefty, ignorant of the botanical significance of his bosky surroundings, would sit on a stone bench by a wall fountain at the point where another path met it at right angles and opened a view of the water. In this retreat he sat undisturbed except for an occasional gardener sloping by. He knew that he should be more appreciative of the costly beauty about him, but he perversely thought how perishable it was and how much better off the world would be if the wages of the gardeners were put into a library. It is not surprising that what he wrote in his sylvan retreat was no better than what he wrote in his eyrie.

Always before when in the doldrums he had sought the wisdom and companionship of older men whom he looked up to, but with one exception the older men at Newport made him think of aging artichokes putting forth luxuriant purple flowers in their senescence. The exception was Dr. Roderick Terry, a Keys man of the class of 1870. He was big, bearded, and amiable, a retired Presbyterian minister who lived in a Victorian fortress called "Linden Towers." He was a bookman, an outstanding collector who had revivified Newport's Redwood Library, which was founded in 1747. He was eighty, Lefty thirty-three, but the difference in their ages need not have precluded a friendship. Dr. Terry was in excellent health, the two shared common tastes and sympathies, the junior put himself respectfully forward as juniors should do, but the friendship was not formed. At eighty the ardors and enthusiasms of youth are fatiguing even if one is sound in mind and limb. Dr. Terry had become more interested in Newport and Rhode Island history than in English literature and the younger man was not yet awake to its significance. They met once or twice, waved, and went their different ways.

By the end of the summer of 1928 it seemed to Lefty that what he was doing was on a par with the lifework he learned of at Bailey's Beach on his sole visit to its solarium, a section of the bathhouse roof screened off for men who wished in those days of full-dress bathing suits to tan areas of themselves denied to the sun in public. The habitués of the solarium might look like saurians sinking into the primordial ooze, but they were not resigning themselves to inevitable extinction, they were making a laudable effort to survive: the sun would improve their looks and increase their vitality. On Lefty's visit to this establishment he found an empty cot next to its high priest whose dedication to the cult had earned him the name "Mahogany." As Lefty lay down on the vacant cot he observed, "That's a very fine sunburn you have, sir."

Mahogany surveyed himself appreciatively. "I am glad you like it," he said simply.

"It takes constant attention?" Lefty asked.

"Oh, yes," Mahogany sighed. "My sunburn's becoming a good deal of a problem. Age, you know," and he looked at Lefty meaningfully.

Lefty didn't know.

"Oh, yes," Mahogany repeated. "One of the disadvantages of growing older is that each year sunburn is harder to get and harder to retain. October and May are my bad months: October is too late for Newport and too early for Palm Beach; May is too late for Palm Beach and too early for Newport. And now in May and October I lose ground I never *quite* regain."

At the end of the summer Lefty's arthritis returned. During this illness he revolted against Horace Walpole with whom he had become so identified that when he saw "Strawberry Hill" he read "Farmington" and when he saw "Horace Walpole" he read "W. S. Lewis." After the new library at Farmington was finished and the Walpole books put on its shelves he could hardly bear to enter it. He went back to Dr. Hinkle and learned that this strong reaction was salutary, a protest against being dominated by a man who had lived two centuries earlier, and that if he was to leave his own footprint on the sands of time he would have to be more than Walpole's ghost. He could not return to the eighteenth century and it was wicked as well as idiotic to want to do so. He must keep one foot planted firmly in the present.

He bought a fresh supply of notebooks and proceeded to fill them. What the confessional is to a Roman Catholic, full communication to a notebook can be, in part, to a Protestant. The act of putting down on paper a statement of what is troubling you eases the tension that has caused the illness. Anger, vanity, and all the other serpents of the mind uncoil and slither away, at least for the time being. Lefty discovered that "illness tells us what we are," and he was reminded that a sick soul produces a sick body. His convalescence was speeded by the discovery of Matthew Arnold's poems. The Palladium-soul, remote, serene, too seldom visited, and the unregarded river of our life flowing to the sea helped him and Annie Burr, too. They read

Most men eddy about
Here and there—eat and drink,
Chatter and love and hate . . .
Striving blindly, achieving
Nothing; and then they die—
Perish;—and no one asks
Who or what they have been,
More than he asks what waves,
In the moonlit solitudes mild
Of the midmost Ocean, have swell'd,
Foam'd for a moment, and gone.

But they took courage on learning that

tasks in hours of insight will'd
Can be through hours of gloom fulfill'd

and Lefty resolved to find the tasks that would save him from oblivion.

During his convalescence he could read only what Virginia Woolf calls "upstairs" books, the Bible, Shakespeare, Wordsworth, Matthew Arnold. Critics seemed to agree that *Lear* is Shakespeare's greatest play. It occurred to Lefty to read it through the eyes of one of its lesser characters, and *Lear* helped him pass the next summer at Newport, a novel escape in that envied place. He chose Goneril's husband, the Duke of Albany, who is marked for favorable notice in the first line of the play.

Albany is an amiable, easygoing young man with every advantage of birth and circumstance. Lear's foolish division of the kingdom and Albany's discovery that his beloved wife is a "gilded serpent" who has only contempt for him as a "milk-livered man," bring out the best in him; he becomes the pivot upon which the rest of the play turns and at the end he represents virtue triumphant. A thoroughly nice man neither very good nor very bad in the humdrum of everyday life, in the cataclysm his courage and decency show what an ordinary man can do when put to the test. Lefty, exploring the Redwood Library, was surprised to discover how little critical notice had apparently been taken of this significant creation. Solutions of the textual puzzles in the play that concern Albany become clear once his character is understood. Could a tyro blunder into Shakespeareshire, of all counties, and see something that Dr. Johnson, Coleridge, Hazlitt, and a thousand Germans had missed? Probably not; what mattered for Lefty was that he had learned to read the great books in our language on his own.

Mrs. Auchincloss had Annie Burr's portrait painted for Lefty by Ellen Emmet ("Bay") Rand in 1930. It is a large portrait, painted to hang over the fireplace in the new library. No one liked it, but Bay died before she could do it over. Annie Burr is sitting on a bench, looking at the viewer, her hands in her lap in the way she folded them. The accessories are pleasing—a golden chiffon dress that matches her hair, a jade necklace—but she appears cold and discontented. The colored photograph of her that Lefty took in 1958 on the last Christmas morning of her life does her greater justice. She had been back from the hospital two weeks and both she and Lefty believed that the cancer was all but conquered. Lefty had found a nineteenth-century iron figure of George Washington (AB had succeeded her Aunt Annie Jennings as Vice-Regent for Connecticut at Mount Vernon) which he had placed in the garden to surprise her when she put up the blinds in their room on Christmas morning. Later he got her to stand beside it and to set the camera for him (she was the photographer in the family.) The poodles milled about and jumped up on her. Lefty snapped the camera at once while she was amused by his protests that none of his pictures ever came out. The result is all that a professional could wish, a moment of joy and hope; but it did not last.

XVII

1929–1932

During the early years of their married life the Lewises were at rather loose ends. They lacked the discipline imposed by a growing family and a paid job. When you can come and go as you please you are in danger of "eddying at large in blind uncertainty." The Lewises were not content to live for sunburn, but were nagged by higher aspirations and Puritan consciences. Aunt Annie Jenning's unflagging engagement in good causes was before Annie Burr; Lefty recalled a drawing in the old *Life* of a boy who was offered the choice of ploughing in the hot sun or lying like a pig in the shade.

The turning point came in 1930 when he read a month-old unanswered letter to Annie Burr from Mrs. Charles Sabin, the head of the Women's Organization for National Prohibition Reform, inviting Annie Burr to help organize its Connecticut branch. Her husband urged her to accept and she did so. The WONPR's Chairman was a Farmington schoolmate, Babs Robinson of Hartford; Margie Clement of New Haven was its Secretary; Annie Burr became the Treasurer. These three showed what able, attractive, and determined young women (all three were under thirty) can do when their energy and intelligence are enlisted in a cause. Their "education" was the kind now laughed at as "Finishing School"; yet if girls' private schools of fifty years ago are judged by their results they were a success. They did not produce Quiz Kids but women who could go to the heart of complicated matters and deal with them effectively.

Treasurer Lewis's latent aptitude for the conduct of affairs came rapidly to the surface. "Clearing," "going through channels," meticulous attention to detail, were second-nature to her. She had common sense, judgment, resolution, and taste; she was wise in the formulation of policy and skillful in the routine of mangement, but she had one shortcoming, the multiplication table. Azro on a timely visit introduced her to the mysteries of accounting; the Farmington Savings Bank carried her deeper into them. Help was sought at times from an unpromising source. One night as he was dropping off to sleep the Treasurer's husband was asked in a whisper, "Left, how much is fifty per cent?" Before Repeal was voted Pauline Sabin chose Annie Burr to be the Secretary of the National Organization. The accountants who spent ten days going over the Connecticut Treasurer's books after the battle was won proved that knowledge of per cent and all that was unnecessary: her books were not one cent out.

Lefty was also engaged in anti-Prohibition activity, in the Crusaders, a group of younger men. The only good thing that can be said for Prohibition is that it made Americans who took things for granted realize that democracies do not run themselves and that determined minorities can impose iniquitous laws while the majorities sleep. The Lewises were awakened by the evils of the Eighteenth Amendment. They discovered something of how the democratic process works; they learned about sumptuary laws and the consent of the governed; they were impressed by the hypocrisy of the political leaders (Republicans in Connecticut, Democrats in Georgia) who drank one way and voted the other. They learned that recent arrivals in the citizenry disliked them because they were of early English-American stock. Among the dozen original Crusaders in Connecticut was a young Republican of Italian descent who in the course of the committee's first evening stood relaxed by bootleg gin in front of Lu Robinson (the Chairman) and Lefty and loudly informed them: "You Yankees are all through. *We* run the country," but he faded from view before Repeal was achieved. Prohibition turned the U.S.A. into a hard-drinking country, it financed crime and encouraged lawlessness, but the repeal of it showed that when the voters become convinced that a change should be made they are stronger than any professional politicians opposing them and the change is made.

Annie Burr got Miss Amy Coggswell of Norwich, Connecticut, to lay out the Lewises' garden. There is an extensive lawn and a few picturesque apple trees that produce bushels of delicious fruit, a rose garden, beds of annuals (tulips, peonies, pansies, petunias, chrysanthemums are a specialty), and a herb garden; there are hedges of yew and a giant forsythia espaliered against the squash court that is a wonder of the vegetable kingdom. The first gardener was Ernest Scott, a thin-faced Cornishman of uncertain temper who had been Mrs. Cowles's chauffeur. At his own house he grew cocker spaniels as well as flowers. When age forced him to leave the Lewises his place was taken in a happy hour by Bill Day and every year since the garden has become more beautiful. In the winter Bill produces carnations, azaleas, primulas, fuchsias, in the two small greenhouses. Lefty's connection with the garden has been limited to de-budding the roses and to adding figures of America (a Seminole princess with arrow, quiver, and pet alligator), Columbia, and George Washington. Ashamed of not doing more, he one day after he passed sixty got down creakily on his knees and tried a little weeding, a feat that he reported to his wife with some pride. She was touched but alarmed and asked where he had weeded. As she feared, he had pulled up the rare rock plants recently given them. Thereafter he stuck to de-budding the roses and to sitting on the garden benches enjoying his surroundings in the way an eighteenth-century man regarded gardens, as a form of painting. The lawn with the elms and tall hemlocks on one side suggest to him the Constable of Salisbury in our National Gallery, the borders, a Manet a friend owns; above may be a Constable sky.

Annie Burr, who had been brought up with dogs, tactfully and firmly introduced Jason, one of Scott's blue roan cocker spaniels into the household. Lefty was taught as a boy to dislike dogs, a misfortune, but he must get over it. Thanks to AB, Jason did not jump up on guests, eat their fur coats, ruin the carpets, or dig in the garden—at least not often. Lefty became increasingly impressed by his dignity and decency and charming dogmanity. Jason swallowed a tack one day, was sent to the vet, and died that night in a fire that burned down the hospital, and Lefty felt Wilmarth's loss when his rabbits disappeared in Alameda. Jason and his successors have taught their master that each dog has his or her own mannerisms and ways of doing things, that they may be winning, offended, forgiving, and that if they have been abused as puppies they will be ruined for life. Lefty became increasingly tolerant of their misdemeanors, even when Tulipe seized an eighteenth-century letter and, dancing about evading the frantic owner, taught her puppies how to tear a manuscript to pieces. His share in the dogs' lives has been limited to talking to them, scratching their ears, and taking them down the garden, but these attentions have won him a place in their regard. Jason, Samson, Tory (blue roans); Fred (a dachshund); Tulipe, Pom, Fidèle, Mimi, Tray, and Honey (standard poodles), while passing from puppyhood to death have more than earned their keep.

Lefty wrote the play with Winchell Smith that I referred to earlier, *The Tadpole.* It was about a simple—too simple—youth who worked for a dear old Uncle Henry in a greenhouse. Sweetness and light, humor and wistfulness, were the ingredients of a Winchell Smith comedy. Uncle Henry was a sort of wizard who invented new plants. He could even turn the simple youth, so he told him, into the rich young man who lived in the big house on the hill and who was engaged to a beautiful girl. Uncle Henry said he would arrange the transformation, safe in the belief that when the moment of transition came the tadpole would prefer to remain his simple self. Bill had wanted to write this play all his life, but couldn't get beyond the first act. When Lefty suggested that the second act might be set in the big house with eccentric and expensive characters, Bill asked Lefty to try it with him. It was like being asked by Henry Ford to make automobiles.

Because of Bill's ill health the team could work only two hours in the mornings, but Lefty learned more about writing then than at any other time in his life. Bill showed him that he should plan his work and avoid irrelevant embellishment. Never did the master make the tyro feel like a tyro; he was the gentlest and most encouraging of collaborators. When the play was ready he assembled the company, which was easy because everyone wanted to work for him. Harry Ellerbe played the boy; Jane Wyatt (in her first professional part), the girl; Harry Davenport, Uncle Henry; Porter Hall (later "The Thin Man") and Jean Adair (later in *Arsenic and Old Lace*) were also of the company. Lefty found out how a play comes to life as the actors grow into it. He was impressed by their immersion in its welfare, not just for the sake of their jobs, but as professional artists. Since there was no star everyone was as good as everyone else and most were eager to do his or her best for Bill, who directed the play himself. Then on the ninth day of rehearsals he had another coronary. John Golden, Bill's partner in earlier plays, had been watching the rehearsal, in which Lefty had taken part, when Bill was stricken. In the latter's bedroom it was decided that Lefty should become the director. He was startled, but the older men were firm. The troupers in the company and Jane Wyatt were patient and helpful; temperament flared in others. When one woman had hysterics, a second followed suit. Entrances and exits and crossings had to be changed, new lines written, new business invented—routine difficulties, but disconcerting to the tyro. Meanwhile, Annie Burr, who was acting as Mistress of the Wardrobe, was having her troubles: the hysterical ladies wouldn't wear the expensive dresses that had been made for them. This was the theater.

After a dismal week in Jackson Heights, *The Tadpole* moved to Hartford where it opened in a benefit for the Connecticut Children's Aid Society. The old Parsons Theater was packed; the audience was in its best clothes. A youthful fantasy of Lefty's had him sitting at the opening night of one of his comedies listening to intoxicating laughter and being dragged on to the stage after the final curtain, bowing and beaming to tumultuous applause. The night *The Tadpole* opened in Hartford he sat at the back of the theater, his head in his hands, and when it was over there was no cry of "Author!" "Never mind," said Bill, "we can fix it." In the following spring, in 1932, the collaborators began again. Bill generously conceded that the tadpole should be a little less simple. The rewriting was going well, although on an even more curtailed schedule, and then Bill had still another coronary and the three expensive sets were sold for $100. *The Tadpole* began and ended Lefty's connection with the professional theater, but he went on thinking up scenes for plays that would never be written.

In 1931 he was still pottering with a novel; he edited Walpole's *Fugitive Verses* and revived *Miscellaneous Antiquities;* he edited 114 unpublished letters to George Selwyn that he owned. These last were from the same people who appear in Jesse's *Selwyn*—to which Lefty had been introduced by Lady Louisa Stuart—and he felt at home with them. He learned that even a scrap may be rewarding, such as an announcement from the Duke of Queensberry dated "Dec. 9, 11 a.m. 1755. The Duke of Queensberry late last night received a letter from his son [Lord Charles Douglas] wrote by himself. *Safe and well* on Board a ship the letter dated the 5 of November: this paper is sent and to be left at Arthur's, that any of his friends may partake the intelligence and comfirt who may happen frequent that house." Lefty's notes on this read: "The consequences of a similar message are told by Walpole: 'We want the French to put a little vivacity into us. The Duke of Newcastle has expected them every hour: he was terribly alarmed t'other night; on his table he found a mysterious card with only these words, *Charles is very well, and is expected in England every day.* It was plainly some secret friend that advertised him of the Pretender's approaching arrival. He called up all the servants, ransacked the whole house to know who had been in his dressing-room—at last it came out to be an answer from the Duchess of Queensberry to the Duchess of Newcastle about Lord Charles Douglas.' " Lefty quoted one of Mrs. Toynbee's rare notes on the passage: "The meaning of the Duchess's message probably was that Lord Charles was returning from Lisbon, where he escaped death in the earthquake of 1755." Editor Lewis added that "The earthquake occurred November 1, 1755, and was followed by a tidal wave and fire which entirely demolished the city, with a loss of thirty to forty thousand lives." He had learned that the first person to turn to for help in the eighteenth century is Horace Walpole. Did Chapman think that it was desirable to publish these letters to Selwyn? Chapman thought it was desirable, but that no publisher on earth would do it and the project was dropped.

Lefty started a biography of Walpole that he proposed to

call *Horace Walpole, Historian,* a title that he explained to Chapman "cuts through at the start all the previous patterns set for him . . . and puts the chief emphasis where it belongs," but he was unable to stick to his plan. "Why," he asked himself, "should I try to say all this when Walpole had said it so much better?" The life became a scrapbook, scissors and paste, and was wisely abandoned. A more modest undertaking that appeared in the third number of *The Colophon* was "A Library Dedicated to the Life and Works of Horace Walpole." It is full of bounce, but the young collector's division of his books into twelve sections was helpful twenty years later when his library was put in order by professionals from Yale.

Instead of going to Newport in 1931 the Lewises rented Lillah McCarthy's house outside Oxford on Boar's Hill. The weather was wet and cold and they both had the flu twice, but the summer added to their circle of intimate friends S. C. (later Sir Sydney) Roberts, Leonard Whibley, and Wyndham Ketton-Cremer. Lefty met them when Chapman took him to the Johnson Club dinner at Cambridge, July 4, a date chosen to honor the three American guests, Colonel Ralph H. Isham, Professor Ronald S. Crane, and W. S. Lewis. The latter stayed with S.C., who was then Secretary of the Cambridge University Press and who as "Prior" of the Club presided at its dinner, which was held in the "Parlour" of his college, Pembroke. The dinner was memorable for the essay, "The Unknown Johnson," which was beautifully written and read by A. S. F. Gow. When Gow sat down there was dead silence for what seemed an eternity of embarrassment to W. S. Lewis. How different, he thought, from a similar occasion at home where half the table would have something to say as soon as possible. He realized that as a guest he must not speak and stared at the tablecloth with everyone else. S.C. whispered, "Chapman?" Chapman answered loudly, "Not ready yet," and went on staring at the tablecloth. At length someone rose at the farther end of the room. There was a ghostly tapping on the table by way of encouragement. The intrepid speaker said in a tense voice that the paper was a very interesting one and sat down. Ghostly tapping of applause. Isham passed a note to S.C., on whose left he was sitting, and was introduced as not only a welcome transatlantic guest on the anniversary of America's Independence but as the new owner of the Boswell papers recently discovered in Ireland. Isham sprang to his feet and talked for an hour. Whibley, the Senior Fellow of Pembroke, a tiny little man with large eyes and a solemn expression, asked Chapman and Lefty to his rooms after dinner and Lefty's friendship with him began.

Annie Burr was driven from Boar's Hill the next day and met these new friends who were to add so much to the Lewises' summers in England. Visits to the Whibleys at Frensham took place over August Bank Holiday, and since the Lewises always brought "anti-cyclone" weather with them, bridge was played under the oak in the garden. Whibley, who was editing Thomas Gray's letters, was close to Walpole; Gray and his friends were never long absent from his talk. He was always present when Whibley and Lefty took the dogs for walks in the Surrey fields and as they climbed over stiles and stumbled across uneven ground the younger man was reminded of Professor Clay and the Hyksos at Yale. On one of these visits Whibley gave Lefty a recently published short history of Pembroke from which the latter learned that Roger Williams had been a member of the College. This fresh tie with Pembroke so impressed Whibley that he suggested that Lefty give the college a piece of plate; if this were done they would make him a member of Parlour, that is, he would have "dining rights" there. Lefty gave a reproduction of a seventeenth-century caudle cup in Keys, the first of its kind, apparently, in America. When in the following year, 1936, he was introduced to Parlour at a dinner, the Master, Sir Montagu Butler, pointed out that he was the descendant of the only Pembroke man ever to appear on a postage stamp, an honor that had just been accorded Williams in Rhode Island's tercentenary year. When Lefty went down to Frensham in 1942 to see Whibley's widow she returned to him the many letters that he had written the little man and pressed upon him as many of her husband's books as he would take, memorials of an endearing friendship.

Thanks to Whibley and S. C. Roberts, the Lewises became very much at home in Cambridge where they stayed at Pembroke with the Butlers and, after S.C. succeeded as Master, with the Robertses. S.C. would punt them along the Backs, the most beautiful man-made half-mile in the world. From Queens' to Magdalene every foot of the way opens new enchantments, a shifting of perspectives in which one picture slowly succeeds the last: the glory of King's Chapel revealed after fifteenth-century Queens', the lawns and gardens on either side, the bridges, the bend in the river at Trinity, and the passage through the crowding walls of John's. On their return up the river they would stop opposite Trinity where Marjorie Roberts was waiting on the bank for them with tea. S.C.'s library was formed with skill and imagination; it was filled with out-of-the-way books in fine condition that add to the great eighteenth-century mosaic. At the end of his life he formed an intimacy with Max Beerbohm; it was he who arranged the Lewises' visit to Rapallo in 1954. When he died recently Lefty lost a friend of thirty-five years in whose company he always delighted and from whom he always parted with regret.

At the Johnson meeting in Cambridge Wyndham Ketton-Cremer told Lefty that his neighbors in Norfolk, the Walpoles of Wolterton who were descendants of Old Horace, had some things Lefty should see, chief among them being the manuscript catalogue of Walpole's library. Wyndham arranged for the Lewises to lunch at Wolterton and so began another Walpolian association. The Lewises became annual visitors to his beautiful and beloved seventeenth-century house, Felbrigg Hall, from which they would set out on excursions to the great neighboring Walpole houses. At the end of their first visit as they were walking in the park Wyndham asked Lefty if he was planning to write a life of Walpole.

"Not for twenty years at least."

"In that case would you mind if I write one? It would be forgotten by then."

"You don't have to get my permission to do it. The Republic of Letters is a free country."

"Oh, but I do!"

The "permission" was given on condition that Wyndham would go to Farmington for three months to use what was there and to talk about the questions that would arise. He went and his *Horace Walpole,* which he dedicated to Annie Burr and Lefty, was the happy result. He has made several later visits to Farmington during one of which he spent a month working on his life of Gray. He has been tireless in seeking out and giving rariora to the Lewis Walpole library and in making additions and corrections that only he could make to Lefty's later work. In such ways the friends have exchanged cheer and counsel over the garden wall.

Another newcomer of the summer of 1931 who affected the course of Lefty's life was Karl Young. His call to Yale marked a turning point in the history of the University's English Department. Before he arrived its senior members were usually graduates of Yale College to whom Yale was "This precious stone set in the silver sea," a state of mind that Karl thought was insular and he said so: Yale was "covered with moss and ivy." He was interested in English studies everywhere and delighted in the meetings, committees, and journals of learned societies. Whereas Tinker spoke of "The Department," meaning the English Department and ignoring the rest, Karl thought of the University as a whole. "We don't have to worry about biology," he pointed out to Lefty one day, "so long as Harrison is here." He was in Oxford during the summer of 1931 seeing his great work on the origins of the drama through the press. His evenings were lonely without his family and the Lewises had him often at Boar's Hill where he played Liszt until the grand piano seemed about to explode. When he discovered that Lefty was never separated from his annotated copy of the Strawberry Hill sale catalogue he was favorably impressed.

The Lewises returned to Newport for the summer of 1932. During it they made the decision that directed the rest of their lives. *The Tadpole* had been buried and would remain in its grave, despite John Golden's exhortations to exhume it. The Walpole library at Farmington had grown to impressive proportions. With Paget Toynbee's death that spring Lefty was free to do the new edition of Walpole's letters that had been in the back of his mind and it began to loom as an enterprise that would give shape and purpose to his life, something for which he was prepared by eight years of collecting and study. In his thirty-seventh year the Lewises must decide which road they should take, the one leading to "Theater" or the other to "Horace Walpole"; they could not take both. Although Lefty's experience with the professional stage was limited to one failure, Bill Smith and John Golden had said, "You ought to be in the theater," and Annie Burr preferred it to Walpole. "The theater is more exciting," Lefty said, "but very uncertain and Walpole is sure." I see now where they paused in their walk and stood for a moment when Lefty summed up their situation.

"Well," Annie Burr decided a little reluctantly, "it had better be Walpole," and they left at once for London.

XVIII

THE YALE WALPOLE I

When the Lewises got there Lefty hurried round to Messrs. Maggs Bros. in Conduit Street as he always did, not to receive a warm reception—the atmosphere was controlled in conformity to the immemorial deference of English shops—but to touch base. On his separation from X he asked Maggs to bid for him "in the rooms" because they were the strongest firm buying in the eighteenth century and he wished to eliminate their competition. Their ten per cent commission was hardly worth bothering with on his purchases, but it is a show of strength to be active at auctions. Instead of trying to conceal the identity of his agent, as X had warned him to do, Lefty told his friends in the trade that he had given his bids to Maggs. In this way he avoided the subterfuges that dealers see through sooner than later and established a reputation for aboveboard dealing. For thirty years the other booksellers did not bid against Maggs on unique Walpoliana unless one of their customers instructed them to do so, which was rare. The result was that Walpole prices stayed virtually stationary while the prices of other authors soared.

There was usually something put aside for Mr. Lewis at 34 Conduit Street to await his arrival. He would buy it promptly;

his enthusiasm would be received courteously by Mr. Ernest Maggs, who wore a reddish Van Dyck beard and spectacles and stood respectfully during a caller's visit. On its conclusion he marched in step, silently, martially, with the visitor down the red carpet to the front door of the shop and bowed him out. The camaraderie that was springing up between collectors and booksellers elsewhere did not flower in Messrs. Maggs Bros. They were in the bookselling business because their father had been in it and to make money. Lefty refused to be chilled, but he was disappointed in 1932 when for once nothing had been put aside for him. "No, nothing for you this time," Mr. Ernest repeated. There was a pause and Lefty could hear him wondering, "When will he go?" The young man was in no hurry. "I think," he said with a sudden inspiration, "I ought to have a letter of Walpole's every year of his life."

"Oh, *well*—!" Mr. Ernest briskly ordered up the Walpole letters for Mr. Lewis. Forty of them appeared. They had been offered in many catalogues, but had gone unsold although they were of high quality. Mr. Ernest suggested a price for the lot that was less than the firm paid for them at Sotheby's eleven years earlier. He also kindly gave Mr. Lewis the catalogue his late brother Charles used at the sale. Mr. Lewis hurried about London and bought all the other Walpole letters he found including thirty-six that X had recently acquired. On getting back to New York he got twenty more from Gabriel Wells, a total of 103 letters in a month at an average cost of about fifteen dollars apiece, a fraction of what they would bring today.

In the collection were twenty letters to Lady Ailesbury that had undergone the methods of Walpole's earliest editor, Mary Berry. She deleted in ink proper names, sentences, and paragraphs because she thought the letters were better without them. These letters had been seen by Toynbee and Lefty took it for granted that he restored the deleted passages in one of his supplementary volumes to his wife's edition, but months later, feeling rather impertinent to be checking up on the great scholar and a friend, Lefty found that he had not restored Miss Berry's deletions. This discovery was a pleasant surprise: great scholars are fallible, after all. And if Toynbee could be careless, think of the transcriptions made by the bluestockings, prudes, and owners who copied their letters for the editor of the moment. Toynbee also expurgated the "new" letters that he discovered. The passages he omitted were stories and phrases that he said to Lefty one day with a look of horror were "unprintable." When the young man observed cautiously that the omitted passages in Mrs. Toynbee's edition were witty and would no longer be considered "improper," his host replied sternly that "a lady could not restore what had been deleted by male editors" even if they were nineteenth-century male editors.

Restoration of the complete and corrected text was the third reason Lefty discovered for a new edition of Walpole's Correspondence. The two reasons he already knew were that comparatively few letters to Walpole had been printed (apart from Mme du Deffand's) and that his letters were virtually unannotated.

The letters to Walpole, many of which are notable in their own right, solve puzzles in his letters that cannot be solved in any other way. Without them it is like listening to one side of a telephone conversation. Walpole's major correspondents were people he chose because he could write to them with ease and affection on the subjects that interested him most—politics, the great world, the new books and painters, and antiquarianism. He always had one major correspondence going on each of these subjects: when Gray, to whom he sent his letters on literary matters, died he took up Mason; when Montagu, an Eton contemporary, stopped answering his letters, which were chiefly about the life of fashionable London, he sent them to Lady Ossory who, divorced from the Duke of Grafton for adultery with Lord Ossory and buried in the country, was hungry for news of the world she had lost. He shared his passion for antiquities with Cole, another Eton and Cambridge contemporary, who lived in the Fens amassing genealogical and heraldic notes in 114 folio volumes. For forty-five years he kept Horace Mann, the British Minister at Florence, in close touch with political events at home and foreign affairs as seen from London.

Walpole's letters can be read as entertainment and enjoyed as works of art even if one knows little about the people and events that appear in them. They may also be treated as a major source for study of the eighteenth century. They were written to inform and divert his correspondents, but Walpole also had a wider audience in mind, posterity, ourselves. "Nothing," he wrote "gives so just an idea of an age as genuine letters; nay, history waits for its last seal from them." He began writing such letters in his eighteenth year and continued until he died in his eightieth. His qualifications to be the historian of his age were many: his father was Prime Minister for twenty-odd years; he was the relation, friend, or acquaintance of most of the leading figures of his day; he was unexcelled as a reporter of big and little events; he had a remarkably wide range of interests; and he wrote superbly. To make the labor of his future editors easier he got back hundreds of his letters and annotated them. The result is what he set out to write, a full, accurate, and entertaining history of his time. In 1932 it had not been edited with anything remotely approaching the care that it deserves nor was this lack felt by the generality of scholars.

The letters began appearing in 1798, the year after Walpole's death, in the five-volume edition of his *Works,* which Miss Berry saw through the press in accordance with his wishes.

They went on appearing, some in single correspondences, three in "complete" editions, but the specialist in 1932 still had to elucidate the text himself although as early as 1848 John Wilson Croker pointed out that "what the reader most indispensably needs [when reading Walpole's letters], and what registers and magazines cannot supply, is the explanation of small events, slight allusions, obscure anecdotes, traits of individual characters, the gossip of the circle, and all the little items and accidents of domestic, social, and political life, which constitute in a most peculiar degree the staple of Walpole's correspondence—the most frequent occasions and chief objects of either his wit or his sagacity, and without some knowledge of which his best letters would be little more than a collection of riddles." The case for the new edition could not have been put better, but Walpole's editors must also have the "registers and magazines," Parliamentary reports and journals, catalogues, reference books and bibliographies, the memoirs, letters, travels, literature, and prints of the period, as well as access to contemporary manuscripts that throw additional light on the events and persons that Walpole wrote about. He himself said that the sources he had not seen would substantiate his own work, and they have. The scrap from the Duke of Queensberry quoted in the last chapter is a case in point.

The first time I remember Lefty speaking of a new edition was in 1929 when Chapman and Milford were staying at Farmington. This was before anyone suspected that the text of the extant editions was faulty. At that time the Toynbee edition was believed to be all that was needed or ever would be needed. Lefty pointed out its two obvious deficiencies to Milford and Chapman, its one-sidedness and its lack of annotation. "You should get out a new edition," he said half seriously. Milford was dismayed, "Good Lord!" "You could have it out by 1950," Lefty went on, a date as improbable then as the edition itself.

Lefty did not say so, but he believed that if he did not do it no one else would. As the years passed he saw that a new edition of Walpole's letters would be justifiable only if it were done on an encyclopedic scale, by which he meant identifying all the people and books mentioned in it, explaining in so far as he could the allusions and references with which the letters abound and enriching the annotation with material pertinent to it. Eighteenth-century letters had not been edited in that way, but Walpole's should be and Lefty did not doubt that he could do it. He was a little apprehensive of his lack of engrossing interest in politics and suspected that there were unpublished political letters and journals of other men in private hands that would throw light on Walpole's letters, but he trusted that such correlative material would, somehow, appear when needed. He thought of Walpole's letters as a gigantic jigsaw puzzle of his time and saw himself putting it together to fulfill Walpole's grand design. This was the work that he, Wilmarth Lewis, had been born to carry out. "The Edition," as he and Annie Burr began calling it, would be the justification of his life.

In the fall of 1932 he told his friends at Yale that he would do the Edition at the Lewises' expense if Yale would sponsor it. Yale's backing was essential to make the undertaking respectable academically, to recruit the staff the editor would need, and to open to it the resources of the Yale Library, which is particularly strong in the English eighteenth century. The undertaking was unprecedented, Lefty was technically outside the profession, but he was no stranger to the senior and junior members of the English and History departments, many of whom came to Farmington and knew what was there.

In December of that year Fred Pottle arranged for the aspiring editor to read a fifteen-minute paper, "Proposals for a New Edition of Horace Walpole's Correspondence," at a meeting of the Modern Language Association. Lefty pointed out the three defects of the previous editions: a faulty text, the absence of letters to Walpole, and the lack of annotation. Apropos to the need for elucidation he wrote, "An eighteenth-century specialist may open any edition of Walpole's letters and be stuck half a dozen times on the first page he reads." After writing this pronouncement he wondered if it was true. He opened the Toynbee edition at random and read Walpole's letter to Cole of 7 April 1773. It sustained his case: the text was faulty (the misprinting of a proper name in it makes one paragraph nonsense) and the copies of Cole's unpublished letters to Walpole in the British Museum (of which Lefty had photostats) explain references and allusions that could not be understood without them. To make the letter fully comprehensible it needed Cole's letter that preceded and followed it and sixteen notes, which were fourteen more than were provided by earlier editors. The letter also showed the value of a special collection: Walpole's marginalia in a sale catalogue at Farmington give the prices he paid for the pictures mentioned in the letter. The future editor worked on his paper as if his life depended on it, but its reception was not auspicious; the audience had the amused air of listening to a fairy tale, and when one of the men asked at question time, "Will you read us some of the suppressed passages?" a titter ran around the room.

Lefty's *Lady Louisa Stuart's Notes on the Selwyn Correspondence,* his work on the unpublished letters to Selwyn, and *Walpole's Fugitive Verses* had introduced him to the problems of editing. To prepare himself further for the new edition he spent the next six months making an index to the first of Walpole's unpublished Paris Journals, kindly lent him by Percival Merritt of Boston. This would have been a formidable task for a professional indexer because of the references to scores of persons often difficult to identify in the sketchy (by English standards) French peerages. It was no small matter for

Lefty to straighten out twenty-eight Montmorencys, thirty-three Bourbons, and thirty-five Choiseuls. Laura Hadley Moseley was later to show him what a good index is and Warren Hunting Smith to improve what he had done, but the hours spent regularly day in, day out, for six months were a voluntary submission to discipline that did him good. It is seldom clear in biographies where the turning point in the subject's life was reached. You see him poor, deserving, unknown, and then—presto!—he has arrived. (At this point the readers' attitude towards him may alter: they liked him more easily when they felt superior to him; from now on he must not appear pleased with himself.) The slow laborious steps that carried him forward are so numerous, dull, and apparently insignificant that the subject himself has forgotten most of them or got them wrong. If he is ashamed of or embarrassed by them he may have deliberately or unconsciously suppressed or altered them. The index was a forward step in Lefty's life that led him to the Yale Walpole. Another step in the same direction was "The Genesis of Strawberry Hill," a monograph that was proposed by W. M. Ivins at the Metropolitan Museum and was printed in its *Studies* in 1934. It showed the Gothic sources of each room in the house and was illustrated by the architect's drawings (in the writer's possession) and the prints that inspired them. This study and the index supplied some of the training that Lefty lacked. He realized that he needed to complete a task that was hard for him to do and daily application to an unglamorous job. He must, he told himself, lose himself to find himself. This dedicated and puritanical spirit made the chore a pleasure.

In the spring when the Lewises had the heads of the Yale Library staff for dinner at Farmington they included Karl Young as the guest of honor. After dinner Mr. Keogh asked Lefty to talk about his library. Karl listened intently in a corner. Shortly afterwards Yale approved the new edition enthusiastically and the new editor was given academic standing as a Research Associate. He took no salary for himself, but one was provided for his assistant, Dayle Wallace, by the University out of its grant from the General Education Fund of the Rockefeller Foundation. The Yale Edition of Horace Walpole's Correspondence had been launched, largely owing, Tinker later confided and Pottle has confirmed, to the strong and persistent endorsement of it by Karl Young.

XIX

THE YALE WALPOLE II

Work began July 5, 1933, in room 331-b of the Sterling Library. As I recall it, there was one desk for the sole assistant, Dayle Wallace who had just taken his Ph.D. under Tink. Today, thirty-four years later, there are desks and tables for six, filing cabinets, a safe, and some 1,500 books on the shelves. The room next door is shared with our neighbors, the Yale Edition of the Private Papers of James Boswell.

Lewis was faced with technical questions: Should the letters be published by correspondences or chronologically? Should the text be "normalized" or should the misspellings and erratic punctuation of the writers be reproduced? Professor Nichol Smith of Oxford settled the question whether to publish chronologically or by correspondences: "You *can't* publish chronologically," he said. I remember where we stood in the High at Oxford and how the buses and lorries thundered by to Carfax as he said it. He had in mind the new letters that would be turning up out of chronological order and the difficulty of steeping oneself in the affairs of the individual correspondents if one went skipping about from one to another. The question of normalizing was much more deeply felt. Whibley and other literary scholars were strong for a *verb. et lit.* transcription; the historians, Wallace Notestein and L. B. Namier, opposed it with matching vigor. They said it was pedantic to treat an eighteenth-century text as if the language were still being formed. Chapman pointed out that to reproduce the misspellings and erratic punctuation and to puzzle over whether Walpole and his friends intended a capital letter or not would be costly as well as unsightly. As to "flavor," that was bogus, since it would be investing Walpole and his correspondents with a quaintness they did not have. Literal transcription of an eighteenth-century text Lewis came to see was Tea Shoppe Scholarship and he sided with Notestein and Namier. When the first volumes appeared there were cries of pain from literary scholars, but these noises have long since died away.

There was also the question of "style." Lewis spent weeks discussing it with Carl Rollins: the nature and inwardness of ibidem and idem (or ibid., *ibid.,* ib., and *ib.*) and the firefly of the scholarly swamps, cf. "Functional" Lefty said to Carl Rollins at one of their lunches, that was what the style of the Edition should be. He wasn't quite sure what he meant by the word, but he believed that skilled management of these minutiae would raise the status of editing eighteenth-century texts. How low that was Tink showed by a story. One day when the professors of "The Department" were discussing a graduate student Karl Young said that he was "only fit to edit eighteenth-century letters," a remark that Tink, the editor of Boswell's letters, found wounding. Eighteenth-century studies, like the collecting of eighteenth-century authors, was lower middle-class. Lefty hoped that the Yale Walpole could climb higher by perfecting the mechanics of style as well as by full elucidation and enrichment of the text.

The new editor began with Walpole's letters to and from

Cole because it is the most complete correspondence. It also, as Lefty pointed out to Chapman, helps to get Walpole in better focus by showing his preoccupation with antiquarianism. "In the course of my reading your book [*Anecdotes of Painting in England*]," Cole began, "I met with two or three errata or false printings, which I hope you will excuse my pointing out. . . . With these I have put down two or three trifling observations of another sort." His observations required sixty-eight notes. Scores of books were needed to write them. Most of the books had not been off the Yale shelves in years, but when they were needed there they were.

Now, three and a half decades and tens of thousands of footnotes later, the problems of editing are as absorbing to W. S. Lewis as they were in the beginning. Each correspondence he was to learn has its peculiar difficulty, but certain general principles have emerged of which the most important is: Do what is best for the reader. From this follows the negative rule, Do not annotate the annotation. "Thoroughness," he learned, is a lethal delusion. If an editor yields to it he expands his footnotes into appendices, into monographs, into books, until he sinks into the morass of his own references, cursed by his exhausted readers. Lewis realized early that one of the most difficult problems is what to explain and what to leave alone. This question is heightened by the Edition's readers being on both sides of the Atlantic. Those who live in England think redundant a note stating that Twickenham is ten miles from Hyde Park Corner, yet readers in the Dakotas may welcome this intelligence; members of the Church of England and the Protestant Episcopal Church of America may be irritated by a note that identifies a quotation from the Book of Common Prayer, yet it could save a Texas Baptist hours of search. The editors give the locus of a quotation from *Titus Andronicus,* but should they give it for "To be or not to be"? It isn't yet necessary to say who Minerva was or St. Paul, but what about Ariadne and Barnabas?

The editors have tried to give information tactfully if a thumping flat footnote would destroy Walpole's wit. When he wrote to Lady Ossory to announce the death of "Capability" Brown, the landscape gardener, "Your Dryads must go into black gloves, Madam, their father-in-law, Lady Nature's second husband is dead," the editors did not intrude with inexorable elucidation, but contrived to let the reader know that Brown designed the Ossory's new garden in Bedfordshire; and when Walpole reported, "I roll about Paris in a chariot decorated with cupids and look like the grandfather of Adonis," they did not help out with a note on Adonis and the explanation that the grandfather is a joke. They have been comforted by Dr. Johnson's wistful conclusion after editing Shakespeare that "It is impossible for an expositor not to write too little for some and too much for others. He can only judge what is necessary by his own experience: and how longsoever he may deliberate, will at last explain too many lines which the learned will think impossible to be mistaken, and omit many for which the ignorant will want his help. These are censures merely relative, and must be quietly endured." W. S. Lewis has also learned that an editor must be on his guard against ostentatious pedantry, that he must resist the temptation to invent ingenious devices in presenting his notes and indexes, that he must on no account be clever. Sir Henry Maine's "Lucidity, simplicity, system" describes the essence of good editing.

Lewis discovered the satisfaction of going beyond routine obligation and proving or disproving his author's statements by contemporary evidence. Such evidence is found in printed sources—government reports, trials, prints, newspapers, magazines—and in unpublished letters, diaries, and the marginalia of the books owned by his correspondents. But contemporary sources of apparently unimpeachable authority can be misleading. Two copies of the *Description of Strawberry Hill* at Farmington, one Cole's, the other Walpole's, illustrate this point. Cole, a formidable witness, wrote in his copy that Walpole paid Conyers Middleton only £20 for his collection of classical antiquities. Left at that Walpole appears as a rich young man who was ungenerous to an impecunious old scholar to whom he owed much, but Walpole wrote in a copy of the book that he paid Middleton £125 for it. That settled the matter until the receipt for the transaction signed by both parties reached Farmington. It proves that Walpole gave Middleton not £20, not £125, but 125 guineas (£131 5*s.*). To produce such evidence when he can is part of the editor's job. It is easier than to reach his ultimate goal.

This ultimate (and unattainable) goal is for the editor to become so intimate with his author and his friends that he shares their thoughts and hopes and fears. Editors of Walpole must place themselves in his chair as he sat in the library at Strawberry Hill writing to such dissimilar people as Cole and Lady Ossory. We have the advantage of knowing every object in the room including the 4000 books and where each stood on the shelves. Some forty per cent of them are at Farmington. To open one and come upon a note or mark in the margin written in Walpole's free or elegant or gouty hand is to enter into his mind. They help his editors reach the intimacy sought by Henry James's young man in *The Sense of the Past* who "wanted the very tick of the old stopped clocks. He wanted the hour of the day at which this and that had happened, and the temperature and the weather and the sound, and yet more the stillness, from the street. . . . He wanted the unimaginable accidents, the little notes of truth for which the common lens of history, however the scowling muse might bury her nose, was not sufficiently fine. He wanted evidence of a sort for which there had never been documents enough, or for which documents mainly, however multiplied, would never *be* enough." Walpole's books, manuscripts, drawings, and prints at Farmington—many of which supplied details of his life that he had forgotten—helped Lefty to approach this intimacy, but he could not reach the ultimate goal because one cannot enter completely into the life of an earlier age: each generation differs from its predecessors and we are on fairly sure ground only with our own. It is possible to learn a great deal about a former age, as Samuel McChord Crothers suggested in the Thacher School parlor, but one cannot hope to be completely at home in it or to divest one's mind of all that its people did not know. We may think we can picture a world without anesthetics, a world in which duels were still fought, where paupers' graves lay open for weeks and highwaymen were hanged in chains in the public way, yet if we were magically conveyed back to the eighteenth century we should be confused and appalled by innumerable circumstances. Nevertheless, some things do not change and human nature is one of them. Love and hate, fear and courage, the offending eye and the itching palm, these are bonds between the ages. The more the editor learns about himself the better he will know his author and be able to explore what William James called "the crepuscular depths of personality" where "the sources of all our outer deeds and decisions take their rise."

"Psychologizing" has many pitfalls for the layman and is still annoying to many. The study of handwriting is regarded as more risible than annoying, a view shared by Lefty until he learned how much it can contribute. Lewis Namier introduced him to this subject in 1938. "Do you use psychographologists?" he asked one day at lunch and Lefty would not have been more surprised if he had asked, "Do you use astrologers?" Namier sent to Brown's a young adept in the science who had just escaped from Vienna. He studied a letter of Walpole's (of whom he had never heard) and gave a good description of his interests and character. Lefty failed to pursue this resource for nearly twenty years. Then on Namier's urging, he consulted Dr. J. H. Mannheim, a Harley Street psychiatrist who uses the study of handwriting as a shortcut to his patients' problems and to whom Namier turned for constant help in his own work. Dr. Mannheim's extended reports on Walpole and his family and friends seemed miraculous to Lewis because he saw in a few hours what it had taken Lefty years to discover by himself. Nor were Dr. Mannheim's revelations merely confirmatory; they illuminated Walpole's relations with his father, made clearer why he was preoccupied with the past, and accounted for apparent inconsistencies in his conduct. What had seemed fantastic appeared rational when Lewis realized that no two handwritings are the same, just as no two fingerprints are the same, and that during the past century a vast amount of clinical information on the subject has been collected. The use of this new science has become routine in many of the biggest European industrial firms. When scholars overcome their fear and ignorance of psychoanalysis and graphology they are able to know their authors better than their authors knew themselves.

In addition to studying the problems of editing Lefty was pursuing his first and continuing obligation to find the original manuscripts of all the letters to and from Walpole in existence, no matter how slight they might be, and to secure permission to publish them when they could not be bought. He had learned that his predecessors had tampered with the text and that until he saw the letters that went through the post he could not be sure of what Walpole wrote. In the Toynbee edition there are nearly 3500 letters from Walpole and about 1000 to him, counting Mrs. Toynbee's edition of Mme du Deffand's letters. Of these 4500 letters the whereabouts of roughly 2500 were known to the new editor in 1933. He must try to find the missing 2000 and the hundreds, perhaps thousands, of letters not yet published. How was he to go about it?

The letters would be, he knew, in three places: in the book trade, public libraries, and private hands, to name their owners in order of their accessibility. He also knew that booksellers owned the fewest and that private persons might have letters buried in their closets and cupboards.

Editors who are collectors start with an advantage. Collectors are members of a small fraternity that has its chapters round the world. By 1933 Lewis was a member of this sodality and had acquired three merits that are esteemed by booksellers: he paid his bills promptly, did not haggle over prices, and did not return what he had bought (after his experience with Mr. X). Furthermore, as a specialist he knew more about his subject than the booksellers and was respected by them accordingly. He called on them regularly to buy and chat, he read their catalogues and ordered from them, and he stimulated their interest in Horace Walpole. He had not forgotten the instruction given him by Mr. X on the one hand and by Evans on the other. He did not want to be an easy mark, but he knew how much a friendly bookseller could help him and he tried to behave as he would want a customer to behave were he a bookseller. By 1933 the editor of the Yale Walpole could count on the cooperation of the trade.

Librarians it turned out are more difficult of access. They are primarily concerned with keeping books and manuscripts, not disposing of them; they are permanent, not temporary, custodians, and they must protect what has been placed in their charge: Miss Argus of the Alameda Free Public Library *vs.* Wilmarth Lewis, but by 1933 the latter had learned that librarians are more than jailers and truant officers on the prowl for delinquents and he had become impressed by their faith in and loyalty to their underpaid profession. In 1933 he knew of some 1500 letters to and from Walpole in public libraries and believed that there must be many more in other public libraries. On Mr. Keogh's suggestion he wrote to all libraries that might have Walpoliana to solicit their help with the new edition. The result did not fulfill the editor's modest expectations: the 800 letters brought only eight replies, and only one, the National Library of Victoria at Melbourne, reported an unrecorded letter. Yet he was lucky to hear of it, I now realize, because librarians have an understandable distaste for persons who ask them and their overworked staffs to do what they believe the inquirers should do themselves. Later Lewis found and friends found for him letters to and from Walpole in several of the libraries to which he had written.

He was taught the difference between American and French library practice at the Archives des Affaires Étrangères in Paris when he went to see the copies of fourteen letters from Walpole to Mme du Deffand that had been made by the French postal authorities in the 1770's. The Archives was open only in the morning from ten to twelve. M. Abel Doysié (a friend of Aunt Annie Jennings) kindly acted as Lefty's guide. He threaded the mazes of the catalogue, found the letters in it, and handed the slips for them to the beautiful young librarian in charge of the empty room. It would take twenty-four hours to find the letters. The following day when MM. Doysié and Lévis returned she greeted them with peals of musical laughter: the old soldier whose duty it was to fetch the letters requested by visitors had brought the *wrong* letters! It was ridiculous, but the gentleman would have to come back on the following morning and hope for better luck.

The Lewises were leaving for England in the morning and could not change their plans. What was to be done? Did M. Doysié think that the old soldier's skill might be sharpened by a present? M. Doysié thought that the suggestion was inspired. How large should the present be, one hundred francs? M. Doysié was horrified. Ten francs (thirty cents at the time) would be princely, and he would undertake to deliver it himself. The beautiful young librarian entered into the conspiracy. She dropped her piercing voice to a whisper: the old soldier was dozing in a *fauteuil* just inside those swinging doors. What a delightful surprise! It was delivered. The old soldier sprang into action, the letters were produced in no time and arrangements for photostatting them were rapidly concluded. When the visitors left the young librarian and the old soldier waved them on their way. *"Au 'voir!" "Au 'voir!"* was called back and forth. The Archives des Affaires Étrangères sparkled and danced with international good will.

Private owners can be divided into those who have collected their letters themselves and those who have inherited them. Collectors of letters are well known in the book world; they may write voluntarily to the editor to offer him their letters for his use; several of them (including some strangers) have sent their Walpole letters to his editor as a present. Owners who have inherited their letters are usually willing to let an editor reproduce them if he appears to be a responsible person even at considerable trouble to themselves; they are more apt to do so if he is introduced by a common friend. Here Lefty's ever-spreading acquaintance in England was invaluable to him. No owner who has collected his letters has denied their use to the Yale Walpole and only one who inherited them has done so, a man who had a letter from Walpole of one page. He wrote through his agent:

Sir

In reply to your letter dated 30th July addressed to Lord ——.

I am instructed to say that the bookseller —— informing you of details of the —— Park Library is gross impertinence and a breach of his professional trust.

His Lordship refuses you your application.

A relation of Lord —— confirmed the suspicion that all was not well with her cousin's liver, but Lefty, after he got through endangering his own health by composing unsent replies, wondered if his letter, of which he kept no copy, may not have taken the owner's compliance for granted. If so his snub was deserved. He had by then learned the steps in the minuet of British correspondence and there was no excuse for him not to perform them gracefully. Offsetting this failure (which was retrieved thirty years later in the sale room), are the many other owners who have generously allowed him to reproduce more than a thousand letters in their possession. They live all over the world. Letters to and from Walpole have turned up in Copenhagen, Geneva, Cape Town, Lima, Honolulu; Dunedin, New Zealand; Armidale, New South Wales; and one day a stranger in Colombo, Ceylon, wrote that he owned 200 letters to Walpole from his cousin and closest friend, Henry Seymour Conway and his wife. There may be still others in Singapore and Butte, Montana, but it is more likely that they are in Shropshire or Fife. It would be remarkable if among the readers of this page there are none who do not own or have in their custody a letter to or from Horace Walpole.

At the outset Lewis sent the ritual appeal to the London *Times Literary Supplement* that announces the writer's design and asks for help. Although its editor gave his letter the place of honor at the head of the correspondence columns no one replied. Another gambit that failed was will-searching in Somerset House. Articles in magazines, lectures, and broadcasts brought to light a dozen letters; advertising in the Agony Column of the London *Times,* about 500; auction sale catalogues, over 1000. Friends and strangers in the trade, libraries, museums, and universities reported letters. Thanks to friends among the appraisers of English country-house libraries for probate there was a time when news of a Walpolian discovery reached Farmington almost as soon as it reached the heirs. After thirty-five years of search letters still turn up, "new" letters that have been mentioned in sale catalogues or printed in out-of-the-way publications, or come out of hiding for the first time. We don't know how many letters to and from Walpole survive, but if no big cache is found the total printed in the Edition will be between 7000 and 8000. The originals of about 3000 of them are at Farmington; photostats of 3000 in other hands have been secured; about 1000 letters printed by earlier editors have disappeared.

The Cole correspondence was published in 1937 on the 220th anniversary of Walpole's birth. In the afternoon the editor delivered a Bergen Lecture on him at Yale; in the evening he gave a dinner to the members of his Advisory Committee. Chapman and Milford were present and the new President of Yale, Charles Seymour. In the course of the dinner Tink rose as Public Orator and presented the editor for the honorary M.A. degree, *privatim*.

The formation of the Advisory Committee of English and American scholars was prompted by the editor's need to have something more official than Brown's Hotel letter paper or his own when writing to strangers on Walpolian business. Backwoods Britons in 1933 might not have heard of Yale, but they had heard of Oxford and Cambridge, the British Museum, the National Portrait Gallery, and the Royal Library, and would accept the Yale Walpole on the strength of its British supporters. Besides Chapman, Whibley, and Wyndham Ketton-Cremer, the English members were Robin Flower, Deputy Keeper of Manuscripts at the British Museum; H. M. Hake, Director of the National Portrait Gallery; Owen Morshead, the

King's Librarian; Professor L. B. Namier, and Lord Waldegrave. At Yale the earliest members were Albert Feuillerat, E. S. Furniss, Keogh, Notestein, Pottle, Tinker, and Karl Young. Carl Rollins produced a letterhead that left comparatively little room for the letter. Among the successors to the original group who have been particularly helpful are C. K. Adams, Hake's successor at the Portrait Gallery; David Erskine; A. N. L. Munby, Librarian of King's; and Romney Sedgwick in England, and at home Leonard Bacon, Allen T. Hazen, Bernhard Knollenberg, H. W. Liebert, and J. M. Osborn. Many have read our proofs, all have saved us from error and enlarged our knowledge. Owen Morshead's assistance on one occasion was spectacular. He volunteered to find Walpole's letters to Miss Anne Pitt, which had not been seen since they were first printed. Were they still at Dropmore? He went there to find out. All cabinets and cupboards flew open before the King's Librarian, the searchers got hot and dusty, but the letters did not appear. The last cupboard was reached. It was locked. "I am afraid," said Owen, "that we must break the lock. Lewis says the letters are here and so they must be." The lock was broken and, fortunately, there were the letters. Lewis Namier, a veteran explorer of muniment rooms and family papers, found many letters that Lefty would have missed and reported them promptly. The Committee has been a bridge between the two countries over which the small and amiable company has passed and repassed, dining whenever occasion offered in London and New Haven with full attendance by the natives each time. Societies such as these may take themselves too seriously, the subject of their gatherings tends to become canonized, but the shade of Horace Walpole has not been embarrassed, I think, by the Advisory Committee's enlistment in his posthumous career.

Chapman's review of the Cole correspondence in the London *Times Literary Supplement* was given the place of honor (which was then on the front page). He wrote that the Edition "may well eclipse the Variorum Shakespeare as the greatest achievement of editorial scholarship in the United States." This welcome appraisal was seconded by Virginia Woolf and other reviewers. Later the Edition was criticized with justice here and there for carrying its annotation too far, a mistake made less often in recent years. We have also been taken to task for not enlarging upon the significance of great events such as the American Revolution, but had we done so the number of volumes would have been nearer five hundred than the projected fifty and the appearance of the final index would have been postponed indefinitely. It is not the business of the editors to write all the books that may be written from their work.

Without my colleagues, senior and junior, there would be no Yale Walpole. Tinker once said of them that "they lead dedicated lives." Full acknowledgment to them would require a long chapter, but in addition to Dayle Wallace I must speak of Warren Hunting Smith, another of Tinker's students, who joined the Edition in 1934 on a nominal salary and George L. Lam, who came in 1937. Warren is the Associate Editor and presides over room 331-b in the Sterling Library. He has edited the six volumes of the correspondence with Mme du Deffand and, partnered with George Lam, the ten volumes with Mann. With knowledge, taste, and judgment he achieves the nice balance between annotating too little and too much. For thirty years he has chaperoned the Edition through the press, quietly vigilant, mindful of the infinite number of small details of editing, the mishandling of any one of which is a blemish. A coordinator does not always inspire affection; that Warren does so is another proof of his exceptional quality. When in the future some curious traveler to Walpoleshire explores the history of the Yale Edition as the histories of its predecessors have been explored he will see how great a part was played in it by Warren Smith.

George Lam arrived in this country from his native Hungary after rigorous early training in a *gymnasium.* Here he went to Bowdoin and took his Ph. D. at Cornell. In addition to editing the correspondence with Gray and co-editing that with Mann he discovered in the Public Record Office in London and the Uffizi in Florence hundreds of the collateral political letters that Lefty worried about at the outset. He has also directed the undergraduate assistants, who are supplied by bursary appointments from the University and who have produced several hundred thousand slips of reference to our indexes, etc. George has been in charge of the Edition's bulldozing operations that have deferred its completion for years but have extended immensely its exploration in depth. His knowledge of languages, ancient and modern, was impressed upon W.S.L. one day when he was given three of George's letters to sign. The first, in Italian, was to the Director Emeritus of the State Archives in Florence; the second, in German, to the Librarian of the University of Munich; the third, in Latin, to a cardinal at the Vatican. In this last George confessed that we had pursued the problem on which we were soliciting the cardinal's help "diligenter sed frustra," a phrase that became the motto of the Edition.

I must also speak of Laura Hadley Moseley and Allen T. Hazen. Laura Moseley made our first indexes that set the pattern for those that followed. Since the Yale Walpole is and will be read chiefly from its index it should indicate what each entry is about. Accordingly, subjects have been included and analyzed as well as persons, places, and books. In the Montagu correspondence, for example, under "Medicine" there are fifty-nine cross-references from ague to wine. When all the separate indexes to each correspondence are brought together in at least six volumes they will supply the key to the entire work. Allen Hazen has produced two volumes that are ancillary to the Edition. A *Bibliography of the Strawberry Hill Press* and a bibliography of Walpole's work that was not printed at it. In 1949 he began his catalogue of Walpole's library, which will be, like the two former, a bibliographical landmark. It will show virtually every book in Walpole's library, where it stood on the shelves, the history of each piece in so far as it has been recovered, its owners and appearances in sale rooms and booksellers' catalogues, and the use that Walpole made of his library in his works and letters.

We are now, counting part-time assistants, never less than a dozen. It has been a happy and contented society, in part because the seniors have been left pretty much alone after their period of learning what was wanted in the Edition, in part because the funds, which were chiefly provided by Annie Burr, have solved the financial problems usually forced upon such undertakings; but most of all because we have believed that the work is worth giving our lives to it and because each of us has made his or her special contribution, which no one else could have made so well. The Edition has taken longer than was anticipated at the start when 1950 was set as the year of its completion, nor was thirty volumes a good guess. Thirty-one have been published and a dozen more are well along, but the appearance of the final volume, volume 50 (?), has had to be advanced from 1950 to November 14, 1975, the senior editor's eightieth birthday. We may just make it. There will be a dinner and on the following morning we shall proceed with volume 51 (?), the volume of additions and corrections.

The Edition's readers are chiefly professionals working in the eighteenth century. That there are others was proved by the Librarian of the House of Commons who told Lewis that when the House is sitting the Edition is consulted daily. We have now upwards of 500 subscribers, which are for the most part public institutions. All the States in the Union have at least one set except Alaska, Hawaii, Montana, and South Dakota, but if the

Yale Press has its way these gaps will be filled. Although there are no subscribers behind the Iron Curtain or in the Far East, we have them in Ghana, Nigeria, Israel, and Peru and it is pleasant to think of readers at Achimota, Adelaide, and All Souls consulting our work. Except for dedicated Walpolians (not a large number), few have read or will read through all the volumes, but we are not being fatuous, I hope, in picturing scholars turning to our indexes as long as libraries survive and being led to information that will help them place history's last seal upon their labors. The way for these readers, I like to recall, was prepared by one of the charter subscribers to the Edition, Waldemar Westergaard, who introduced Wilmarth to the study of history at the Alameda High School in 1909, who came twice to Farmington to visit the Lewises, and who on his death left his set to his alma mater, the University of North Dakota.

The Edition has shown that Walpole is not only a brilliant writer, but an historian who must be taken with utmost seriousness. His reputation as a person has also been raised even though familiar letters expose one to easy criticism: indiscreet remarks, bursts of spleen or silliness, instead of floating away in conversation may become the subject of a monograph three hundred years later in Achimota. Walpole has suffered from his openness, as he feared that he would; readers may pounce upon a remark that he dashed off in a fit of ill-nature or frivolity and confer upon it the weight of an opinion by Lord Mansfield; but whether one likes or dislikes Horace Walpole one can honor his wish to transmit to future ages a true history of his time and applaud his success in carrying it out. The Yale Walpole has tried to cooperate with him. He could correct and amend it in a thousand places, but he couldn't help but be pleased that "giant posterity" has studied his work with close and prolonged scrutiny and pronounced it excellent.

XX

METHOD

The Edition led Lefty's education into regions that he would not otherwise have explored. He had, for example, to get his materials—books and manuscripts—in order. His first attempt to do so was in 1924. Corinne Alsop was faced with the problem of her son Joe, aged fourteen, who was home from school with nothing to do and much too fat. Couldn't he work in Lefty's library? At that time it had only about a thousand books, but any library can do with a catalogue and it was settled that Joe should bicycle each morning the six miles (up and down hill) from Avon and combine reduction in weight with instruction in librarianship. Since Lefty knew little about it his contribution to the summer program ran second to Joe's bicycle. The future journalist, already an ardent Walpolian, was more interested in reading the books put before him than in transcribing their title pages on little cards. It cannot be said that he earned his fifty—or was it twenty-five?—cents an hour, but a year later while lunching with his mother and grandmother, Mrs. Douglas Robinson, at Lefty's he proved that his horizon had been widened. The bigamous Duchess of Kingston was mentioned. "The Virgin Chudleigh," Joe murmured quoting Walpole. He then gave the details of one of the most complicated trials of the eighteenth century, an account of which he had "catalogued" the previous summer.

With the launching of the Yale Walpole in 1933 Annie Burr and Lefty went to Paris to consult Seymour de Ricci, who was the last word on tracking down manuscripts and rarities of all kinds. He was a tall man, a rather alarming man, an amalgam of learning and races, French, English, Italian, Jewish, just the man to summon Walpole's correspondence from the vasty deep. He lived on the ground floor of an apartment house in the rue Boissière; only a *rez-de-chaussée* could support the weight of his 30,000 auction-sale catalogues. Mme de Ricci appeared during Lefty's first session with her husband. The walls of the room were lined with catalogues. Catalogues were also on the tables, chairs, sofas, and floor. "Books!" Mme de Ricci cried, glaring around with loathing. "Would you like to see where I hang my dresses?" Lefty followed into her bedroom. She threw open the closet door. Within, leaving no space for a single dress, were rows and rows of catalogues. "Books everywhere!" she shouted and left abruptly.

De Ricci looked calmly at the floor. "You have some questions for me?" he asked when the door slammed behind his wife.

Lefty hoped that he knew where Mme du Deffand's letters to Walpole were. De Ricci answered at once. "They were sold in the Strawberry Hill Sale, April 1842, sixth day, lot 107, to a Eurasian named Dyce Sombre of Meaford Hall, Stone, Staffordshire. They were resold in the Parker-Jervis Sale at Sotheby's, March 12, 1920, lot 387, to a bookseller for Paget Toynbee for twenty pounds. He gave them to the Bodleian where they now are." De Ricci gazed at his visitor, as impressed as Lefty was by this display of knowledge and memory. He could not answer the next question, "Where are Cole's letters to Walpole?" but when Lefty told him that they had been bought at the Strawberry Hill sale by Henry Colburn he went on smoothly. Colburn and Richard Bentley were partners in the great nineteenth-century publishing firm that specialized in eighteenth-century memoirs and letters. Bentley's grandson, the present Richard Bentley, was living at The Mere, Upton, Slough, and de Ricci suggested that Lefty write him. During the summer Dayle Wallace in the Yale Library found that the letters had been given to the Victoria and Albert Museum by Colburn, but Lefty's letter to the current Richard Bentley at Slough produced eventually over 1100 letters to and from Walpole and a cache of Walpole's manuscripts. The value of what de Ricci called "my methods," the systematic pursuit of "provenance," was demonstrated.

In 1933 he convinced Lefty that a search should be made for Walpole's correspondence in the London and New York auction catalogues and produced an assistant who began it. He also made it clear that the results of this search should be filed and catalogued methodically. De Ricci's collection of catalogues was the finest in private hands, his knowledge was vast, his powers of deduction and induction were unexcelled, yet these advantages would have been all but wasted without an effective catalogue. Lefty thought with shame of how he dropped his letters and manuscripts into a box or book and had no record of what or where they were or when or from whom he had acquired them or how much they had cost. He would be getting many more manuscripts and photostats of originals; they must be catalogued, housed, and immediately accessible. The need to put his library in order was brought home to him after his return to Farmington when on opening his copy of Spence's *Polymetis* a letter fell out of it on to the floor, a letter from Spence to an unmentioned correspondent. It was mostly about Richard I and might have been to any antiquary, but that it was not was shown by Spence's closing words: "May the press at

Strawberry Hill ever flourish and abound." Walpoliana may be anywhere.

By 1934 the new library at Farmington was about filled and more books were arriving regularly. Annie Burr, alarmed by a fire that nearly destroyed a 1740 house on the village street that she had rescued and restored, added a sizable fireproof room, the "North Library" off the long hall for the unique Walpoliana. Here was a chance to have a "functional" library in the modern spirit at the other pole from Billy Delano's Georgian room. Dick Kimball was willing to design it, but had to be told how many drawers and card trays would be needed and Lefty did not know. Although de Ricci had demonstrated the excellence of "my methods," Lefty thought he should find out what the standard American practice was for handling manuscripts. He assumed that Mr. Keogh could tell him, but in this he was mistaken. The Yale Librarian listened patiently to Lefty's problem and then said, "I'm afraid I can't help you."

Lefty was astonished.

Mr. Keogh explained crisply. "Your collection will not be available to the public and your cards will be right next to the originals to which they refer. The American Library Association does not provide for cases like yours."

The Lewises went out to the Huntington Library in California for a week and in that enchanted place Lefty got more help. The Huntington had been open only a few years, its vast stores of English family papers were still being catalogued and calendared, but Lefty found Herman Schultz and Miss Norma Cuthbert eager to help him. It became clear that a specialized collection must work out its own salvation, and so on his return to Farmington Lefty turned to A. L. Burt of Hartford who provided the steel furniture for the North Library. American business was then well ahead of librarians and university scholars when it came to devising methods for storing and finding records: if Mrs. Smith of Tucson, Arizona, lost her piano someone in Hartford, Conn., would find out all about it in one minute. Could Mr. Burt adapt this wizardry to Lefty's needs? He would try and would enjoy doing it because so far as he knew it was the first time that business methods had been applied to scholarship. A special card was printed for Walpole's correspondence. Experience has shown how it could be bettered, but its merit was soon proved by a presentation copy of a Strawberry Hill imprint with Walpole's accompanying letter bound in that turned up mysteriously at Goodspeed's in Boston. Lefty could have the book and letter for $45. There was a card at Farmington that showed the letter was unpublished and that gave its history from the day it left Strawberry Hill in 1783 until Quaritch sold it to Frank B. Bemis of Boston for thirty-five pounds in 1926. Lefty recalled tardily Mr. Bemis telling him the last time they met that he had a book (not saying what it was or mentioning the letter in it) of Walpolian interest that he would show him. He left it at Goodspeed's for the young man to see on his next trip to Boston, which did not take place until after Mr. Bemis's death. Lefty sent the book and its letter back to George Goodspeed with its history, adding, "You, alas, have no right to sell it and I no right to buy it," but he hoped that the executors of Mr. Bemis's estate would consider letting him have it; he would gladly give what Mr. Bemis paid Quaritch for it. The executors were pleased to recover the book, the only one missing from the library, and sent it back to Farmington saying they would not think of asking Mr. Lewis to pay more than Goodspeed's price.

There are now at Farmington and in the Walpole Room at Yale over 100 categories of index cards, the most unusual of which is a case history of Walpole's thirty-six attacks of gout (which Harvey Cushing said may be compared with Montaigne's history of the stone for clinical interest). There are several special files, such as a "diurnal" that will show when finished what is known every day of Walpole's life from his twenty-second year to his eightieth, and "The Black Books," which register the Walpoliana not at Farmington and their owners. The file that means most to Lewis records "HW Gifts to WSL": Walpole's letters and manuscripts, and books, drawings, and prints from Strawberry Hill. Seventy donors have given 130 items: six of the donors were public libraries; three were bequests from virtual strangers in Stonington, Conn., Co. Wicklow, and Portugal. The 7 original drawers installed in 1934 for manuscripts and correspondence have grown to 47; the 12 original card trays to over 500 in which there are 850,000 cards with room for 350,000 more; some five miles of microfilm have been acquired. All this was started before the days of "information retrieval" systems and their miraculous devices, but Lefty has been reassured by one of their inventors that the "wet-thumb" system is the best there is. Certainly the Burt–Lewis–Lam System is an advance over Wilmarth's initial venture into method sixty years ago, the cigar box for his collection of houseflies.

To get the books properly catalogued was more difficult. By 1947 Lefty was having trouble finding what he wanted and he was buying unwelcome duplicates. Professional help was provided by the new Yale Librarian, James T. Babb, who asked Mrs. Dorothy Livingston and Miss Dorothy Bridgwater of the Cataloguing Department to work out with Mr. Lewis a "classification scheme" for the Library's future annex in Farmington. This collaboration introduced Mr. Lewis to such arcane matters as Cutter Numbers and Shelf Lists and the layman's pleasure of being talked to by professionals in their own language. What I recall chiefly of our discussions (which took place over several months) is the tact and common sense of my two collaborators and how much they taught Lewis about his own library. They fitted the classification scheme to its probable development instead of making the library conform to a Procrustean bed of standard measurements. Miss Mabel Martin, who had been Librarian of Bennett Junior College, arrived, and now some 14,000 titles (19,000 volumes) have been catalogued with an average of ten cards to a title, three of which are at Yale. The library continues to grow: three new rooms for 15,000 additional volumes have been added and suitable provision made for visiting scholars.

Lefty's knowledge of method was increased during the academic year 1937–8 when Karl Young and Wallace Notestein persuaded him to give a seminar in the Graduate School on "Horace Walpole's England." He still liked the idea of teaching: a teacher if he is any good is master of his classroom; he directs, rewards, punishes; he is treated with respect, fear, and affection; he enlarges the minds of his students, the best of whom stimulate his own mind: but Lefty hesitated to give the course. Wouldn't the younger men in the English and History departments resent it even though he would not be a drain on any budget or stand in the way of their advancement? No, no, his two professorial friends assured him, they would take care of all that. They would send him their best students and it would be good for Yale if he gave the course. So, flattered, he who declined to take a Ph.D. himself agreed to teach candidates for it. His two senior friends each sent one student; a third, Ralph Williams, came on his own. The class therefore totaled four, including the instructor.

It was frankly experimental. What interested Associate Professor Lewis most in the eighteenth century was the way its people lived and thought. As a traveler on his first visit abroad notices similarities to and dissimilarities from his own country, so Lefty was struck in Walpole's letters by the familiar and the strange. The familiar included displays of the old Adam such as when Princess Amelia accused Walpole at the card table of being a political timeserver. We feel his embarrassment and anger, since he was not a timeserver, and his helplessness, because he could not answer back to royalty. We can sympathize with his human predicament, but we are in the dark about the details of the evening. When did the guests arrive? what happened before they went to dinner? how were they seated at dinner, man, woman, man? and how did they talk, first to one side then to the other, or was there general conversation? These tacit assumptions that everyone took for granted have to be ferreted out in the journals and letters of foreign visitors to England who commented on what was strange to them, in newspaper advertisements, in prints that show streets, vehicles, rooms, and costumes with photographic accuracy. Trials for adultery disclose the details of the principals' lives, when they got up and went to bed, what they had for breakfast and when they had it, and the routine of their day. Lefty hoped that History 155 might reveal the tacit assumptions of the age and that his students (and he) would become so familiar with the eighteenth century that they could hear, in G. M. Young's phrase, its people talking.

The class met once a week for two hours. Professor Lewis assigned a newspaper or magazine to each member of it, including himself. To keep the study within bounds he limited the search to 1747–57. The class recorded every figure that threw light on the life of the time, typing out its notes in quadruplicate. When it met the notes were distributed and put into the expanding file kept by each of the four. The determination of categories under which to file the notes had to be done first. Certain categories, such as Law, Medicine, Food, were easy; others, such as Accessories (buckles, buttons, fans, etc.) and Household Effects, were portmanteaux. The categories could have been refined, but they served their immediate purpose, which was to get the jumble of material in workable order. After three months of this collecting one category stood out as more promising for further study than the rest, private charity, the gift of money, food, clothing, etc., to persons who had no legal or moral claim upon the donors. The class was pleased when it found Lecky saying that such altruistic philanthropy did not exist before 1760.

History 155 went better and better as the year progressed. It had enlivening glimpses of the time such as when on Twelfth Night 1747 "His Majesty and the royal family with several of the nobility played at hazard for the benefit of the groom porter," or when on Christmas Day 1756 "the Rev. Dr. Bullock, Dean of Norwich, gave a dinner of roast beef and plumb puddings, with two barrels of beer, and sixpence each man, to seventy of the oldest soldiers that were at the siege of Minorca." Lefty thought that others might like to see what the class had done and published the results of its work through the Yale Press. The final outline of *Private Charity in England, 1747–1757* begins:

I. Impulses.
  1. Enlightened Selfishness.
    A. Mercantilism.
      i. Wages and Cost of Living.
      ii. Alms-giving.

and ends,

VIII. Results.
  1. Benefits and Achievements.
  2. Fraud and Imposition.

Illustrations from the periodicals were furnished for each entry. Ralph Williams was the joint editor. Carl Rollins designed an attractive little book that sold for two dollars a copy. Lewis concluded his Preface, "We are publishing the study in the hope that it may . . . encourage those whose primary interest is in history or literature to venture into a field which at first view may appear to be the exclusive province of the economist. Whatever value may be ascribed to the results of such researches, we can say from our experience that they give to those who engage in them satisfaction and pleasure." The reception of the book was equally modest. Harold Laski told the senior editor that *Private Charity* broke new ground in eighteenth-century studies, and that he had his class at the London School of Economics read it, but he was the sole scholar to mention it to anybody, so far as I know. Reviewers passed it by in total silence. Two copies were sold almost at once in Canada, a promising start, but it was only a flash in the pan. The editor's hopes of leading to a fresh field of research were not fulfilled.

Associate Professor Lewis got so much out of the course that he was ready to continue it. He planned to spend all the second year on one of Hogarth's prints in The Rake's Progress, the fourth episode where the rake is arrested for debt. However, no one stopped at Professor Lewis's door to register for the course and somewhat to his relief History 155 expired. It was a pioneer that ventured into new country and was never heard of again.

Lefty's experiments with method taught him that, like money, "system" gives pleasure, independence, and power. Keeping pace with his collecting, editing, and curating, was his increasing knowledge of libraries, of the Yale Library, above all.

XXI

THE YALE LIBRARY

Lefty's introduction to the Yale Library was inauspicious. In 1914 it was still housed in a building with an 1843 neo-Gothic wing. On his first morning as an undergraduate he went to it under the impression that it was where Daily Chapel was held and had to be directed with smiles of amusement to Battell across the Campus. Although the Library's ecclesiastical appearance had misled other Freshmen before him, he regarded it thereafter with suspicion until he began collecting Walpole ten years later. Then its architectural descent from Strawberry Hill made it a place of pilgrimage for him. Walpole would have found its towers and "gloomth" congenial and as a friend of America he would have been pleased that a child of Strawberry should be at the heart of a university in the hemisphere where he prophesied that the next Augustan age would dawn.

Lefty began to feel at home in the stacks after Mr. Keogh opened them to him. They were like a huge bookshop where he could wander at will. The books were not for sale, but he got other copies of those he wanted. He was like a Henry James character moving about in a great and dimly lit house, more and more aware of a following presence just beyond the long shafts of light that filtered through the lancet window. The gathering apparition was not sinister; quite the contrary, it encouraged and guided the young man amicably from a discreet distance.

Lefty became increasingly conscious of the bookplates that named the donors of funds for purchasing the books that he held in his hands and who had by their gifts helped make Yale a place where study in any subject might be pursued. More slowly he came to appreciate the skill of the staff in their meticulous and exacting profession and to marvel at their loyalty to it. He learned that a member of it who had risen to one of the highest posts earned no more than an assistant athletic coach and that pensions were given to those only in dire straits. Their profession was not attractive financially, especially when one had to support an ailing relative as well as oneself. Yet they accepted their lot cheerfully; "library work" and poverty went together. They did not presume to question the University's indifference to its most valuable possession.

The head of the purchasing department was May Humphries, a shy man whose desk was cluttered with the catalogues of antiquarian booksellers and pending auction sales. He took a fatherly interest in Lefty's collection, listened carefully to his reports of new acquisitions, and one day told him gently that regions of knowledge and collecting would open to him of which he had not yet imagined, a prophesy that the young man, slightly abashed, was to fulfill. May Humphries did not share the views of the professor who said to Mr. Hadley that the chief use of a university library is to lend an occasional book to a professor who does not happen to have it on his own shelves. He and his forgotten predecessors built up the University's collections, book by book, with the zeal and piety of thirteenth-century Christians piling stone on stone to raise their cathedrals to the glory and service of God.

In 1924 the Library was Cinderella, friendless and forlorn, but a Prince Charming arrived in the person of Professor

Tinker and he took her to the ball. On Alumni Day of that year he made the chief speech to the returning graduates. His subject was the Library. "There are three distinguishing marks of a university," he began: "a group of students, a corps of instructors, and a collection of books; and of these three the most important is the collection of books." This was unfamiliar doctrine to most of his audience. Yale was about to spend several of the Sterling millions on a new library building he pointed out, but nothing "for books, binding, or service to readers. . . . If we are not willing to compete with the best libraries in this country, it is folly for us to attempt to be one of the great universities, for scholars and teachers, graduate students, and, at last, undergraduate students will go where the books are." The Yale Library was slipping from second place into the fifth or sixth among American university libraries. It was to be hoped that the University's administration would arrest this decline and that the alumni would help them do it. What could individual graduates do? They could make themselves responsible for one of the weaker spots in the Library and build it up, a suggestion that influenced Lefty's decision later to collect Horace Walpole who was but feebly represented there.

The latter-day enrichment of the Library (and Yale's resultant increased strength as a center of research) came about in consequence of Tinker's speech. Frank Altschul who had made the outstanding American collection of Meredith was so impressed by what Tink said that he invited a dozen book-collecting alumni (chosen by Mr. Keogh) to dine with him and the University administration at his apartment in New York to learn how they could carry out Tink's proposal. The junior member of this group in every sense was W. S. Lewis. All twelve of the alumni came—W. S. Mason from Chicago; Leonard Hanna from Cleveland; Conger Goodyear from Buffalo; the

New Yorkers included Dr. Samuel Lambert, Starling Childs, Robert Hartshorne, Russell Leffingwell. The President, Treasurer, and Comptroller of the University came. Not since the original ten trustees met at Branford in Pastor Russel's house in 1701 and laid their books on a table "for the founding of a college in this Colony" had the future of the Library been so bright. After dinner the prospective benefactors sat back to hear what the University authorities would like to have them do. They knew that they had been included because they had money as well as interest, for the rich can see the glint of a rifle in the thickest underbrush miles away. All except W. S. Lewis were used to being shot at, but their loyalty to Yale was stimulated by what appeared to be an effort on the part of the University to strengthen its foundations and they were willing as well as visible targets.

President Angell spoke first and at some length. It was very good of everyone to come, the Library was certainly a fine thing and the University officers welcomed this show of interest in it by so many distinguished graduates, but, gentlemen, Yale was about to launch a drive for twenty million dollars and, well, the applecart must not be tipped over. Mr. Keogh then crisply handed about what seemed through the soft mists of Frank's Lucullan dinner to be a mountain of papers. He had kept in training during the evening, had prepared his remarks, and went into them with the speed of a racehorse. The papers, it appeared, showed where the Library stood in relation to the other chief university libraries in the country, the number of books on their shelves, the size of their staffs, their budgets, annual expenditures for binding, cataloguing, new accessions, the cost of stationery, telephones, postage. At last he reached his crucial question, Should the Library be kept open until ten at night for graduate students? When in a few weeks a special meeting of the Committee was held in New Haven to visit the

Library Frank and Lefty were the only members of it who came. The applecart had not been tipped over.

It took more than these fiascos to stop Frank. He went right on giving annual dinners for the dozen would-be friends. There were always high university officials in uneasy attendance. They did not feel as strongly as the head of a sister institution who shook his fist at its famous library and cried, "Pack-rats! I'll get 'em!" but they offered no encouragement even after the twenty-million-dollar drive had been completed and the apple-cart was safe. One muttered something about booksellers being "tricky," but for the most part they kept a watchful silence. Anxiety about the Library Committee, as it came to be called, reached up even to the Corporation, Lefty learned one day, when a member of it asked him, "How many books do you need in the Library, anyway?" (That man subsequently became an active book collector and was then able to answer his own question.) What, Lefty would ask Tink, was the matter with these people? Instead of being intransigent why weren't they urging the enthusiasts on? Tink had no idea and Lefty was slow to find two explanations: most administrators do not realize that research is dependent upon objects—books, manuscripts, pictures, prints, fossils, bird skins, or whatnot; on collections, in short—and administrators naturally dislike outside pressure. They run the place and they do not intend to let anyone else run it. Nevertheless, the Alumni's Library Committee had to be treated with care: its members were wealthy and influential; they had bees in their bonnets, but they mustn't be sent away mad. As I look back on these meetings now I see them as a version of the Mastick War in which the members of the Committee were the aggressors and the administrators lay on the ground hoping that when the charge was over the aroused alumni would transfer their attention to concerns of the officers' choosing. A dissertation of more than usual interest might be written on "Pride and Prudence in the Management of American Universities."

The administration's fear of the committee was easier for Lefty to understand than Mr. Keogh's fear of it. This, it gradually dawned on him, came from a similar alarm lest these high-powered amateurs disguised as friends should prove to be aliens in his domain that he could not control. Might they not think that their gifts gave them the right to meddle? They didn't know how the library was run or how much their gifts cost in time, trouble, and money. Mr. Keogh once told Lefty by way of mild complaint that every book given cost the Library at least three dollars to "accession." This seemed a small price to pay for something that would usually be worth many times three dollars and might be just the book a scholar needed in his work, but the funds for accessioning were already overtaxed and the Corporation (the whipping boy of the University) would not give the Library any more. Most librarians could make better use of an extra cataloguer than of all the Books of Hours in Christendom.

It took Lefty still longer to find out why members of the teaching profession dislike books. To many of them bibliophilism appears precious. All that scientists and mathematicians want are the current publications in their subjects unless they are interested in the history of science, which few of them are. Humanists take pride in showing that their books are falling to pieces: a tattered book, like a tattered battle flag, proves it has been in use. If scholars do not know why bibliography is helpful—and most of them do not—the talk of "condition," of uncut and unopened pages, of cancels, of original boards and binding variants, of "provenance," is irritating. All they are interested in, they will say, is what is inside the book, adding that "The last edition is the best," with childlike faith in its editor. Also, the scholar may have had the bad (and rare) luck to run into a collector who refused to let him print an unpublished manuscript of an author that the scholar regarded as "his." Whether or not publication of an unpublished manuscript reduces its monetary value is a moot point; booksellers are not agreed on it; but it is not debatable that the manuscript is the owner's property and that if he chooses to withhold it from publication the scholar is not apt to make him change his mind by being disagreeable about it.

The Library-graduate problem at Yale was solved by its new Provost, Charles Seymour, whose attitude towards the Library was quite different from that of his colleagues. Lefty discovered this one day in 1930 when he ran into the future President on the train to New York. "What a pity," the younger man said, "that you people killed the Alumni's Library Committee!"

"I agree," Charlie Seymour replied. "Why don't we start it up again?" The Sterling Library would soon be completed, there would be a rare book room in it, Why shouldn't Tinker be its Keeper?

Frank and Lefty needed no further encouragement. With the examples before them of Les Amis de la Bibliothèque Nationale and the Friends of the Bodleian they formed the Yale Library Associates, the first organization of its kind in this country. Twenty-four graduates became its trustees; several hundred members were recruited at a minimum annual subscription of five dollars or gifts in kind. Frank and his Vice-Chairman, Starling Childs, established large funds to purchase books. Gifts of books and collections, large and small, came in rapidly; the annual gifts of cash rose high into five figures (it is now over $200,000). The Keeper of Rare Books was supposed to spend this money in consultation with the Head of the Purchasing Department and the Chairman of the Associates, but from the first Tink made it plain that he would do nothing of the kind. When a book that the Library should have appeared in a catalogue he wired or telephoned for it at once without consulting anybody and so secured many rarities that might have been lost if he had delayed. "The Keeper must be free to act at once," he said. "A committee can't build up a great library!" He was equally firm in his stand against those who maintained that photostats and microfilm serve the scholar as well as the book itself. "No photostats in the Rare Book Room!" he cried. "People who talk about photostats have no knowledge of bibliography and no feeling for *books!"* Tink spent the Associates' money as he pleased for twenty-five years to the immense gain of the Library, where he will be honored long after the last of his thousands of grateful students are dead. He had a little office in the Rare Book Room, the Keeper's Kosy Korner, to which he would repair with the air of one entering into his kingdom. Current book catalogues were on his desk. Booksellers called. Part of his success was owing to his making much of booksellers. "They are learned men," he would say, "they know dates." He treated them with confidence and respect; first names were reached in short order. It was natural that the trade preferred Yale to the institutions that still treated it with suspicion and condescension.

When Lefty succeeded Frank Altschul as Chairman of the Associates in 1933 the new Library was in full swing, Tink in the Kosy Korner, but all was not right with the world. There was what is known in the genteel language of "management" as "a personality problem," and the problem was Tink. He didn't like his senior colleagues; in fact, he might not speak to them for days on end. The one who was most often out of bounds was the Head of the Purchasing Department, a kindly man who mispronounced English place names. The Keeper of Rare Books would in the ordinary way have been in constant touch with him, since the Keeper spent the Associates' money for books that the Library could not afford to buy, and the Head of the Purchasing Department was the man who decided whether it could or could not afford to buy them, but when one day that unfortunate official pronounced Salisbury "Sal-lis-berry" communication between him and the Keeper ceased. As Mr. Keogh was also out of bounds at the time, the business of the Kosy Korner with these key persons had to be conducted through Farmington.

The role of administrator was as new to Chairman Lewis as it was to Keeper Tinker. When he was a Freshman sitting under Tink, Lefty never dreamt that one day he would have to admonish the great man, yet one day, his heart in his mouth, admonish him he did. "The first story I ever read," he said when he got to the Kosy Korner during the Sal-lis-berry crisis, "was of the wager between the wind and the sun. The question, you remember, was, Which of them was the stronger? They agreed that the winner would be the one that could get the cloak off a man walking on a plain. The wind blew and blew, but the harder it blew the tighter the man clutched his cloak about him and the wind gave up. Then the sun had its turn. It beamed and beamed and the man took off his cloak." It wasn't much of an admonition. Tink merely stared and went right on being a personality problem.

He was very happy in his job in spite of his colleagues. He loved having the great booksellers of England and America come to him cap in hand; he loved to handle the books that they brought him; he loved filling in gaps in the Library's collections and substituting a fine copy for a poor one. He was sensitive to any hint that he favored English literature, especially books from Richardson to Henry James, the period covered by his own library, and when the Ionides collection of Greek and Latin authors came on the market he presented it to the Library at the cost of a year's salary.

With the arrival of Harvey Cushing in the thirties Yale acquired a learned book collector as well as a world-famous neurologist and the Library a friend and advocate who was used to getting what he wanted. He started a monthly lunch at Mory's of the local trustees of the Associates. Tink would bring a book that had recently come to his desk and that the Library had to have, perhaps an early Ptolemy, perhaps a tract by Servetus. They were expensive luncheons. Cush's library was in the great medical humanist tradition. To make it even stronger he merged it with the libraries of John Fulton and Arnold Klebs, "The Institute" they called it, and agreed to give it to a university, preferably to Yale if it would add a wing to the Medical School for it. This the University, reluctantly, finally did.

The Chairman of the Library Associates was made an ex-officio member of the Alumni Board, which had upwards of a hundred branches throughout the country. Lefty formed subcommittees in several of them on the Library and Museums, some of which had active chairmen who sent to New Haven welcome gifts. That a salesman may be too successful was shown at his first talk to the alumni on this subject. He gave it in Chicago in 1934 at a large luncheon got up for him by his classmate, Lester Armour. When he finished, a graduate who had unearthed dinosaurs on his property near Peoria charged up and said, "Now at last Yale is making sense. I will give you *all* my dinosaurs!" an offer that had, alas, to be declined because it overtaxed the stabling capacities of the Peabody Museum. Chairman Lewis hoped that the subcommittee would send to Yale collections of local and regional material and some did. The alumni even at the dinners where football movies were the main attraction were interested to hear that a university's strength as a place of learning depends upon its collections, that Yale's are superb and should be augmented further.

Serious-minded graduates who rarely went to Yale dinners came: it was novel to have someone from the University assume that they were adults and not jolly Sophomores singing on the Old Yale Fence. It was a yeasting time for the Yale Library. The graduates were determined to help it and so were a dozen members of the faculty who were creative book collectors, an unusually large number for any university. In this galaxy besides Tinker, Cushing, and Fulton, there were George D. Smith, Clements Fry, Clarence W. Mendell, F. W. Hilles, James M. Osborn, von Faber du Faur, Louis Gimbel, Richard Purdy, and Norman Pearson. On the Library staff there were Donald T. Wing, H. W. Liebert, Warren Lowenhaupt, Thomas E. Marston, Alexander O. Vietor, Donald C. Gallup, and at their head, James T. Babb who as a collector of collectors has been unexcelled in this country.

With the tax advantages that American owners of valuable books and objects of art enjoy it is inevitable that collections will gravitate to public institutions, and it is suicidal for a university not to try to get its full share of them. It so happens that in recent years a large number of outstanding collectors of all kinds have been Yale men or friends of Yale. The Yale Library Associates and the Associates of the Yale Art Gallery have been a channel through which their books and pictures have passed to the University. Yale would have been given some of them anyway, but many would have gone elsewhere had the University failed to impress upon their owners that it wanted them. A university is not concerned with the market value of its collections, yet it is of academic interest that the gifts made through the Library Associates and its sister Art Gallery Associates now reach well into eight figures in each institution, a sum that has shown those in authority that bees in bonnets may eventually produce sweet honey.

As I turn over Lefty's extensive correspondence on the Yale

Library with graduates all over the country I am impressed by his ardor. Why did he get so emotional about it? How had it become for him a fortress, cathedral, palladium? Absorption in the past, we are told, is an expression of infantile "fixation" with one or both parents and an attempt to escape from a personal past. This is the most subterranean explanation. More obvious is that he was a bookman, a Yale bookman, and that Tink (and Carlyle) had made it clear to him that the library is the heart of a university, a figure of speech that was not in 1924 a cliché. Opposed to Tink and the forces of light were the forces of darkness who were blind to the Library's significance and who kept it an underdog. Lefty was by instinct against authority and for underdogs, even though he liked having authority himself and hated being an underdog. He was not a librarian, but he was a book collector and book collectors are also looked at askance by most administrators. So Lefty's dedication to Tinker's crusade was strengthened by edginess as well as a love of the past. He had substituted Yale for God and made the Library its Church. His aborted religious fervor had to go somewhere. Tink led it to the repository of Learning, Beauty, Truth, and Rarity, an unimpeachable cause in which to expend one's aggressive energy. Lefty had been trained for this crusade at Sunday School when Wilmarth, clutching his five-cent piece, marched round the room singing:

Hell's foundations quiver
At the shout of praise;
Brothers, lift your voices,
Loud your anthems raise!

The heathen might rage, but the Library would prevail. The Associates have prevailed and have set an example followed throughout the country by many other libraries. If Miss Argus of the Alameda Free Public Library were alive all her eyes would blink to see how much the relations of librarians with the public have improved since she made life as hard as possible for Wilmarth Lewis.

He might have become a librarian himself. His first chance to be one occurred in 1937. Alumni interest in the Yale Library had by then reached the point feared by Mr. Keogh; in fact, the situation had got so out of hand that Charles Seymour, the new President, wanted someone to speed the momentum started by the Associates to build up the Library even if he was not a librarian. Lefty had foreseen that such a course might be followed and that he would be among the many who would be considered as Mr. Keogh's successor. This possibility occurred to him with clarity one day in the summer of 1934, six years after he and Annie Burr were married. Azro was motoring them from the Yosemite to Lake Tahoe. The moment of clarity came while they were picnicking at a light-headed height of 10,000 feet amid the peaks of the nearby Sierras. Lefty decided then that if he were asked to be Librarian he would accept, but when four years later he was asked to be it he had learned enough about himself to realize that however much he would enjoy building up the University's collections and the prestige of the position, once the glamour of it had worn off he would hate the confinement of the office and restraints of still higher authority. He recalled how once Mr. Keogh told him that librarians have no time to write books or engage in scholarly publications; that is, if Lefty took the librarianship he would let down the Yale Walpole. Fortunately for him, for the Yale Walpole, and the Yale Library, sea-level common sense vetoed his decision made in the high Sierras and he retained his independence and freedom when the Yale Librarianship was pressed upon him in 1937.

President Seymour then asked him to serve on the committee to recommend Keogh's (and his own) successor. Its chairman was E. S. Furniss, the new Provost of the University; the other members were Harvey Cushing, Karl Young, Roy Angier, and Carl Lohmann, its secretary. (Tink, who would normally have been on it, was at Harvard giving the Charles Eliot Norton Lectures.) The committee met nearly every week for six months. At the outset it agreed that what the Library needed was a man who could build up its collections and who would adopt a more generous attitude towards their use. Mr. Keogh had been an outstanding reference librarian; he had got Yale's collections arranged on the shelves for the maximum advantage of scholars; but he took the line that the Library was for Yale's faculty and students and not for anyone else. Accordingly, when the Library of Congress set up its Union Catalogue of books in the leading American libraries he refused to report Yale's holdings to it with the result that they were not known nationally. Since in the learned world the strength of a university, especially in humanistic studies, is gauged by the strength of its library, Mr. Keogh's stand injured the University professionally. "Why should anyone bother with the Yale Library?" a bookman of international reputation, Thomas W. Streeter, asked Lefty in 1944, "Yale hasn't any books." When on Lefty's invitation he went to the Library he conceded gladly that it was in the same rank as the Library of Congress, the New York Public Library, and Harvard. Thereafter he became its active supporter and facilitated the migration to it of his great Texas collection. The committee to choose Mr. Keogh's successor wanted a man who could not only increase the Library's resources but make them more accessible to scholars everywhere.

Harvey Cushing and Lefty went down to Washington to get the advice of Herbert Putnam, the Librarian of Congress and dean of American librarians. When he heard the sort of man that the committee had in mind he said he would not be found among librarians. "I suggest you look for him in Wall Street," he said. "He will probably be a lawyer—I was once one my-self—and he must of course be a man who knows and values research."

"If we pick such a man," Lefty explained, "the present second in command will resign. The new number two must be a professional?"

"Oh, no!" Mr. Putnam was equally clear on that point. "The Yale Library is so well organized that the heads of its departments can run it," a remark that later resulted in the appointment to the second post of James T. Babb who was then a stockbroker in New Haven, a collector whose dedication to the Library could not be taught by all the library schools in the world. The committee after canvassing the nation's librarians recommended the appointment of Bernhard Knollenberg, an outstanding lawyer in New York and student of the American Revolution. How ardently the librarianship was coveted was shown by four senior members of the faculty who let it be known that they were available for it.

Members of such a committee meet in a pleasant frame of mind: their appointment to it is recognition of their own stat-ure and their ability to wield and confer power disinterestedly for the welfare of the institution they serve. They embark upon their task with a sense of well-being buttressed by humility. They are out to get the best man for the job and they mean to find him. They are prepared to give disappointment to many, pain to a few, and joy to one. Their discussions will be the subject of much speculation outside the committee; rumors will escape from its confidential sessions and flying abroad will become more and more distorted as they fly, an annoyance that underscores the importance of what the committee is doing. When things go smoothly a feeling of brotherhood develops; the sessions become relaxed and expansive, pleasantries ripple forth; the committee are kingmakers off on a spree. Lefty loved the meetings, which reminded him how a candidate's mannerisms and traits of personality may rise up, especially after dinner, to make or mar his career at a critical juncture in his life.

The leaders of the library world were not pleased with the committee's choice of one outside their guild. Each member of the Corporation received an anonymous letter from Brooklyn in which the writer made it clear in what low esteem he held that usually respected body. The *Library Journal,* the organ of the American Library Association, printed an angry and sarcastic editorial that assumed the Corporation had chosen Mr. Keogh's successor by lot; the result was to turn "the clock back to an earlier generation." If so, it was just what the Library needed. Bernhard Knollenberg as Librarian and James T. Babb as his associate realized the committee's hopes for what the Library might become. During his four years in office Knollie introduced a department of manuscripts and made the would-be benefactors of the Library welcome. When he resigned Lewis was the chairman of the committee to chose his successor. It met once for twenty minutes and chose Jim Babb. Then the Library entered upon an era of golden harvest that culminated in the Beinecke Library, Tink's and the original trustees' fabulous dream come true.

XXII

1933–1938

The Yale Walpole gave Lefty the employment that he wanted and needed. It increased his correspondence and furnished him with homework brought from Yale on his Wednesday visits there. In New Haven he would lunch with Tink or Karl Young or Fred Pottle or at Calhoun College (which opened in 1933), with the Master, Arnold Whitridge, and the Fellows, of whom he was one. The ten-year-old daughter of a Calhoun colleague introduced him to the excitement of collecting matchbooks, a subject he had regarded as the nadir of all collecting. Lefty's most valued contribution to her collection was the matchbook of Jack Dempsey's restaurant autographed by the proprietor "For Loraine Fairchild."

Other projects appear in one of Lefty's notebooks in 1935:

> *1. The Edition.*
> *2. The Yale Collections.*
> *3. The Yale Library Associates.*
> *4. Photostats of English family papers*
> *[of which nothing came].*

He failed to include the project that he took for granted morning, noon, and night, his library. He was buying not only

Walpoliana, the books Walpole wrote, printed, and owned, but the novels, plays, poetry, histories, biographies, memoirs, and letters of the period, its magazines, and whatever was of interest to Walpole such as certain trials and topographical works. All were available during the depression for as many shillings as they fetch in pounds today. Such wholesale buying imposed an unwelcome burden on the Farmington Post Office whose aging postmistress complained to the collector one day as she shoveled out through her narrow window the first 302 volumes of the *Gentleman's Magazine,* "Here you go on, Mr. Lewis, buying *books,* and all the world *crying* for bread!" There was in this collecting the passion of the zealot, the recklessness of the gambler, the rapacity of the miser. His library was for Lefty the road to salvation. At one point he was tempted to collect Matthew Arnold as well, but wisely drew back: recollection of Josh Billings's admonition to stick to one thing until he got there held him to his main purpose.

The Lewises' guest book recorded more and more visitors, but most of the 378 people who spent at least one night with them from January 1, 1933, to January 1, 1939, were old friends who came for weekends of tennis, golf, croquet, bridge, and the prattle that is one of the most agreeable features of life. As I look back on the thirties I think with particular pleasure of the theater. The Lewises saw virtually every play in New York during the season. They would stay with Mrs. Auchincloss and had the use of her second car and chauffeur, a provision that removed any difficulty of getting to and from the theater. Nor was there any difficulty about getting tickets through a club at a small advance over the box-office prices. They would dress, dine with friends at home, and be in their seats before the curtain went up. There were always other friends in the audience and the evening had a social as well as theatrical aspect.

The Lewises' library and its expanding use did not obtrude

on most weekends, intimate friends rarely know much about each other's chief occupations, yet as time went on and the library grew it became something of a problem with newcomers who had heard of it. Annie Burr would say, "*Don't* begin on the pictures in the hall going up to dinner," a reasonable injunction. On the other hand she might caution, "Don't forget to show —— something later" because —— would be wounded if tribute were not paid to her intellect. The golden mean between showing too much and too little was found at last or, rather, five golden means for the five classes of visitors. The classes were (and are): (1) those who are afraid they may have to look at the library; (2) those who merely want to say they've seen it; (3) the gushers; (4) the uninformed but interested; (5) the experts. The first class is no problem. The rest are taken into the North Library. Classes 2 and 3 gasp in surprise: "Oh, my!" The steel door closes emphatically. The uncertain look back at it anxiously. Are they locked in? The merely curious advance cautiously, glance uneasily around, smile, and are eager to depart: they have seen the library. The gushers (always female, I'm afraid) go a step further. "Lovely leather bindings," they will murmur with half-closed eyes and ask archly, "May I touch one?" The one they touch is the least interesting binding on the shelf. Having paid tribute to beauty, learning, and rarity they, too, are ready to go and leave with a sweeping glance of ecstasy round the room. Classes 2 and 3 are taken care of in five minutes. Class 4, the uninformed but interested, is a pleasure. Its members have no pretense or silliness; they really want to see something of the library and are given what John Carter calls "a Walpole Wallow" that may last an hour. Class 5, the experts, are the most welcome of all. The material on their subjects whatever it may be—Lord North, the Quakers, carriages—is assembled before they arrive. Their surprise at finding, usually, more than they expected is gratifying; if they are disappointed the owner tries to fill the gap as soon as possible. This professional perlustration proceeds from one book or manuscript or print to another until the explorers can endure no more.

Annie Burr was as easy with the experts as with old friends. She made not the faintest shadow of pretense to knowledge that she lacked and took what she had (which was far more than her old friends realized) as a matter of course. One Sunday evening in 1936 she proved this to Michael Sadleir, John Carter, and her husband who had proposed a bibliographical guessing game. Lefty picked out books in bindings from the early seventeenth century to the late nineteenth century that the company agreed were contemporary with the books' publication and the four wrote down their guesses of the dates when the books were published. (The books had no visible titles.) I see Annie Burr now sitting in the corner of the sofa by the table beside the needlework picture of Strawberry Hill, her first essay in the art, which a visiting textile expert mistook for "an example of the finest early nineteenth-century needlework"; I see her quite quietly writing down her answers that proved to be the nearest right even of the mid-nineteenth-century books, to the astonishment of her English visitors, the two greatest experts on Victorian bindings alive.

The Lewises spent March with Mrs. Auchincloss at Jekyll Island, a club off the coast of Georgia, the most beautiful club, I suppose, in all the world. It had a large clubhouse built in the eighties and cottages, some of them ample. There was golf, a beach and a pool and shell roads that wound round the island through palmettos and oaks festooned with Spanish moss. There was a great deal of tennis—indoors and outdoors. Lefty won three tournaments, the last with Annie Burr in the annual mixed doubles. He also won the backgammon tournament one year and so added four pewter cups to the copper stein Ed

Woods won for him at Duxbury in 1907. There were always old friends and everyone appeared at their most relaxed and best. This was not merely getting through the calendar. In the evenings of his last visit (the club was sold to the State of Georgia during the war), Lefty played tense backgammon with its president, Mr. J. P. Morgan, who was supposed to go to bed at ten but who often stayed later to talk about the Morgan Library. Lefty was impressed by his knowing all the Walpoliana in it and when his father acquired them. His affection for the Library, to which he went every day when in New York, was touching, and Lefty realized that his modesty and shyness concealed one of the keenest collectors of our time. Perhaps a social historian will unearth the history of the Jekyll Island Club where a few score responsible Americans met for the latter part of the winter to enjoy a well-earned rest. It will not be easy to convey its tone and atmosphere to a generation as unfamiliar with it as with the Court of the Great Mogul.

Annie Burr's extracurricular activity at this time centered on Miss Porter's School. She encouraged its Principals, Robert Porter Keep and his wife, to start a "College Preparatory Course." More and more daughters of "ancients" were going elsewhere to get one: the "finishing school" was finished. She also founded the Alumnae Association, employing the knowledge and skill she gained working under Pauline Sabin Davis in the anti-Prohibition movement. Branches of the new Association were formed throughout the country, committees on the library and other aspects of the School that alumnae may properly help were formed, meetings were held, annual giving, that blessed emollient, was begun. After three years, the ideal term for the chairmanship of such an undertaking, she resigned, thus setting a good precedent.

The Lewises went to England every year. On their travels Annie Burr carried the tickets and passports, surrendering them to her husband only on demand at gangplanks and gates and restoring them to the security of her handbag as soon as possible. When they were engaged Lefty told her that he liked being punctual, a warning that he was to regret. The Lewises never got to dinner in time for lunch or to lunch in time for breakfast, but they regularly caught the train ahead of the one they set out to take and once they caught an earlier boat and found themselves bound for Nantucket instead of Martha's Vineyard.

In London they stayed at Brown's in "Queen Wilhelmina's Suite," which had enormous cabinets filled with hideous objets d'art, a constellation of electric lights, and mice frisking about at night. Holmes, Turner, and the Boadicean housekeeper were gone, but Nice had been promoted to the Albemarle Street side and provided continuity with the past. There were always American friends at Brown's; occasionally English ones came up from the country for a day or two; it was more club than hotel. The Lewises' visits to English friends increased. At one house where they were the only Americans of their hosts' acquaintance the parties grew larger and larger with each passing year. On their last visit before the war their hostess said while tea was being cleared away, "You poor darlings, you have had *no* cocktails all these years. This time we have a surprise for you!" and the butler returned with a tray of martinis to get the temperature of the room before dinner three hours off. American ways were being adopted in England.

During this six-year period Lefty secured some 1400 letters to and from Walpole and about an equal number of titles from Walpole's library. That knowledge of Lefty's collecting had spread beyond the book trade was proved by the barber at Brown's who one day said to him, "I understand you are a book collector, sir. I have some of my collection here to show you." He paused in his snipping. "I collect all kinds of books, sir.

Here is my Barrie," and he picked up from behind the bottles of lotion a copy of *Quality Street.* Mr. Lewis opened it cautiously to keep the back cover on. The title page was torn in half and a child or an idiot had made zigzags throughout the book with colored crayons. Mr. Lewis was not the first person who had been shown it while his hair was being cut. "And here," the barber continued, again suspending his scissors, "is part of a sporting work, *Jorrocks,* sir." "Part" was the word, for not only was there but one volume, half of that was missing.

"Oh, yes," Mr. Lewis murmured.

"I can't stay out of bookshops," the barber resumed his snipping; "no more than you, sir. Of course I don't go to the West End people, Quaritch and such, but I like to browse along Charing Cross Road," the snipping stopped. "By the way, sir, would you care to buy my library? I'd let it go cheap, sir, to you." Mr. Lewis thanked him, said no, he thought not, but that he would have a shampoo. As he stepped out of the chair the barber looked at him coldly. "Is it that my collection is not good enough for America?" he asked.

The book trade itself became increasingly mindful of Horace Walpole. Several of the clerks in the big firms, modest men often kept in the lower regions, made it a point to be on the lookout for books, manuscripts, and prints that they thought might be of interest to Mr. Lewis. Such a man was Edgar Rogers who for over twenty years sent to Farmington lists of possibilities in longhand, items that Mr. Lewis was glad to have and that he would otherwise have missed. Special help was given by two friends at the British Museum, A. J. Watson in the Department of Manuscripts and A. W. Aspital in the Department of Prints and Drawings. These sergeant-majors of the staff had acquired through years of devoted and vigilant service great knowledge of the contents of their departments. They became eager volunteers in the Walpolian quest, answering innumerable queries and finding Walpoliana that had not been identified previously in the vast stores within their territories. No one anywhere was more concerned for the welfare of the Edition. Two of Watson's humbler colleagues in the Department of Manuscripts made Mr. Lewis as welcome on its outskirts. One of them, Maxwell, had been wounded at Mafeking; the other, Keenan, at Gallipoli. Maxwell was the more outgoing of the pair. His greeting lighted up the murk of Bloomsbury. If Mr. Flower or Mr. Watson was busy when Mr. Lewis arrived, Maxwell escorted him into the glass box where the visitors waited. He was the perfect host, solicitous, affable, informative. Keenan, a preoccupied man, seldom spoke and never smiled. One day when Mr. Lewis was in the box Maxwell confided to him that Keenan had a silver plate on the top of his head as a result of Gallipoli. "He is very proud of it, sir, and he don't let everybody touch it." After a decent interval Keenan advanced and took off his cap. "You may press the top of my head, sir," he said solemnly and bowed. Mr. Lewis pressed the top of his head gingerly. The silver plate gave slightly. Maxwell beamed. Mr. Lewis had received the accolade.

It was during this period that Lefty acquired his first unique Walpoliana from public libraries. Their officers and trustees approved the innovation because Lewis's collection would eventually belong to Yale, scholars would gain by having Walpoliana concentrated in one place, and their own institutions would gain by getting something they would rather have than their Walpoliana. Nineteen American and four British libraries followed Yale's lead and have been pleased by the exchange. For example, the Folger Shakespeare Library was enabled to buy an eighteenth-century reproduction of the Chandos portrait of Shakespeare that it could not otherwise have had, so its director, J. Q. Adams, wrote. "In my judgment," he added, "this is far more valuable to students than the

Chandos portrait as it now is. And the price we paid was almost exactly the same represented by your check. Thanks!"

Lefty spoke often before and after dinner on collecting, libraries, and editing, but he began to wonder just how effective these appearances were, a question answered symbolically at the meeting of the Modern Language Association in Chicago, December 28, 1937. His subject was "Problems of Editing Eighteenth-Century Correspondence," which he concluded with a proposal to establish a clearinghouse in London that would help American scholars gain access to private owners of material the scholars wished to use and which, unassisted, they might never see. The talk was in the ballroom of the Drake Hotel before about 300 people. By the lectern was a small frosted glass ball on a long rod to which Lewis, like his predecessors, addressed himself distinctly and conscientiously. After he finished he followed the cord that came out of the rod across the platform to where its plug rested quietly on the floor before an outlet. Whether the glass ball was an amplifying device or merely a Yuletide decoration he did not learn, but nothing came of the clearinghouse and the speaker thought of the ball as symbolizing the futility of much learned discussion.

Lefty's fortieth birthday was celebrated in the new library at a dinner for forty people and a dance afterwards to which many more came. All were dressed in the style of their fortieth birthday, a costume that gave the younger guests a chance to exercise their imaginations. The host wore his Bachelor of Arts gown to indicate his modest academic affiliation. He sensed dimly that his long preparation was over but that his education was not. He did not realize that older people were determining his future, yet he was reaching that point as he was shortly to learn.

XXIII

THE FRESHMAN TRUSTEE

On Saturday, February 12, 1938, Lefty received a telephone call from President Seymour of Yale to tell him that he had been elected to the Yale Corporation. This was one of the events in his life by which he later measured time.

The President and Fellows of Yale University, "the Corporation," compose the governing board of the University. There are nineteen members of it of whom three are *ex officiis:* the Governor and Lieutenant Governor of Connecticut, who rarely come to meetings, and the President of the University who presides at them. Six of the Fellows are elected by the alumni for terms of six years; the remaining ten and the President choose their own number in succession to the original ten Congregational ministers who founded the Collegiate School in 1701. The "Successors," of whom Lefty was one, serve until the Commencement following their sixty-eighth birthdays. Normally, the Corporation meets eight times a year on the second Saturday morning of the month, the standing committees the day before.

Lefty was not among strangers: Henry Coffin, Henry Sherrill, Trubee Davison, and Dean Acheson welcomed him. As he walked up the stairs in Woodbridge Hall with the latter to his initial meeting in the Corporation Room he hoped he would not die with joy before he reached it. He got there safely and was precipitated without warning into action. The President reported the recommendation of Mr. Knollenberg by the ad hoc committee on the new Librarian, nominated him, and asked the Provost, Mr. Furniss, the chairman of the committee, to comment. Mr. Furniss rose and commented. Then Mr. Lewis was asked to speak as one of the committee. Since no other member of the Corporation had spoken he did not know whether he should stand or sit. He stood; a mistake, but it did him and his candidate no harm. Mr. Knollenberg's appointment went through smoothly. The meeting continued for two hours with the reports of the President, Provost, Secretary, Treasurer, and standing committees. Although Lefty had been closer to the University than most freshman Fellows he saw that he had a great deal to learn. Conference maketh a ready man, but only after much listening. Lefty had the sense to keep quiet. Another newcomer, a more experienced man, was less prudent and made a motion at his first meeting. Afterwards Henry Coffin, a much respected senior, said to him, "New members of the Corporation are not expected to make motions at their first meetings—and you are a new member for a long time."

The President at the head of the long table was flanked by his officers, the Provost, E. S. Furniss; the Secretary, C. A. Lohmann; and next to him the Comptroller, T. W. Farnam. The Treasurer, G. P. Day, had been demoted to the foot of the table. Down its sides sat the Corporation more or less in the order of their election. The Clerical Bloc, Henry Coffin, Arthur Bradford, and Henry Sherrill, were effective supporters of liberal positions; Judges Thomas W. Swan (the former Dean of the Law School who brought it to the top rank) and Thomas D. Thacher were other much respected members. Tom Thacher was a nephew of S. D. Thacher. He was endowed with his uncle's sense of moral rectitude, but added to it conviviality on suitable occasions. Edward B. Greene of Cleveland and James Lee Loomis of Hartford were businessmen with a clear vision of what a university is, the former in part because he was a collector (of prints), the latter, because he had been through law school. R. A. Taft, who was soon to be elected to his first term in the Senate, and Dean Acheson were with Lefty at the junior end of the table. Their impatience with the controlled pace of progress increased as time went on.

Lefty was helped in his early days on the Corporation by Ed Furniss, who asked him to the Furnisses' apartment in the Graduate School Tower to talk things over on his weekly Walpolian visits. (Lefty and Ed did not realize that these delightful meetings were not correct, that a member of a governing board should not confer regularly on matters of policy with any administrative officer except its president or chairman of the board.) The two hours in the Tower flew by and Lefty would drive back to Farmington elated by a sense of accomplishment. From these talks came the support for the Historical Library in the Medical School, the reorganization of the University Press, improved alumni relations, and other desirable results. Lefty was reminded of the lesson he learned in elementary physics that the end of the lever's long arm is the most effective place to exert power.

At that time the Corporation did not dine together before the Friday evening meeting, but alone or with the Master of the College with which they were affiliated. Ed proposed to Lefty that he and a few others dine with him in the Tower, an invitation that was eagerly accepted by Henry Sherrill, Tom Thacher, Dean Acheson, and by George Van Santvoord and Morris Hadley when they were elected to the Corporation. This group, which called itself "The Cabal," continued to meet until the war. It provided champagne and got to the evening meeting later and later, to the justified annoyance of the President. After the war the Corporation was invited by the President to dine together at the Graduate Club or Mory's and The Cabal was no more.

Lefty was appointed to three of the Corporation's standing committees, Educational Policy, Honorary Degrees, and the Library and Museums. What, he asked Carl Lohmann, does the Library and Museums Committee do? "Nothing," Carl replied promptly. "It ought to be abolished!" but instead of being abolished it met regularly, visiting the Library, Art Gallery, Peabody Museum of Natural History, and other major collections in the University. The Committee learned some surprising things, such as that the Peabody Museum is really two museums, Anthropology as well as Natural History, a fact that had been lost sight of for years by the President and Fellows. The anthropological collections came from every corner of the earth, but they had lacked friends at court and so had never got a museum of their own. When the new Peabody Museum was designed their most valuable objects were squeezed into a fifth of it and the rest were stored hither and yon about the University in combustible structures. This waste of educational material showed Lefty how the hopes of benefactors may be frustrated by ignorance and indifference and the daily intrusion of more pressing affairs. He used to wonder how he could protect the Lewis Walpole Library from neglect when it would belong to the University after his death.

He learned that as a member of the Corporation he must not be exigent about the Library and Museums. A trustee who becomes a partisan of a segment of the University may build up resistance to it; if he grows emotional and overzealous the resistance may become opposition. Libraries and Museums have to be handled with special care: most speeches for them are as asphyxiating as the baccalaureate gas released from Commencement platforms. Lefty suspected that one of the troubles is the word "collections," which invokes Meissen shepherdesses and the stamps of boyhood, but he couldn't think of an acceptable substitute. He did find a way to enlist support for collections once they arrived. This was his Conscience Speech. "Yale," the speech went, "does not have to accept gifts, but if it does it has a moral duty to take proper care of them." No one could dispute that. When he followed it up by naming the trustees of the Library and Gallery Associates, names to turn any President and Treasurer pale, the most unsympathetic could see that there is something to collections, after all. Lefty's proposals were seconded by several colleagues who knew a great deal about money—Eddie Greene, Jim Loomis, and later Irving Olds, to mention only three. Without their support long overdue cataloguing and binding would not have been done, exhibition cases would not have been acquired, needed space would not have been provided. Successful businessmen—bankers, industrialists—have the power that goes with management of money. When they know that an educational institution cannot be run as if it were a bank or an insurance company and that the libraries and museums are the centers of research it moves ahead.

During the war the Lewises were in Washington, but returned each month for the Corporation's meetings and a weekend at Farmington. The Educational Policy Committee considered what buildings the University should put up when the war was over and recommended an extension to the Art Gallery, an Anthropology Museum, and a plant physiology laboratory. After the list was read Senator Taft, glaring across the table, shouted at Mr. Lewis, "Why should Yale have all these collections? What *good* are they? Why do we need a *Titian?* And these dinosaurs. I don't know what you do with *dinosaurs,* but somebody has to *dust* them, don't they? *And that costs money!*"

Mr. Lewis agreed that the subject was a large one, but the hour was late, and if the Senator wanted to continue the discussion he could do so on the ride back to Washington on the morrow.

The following day Annie Burr had prudently brought a picnic lunch that the Lewises might avoid the overcrowded dining car. Bob Taft appeared as soon as he could with the aspect of a good little boy reporting for his violin lesson. "I really would like to know about the collections, Lefty," he said meekly. The instructor looked out the window when his lecture began. The train was going over the Hell Gate Bridge. At that point Bob was in the kindergarten with respect to the subject, but he had his Ph.D. by Newark. Having secured it he talked about the Senate, how he and Arthur Vandenberg had "divided up the work" there—Vandenberg taking foreign affairs, Bob, domestic matters—how no one tells newcomers to the Senate what the rules are, how one's views of one's colleagues vary with their support or lack of it at critical junctures. He was at his best, and although he knew that Lefty disagreed with him on most political questions, he was grateful for the instruction he had just received on the importance of collections for universities and thereafter he was their staunch supporter. I wish I could recall what Lefty said that was so effective because it is a lecture that must be repeated often. No doubt he emphasized that collections are the scholar's "tools" and he may have added that libraries and museums are the humanist's laboratories, a statement that is usually taken in silently and accepted. "Laboratories" is the magic word. It evokes lean men in white jackets holding up test tubes and discovering the cure for cancer. The analogy between such researchers and those who are exploring Tudor poetry may not be immediately clear, but laymen expect to be mystified. Although "laboratories" is perhaps all that needs to be said it must be said often.

After the war Lefty got the somewhat guarded approval of

the University administration to form a Council made up of the heads of the Library and Museums. He hoped that the Council would bring the four institutions closer together to share their allied problems and to think of themselves not as rivals for administrative favor but as participants in a common purpose. It met once a month to visit the main collections of the University, as the Corporation's Committee on the Library and Museums did. Chairman Lewis asked each of its members what they considered to be the greatest lack in his institution and in some cases was able to show them that what they wanted was already in New Haven: Theodore Sizer, then Director of the Art Gallery, was delighted to find pre-Columbian gold in the Peabody Museum; Cornelius Osgood, curator of anthropology there, learned that the weights and measures he wanted were in the Streeter Collection in the Medical School's Historical Library. All over the University were important collections unknown to members of the faculty who could use them. A two-day Convocation was held in the fall of 1946 to mark the return of the University's collections to normal use. There were addresses by librarians and museum people. The convocation concluded with the conferring of honorary degrees in Woolsey Hall on eight of the visitors. A ninth degree was a surprise for the Public Orator, C. B. Tinker, and was proposed by W. S. Lewis, for whom the occasion was an emotional one.

The latter had spent six months writing a little book, *The Yale Collections,* which Carl Rollins designed. The author gave a brief account of the history and chief contents of the Library, Gallery, and Peabody Museum. He called attention to such early Yale benefactors as King George I, Isaac Newton, Bishop Berkeley. The book was dedicated to the elder Silliman, E. E. Salisbury, Daniel Coit Gilman, and Othniel Marsh, "Builders of Yale's Collections." In his Preface Lewis tried to answer Bob Taft's question, "What is the use of all this stuff?" by paraphrasing Tinker's dictum on collections, scholars, and students. He did not mention the indifference of many of the teaching profession to libraries and museums or tell what happened to the "Gibbs Cabinet," which was the first sizable collection of minerals (some 12,000 specimens) in this country. It was formed by George Gibbs of Newport, R. I., who made it while studying in Germany at the end of the eighteenth century. The elder Silliman raised $20,000 to buy it, a sensational sum for the time. The Gibbs Cabinet became one of the sights that learned Europeans had to see in America; advanced mineralogical studies here stem from it. When Lewis in his turn asked to see it he was met with embarrassment. "I have been dreading this moment," Carl Dunbar, the Director of the Museum, confessed.

"Don't tell me you can't find it!" Carl bowed his head and nodded.

"But how could you lose 12,000 rocks?" It appeared that a curator had decided it should be merged with the University's other geological collections, which had become very extensive. That was all right, but he scrambled them together without marking the Gibbs specimens and so lost their identity forever. The result of this destruction of provenance is that the beginnings of mineralogical studies in this country cannot now be written.

Lewis mentioned the chief collections at Yale, but after his book came out he learned from Sir Frederick Kenyon's *The Story of the Bible* that he had overlooked what is perhaps the most significant single object in the University, the first fragment discovered of Tatian's *Diatessaron,* the second-century Harmony of the Gospels. The leaf from Mark at Yale was unearthed in Syria in the 1930s and settled the dispute among scholars whether the original was in Greek. Although the fragment was known to the Director of the British Museum it was unknown at Yale to anyone outside the Classics Department in whose library it was concealed.

Lewis hoped that the Convocation might inspire interest in the University's collections and that Freshmen might be introduced to them by sympathetic guides as he wished that he had been introduced in his day. The first objective was reached with the informed public, which had no idea that Yale owned such treasures. Yale was not Philistine, after all; in fact, its Library and Museums had become extremely active. Large and important gifts were made to them after the Convocation; several of which were given by non-Yale people: Yale was a place where their collections would be honored and used. A step towards reaching the second objective, familiarity by the undergraduates with the great things about them, was taken by tours of the Library, Gallery, and Peabody Museum arranged for Freshmen, but most undergraduates apparently continue to go through Yale unaware of what they are missing.

Lewis also hoped that the four institutions would join in setting up big exhibitions to which each would lend pertinent material. Such an opportunity was offered by the publication of the Revised Version of the New Testament under the editorship of Dean Luther Weigle of the Yale Divinity School. Chairman Lewis visualized an exhibition in the Gallery where there is the earliest surviving Baptistry in Christendom, a Mithraeum, and other second-century objects from the Holy Land, and the Jarves Collection of Italian Primitives. The Library could have contributed early Bibles and Books of Hours; the Peabody Museum, artifacts and examples of the region's flora and fauna. Such an exhibition would have shown the universality of collections and how they touch and amplify each other, but nothing came of Lewis's suggestion. After he resigned as chairman—he realized that members of a university's governing body should not be on a working university committee—

the Council gave up meeting (its members were very busy) until it was revived by Dillon Ripley while he was Director of the Peabody Museum. During its revival David Challinor made the long overdue inventory of the collections that are scattered about the University, and that is much. It is unlikely that such a treasure as the fragment of Tatian's Harmony of the Gospels will be sequestered in the future.

As we shall see, while in Washington Lefty was active in what he thought of as the ecumenical spirit in libraries. On his return to Farmington he persuaded John Nicholas Brown and Lawrence C. Wroth to let him form the Associates of the John Carter Brown Library in Providence, a library unsurpassed in Americana to 1801. It was started a century earlier by John's grandfather and was given to Brown University in 1900 by John's father who also provided a building for it on the Brown Campus and an endowment that was handsome for the time but that no longer enabled the Library to buy all the books it needed to maintain its premier position. When Lewis gave the Colver Lectures at Brown in 1941 he was shocked to hear the Library called "a Fort Knox" and was saddened to find that some of his Providence friends were unaware of what a great library was in their midst or that in Lawrence Wroth it had a Librarian worthy of it, honored and beloved throughout the library world. This showed him that Yale's comparative indifference to its collections was normal. Although lip service is given to libraries and museums, most people in universities, as elsewhere, must be led to them gently and taught to honor them as founts of wisdom and learning. Thanks to our country's enlightened provisions for income tax and testamentary deductions of gifts to educational institutions the strength of American libraries and museums has increased vastly in recent years. Lefty believed that many in Providence and outside it would be proud to be associated with the John Carter Brown

Library and this proved to be so. The first meeting of its Associates was held at the library in January 1944 with W. S. Lewis in the chair. The big room was not half filled, but at the last meeting of his chairmanship three years later he had the satisfaction of seeing standing-room only and the membership of the Associates extended to half the states in the Union. Brown University made him an honorary Doctor of Letters in 1945. His citation was written by Lawrence Wroth who called him "Friend of Libraries."

Another chapter in the library ecumenical movement was furnished by the Watkinson Library in Hartford to the Board of which Lefty had been elected while in Washington. Among the original trustees were two men of national reputation in the book world, James Hammond Trumbull, Librarian of the Watkinson from its opening in 1863 to 1897, and George Brinley, one of the outstanding early collectors of Americana who was the second President of the Board. So happy a combination of money, knowledge, and authority is rare in library affairs. The result was a library of great strength in the subjects collected. Trumbull and Brinley were model trustees, but not as much can be said of all their successors. For eighty years the best business brains of Hartford administered the Library's funds, gravely, high-mindedly, conservatively, and did it in such a way that after eighty years the endowment of $100,000 had become $80,000.

Before his first meeting in 1944 Lefty spent an hour or so at the Watkinson. It was on the second floor of the Hartford Public Library across the hall from the Connecticut Historical Society to which it was linked by Watkinson's will. The building was a grandchild of Strawberry Hill in the Gothick-Armory style. Its main room was a nave with a ceiling lost in murk. The Librarian's cage might have been the choir in an English cathedral, the narrow balcony, a triforium. Lefty shrank back from the edge of it in alarm. There was nothing between him and the floor far below but a flimsy knee-high rail. Suppose he had a dizzy fit, crashed through the rail clutching at the empty air, and plunged down, smash, to the linguistic section beneath—! Cowering back he expressed his fright to the Librarian who confessed that the possibility of toppling overboard appeared to her recurrently in nightmare.

On his first official visit to the Watkinson the new trustee got only a general impression of its wealth and range. There were more than 100,000 books and their quality was evident from even a cursory view. It was a scholar's library that had been assembled according to the predilections of its librarians: bibliography, the Arthurian and Faust legends, our Civil War, Western Americana, Bibles and Prayerbooks, early American textbooks, linguistics, art, ethnology, long runs of learned journals in English, French, German, and Italian. Its sweep and majesty was impressive; the condition into which the books had been permitted to deteriorate was appalling. In the summer they were stewed; in the winter they were baked. The effect upon them of this normal non-air-conditioned American atmosphere was evident. The vellum bindings of the incunabula had stiffened and curled in *rigor mortis,* their spines had split open, and the ubiquitous dust had sifted in. That all five copies of the Nuremberg *Chronicle* were ruined was clear even from the weak light of the grimy bulb that dangled in the hot air some distance away.

The Library Staff numbered exactly one, the Librarian. By the time she had read the reviews of the forthcoming books, had made her recommendations to the book committee of those to buy, "accessioned" and catalogued the few that the Library bought, answered the telephone and the morning mail, received the occasional visitors and got the books they wanted, she did not have much time left over to dust 100,000 books.

The visitors were the least of her problems, for there were only three and one seventh of them a day, including the schoolchildren who strayed in to see the biggest book and the smallest book and the latest book on snakes. Occasionally a reader of the Union Catalogue in the Library of Congress would write to ask for the loan of a book not elsewhere in the country, but such a request was handled quickly: no book was allowed to leave the building under any circumstances. The trustees had recently recognized the Librarian's years of dedicated service by raising her salary to $2,100 a year.

The board met in the office of a trustee with an infirmity that kept him close to his bathroom. More than half the members were present at Mr. Lewis's first meeting. They listened thoughtfully to the sole business brought before them: What should be done with the last quarter's income, three hundred dollars? The presidents of the insurance companies, whose assets totaled billions, considered the matter until one of them suggested the purchase of an E. Bond. Heads nodded gravely in approval (a wise decision), the vote was passed, and the meeting was about to adjourn.

"Mr. President," Mr. Lewis spoke up, "I hesitate to ask a question at my first meeting, but I have one I'd like to ask, if I may."

"Certainly, Mr. Lewis."

"What is the purpose of this library?"

There was a stunned silence, except for an encouraging laugh from Mr. Lewis's Yale classmate, Lucius F. Robinson, Jr. He urged the newcomer to give his views on the Library. Mr. Lewis could not pretend to anything but the most superficial impression of it, yet its riches were obvious and the condition into which they had been allowed to deteriorate lamentable. All the money in the world couldn't replace the Library. The building in which it was housed was one of the worst fire hazards in Hartford; the books were decaying on the shelves; the library was of little use to anyone at present. The Freshman concluded with a variation on his Conscience Speech: "Until we get a modern building and a new catalogue we are not carrying out the wishes of David Watkinson." The stirring of New England consciences was almost audible.

The trustees' first move was an attempt to merge the Watkinson with its neighbors, the Connecticut Historical Society and the Hartford Public Library. Committees of the three libraries met and appeared to be in agreement, the Mayor was eager to help, everything went smoothly in spite of the complications, legal, financial, historical, geographical, and sentimental, until an insurmountable obstacle was met: the Historical Society decided not to go along. Its President was also President of the Watkinson. As President of the latter he voted for the merger. Then he walked across the hall and voted against it as President of the Historical Society. This was an example of conscientious trusteemanship: he believed that the Watkinson would gain by the merger and that the Historical Society would lose and he voted accordingly. The merger did not take place; all the meetings, all the resolutions, all the conversations after dinner, all the luncheons of creamed chicken and peas, all the telephoning, letters, and carbon copies had been in vain.

What was to be done? A Friends of the Watkinson was suggested, but people shouldn't be asked to give money for books in a firetrap. The trustees' first duty was to get them into a modern building.

Hartford had then no university, but it had Trinity College, whose President is an ex-officio member of the Watkinson Board. It needed a new library building badly. Lefty called on Keith Funston, its President. If Trinity built a library to include the Watkinson's books and recatalogued them there was a possibility, Lewis thought, that the Watkinson trustees would hand over their books and endowment. He pointed out that were the books at Trinity its library would be nearly doubled in size and vastly strengthened in quality; in fact, Trinity would overnight become one of the strongest smaller liberal arts colleges in the country.

Keith Funston was impressed. "But," he said, "we are in the middle of a fund drive."

"For what?" Lewis asked.

"Well, we've got to do something about our library, but most of the money will go to a field house."

After the field house was built Lewis met the President by chance on a train. "You remember our talk about the possibility of the Watkinson coming to Trinity?" he asked. To get the Watkinson was now his first objective, he said. The College had the land and some money for the Library, but four times as much was needed to build a suitable building and endow it. Before he tried to raise it he would have to be assured by the Watkinson trustees that they would give their books and endowment if the building were provided.

The trustees gave the assurance, Paul Mellon's Foundation, the Old Dominion, gave the money, the State Legislature and the Superior Court of Connecticut approved the transfer of the books, endowment, and Librarian, and the new Library was built to Trinity's immense gain. The history of the Watkinson taught Lewis that a fine library will languish when its founder dies if the trustees do not understand its purpose and are primarily concerned with protecting it from use. He also learned that the best financial minds may go astray and that they may be guided by an obvious question from one who knows nothing about the management of money.

By the time he was fifty Lewis had become a junior member of several other boards including the Institute for Advanced Study at Princeton. The boy who was the despair of Mr. Dodge at Thacher had become the nominal boss of Einstein. At his first meeting he was called on to decide whether the Institute should contribute $300,000 towards the construction of the first of the electronic computers in this country. If it did the Navy would give an additional $800,000. Lewis was invited to Princeton the night before the meeting to learn about the computer from its designer, John von Neumann, and two of his colleagues, a trio with low voices and eyes that looked deep into the mystery of things. Von Neumann was the man in the Manhattan Project who decided where the bomb should be exploded over Hiroshima. If it was exploded at the point he recommended he explained what would happen—so many buildings blotted out, so many people killed, so many maimed. The bomb was exploded at that point and everything happened as he said it would. On the night of Lewis's first visit to the Institute he described the mechanical and mathematical niceties of the computer three times to the new trustee, each time in a louder voice. After the third repetition Lewis was ready to vote for the project on one condition. What was it? "That you do not explain the computer to me a fourth time." When it was given its first problem Lewis happened to be again at Princeton. Robert Oppenheimer, the new Director of the Institute, asked him, please, to witness the demonstration; it would mean much to everybody if he would; people were working all night to get everything ready for him—just as they had at Camp Kearney. It was no time for protestations of ignorance. In the morning he was led away to the little building where the historic trial was to take place. The atmosphere was as tense as in the Camp Kearney dugout. The men who had been up all night were unshaved and bloodshot with fatigue. Mr. Lewis was led up to the computer, a Frankenstein of wheels and sprockets. As soon as he was in place the countdown began, "Ten, nine, eight . . ." At zero there was a blue flash—and that was all. The silence that followed was tragic. Lewis bowed and left. He had learned when a trustee should say nothing.

XXIV

WASHINGTON I

Chance plays a part in one's education as in everything else. If Dunham Barney's prospective roommate at Yale had not flunked his Virgil exam Lewie would not have been Dunham's roommate. Lefty's purchase of Lady Louisa Stuart's notes on Jesse's *Selwyn* at York was the end of a long chain of chances. He just happened to walk down Chancery Lane and into Hodgson's the day before the sale in which Walpole's letters to Pinkerton were sold; and it was by chance that the Lewises lunched with the Archibald MacLeishes at Conway, Mass., on the day that a former Archivist of the United States called Archie on the telephone.

This particular intervention of chance occurred in August 1941. Archie, then Librarian of Congress, was helping William J. Donovan start the agency that was at first called the Coordinator of Information and later the Office of Strategic Services. The Lewises had barely heard of it, but their host convinced them of its importance once we were in the war (no one at the table doubted we would be in it eventually). What would the new agency do? Gather information and receive the reports of other government agencies and departments, write reports and send them direct to the President, whose intelligence agency it would be. Would there be spies? Yes, probably, but they hadn't got to spies yet. The novel thing about C.O.I., Archie explained, was the mobilization of scholars to deal with intelligence. President Baxter of Williams had joined up and so had William L. Langer and Edward S. Mason of Harvard, Geroid Robinson of Columbia, Conyers Read of Pennsylvania, Robert Gooch of Virginia, Calvin Hoover of Duke and many more from all over the country. Who was there from Yale? Nobody as yet. Yale, Archie said, was not as well thought of outside its family as within it. What was essential, he added, was a system for filing and indexing the government reports and documents that the C.O.I. would be getting so that they could be found quickly. Such a system was unknown in Washington and the success of the new organization depended upon its having one. Archie and Bill Donovan thought they had just the man to invent it, a former Archivist of the United States.

The telephone rang. It was the former Archivist who turned the job down. Gloom descended on the MacLeish luncheon table, the one and only time it has ever been there.

Riding back to Farmington Lefty discussed with Annie Burr the possibility of offering himself for the rejected post. The Lewises were what the isolationists of the time called "warmongers." They believed that we should be in the war and that the sooner we were in it the better. Lefty joined a group to combat isolationism and wrote a letter to *The New York Times* that was printed at the head of its correspondence column. He received several anonymous replies, one of which ended, "It is evident what you are, a Jewish munitions maker." When a group of faculty people at Yale invited Oxford to send mothers and children of dons to safety in and about New Haven the Lewises arranged for eighteen of them to move to Farmington, of whom eight, who became intimate members of their family, were under their immediate protection in a house close by. On hearing that the Lewises were planning to have them in the old part of their own house Ross was startled: "In *this* house, sir? But you and Mrs. Lewis are not used to children and you will find them very trying," and so he saved the Lewises, their protégés, and himself much suffering. Relations were strained when Felicity, aged ten, was discovered twice smoking in a barn. In the ensuing contest of wills Uncle Lefty, pitifully inexperienced as a disciplinarian of the young, could claim only a draw. Annie Burr gave a mobile feeding kitchen during the blitz in memory of Horace Walpole, a novel memorial, but perhaps one not inappropriate for the man who had imagined "some curious traveller from Lima" giving a description of the ruins of St. Paul's.

Lefty thought he could do the job that Archie had talked about. The Edition would go smoothly in New Haven with Warren Smith, George Lam, and Charles Bennett until the war came, and he would read the proof in Washington of the two volumes that were going through the press. At any rate, it was no time to think of one's private concerns. (Lefty's attitude towards the pending war was very different from what it had been in 1917.) Annie Burr listened quietly on the two-hour drive back to Farmington and when they got there she encouraged him to offer himself for the archival post. He did so that night: his experience, Archie knew, was limited to devising the files and indexes at Farmington and to giving the course in the Yale Graduate School on the management of historical material. In a few days he was on his way to Washington as Chief of the Central Information Division of the Research and Analysis Branch of the Coordinator of Information, a Division that then consisted of one person, himself.

Annie Burr followed soon with the household, which was augmented by Bruno, a chauffeur who had been with Mrs. Auchincloss, and the two poodles, Fidèle and Pom. Ross viewed the move with some disappointment. "I had hoped, sir," he confessed, "that we would be going to the Court of St. James's." The Lewises rented a small 1820 house in P Street, Georgetown. Although they liked it, Ross found it disappointing. "It's only camping out, sir," he said, "but it is for the cause." Pom did not care for the house, either, because there was only one staircase. He was used to having a staircase of his own at Farmington and since he had come to the Lewises first he would not allow Fidèle to go up it. Fidèle, the heavier dog, sent him to the hospital. On his return Pom was taken back to Farmington. Ross's grief was articulate: "He is my closest friend," but Mr. Lewis stood firm. He was to learn that the difficulty of Pom and Fidèle about the staircase was not unusual in official Washington. The reflecting pool in the Mall in which Ross won yacht races consoled him for the loss of Pom and his employer's lowly status and he discovered a radio station that nobody else heard. Only the most horrible news came over it such as, "Sweden has declared war on us, sir." Mr. Lewis brushed off his report that the Japanese had bombed Pearl Harbor until Ross with dignity turned on Mr. Lewis's own radio for confirmation.

In a few months Lefty bought a larger 1790 house at the corner of N and 28th streets and was able to renovate it before the building restrictions were in force. When the house next door, which had originally been a part of it, turned out to be a Negro brothel he had to buy it also, paying something for the good will that was of little use to him. Washington real estate has always been uncertain.

Pauline Sabin Davis, who had become National Chairman of the Red Cross Volunteer Services, asked AB to be the head of two of them, Staff Assistants and Home Service. Marie Bissell, Ada MacLeish, Dot Davison, Helen Lippmann, and Grace Eustis headed other services. AB was very happy. It was the busiest interval of the Lewises' lives together. Washington was full of old friends with whom they dined and they made new intimacies, chief of whom were with Ray and Maude Atherton. On weekends the Lewises played tennis and croquet and bowled in the Georgetown alleys. The gasoline shortage kept them close to home, but they could get out to Merrywood, Hughdie Auchincloss's beautiful place on the Potomac in Virginia, for Sunday lunch and croquet.

Lefty found himself with an agreeable group of men during the week, all of whom were strangers to him except Sherman Kent, the sole member of the Yale faculty chosen at the outset for the Research and Analysis Branch. They had disrupted their lives and the lives of their families because they believed that the country must get into the war as soon as possible. Most of them were too young to have been in the earlier war and regretted it. Here was their chance to show that teachers—the respected and scorned—could be of use in wartime. Confusion, delay, compatibility, brought the new colleagues rapidly together. There were interminable interviews with Civil Service officials and complicated "job descriptions" that had to be written in a jargon as odious as the academic jargon. The newcomers were discovering how the government is run. For years they had been telling their students why Charles the First lost his head and where Wilson went wrong in 1919, but of the machinery that runs governments most of them knew little. They discovered that whereas it was easy at the outset to set up jobs and determine salaries they were to learn later that to get an extra much needed clerk at the lowest salary required as much preparation as writing a new lecture and that they might be denied the clerk in the end. They were professionals in universities, but to the Army, Navy, and State Departments they were unwelcome amateurs who were tolerated only because they were protected by the President. Yet the newcomers in Washington during the six months before Pearl Harbor look back to that time with particular satisfaction.

Then none was for a party,
Then all were for the state.

The one stipulation that the new Chief of the Central Information Division made before he took the post was that he should have an experienced member of the Civil Service as his assistant, and that is what Laurence Egbert was. The Division filled up with stenographers and clerks. (Egbert said that one reason why it was easy to get them for the Division was that the Chief stood up when they came to be interviewed and when they left, an unheard of courtesy in the Civil Service.) Lefty recruited on his own George Young and Kenneth MacLeish who brought Howe Bancroft, and the four produced the new system. It was gratifying when they were able to answer their first test, What electrical current is used in Surinam? in record time. C.I.D. made a good name for itself; after a while the "old-line" Departments came to see their own documents there because it was quicker for them to cross half Washington than to hunt for them in their own files. The Division was pleased but not surprised when a committee of the War College surveyed all filing and indexing systems in Washington and chose it as the model for its own.

After the C.I.D. was running along on its own steam Lefty spent much time with Colonel Frank Ross and Commander Francis Denebrink who were assigned to the C.O.I. as liaison between the Central Information Division and the Army and Navy. After the Division was running smoothly they had little to do except to meet in Lefty's office, close the door importantly, and color their meerschaum pipes, which Lefty had provided. Pearl Harbor ended these meetings: Frank was sent to San Francisco; Denny, who became a Captain, an event Lefty celebrated at the Metropolitan Club with a dinner, was asked by Admiral King to stay and draw up a plan for the reorganization of the Navy Department. Thereafter for several months he and Lefty lunched together each Tuesday, alternating between the Army and Navy Club and the Metropolitan. Denny would tell with never a needless word long and funny "Episodes" in his life. Lunch over they would go to his large office in the Joint Chiefs of Staff building where an elaborate chart of the different elements of the Naval Command covered a blackboard. New names were wanted for old groups. Denny is a big man with glasses that assumed an owlish expression as he stood in front of the board, chalk in hand.

"Our problem today, Lefty," he would say solemnly and distinctly, "is what are we to call this group?" and he would indicate it on the board.

"What do they do?"

After Lefty was told what they did he would suggest a grandiose government word. If Denny approved it he would purse his lips, nod, and write it in; if the word was not acceptable Denny would shake his head slowly. "No, I'm afraid that's not quite it. Please try again." Denny reported the results of this collaboration to Admiral King. When the plan was finished it went to the White House where it was turned down immediately by the Commander-in-Chief. However, Admiral King was able to carry out most of its proposals, including the transfer of the O.S.S. to the Chiefs of Staff, a course that Denny has recently affirmed was owing to Lefty's conviction that the Research and Analysis Branch deserved to be used at the highest level instead of being held suspiciously at arm's length. Denny's reward was immediate: within twenty-four hours after the President's rejection of his plan he was Captain of the *Brooklyn* on his way to take part in the Battle of Casablanca.

He ended the war a Vice Admiral. These friendships were Lefty's introduction to the high quality of our regular military officers, their sense of profession, the range of their training, their modesty and companionability.

Lefty also acted as the editor of the reports issued by the Research and Analysis Branch. I can recall only two of them, the one by Ralph Bunche on the American Negro and Sherman Kent's on Madagascar, which was made up of biographical sketches provided by a salty character who had lived there for years and knew the worst about everybody. The difficulty Lefty had in trying to understand what some of the others wished to say led him to formulate a style sheet with the assistance of a dozen of his colleagues. He wrote the preface to it, the only one of his O.S.S. compositions that he kept. "The style sheet," he wrote, "represents a certain amount of compromise, since our language and its usage are continually changing and no two people, no matter how experienced, follow the same style. It doesn't much matter what style we adopt so long as we all make every effort to follow it. It may be true that 'with consistency a great soul has simply nothing to do,' but the less soul in government reports the better.

"The chief fault with the style of our reports has not been its inconsistencies, wide as they have been. It has not even been the perpetration of hanging participles, elegant variations, abnormal inversions, and the other stylistic misdemeanors which are exposed in Fowler. All these and much besides are to be found on our record, but they are peccadilloes compared to the offense of our turgidity and wordiness. All of our reports could have been written with fewer words and all would have been improved by the resulting clarity. There is some tendency to regard careful writing as a frill which may be regarded indulgently by a world at peace, but which is to be jettisoned in wartime. Our verbosity has frequently led to misunderstanding. Hundreds of our sentences must be read more than once to be understood, not because of the profundity of the thought, but because of the ambiguity of its expression.

"The answer is to write short sentences, for few people can remain articulate with too many clauses under the belt."

This spirited performance was sent by Felix Frankfurter to his brethren of the Court, where it made as little impression as it did in the O.S.S. The flood of bad academic writing was not to be swept back by one little broom.

Lefty also edited a series of pamphlets that were written to inform troops about the foreign countries where they were to be sent. The authors of them were specialists who gave advice that the average American soldier needed, such as not to get ideas about Moslem women or to urinate on mosques. With the pamphlet on Britain Lefty had more to do. Lord Halifax kindly offered to look it over for him and, very courteously, made two or three suggestions such as that it might perhaps be as well not to say that Leeds was in the Midlands. While Lefty was on vacation his uncorrected typescript was rushed through the press and a million copies of it printed with none of Lord Halifax's corrections. It was boiled down and printed in the *Reader's Digest*. He was led to doubt the effectiveness of his most widely circulated work when flying to England in September 1942 one of his fellow passengers, an Air Corps Captain from Oregon, mentioned the article and said that the English were "different."

"In what way?" the author ventured to ask.

"Why, look," the Captain explained, "their Queen is a Rumanian, isn't she?"

Lefty was more successful in carrying out Operation Telephone Book in London, whither he went with Bill Langer and Conyers Read to help set up the O.S.S. branch in Grosvenor Street. The flight by hydroplane took nineteen hours, and gave

Lefty a disconcerting sense of the time machine spinning backwards: England, which had always been about a week away was now less than a day and had lost something in consequence. In London when he was shown into his office he closed the door and wondered what he was supposed to do. While waiting to find out he thought he might as well telephone friends and asked the switchboard operator to get him Robin Flower at the British Museum.

"Certainly, Mr. Lewis, but it will take about two hours."

"Two hours!"

"At least. You see we have no telephone book and unless we know the number we have to go through Enquiries. It takes just on two hours."

"Can't we get a telephone book?"

"Oh, no, I'm afraid it's quite impossible." Lefty saw a chance to serve his country and justify the use of the taxpayer's money in sending him abroad. He went to the National Portrait Gallery.

"Would you care to make a contribution to the American War Effort?" he asked its Director, H. M. Hake, a charter member of the Yale Walpole Advisory Committee. Hake hesitated. "Have you an old telephone book?" Back in Grosvenor Street Mr. Lewis received the plaudits of a grateful office with a modesty that heightened the mystery he preserved round his achievement.

He was appalled by the war damage. Maggs's old shop in which he had spent so many hours was gone and so were Dobell's and Dulau's. Nothing was left of St. Anne's, Soho, in whose courtyard he and Annie Burr had spent that idyllic Sunday afternoon, except a fragment of its west front on which still stood Walpole's memorial to King Theodore of Corsica. The houses with their exposed bedrooms stained by rain and pigeons took him back to San Francisco after the Fire. The change of attitude towards Americans was also marked. It struck Lefty one day when he hurried into an office building to escape a sudden shower. The entrance filled up rapidly with dingy people in waterproofs. At last a G.I. dashed in, a slight youth with a pleasant smile. He watched the rain unaware that he was being gazed at with curiosity and respect. Lefty sensed the English instinct to ingest alien bodies. Saxons, Angles, and Jutes, Romans, Danes, and Normans had been absorbed, and now he saw the ancient visceral machinery going to work on the young American. When the shower stopped the G.I. asked a neighbor a question. The man eagerly pointed up the street and jerked his thumb to the right and the boy was gone; so a cardinal in a bird feeder might fly away from sparrows. For a few minutes the young G.I. was the symbol of hope to a group of everyday Britons. I have often wondered how he fared on Omaha Beach.

The most memorable occasion of this visit for Lefty was a dinner of the Biblios, of which he was "the American corresponding member." The Biblios is a club of book collectors and dealers that was then presided over by Michael Sadleir and John Carter. After the dinner John Sparrow walked back to Brown's Hotel with Lefty through the blackout. The future Warden of All Souls had something to do with Intelligence, just how much Lefty couldn't make out. The keeping and guarding of secrets was as firmly implanted in the members of O.S.S. as it was in Yale undergraduates, but on that night Lefty made a remark that he should not have made. When John wondered why the Allies didn't invade Europe Lefty, who knew of the forthcoming African landings, said significantly, "Europe isn't the only continent," and agonized when he thought of his indiscretion until the landings had been safely accomplished.

Apart from the telephone book, his mission for the O.S.S. accomplished little, but when he flew home he did carry with him three folio volumes of Walpole's unpublished manuscripts.

Parkinson's Law operated rapidly in C.I.D. Lefty was able to secure a French library of ten thousand volumes, which greatly enlarged the resources of the Division. A Section called Pictorial Records was transferred to it from New York where it had been under the direction of a regular army colonel who never missed a matinee. The budget of Pictorial Records in New York was just under a million dollars. This provided for expensive office space and over a hundred personnel who were not very busily engaged in collecting "strategic photographs" of military targets in Latin America and the British Isles just in case the Germans occupied those territories. Pictorial Records was less concerned with Italy, France, Belgium, Holland, and Germany. The colonel was disposed of and all but thirty-odd of his staff were moved to Washington. The budget was reduced by over $800,000, a saving that more than paid for the trip to England of the Division's chief. He engaged Tony Garvan and Alec Vietor to explore the Italian engineering publications in the Yale Library, which abounded in photographs of hydroelectric plants, docks, and other targets, a large and informative collection. These photographs, he trusted, would prove to be more useful than similar views of Liverpool and Montevideo. Further progress was made when American tourists were encouraged to send to Pictorial Records snapshots they had taken in Europe in the hope that among them might be some of strategic significance. The plea was all too successful. Hundreds of thousands arrived showing equestrian monuments and sea gulls, but there were also some photographs that were welcome. How to handle them? John F. Langan, a man of infinite resource who brightened the official life of C.I.D.'s chief, asked if he might experiment with inserting a microfilm picture of the photographs on an IBM card. He succeeded, and it is pleasant to record that today the Langan Aperture Cards are used by the Department of Defense and have brought their inventor a well-earned reward.

As the staff of C.I.D. grew the Division was subjected to tightened control by the Civil Service Commission. Lefty's interest in it languished. Warren Smith came down from the Walpole Room and the central part of the Division was therefore in the best possible hands. I see Lefty sitting one day at his desk and thinking that he should revive his interest by pouring into his work the "libido" he had summoned up for the index to Walpole's "Paris Journals." He failed to do it because he was spending half his time in a job that was more interesting to him at the other end of Washington.

XXV

WASHINGTON II

Soon after the Lewises moved to Washington Archie MacLeish began urging Lefty to have some connection, any connection, with the Library of Congress. The newcomer pointed out that Archie had got him down there for quite a different purpose, but the Librarian of Congress replied, "I am going to call you every night until you have found something to do there," and he did. Lefty's introduction to the Library had occurred forty years earlier when Wilmarth was given postcards that featured its goldleaf dome and marble galleries with Melpomene and Euterpe and their sisters in blue and gold and crimson languishing on the ceilings. He learned later of its millions of library cards that circulate throughout the land, but of its collections he knew nothing. The first glimpse of them under the guidance of Frederick Goff of the Rare Book Room bowled him over. This was the National Library and it was worthy of the Republic that was so largely unaware of it. Why not have a small advisory council of librarians and collectors to whom the Librarian could turn for advice (and possible gifts) and who would act as the Library's friendly emissaries throughout the country? Lefty's proposal was taken up by Archie. The Librarian's Council of the Library of Congress was formed with W. S.

Lewis as its Chairman and an Executive Committee composed of Randolph Adams, Librarian of the William L. Clements Library, Ann Arbor; Julian Boyd, Librarian of Princeton; Miss Belle daCosta Greene, Librarian of the Pierpont Morgan Library; Bernhard Knollenberg, Librarian of Yale; Keyes Metcalf, Librarian of Harvard; Lessing Rosenwald; and Lawrence Wroth, Librarian of the John Carter Brown Library, Providence. Thomas W. Streeter was added soon afterwards.

When the Committee met at lunch on February 27, 1942, it was with an agreeable sense of serving its country in the way its members were best fitted to serve it (they were all beyond the musket-carrying age), as a bibliographical Home Guard. Sixteen other librarians and collectors from all parts of the country were chosen to fill out the Council. Each member of the Executive Committee became chairman of a committee to deal with a division of the Library—Bibliography, Fine Arts, Hispanic America, Maps, Manuscripts, Periodicals, Rare Books, and a new project, Publications. Each Chairman was to select the members of his committee of three or four who were not to be restricted to the Council. Chairman Lewis took Publications as his committee.

He lunched on Mondays at the Library with the Librarian and his chief assistants, Luther Evans, Verner Clapp, David Mearns, and Fred Goff. Soon Lefty was saying "we" instead of "you." Many of the things that were talked about influenced later developments in the Library, including the *Library of Congress Quarterly* and the catalogue of Jefferson's library. Such discussions are the despair of the historian because they have often more influence on subsequent events than the formal meetings where minutes are kept, yet they tend to fade from the minds of those who took part in them and no one is quite sure who said what or when.

Lefty would go to the Library several afternoons a week.

Fred Goff would call up the chief of one of the Divisions and say that he was bringing Mr. Lewis round to see him. The chief had heard something of these mysterious visits of Mr. MacLeish's friend (Lefty was called "Colonel House") and awaited him with curiosity, hope, and apprehension. Here was a chance to advertise the needs of his division, but suppose this stranger failed to understand them—or thought them illusory? How significant *was* his visit? Life in the Civil Service has endless inspections and threats of amputation, was Mr. Lewis a new device to harass and dismay? Despite their natural bewilderment Mr. Lewis's hosts without exception gave him pleasant and instructive afternoons. What he was able to do for them in return was, alas, little.

Two impressions emerged from these visits, the richness of our national library and the desirability of having the leading libraries of the country work more closely with it and with each other. Lewis dreamt of purposeful cooperation. The Library of Congress had already taken a long stride towards it by setting up the Union Catalogue to which all the great libraries had contributed except Yale. Lefty now saw Yale's refusal to cooperate as a denial of its national responsibility.

Working against the cooperative spirit was library competition for rare books, a contest in which Lefty had been as active as anyone, but his experience proved that libraries could be generous and commonsensical about them. If public and university libraries would exchange with a private collector unique books for others more valuable to them as they had with him (on the understanding that the books they exchanged would go eventually to Yale), they might be willing to do the same with each other. This cooperation need not be confined to our own country, as Lewis could also illustrate from his experience with the British Museum. In 1935 Robin Flower told him, "You may be glad to hear we have decided to buy no more

Walpoliana because we want you to have all of it." Lefty *was* glad to hear it and when he had a chance to buy Edward Fitzgerald's correspondence with Fanny Kemble, which the Museum wanted but could not afford, he was happy to give it to them. This in the beginning was his idea of library cooperation, but he came to see that the books being published in Europe during the war offered an opportunity for cooperation after the war was won. Left to themselves American libraries would then buy as many of them as they could afford without regard to what other libraries were doing. There should be in this country a copy of every book published abroad, but many of them are so special and unimportant that no more than one copy need be acquired. Why shouldn't the leading research libraries get together, agree to cover the waterfront, and assume responsibility for the books in certain segments of it? All subjects would be divided among the cooperating libraries and their holdings recorded and made available on call to readers borrowing them through their librarians. Each library would be free to buy any book it wanted as in the past.

This proposed cooperation was advisable to save space as well as money. Most libraries were contending with "a space problem" or knew that they would soon be doing so; a recent study showed that American libraries double in size every sixteen years. Librarians had been like the pioneers pushing west into a land of endless bounty, and it was disconcerting to find that the frontier had been reached. They were fighting back the rising tide of books, knocking out a wall here, stuffing shelves in there, persuading their trustees to build a wing, an annex, a whole new building. The tide was rising higher and higher. Had perhaps the time come, Lewis asked in 1942, to substitute the dykes of cooperation for the broom of rugged individuality?

With these thoughts in mind he welcomed the Executive

Committee of the Council at Farmington on October 9, 1942. This group, it seemed, held the future of American libraries in its hands; at least, if it couldn't get together it was unlikely that any group of librarians ever would. "Library Cooperation" was the first matter on the agenda. Julian Boyd prepared a memorandum recommending that "at least one copy of all books important to scholarship should be available somewhere in the United States, and second, that their availability should be of record. To accomplish these desiderata libraries must accept responsibility for the acquisition and service of materials within every discipline, according to an accepted schedule of distribution on the basis of subject fields." The Council adopted the recommendation; a subcommittee was appointed with Keyes Metcalf as Chairman. This is how, so far as I can recall it, "the Farmington Plan" came into being. Keyes Metcalf's knowledge, imagination, and statesmanship made it a success. On his recommendation the Carnegie Corporation of New York provided the funds that put it into operation on January 1, 1948, with the publications of France, Sweden, and Switzerland. The 1961 edition of the *Farmington Plan Handbook* fills 141 ample pages. It shows that 145 countries from Aden to Zanzibar have become "Farmington Countries" and names the American library that is responsible for acquiring each country's publications: Northwestern takes care of Angola, the University of Florida, Surinam; the books on sugar crops go to Purdue, those on soap to Wayne. The Farmington Plan is affording employment to many people around the world today.

Lefty's connection with the Library of Congress faded after the war. The status of the Librarian's Council was not clear. Who paid its modest expenses? How did it fit into the governmental scheme of things? The Council disappeared, but it had helped its Chairman to realize that the Yale Library is not the only library in the country. He saw that what he thought of as the ecumenical spirit can be effective if all the institutions concerned are generous-minded, but that if the largest and richest take the attitude, "We are all for unity; you join us," altruism withers rapidly. The widening of Chairman Lewis's horizon did not end with libraries; it extended to all humanistic research. Scientists were performing their miracles by using each other's "disciplines," and historians, classicists, sociologists, and students of literature could do the same if they would be willing to learn from each other. Medical humanists showed the way. A coda to Chairman Lewis's connection with the Library of Congress was a lunch with Bernhard Knollenberg at the Metropolitan Club in 1944 after Knollie was asked by the White House to recommend Archie MacLeish's successor as Librarian. Knollie said that he would like to propose W. S. Lewis. Lefty was of course pleased, but returned the same answer that he had made to Charlie Seymour seven years earlier, and I am sure that it was the right answer in both cases.

The summer of 1942 had fifty-four days of 90 degrees and over in Washington. Lefty was able to get an air-conditioner for his office and two more for 2726 N Street, but his *malaise* was not to be cured by air-conditioners. When he went to Washington he cautioned himself against the state of mind that would lead him into illness when things went the way he did not want them to go, yet when the crises came he failed to curb the destructive forces. After a year and a half in Washington he began losing weight and gaining irritability, the normal effects of government service. C.I.D. was going well, someone else could run it better, and Lefty resigned. The Ray Athertons asked him to join them at Ottawa, where Ray had been sent as our first Ambassador, and Lefty went for a few weeks, grateful for their timely demonstration of friendship. He did something (I can't remember just what) about Canadian-American cultural relations and was reintroduced to bridge with the Goren count. Lefty's job took the Lewises to Washington in 1941, but they stayed until June 1944 for Annie Burr's.

David and Marjorie Finley sent them off to Farmington with a little dinner at which were the Achesons and Frankfurters, and the six stood on the steps waving good-bye when the Lewises left for the station. The three years in Washington had got them away from their Farmington–Yale–Walpole routine and showed them that life outside an ivory tower is not too bad; that, in fact, life in an ivory tower is improved by a vacation from it. On looking back at the Lewises' sojourn in Washington I view with satisfaction Lefty's C.I.D. filing and indexing system, which I understand is now used by the State Department, and his proposal of the Farmington Plan, which drew the nation's libraries closer together and so strengthened its educational system. Another contribution that he made was a phrase that he used to describe the most secret branch of the O.S.S. and that came to be applied to the O.S.S. itself and similar intelligence agencies. He picked it up from Admiral Pott, the British Naval attaché, who used it to describe a member of the Embassy. The phrase was "cloak and dagger." I look back on three weekly engagements—lunch with Denny (on Tuesdays), Ray Atherton (on Thursdays), Wednesday matinees with Fritz Liebert at the O.S.S. movie—with particular pleasure; the Metropolitan Club was a daily relief from office routine; small dinners at which everything was discussed but the war (*that* we had all day) were relaxing.

A lunch with David Finley paved the way for Lefty to resume an official connection with Washington twenty-two years later. David, as Director of the National Gallery, had just acquired the use of the old Federal Court Building and he asked Lefty what he would do with it. The latter announced promptly, "Make it into a National Portrait Gallery." David thought well of the solution and set the machinery in motion to bring it about. The wheels ground for twenty-one years before the Congress voted it into existence as a branch of the Smithsonian. David had saved the old Patent Office Building from demolition for a parking space, and the National Portrait Gallery was assigned its ground floor. Messrs. Finley and Lewis were appointed to the Commission on it; John Nicholas Brown, a Regent of the Smithsonian, was its Chairman; Julian Boyd was another old friend on it. The hour was late to begin the National Portrait Gallery, hundreds of portraits that "ought" to be in it had been given long since to other galleries, but a start had been made.

The "setting up" of the Gallery's staff took Commissioner Lewis back to the first weeks of the O.S.S., the "job descriptions" of the Civil Service and the difficulty of knowing what is going to be wanted once the new institution is functioning. The jobs had been set up before the Commission was appointed and did not provide enough rank and salary for the Associate Director, who was to be in charge of the library and research activities of the Gallery. These, the commissioners believed, should make the N.P.G. the clearinghouse for iconographical studies of Americans. An imaginatively picked library of books, prints, photographs, and microfilm is essential for this purpose. If it is created American studies will be enabled to make a wide and fruitful expansion. The Civil Service Commission held a hearing on raising the Associate Director's grade. Lewis did not know what were the current golden words in the Civil Service vocabulary—"librarian" and "research" he suspected were no more honored than they were in 1941—and guessed correctly that he could not go wrong with "science" and "laboratory." "Iconography" was an inspiration, an unusual, scientific-sounding word, that impresses anyone whether he understands it or not. The desired increase in grade was granted.

John Brown put Lewis on a committee with Julian Boyd, Richard Shryock, and Catherine Drinker Bowen to draw up rules to guide the Commissioners in determining which individuals will be represented in the Gallery, an agreeable task that made the committee feel that they were doorkeepers to posterity. It had been settled that the overriding criterion should be the national importance of the sitter rather than the quality of the portrait: a fine Copley of a Boston merchant belongs in Boston or in whatever gallery can get it; the first Governor of Idaho belongs in Boise; but photographs of their portraits should be in the Gallery's library. Besides the obvious candidates, the Founding Fathers of the Republic and the Presidents, the leading writers, artists, jurists, medical men, and so on, the committee envisaged rooms in which outstanding figures in sport and crime will be displayed. There will be countless problems and difficulties. What can be done about the earliest explorers and settlers such as Roger Williams, of whom no authentic portrait is known? Thanks to Andrew Mellon who saw that there would one day be a National Portrait Gallery and who collected some eighty portraits for it, the nation has Pocohantas, but the Puritan maiden Priscilla is yet to be found. The Gallery must have a large fund for the purchase of pictures raised by private subscription so that it can buy portraits of Booker T. Washington, say, without a congressman from Alabama shutting off the Gallery's federal funds. Commissioner Lewis is grateful for this new connection in Washington. It helps enrich what Felix Frankfurter called "the great decades." "Welcome to the Great Decades," Felix wired when Lefty reached his sixtieth birthday.

Lefty met Felix first in 1940 while the Lewises and Achesons were staying with the MacLeishes at Conway. The Frankfurters were spending the summer at Heath nearby, a pleasant, but not very conversational place; an evening at Conway released pent-up ebullience in the Justice. He had taught Dean and Archie at the Harvard Law School and was a major figure in their lives. He regarded the Lewises on the first evening with some reserve. Were they, perhaps, on the conservative side? When at dinner Dean raised the question put to him by his son David, "What is all this about the Great Man? Are there any today?" Felix held forth at once on Holmes. Then Lefty diffidently suggested Thomas Mann. "Oh, no!" Felix burst out. "No! No! No!" When Archie supported Mann he received the same answer. Then he asked Felix, "Have you ever read any of Mann's novels?" Felix ignored this question and went on with his general expostulation. Whereupon Lefty pointed out, "That, Mr. Justice, is a question that can be answered 'Yes' or 'No,' " and their friendship had begun.

In Washington Lefty spent every Sunday morning with him from eleven to one. They had an "agenda," but never got beyond the first or second items on it. *Felix Frankfurter Reminisces* catches exactly his tone and manner, the stories, bursts of laughter, noise, and delight with what he was saying or hearing. People were black or white, there were no pastel shades: the black were of an unrelieved blackness, the white—apart from the gods, Holmes and Stimson—were not exempt from humorous and affectionate discrimination. He studied our language (which he began learning at the age of twelve) with a connoisseur's love. He delighted in wit that exposed pomposity and hypocrisy and in purple passages that rolled and soared. To get a quotation exact he would dart to the book on the shelf, find the page without fumbling, and read it with conviction. These excursions interrupted the flow of talk, but he had no trouble starting it up again, which he usually did by asking a question, not a Socratic question designed to confuse, but one that the questioned could answer readily and so feel pleased with himself. Felix's ebullience led him over hill, over dale, through bramble, through briar. "Come and get Felix out of his fourth parenthesis," his wife called one day, but that sent him into a fifth.

He encouraged Lefty's ecumenical approach to libraries and universities, illustrating his position by the story of how at Harvard he had opposed a move to call an outstanding professor from a Midwestern law school because his departure would have hurt it. "I told them," said Felix, "that we should foster the welfare of all law schools in the country and not just think of our own glory." I can see and hear him saying this to his colleagues as clearly as if I had been present. Very fierce he sounded and very fierce he looked, and though what he said might have been sententious in another I am sure that no one present was tempted to smile.

Why, people who did not know him ask, had Felix so wide an influence? Quickness of mind, a wonderful memory, both wit and humor, a passionate desire to make the world a better and pleasanter place to live in, moral courage, are part of the explanation, but they are not the answer. It was named at the dinner Archie and Lefty got up to celebrate Felix's seventieth birthday on November 15, 1952. They persuaded Judge Learned Hand to preside and hoped that the nine others, Dean apart, would not feel compelled to rise, one after the other, and pay their tribute to the guest of honor because when such compulsion seizes a tableful of people the pleasure of the evening is impaired; but after Dean had told how he could not have got through his ordeal in the State Department without "that little man," and Mr. Justice Jackson had testified what it meant to be with him on the Court, Robert Oppenheimer summed him up in one word: "Many nice things have been said about Felix tonight, but no one has yet used the word that explains him. That word is 'love.' " There was nothing more that could be said, or so it seemed that night, but Archie

MacLeish added a postscript thirteen years later at the "Proceedings Before the Supreme Court of the U.S. In Memory of Felix Frankfurter." "What Justice Frankfurter gave his time," Archie said, "was something more than intelligence, though his intelligence was vigorous and effective; something more than courage, though his courage was unquestioned; something more than affection though affection flowed from him and love was the motive and the motion of his heart. What he gave his time was an enlargement of its human life. As long as he was here in his office in this building, or his house on Dumbarton Avenue, or off at Heath in the Massachusetts hills in the summers, the world had an extra dimension for us all. Whatever we did or wrote or said was somehow more significant because he knew of it or might have known, approving or disapproving—a phone call late at night or an all but illegible note scribbled on one of those little squares of memorandum paper or just a message through a friend. What mattered was not the word sent, the reproof or the commendation. What mattered was the fact that there was someone listening—someone who cared not only about you but about the world, about the country—above all about the country."

Some months before his eightieth birthday Felix had a stroke that paralyzed his left side, but mercifully spared his right side and his brain. He was able to get to the Achesons' for his birthday dinner. Dean and Alice asked Lefty to it (he and Felix made a point of their birthdays, which were only a day apart) and Lefty saw him whenever he was in Washington. As he was leaving the last time Felix called him back (a favorite trick of his with departing guests), put his right hand on Lefty's arm and said, "I hope you know how much your friendship has meant to me." As Lefty reached the door again Felix recalled him a second time. "Put our friendship in a book," he said. "Just a little book."

XXVI

TWO MISSIONS

The word "educational" may be stretched, the dictionaries imply, to cover any experience that enlarges the mind or provides it with fresh insights. When the enlargement is exotic its effect is heightened. One such enlargement for Lewis was a State Department mission to Peru in August 1943 after its National Library was destroyed by fire, a disaster hardly to be imagined by North Americans, for the Library was much more than the country's chief repository of books and manuscripts. If the Library of Congress was destroyed the sources of our history would not be disastrously diminished because they are spread widely in many other American libraries. Furthermore, the National Library was a symbol of Peru's cultural seniority in the Western Hemisphere: the country was conquered a century before the Pilgrims landed on Plymouth Rock; the University of San Marcos was founded eighty-five years before Harvard; even their Indians, the Incas and their gifted predecessors, make our Pequots and Apaches seem very backward. Because the Library was established by San Martín in 1821 when Peru won independence and was opened at once to any Peruvian it was also a symbol of intellectual freedom. Archie MacLeish as the Librarian of Congress felt strongly that the United States should be the first American Republic to go to the aid of its stricken sister. A committee to Aid the National Library of Peru and the Lima Geographical Society was formed with three additional persons, "one of whom should be the secretary, one as competent consultant on library matters generally, and one a representative scholar with a particular interest in libraries." They were to proceed to Lima where they were instructed to discuss with the appropriate officials of the National Library of the Government: (1) the establishment of a library school at Lima [it would be the only one in South America], (2) sending the Peruvian architect to the United States to inspect and study libraries there, and (3) a gift of many thousand American books on all subjects to the new library in a room to be reserved for them. It was believed that the money for all this would be forthcoming from private American sources. The sole expense to the American government would be the emissaries' transportation and seven dollars a day to each of them while they were in Peru. They were told not to take evening clothes although they were going in the height of the Lima season. The State Department justified its outlay of public money on the grounds that the reception of the transparently innocent emissaries would be a weathervane to gauge the attitude of the Peruvian government to the United States and that the gifts they were taking would help to counteract the subversive influences, Japanese and German, that were creeping about Latin America. Lewis's colleagues were Keyes Metcalf and Lewis Hanke, who was the Director of the Hispanic Foundation in the Library of Congress. It was as companionable a trio as ever went on a mission with or without proper clothes.

Their reception at the Lima airport was not unclouded. On a bit of red carpet were standing a welcoming committee of seven officials: George Vailliant, the Special Cultural Attaché at the American Embassy representing the Ambassador, dignitaries representing the President of the Republic, the Secretary of Foreign Affairs, and four other notables. Reporters buzzed about; photographers squatted and flashed. The *emisarios* were escorted to the *aduana* where everyone rose on their entrance except two men seated at one side who studiously ignored the new arrivals. They were the Archbishop of Peru and the Papal Nuncio who had come to greet a former President's daughter returning to have a baby. The customs officials offset this ecclesiastical rebuff with an apologetic and perfunctory examination of baggage that permitted the Americans to be rushed to their Embassy with little delay. There the Ambassador, R. Harry Norweb, told them the facts of life: the success of their mission depended on three people: the President, Manuel Prado, José de la Riva Agüero y Osma (the leading Peruvian historian, Chairman of the National Committee for the Restoration of the National Library and the last of the *conquistadores*), and a lady, Mrs. Gallagher de Parks. Of these three the most important for the emissaries was the last. A member of one of the oldest Peruvian families, multilingual, traveled, rich, her favorable notice was essential to success in the arts and letters. If she failed to give it to the visitors they should lose no time in returning to the Estados Unidos.

Meanwhile, they were to be engaged morning, noon, and night calling on the highest dignitaries of Church (turning the other cheek) and State, visiting museums, comforting libraries. They were to radiate culture and good will, and thanks to the knowledge, fluency, and good will of Lewis Hanke, this is what they did. Their every move was reported daily with photographs in all four of the Lima newspapers. "Los Bibliotecónomos Norteamericanos" were invariably presented in a litany that went, "Señores Doctor Keyes D. Metcalf, Presidente de The American Library Association y Director de la Biblioteca de la Universidad de Harvard, Lewis Hanke, Director de la Fundación Hispánica de la Biblioteca del Congresso de la Union, y Milmarth [sic] Lewis de la Universidad de Yale y Presidente del Consejo Consultivo de la Biblioteca del Congresso de los Estados Unidos."

The second and third days were the crucial ones, as I am reminded by the "Schedule of Emisarios" that Lewis Hanke summarized when the mission was completed:

Thursday, August 12

10:00	*Talk with Ambassador*
11:00	*Visit to Ruins of National Library*
12:00	*Interview with Foreign Minister*
1:00	*Luncheon at Embassy Residence*
3:00	*Talk with Dr. Belaunde [the statesman and cultural leader] at his home*
4:00	*Talk with Dr. Laroza, Minister of Education*
7:00	*Interview with President Prado at Palace*
9:00	*Dr. Lewis—Dinner at Jockey Club with Mr. Frank Truslow [a cousin of Annie Burr's who was getting rubber over the Andes to Callao for the Rubber Reserve Co.]*

Friday, August 13

9:00	*Dr. Morales Macedo, discussion of Geographical Society*
10:00	*Discussion of Library Building plans with Jachomowitz, Dr. Basadre, Hart Terré, and Emilio Delboy*
1:30	*Luncheon with Riva Agüero, Rubén Vargas Ugarte, S. J., Victor Andrés Belaunde, Prof. Cornelius Krusé, Raúl Porras Barrenechesa*
4:00–6:00	*Discussion with Dr. Basadre concerning technical assistance and other related problems*
7:30	*Cocktails at Jefferson Patterson's [the Counselor of the Embassy]*
9:00	*Supper at Dr. Vailliant's to meet librarians.*

It will be noted that during these two crowded days the names of the President and Riva Agüero appear. The visitors to the Palace felt immensely tall (and important) as they marched through a guard of honor of stocky little brown men presenting arms. They felt even more conspicuous lunching with Señor Riva Agüero and his friends in the center of the Bolívar's dining room. So far so good, but two whole days had gone by and Mrs. Gallagher de Parks had made no sign. If she failed to come to the Patterson's cocktail party the Embassy would expedite the northward journey of the visiting librarians.

At 7:30 the flower of Lima society arrived at the Patterson's, but not its crowning blossom. Patterson took Lewis into his library, which opened off the large drawing room, to see his fine post-impressionist pictures, but their minds were not on them. (I seem to remember a Matisse and a Gauguin; possibly even a van Gogh.) Suddenly the babble in the drawing room ceased. "She's come!" whispered Patterson and hurried to greet the great lady. Lewis halted respectfully in the door to watch an entrance that was slow, measured, royal. Mrs. Parks was perhaps in her sixties, with a countenance more intelligent than beautiful. The walking stick that she carried was a symbol of authority, not a required prop. She acknowledged the greetings of the other guests as she proceeded to the middle of the room. There she stopped and looking slowly around asked, "Which is Mr. Lewis?" Alice was not more surprised when the White Rabbit read out her name at the top of his shrill little voice. Emisario Lewis stumbled forward. Mrs. Gallagher de Parks smiled. "I have a letter of Horace Walpole," she said. Recognition by the third and least accessible personage had been gained. How much it meant was shown when the emisarios met the Papal Nuncio in the street a few days later. He had received them politely in his Palace, but on this chance encounter he was more than polite. Sweeping off his green shovel hat with velvet balls dangling from its brim he made an obeisance fit for princes. The Embassy urged the librarians to stay another week.

They were invited by the President to visit his family's museum at nearby Chorrillos. His brother, Mariano Prado, greeted them in the first room, which was filled with the hideous furniture of the 1880s. They made the admiring noises due any cultural object. Their host smiled and opened a door to another room, which was furnished in the style of the 1860s, a better period acknowledged by the visitors' more appreciative murmurs. They also believed, so modest did the adobe building appear to be, that they had come to the end of the museum. In this they were wrong. Señor Mariano Prado opened another little door to a room of the 1840s, but they had hardly started their journey into the past. On and on they were led with each room becoming more ample and magnificent until they finally reached a great hall filled with Incan, Nescan, and Chimu treasures. By then they would not have been surprised had they seen Atahualpa himself seated upon his throne.

Before they reached this ultimate splendor they had gone through a patio on the walls of which were sixteenth- and seventeenth-century pictures of the Cuzco School, a new school to Emisario Lewis. When the Spaniards arrived in Peru they found artists among the natives of Cuzco who had exceptional talent and who were quick to learn from their conquerors. The result was a fusion of the High Spanish Renaissance and native mannerisms. Lefty secured permission from the Ambassador to buy a Cuzco picture if he could find one and if he would pay for it. He sought Mrs. Gallagher de Parks's help. That lady had become assiduous in her attentions. (She did not use the common post or telephone for her communications, but sent them by the hand of her chauffeur, an alert young man in a plum-colored livery.) Mr. Lewis explained that he did not want an altarpiece because he hoped to carry his picture home to his wife as a present. Since, so far as he knew, there was no painting of the Cuzco School in all the U.S.A., the importation of one to Washington would awaken interest in this early proof of Peru's cultural seniority. Mrs. Gallagher de Parks threw herself into the quest. The plum-colored chauffeur rolled back and forth from her house to the Bolívar with reports of no progress. Mr. Lewis's replies were encouraging but hasty, and he was told, "You enjoy the distinction of being the only person of my acquaintance with a more undecipherable handwriting than my very dear friend Count Keyserling." Then came the morning when Mrs. Parks took Mr. Lewis to the shop where she had found his picture.

The "shop" proved to be an enormous private house in the most elegant quarter of Lima. As the visitors walked up its noble staircase to the main floor Mrs. Parks waved at a colossal Apotheosis of the Virgin hanging in the stairwell. "There it is! There's your picture!" What was Emisario Lewis to do? Fortunately, his chaperone was led away by the proprietor to see some eighteenth-century dolls that he hoped she would add to her doll collection. (She was eclectic in her enthusiasms: Shelley, Beethoven, Horace Walpole, and dolls.) Lewis looked desperately round for a small *portable* picture until he found one. It had a superb seventeenth-century gilt frame, but the picture itself was obscured by dirt. "I am interested in this picture," Lewis told the proprietor on his return, "but I can't quite make it out." The proprietor took it away and gave it a good scrub with radiant results. The artist had chosen the incident, which only St. Matthew records, when Joseph learns of Mary's condition, is "minded to put her away privily," and is restrained in a dream by the angel of the Lord. In the picture Joseph is sleeping with one elbow on a table and supporting his troubled head with his hand. A golden palm branch lies on the table with a book. The fair-haired angel stands over Joseph pointing upward to his dream, which appears in a square picture above him. In it Mary, *muy immaculata* at her prie-dieu, is vouched for by the dove of the Holy Ghost hovering above her head. An opening in the blank wall behind Joseph and the angel discloses a Cuzco street. On Joseph's blue and scarlet robes and on the angel's blue and white pelisse and powerful wings are golden Cuzco stars. The remaining third of the picture is a landscape: there are distant hills, more Andalusian than Andean, a town with tall churches and houses at their base; in the middle distance is a shepherd in blue and magenta and a plumed cockaded hat piping to his flock; in the foreground is a pair of peacocks, the male in glory; flanking the landscape are luxuriant Peruvian trees and for good measure scarlet birds. What, Lefty asked himself in alarm, had he let himself in for? He would not be robbed, not even to save the mission and the reputation of the U.S.A. for prodigal patronage of the arts. With his heart in his mouth he asked the price. It was the equivalent of fifty dollars. "I'll take it!" he announced promptly.

"You have a very fine eye," Mrs. Gallagher de Parks congratulated him as they drove away. "That is the best Cuzco painting that has turned up in years." Its arrival in Washington was delayed for months while a grasping official withheld an export license until Mrs. Parks herself intervened. Then it came through at once. Thanks to her, Lewis Hanke, Keyes Metcalf, and Horace Walpole the emisarios' mission was accomplished.

2

Lectures in Australia by American scholars were initiated by Mr. Richard (later Lord) Casey when he was Australian Minister in Washington just before the war. Theodore Sizer led off and brought back the first exhibition of Australian painting, beginning with its aborigines, that was shown in this country. Thanks to Sizer, W. S. Lewis was invited by the University of Melbourne to lecture on Walpole and he and his wife took off in February 1947 on the first direct Pan-Am flight to Australia. In the back of the lecturer's mind (not very far back) was the possibility of finding Walpoliana, since Britons take their family papers with them wherever they go. Dean Acheson, who was then Undersecretary of State, arranged for the travelers to be under the protection of the Embassy, a welcome intervention that secured for them the efficient and amiable services of Robert Burlingame, the Cultural Attaché, who made all arrangements for their accommodation and decided which invitations to speak Dr. Lewis should accept in Sydney and Canberra. Dr. L. went prepared to speak on libraries and collecting as well as on Horace Walpole.

His first public appearance was in the Mitchell Library in Sydney, an experience that taught him that those who do not verify facts, no matter how confidently held, may be punished. His talk was "The Layman and Libraries." Before reading it he gave a present on behalf of the President and Fellows of Yale University. The present was a letter to Sir Joseph Banks, "The Father of Australia," which Lefty had turned over to Yale some years earlier in a collection of Banks's papers. The letter referred in guarded terms to the late mutiny on the *Bounty* and suggested that a second expedition to the South Seas was in order since the breadfruit was still there. When Lefty proposed to the Corporation that it would be a friendly gesture to give the letter to the Mitchell Library, which has the main collection of the Banks Papers relating to Australia, they readily concurred. A case was made for it inscribed in gold, "The President and Fellows of Yale University to the Chancellor of the University of Sydney." On arrival at Sydney Lewis informed Mr. John

Metcalfe, the Librarian of the Public Library of New South Wales, of this gift and within an hour the Lewises were waited on at their hotel by the Chancellor of the University, Sir Charles Blackburn, M.D.

With infinite tact he approached the subject of the pending gift. It was, he said, a most generous and unusual gift; in fact, nothing quite like it had ever to his knowledge been made in Australia. There was one point, however, about which he was not clear. Just to whom was Yale giving the letter?

"To the Mitchell Library," Lewis answered promptly.

Sir Charles nodded. "I am to understand, then, that it is the intention of the President and Fellows of Yale University to give the letter to the Mitchell Library?"

"Yes, that is our intention. We are giving it to the Mitchell Library, which of course we know is part of the University of Sydney and so we are giving it formally to the University in the person of the Chancellor." Lewis spoke as one aware that Yale knows how to do things.

"But you see," Sir Charles began, hesitated, and looked at the donor with infinite kindness.

The donor felt himself getting red. "*Isn't* the Mitchell Library part of the University of Sydney?"

"No," Sir Charles shook his head. "No, I'm afraid not. Actually," he went on, "the Mitchell Library is part of the Public Library of New South Wales. It is as separate from the University as the New York Public Library is from Columbia." Tableau.

What was to be done? Sir Charles had already decided. He, as Chancellor of the University, would be on the platform when Lewis gave his talk on libraries and made his gift from Yale. Mr. Justice Ferguson of the Supreme Court of New South Wales and Chairman of the Public Library's Board of Trustees would be presiding. Lewis would hand the Banks letter to Sir

Charles and he would hand it to Mr. Justice Ferguson; that is, the presentation would be a double lateral pass and like all such maneuvers the sooner it was done the better.

When the Lewises arrived at the Library its auditorium was already filled. So great was the name and fame of Yale and so handsome was its gesture (whatever it was) that the least Sydney could do was to turn out for its representative. On the platform were seated the Trustees of the University as well as the Trustees of the Library (since Yale had united them) and the leading librarians of New South Wales. Mr. Justice Ferguson opened the meeting. After a most generous introduction, he sat down and Dr. Wilmarth Lewis rose and advanced, letter and lecture in hand, to the lectern. But this was premature; he had not been told that there was to be a second introduction and was drawn gently back to his seat. Miss M. Thompson, President of the New South Wales Branch of the Australian Institute of Librarians, then welcomed him on behalf of the librarians. When she finished he was not to be caught repeating his former mistake and remained seated. But this time he should have advanced. The same friendly hands urged him gently forward.

The presentation of the letter to Banks took place. The donor's remarks were brief but confused. When he handed the letter to Sir Charles he was aware even in his fluster that the Chancellor received it as if it were a hot potato. As rapidly as possible he got it into the outstretched hand of Mr. Justice Ferguson. The second lateral pass had been completed. The Justice responded with the ease and confidence of his profession, bowing to Dr. Wilmarth Lewis in conclusion. Photographers sprang up from the floor where they had been crouching, bulbs burst in air, and the donor was on his own at last with "The Layman and Libraries."

The talk was later published in the *Yale Review* and reprinted by the Friends of the Dartmouth Library and the American Library Association. It also came out in *The Australian Quarterly* and was reprinted by the Trustees of the Public Library of Sydney with a Preface that describes accurately Dr. Lewis's appearance there and his presentation of the Banks letter, the gift of the President and Fellows of Yale University. "Dr. Lewis was introduced to a large and appreciative audience of laymen and librarians by Mr. Justice Ferguson on behalf of the Trustees, and by Miss M. Thompson as President of the New South Wales Branch of the Australian Institute of Librarians. The letter in an inscribed case was handed by Dr. Lewis to Sir Charles Blackburn, Chancellor of the University of Sydney, and received from him by Mr. Justice Ferguson on behalf of the Trustees."

The Lewises' stay in Sydney was made by Hugh and Polly McClure-Smith, who were old acquaintances. Hugh was the very able editor of the Sydney *Morning Herald;* Polly's father, Lewis Buddy, was a pioneer Walpolian at the turn of the century. Hugh was a keen collector of Australian pictures, which were then little known outside the country. Dobell and Drysdale were coming into their own and it was with something of the pride of sixteenth-century Venetians showing the work of Titian and Tintoretto to foreigners that the McClure-Smiths took the Lewises to the exhibition at the National Art Gallery of New South Wales.

The respect accorded to one's critical judgments increases the farther one travels from home. Sydney is some ten thousand miles from Farmington; Lewis's passage through the sky and over the waste of waters invested him with the mantle of John Ruskin. Once again he found himself in a role that he was not qualified to play and on that morning he felt stuffy as well as inept in not responding more warmly to the vigorous new Australian School. He told himself that it was right for the young artists to paint their own country in their own way. As in the Lima shop he looked for a picture that would help him to safety and as at Lima he found it. "Oh, there," he said, "I like that one very much. Jeff Smart. 'Tropic of Capricorn.' "

Hugh was surprised. "Really!" he said, gazing at it attentively. "He's a young man in Adelaide." The picture showed a man and woman with a baby carriage on the Tropic of Capricorn. It was carefully painted and had the implication of cosmic significance that surrealism imparts. "Oh, yes," Lefty repeated, "I like it *very* much." "I think," said Hugh, "I shall get a Jeff Smart."

A week later at Canberra while the Lewises lunched with Mrs. Herbert Evatt, the wife of the Deputy Prime Minister, Attorney General, and Minister for External Affairs, Lefty learned that she was also a keen collector of the new Australian School. He spoke of the Sydney show and his admiration for Jeff Smart's "Tropic of Capricorn." Mrs. Evatt looked at him searchingly. "You must have a very fine eye," she said, "that is the best picture in the exhibition. I am getting a Smart for my own collection." A week later in Melbourne the Vice-Chancellor of the University, John Medley, told Lefty that the report of his admiration of Smart had preceded him and that the University had just secured a fine example of the young man's work, its first, from the artist's studio. It appeared that all over Australia the cognoscenti were buying Smarts; and so it was with particular pleasure and gratitude that the Lewises on leaving Melbourne after Lefty's lectures received as a present from the Chancellor and Fellows of the University a large Jeff Smart hot off the easel for the collection at Farmington.

Early on his arrival at Sydney, Dr. Lewis was invited, as Tubby Sizer had told him that he probably would be, to speak on the Australian Broadcasting Company's "Distinguished Visitor's" fifteen-minute Sunday-evening program, which was listened to by a third of the entire country. The ABC suggested that Dr. Lewis talk on "The Treasure Hunt," the subject that he himself would have chosen. However, an awkwardness developed, as the embarrassed manager of the program explained to him a week before the broadcast. Dr. Lewis might have noticed in the newspapers that Australia had been playing England at cricket. The matches were now over, and, well, would Dr. Lewis mind very much standing down a week for the captain of the defeated English side? Dr. Lewis was all compliance, he was certain there was more interest in cricket than in Horace Walpole, but since he would be in Melbourne on the following Sunday his remarks would have to be recorded before he left.

On the evening of his broadcast he and Annie Burr listened to it while dining with the Russell Grimwades and twenty other guests in Melbourne. The wireless had been wheeled into the dining room, the soup was before the guests, and there was Dr. Lewis visible at the table as well as audible above and around it. To hear one's voice for the first time must be disconcerting when alone, but to hear it, as Dr. Lewis was hearing it, in a company of strangers, no matter how friendly, ten thousand miles from home, was paralyzing. He stared, stunned, at his soup. Was this elegant-sounding gent really he? The other guests were sitting transfixed with decorum while their soup cooled. Then Dr. Lewis came to and with great presence of mind picked up his spoon. The rest of the table promptly did the same. After the voice on the air explained who Horace Walpole was and why his editor was eager to find as many of the letters to and from him as soon as possible it told of the letter already reported in the Melbourne Public Library. Perhaps there were others in Australia, at Launceston or Alice Springs, and the speaker invited their owners to communicate with him. "I used to think," he concluded, "how pleasant it would be if I could lean out of my London hotel window, blow a silvery trumpet, and have all the Walpole letters in England float into the room and settle at my feet. Now, thanks to the ABC, I have used a more up-to-date method of announcement." The fifteen minutes came to an end; murmurs of admiration were murmured around the table; the broadcaster tried to look modest and offhand. Recently when I asked Clive Fitts who was present what he remembered of the evening he answered promptly, "Annie Burr, and my relief when you picked up your spoon."

On the following days letters floated in from all over Australia, but none, alas, from or to Walpole. "I wish," several of them said, "that I had a Walpole letter; I would give it to you." One correspondent wanted to give Dr. Lewis Thackeray's *Virginians* in parts, then a twenty-pound book, merely because Walpole is mentioned in it. Another insisted upon giving him some of his family papers that threw light on Sir Horace Mann's dealings with Walpole's niece, the Duchess of Gloucester and her husband in Florence. A third sent a cutting from a recent Sydney auction catalogue that described a "new" Walpole letter. This friendly stranger did not know what had become of it, but the travelers on returning to Farmington found that it had preceded them there by way of Messrs. Maggs Bros. and London.

"Live and learn" we say after discovering something that everyone else seems to know. Such a lesson was learned by Lefty at Healsville, the "natural" zoo forty miles from Melbourne. The Lewises were taken to it as a result of Annie Burr's remark to Sir Edmund Herring, the Chief Justice of the Supreme Court of Victoria, at a dinner given for the Lewises on their arrival at Melbourne by the Caseys. When Sir Edmund asked AB what she would like to see in Australia she answered promptly as others have answered the same question before and since, "A platypus." Sir Edmund, who had been a Lieutenant General during the war, volunteered to take the Lewises himself to the zoo, alerted its Director, Mr. Fleay, of their approach, and enlisted his former aide, John Oldham, as their driver.

The zoo is "a friendly zoo" in which the nondangerous animals wander about without restraint in an atmosphere of trust and good will. After seeing the three platypuses, which were about to leave for the Bronx Zoo, the Lewises were taken along a road to a field where an exhibition of boomerang-throwing had been arranged for them. As they walked Mr. Lewis had an uneasy feeling that something was following close behind him and turning around saw that something was. At first he took it for a certain elderly friend without her diamond dog collar, but then he saw that it was an emu. A wombat gazed at him reflectively as the party passed. It must have been this way in the Garden of Eden and as in the Garden there was the enemy. On the way to the boomerang field the party passed the "Snake House." Lefty, who was hysterically afraid of snakes, foresaw the ordeal before him. Returning from the boomeranging, the party headed for the ominous building. Fleay instructed them to stay outside it by a pen of dingoes, who raged unpleasantly close, and disappeared within. Lefty told himself that he must not faint or run away: he was representing the United States of America. Fleay reappeared with several baby green pythons wreathed about his person. Peeling off one he handed it to Lefty who took it while the dingoes plunged about nearby and Annie Burr stared helplessly. Instead of being cold and slimy the python was warm and dry. It wrapped itself about his arm with an affectionate squeeze. Lefty picked it off gingerly and handed it back. "Thank you," he said, and he has not been hysterical about snakes since.

Of all the trips that Annie Burr and Lefty took together none was more delightful than their five weeks in Australia;

even the weather, the waning Australian summer, was perfect. Heralded by outriders and trumpeters, they were welcomed by the most interesting and delightful people in the land, all bent on making the visitors as happy and comfortable as possible. Friendships ripen rapidly under such conditions. The Lewises learned that a visit of two or three weeks, which is what they had at Sydney as well as at Melbourne, is the ideal length: it is long enough to give the feeling at the outset of settling in and short enough to keep the conclusion in view. Such a visit is like a 220-yard dash, less headlong than the 100, less exhausting than the 440. The Farmingtonians made many friends with whom they were to "keep up" and nearly all of whom were to visit them at Farmington, the Daryl Lindsays, Mab Grimwade, the Hugh McClure-Smiths, Clive Fitts, and John McDonnell more than once.

XXVII

DETACHED RETINA

During the spring after the Lewises' return from Australia Lefty began to have trouble with one of his eyes. It developed into an iritis that put him into the Hartford Hospital for three weeks. When his doctor cut into his eyeball (paracentesis), which was acutely inflamed, without anesthetic he was reminded that the best way to deal with pain is to concentrate on it instead of trying to run away from it and got through the operation by focusing on Goya's studies of torture.

Intense and persistent fantasies are common in serious illnesses of the eye. A globe would appear to Lefty showing a section with water at its center—the English Channel, the Mediterranean, the China Sea—a fantasy that began in light blue and faded to black. The land would retreat until the water covered it in a second Deluge. After an interval of submersion life gradually reappeared. Venerable William Blake sages followed, bearded, motionless, gazing downward. They were on a slowly moving platform that passed to the left and brought them back on the right when they would gravely pass again. The patient's convalescence continued into midsummer when he relapsed into choroiditis, a painless disease that may cause the retina to become detached. He was hurried from Newport to New Haven where Dr. Eugene Blake interrupted his vacation to take care of him. The cause of the trouble was sought with the thoroughness that lends fresh terrors to illness. After a session with a specialist he discovered that the sight in his right eye from five to eleven was gone except for a glimmer of green when he looked down at the green floor. Having read the books on eyes that Dr. Blake had lent him he knew that his retina was partially detached. He was sitting in a wheel chair waiting for an orderly to push him back to his room and felt rather sorry for himself, but also rather important. This was the most dramatic illness he had yet had. A big Italian woman with two straggling children heaved along the corridor, a stretcher with a very sick man on it was pushed past by a tired nurse, two gangling orderlies hurried by hating someone in loud voices. Lefty would have to have an operation, but it would be successful.

Back in his room and his diagnosis confirmed, he was put to bed, a mask over his face. He could move his arms and legs freely, but his head only an inch every eight hours with the help of two nurses. In this confinement he spent six weeks. The books are full of cases where the patient tears off his bandage and runs wildly down the corridor. What sets him off is claustrophobia, a fear new to Lefty, that is heightened by fantasies. Lefty reached this crisis one night when he saw himself being buried alive. Rigid, recumbent, he was lowered slowly into his grave. A glass was slid over his face; earth was thrown down, clump, clump, while he struggled, terrified, to breathe. He did not leap from his bed because he was afraid of being ridiculous; he told himself that he was not in Belsen or Dachau, but in the New Haven Hospital among friends who were doing everything they could to help him. Instead of trying to escape from his grave he thought, "Very well, this is death. I've wondered what it's like; now I am going to find out." After that he had no more claustrophobia and earned the highest praise given to a patient, "cooperative." He needed no pills for sleep or anything else during his sojourn in the hospital.

The images and scenes that followed the reattachment of the retina differed from the earlier ones. They began with an empty stone cellar that had a narrow window at ground level through which was seen a dead landscape with tumbleweed blown against broken barbed-wire fences. It was followed by a deserted prairie town, an unearthed ancient city, a modern city devastated by a tornado or war. There were no human beings or animals in these scenes. Next came a Gothic cathedral, towering, gutted; but presently scaffolding was erected to repair it. The final series showed canyons of city streets, again empty, through which he moved on an elevated track at the same sedate pace that shifted all the scenes. The hour was always night, the buildings were often covered with snow or seen by moonlight. Towards the end lights began to appear in them, but the effect remained the same, light that was no light:

> *yet from those flames*
> *No light; but rather darkness visible.*

This is Milton in *Paradise Lost.* In *Samson Agonistes* Samson says after his eyes are put out, "Dark, dark, dark amid the blaze of noon." Lefty puzzled over the word "dark." Why wouldn't "black" have been more accurate as well as more effective? "Black, black, black amid the blaze of noon." Gloucester in *Lear* also uses "dark" to describe his condition after his eyes are put out, "All dark and comfortless." Lefty asked Tinker who had had an eye removed what the right word is and he said that neither "dark" nor "black" is right, that there is nothing at all. So Shakespeare and Milton got it wrong: Gloucester's and Samson's eyes were removed and they would have had no suggestion of light. Milton's eyes had not been removed; what he apparently had was glaucoma; "darkness visible" was what he saw, and it was the light that shone on Lefty's fantasies. Such speculation helped him pass the time.

It is said that the remaining senses of the blind become more acute. Probably the truth is that the blind make better use of them. When you cannot see you depend more on your ears and nose and fingers than you do normally. You can astonish witnesses in many ways, but none of Lefty's little triumphs was more surprising than his guessing the time within a few minutes, which he did by marking the Battell Chapel clock striking the quarters a mile away. Not to be able to distinguish color is an obvious loss; not to know what strangers look like is worse. Their voices told Lefty most about them—their ages and where they belonged in our classless society. He also got a good idea of their height and even their weight as they moved about the room. He sensed their state of mind, whether they were at ease or nervous, anxious, or secure; whether they were looking at him with curiosity, compassion, or fear. In time he would form an impression of what they looked like, as one does after talking frequently to someone on the telephone whom one has never seen. He discovered later that he had been right about the strangers' ages, height, weight, and general condition in life, but that he had in every case been wrong about their appearance.

Blindness is such a dreadful affliction that it awakens compassion in most who see it. This normal reaction may encourage its victims to become querulous and spoiled, but when they are determined to do the best they can they have the respect and admiration of all beholders: nothing is more gallant than a man or woman striding along with a seeing-eye dog. Lefty's room never lacked visitors when he wanted them. New Haven is full of people who are eager to read what they are writing. In the evening when Annie Burr had gone back to the Lawn Club after her long day at the hospital they would read their works in progress to the patient, who was able to concentrate wonderfully upon them. Fritz Liebert read a paper on Dr. Johnson and arranged with the Library of Congress to have Talking Books sent to Lefty (who, in sober mood, chose *Paradise Lost* and the *Antigone*). Tinker came to read the early chapters of his autobiography. Very good it was and touching when he told how his father led him, a little boy, across the Boston Common to the doctor who was to remove his eye, but when Lefty suggested that he had shown rather too much resentment of the gilded youths in his class at Yale he took the manuscript home and burnt it. Thornton Wilder read large portions of *The Ides of March* (no author ever read his own work better). One night he asked what it was like to be blind and added the substance of Lefty's answer, enriched, in a passage that he called "The Abyss" towards the end of the book.

The one who helped Lefty most was Annie Burr. She would arrive early in the morning and stay all day, reading the newspapers to the patient, arranging for visitors, or just keeping quiet. She proved to be a first-class secretary, taking Lefty's letters with smoothness and accuracy. The heat was intense, the noise of building a new hospital wing deafening, the Lawn Club not home, but she preserved her outer serenity. A few weeks after the Lewises returned to Farmington and while Lefty was still wearing black glasses with pin points in them his eye was again in trouble. Back at the hospital Dr. Blake and another doctor diagnosed the new condition as an edema of the optic nerve. Nothing could be done about it until the morning, but in the morning the edema had disappeared. The doctors called it "a miracle"; other doctors might call it "hysterical"; either way it was Annie Burr's love that effected the cure.

One night after Lefty was entirely recovered the Lewises dined in New York with the Bayne-Joneses. (B-J was then the head of the New York Hospital.) Dr. Thomas A. C. Rennie, the psychiatrist, was there. Apropos of his detached retina, Lefty said that it was a relief to have an illness that was not psychosomatic in origin.

"Oh?" Rennie asked, smiling.

"Don't tell me . . . ?"

"Have you read my paper on eyes in the *Transactions of the American Academy of Ophthalmology and Otolaryngology?*"

Lefty had to confess that he'd missed it. When he read it he found that, sure enough, his detached retina had probably come, like all his earlier illnesses, from emotional stress. The article contained a statement of what psychosomatic medicine is, "the study and treatment of bodily disorders the nature of which can only be understood when emotional and physical facts are jointly appreciated and dealt with. . . . It merely reasserts the principle that has been known for 2000 years, that a human being as a patient must be considered in his entirety, that emotions and feelings are medical facts, that emotions of anxiety, frustration, depression, anger, fear, etc., can throw an entire organism off balance and lead to profound reverberation in somatic upsets of organs or organ systems," eyes included. During the delights of Australia Lefty had lost sleep over the indifference of the Yale Press to works of scholarship (not to the Yale Walpole) and its failure to establish proper relations with the Yale faculty. He had been equally misguided when he was an employee of the Press and he wished to atone for his stupidity. Couldn't he do something about it as a member of the Corporation? The answer was "No," because the administration would not take the drastic steps needed to effect reform. This ineffectual tumult built up poisons in his system that attacked, as they do, the weakest place. In June 1947 that was his eye, which he had irritated during his mild hay fever. Such is the superficial explanation; the deeper one is that the unconscious chooses the organ most vital to an individual and offers it in expiation, a sacrifice that belies St. Paul's assertion "no man ever yet hated his own flesh."

During the 908 hours of immobility with both eyes bandaged Lefty learned to switch his mind from the subjects that generated poisons and to check the impulse to swing back to them. Cure of an ailing spirit he knew, like cure of an ailing body, is effected by getting to the root of the trouble, whatever it is, and dealing with it when it is exposed; yet keeping the mind off the immediate agitation checks the active poisons from festering further while they are still in command of the body. Lefty's detached retina helped him grasp what he had dimly known, that in his case some sort of illness followed angry brooding and that serious illness followed prolonged indulgence of it. We acknowledge the effect of strain when we say, "I worried myself sick," and if illness follows a painful shock or prolonged tension we accept it as the natural result of deep emotional disturbance. Lefty was struck by comment on the relationship between the mind and the body when he came across it in his casual reading from Plato's *Timaeus* onwards. John Donne preached on March 24, 1616, "Plato says—he that will cure an ill eye must cure the head; he that would cure the head must cure the body; and he that will cure the body must cure the soul; that is, must bring the mind to a temperature, a moderation, an equanimity"; God, according to Brother Lawrence in his *Practice of the Presence of God,* "sometimes permits bodily diseases to cure the distempers of the soul," and Hawthorne in *The Scarlet Letter* points out that "A bodily disease which we look upon as whole and entire within itself, may, after all, be but a symptom of some ailment in the spiritual part . . . a sickness . . . in your spirit hath immediately its appropriate manifestation in your bodily frame." It is tempting to add similar quotations, but I'll stop with one more from an eighteenth-century newspaper, the *London Chronicle* for January 11–13, 1774: "Violent passions of the mind deservedly hold the first rank [among "The Remote Causes of Disease"]; for nothing more quickly disturbs the easy regular motions of the solids and fluids. The effects these produce are manifest to the senses; but the mode of their operation is hitherto unknown, and perhaps ever will be so."

After his recovery Lefty was in better health than he had been in years and overcame his addiction to unnecessary operations. The lifelong pattern of retreat into illness in atonement for spiritual lapses was not destroyed, but when physical symptoms appeared he recognized them as warnings and by analyzing and exposing their causes in talks with Annie Burr and confessions in his notebook they "cleared up." He was prepared for this therapy by Dubois's *Influence of the Mind on the Body,* and, earlier, by Lady Macbeth's doctor confiding to the gentlewoman, "More needs she the divine than the physician." Lewis reading this at Thacher thought of his mother's mysterious headaches and poor baffled Dr. Reynolds, but his introduction to the power of the mind over the body had occurred in the backyard at Alameda, when Wilmarth, knife and potato in hand, dealt with his wart. The millennium will have moved closer when physicians—especially general practitioners in the front line of medical practice—accept the fact that much illness is spiritual in origin and treat their patients accordingly. The confirmed neurotic, recognized in common speech as one who "enjoys bad health," must be a terrible nuisance; no sooner is one symptom dealt with than another is produced. After physicians accept the fact that the sick unconscious from which the symptoms emerge should be treated by a psychiatrist they and their patients will be better off.

The Old Testament Apocrypha contributed to Lewis's knowledge of illness. In Ecclesiasticus he read: "Humble thyself before thou be sick"; "He that sinneth before his Maker, let him fall into the hand of the physician"; "For it was neither heat, nor mollifying plaster, that restored them to health; but thy word, O Lord, which healeth all things." It seemed lamentable to Lefty and Annie Burr, with whom he shared these discoveries, that so much wisdom should have been put outside the canon. The Apocrypha sent him back to the Bible, which he read straight through from Genesis to Revelations, skipping only Chronicles. He made discoveries such as that simple statement is more effective than mannered writing and that the songs—Moses', Deborah's, Hannah's—are beautiful. He kept a record of parallels with secular literature such as Isaiah's vision of owls dwelling in the desolation of Babylon and Gray's vision of owls hooting in St. Paul's. The passage that became his vade-mecum was I Corinthians, Chapter 13, verses 4–7, in which are listed the fifteen attributes of charity. Those who live by them will forgive my repeating the familiar passage: "Charity suffereth long, and is kind; charity envieth not; charity vaunteth not itself, is not puffed up, Doth not behave itself unseemly, seeketh not her own, is not easily provoked, thinketh no evil; Rejoiceth not in iniquity, but rejoiceth in the truth; Beareth all things, believeth all things, hopeth all things, endureth all things." Of these the one that he henceforth tried to remember when put to the test was "not easily provoked."

Lefty's religious life had ebbed and flowed. On his return to New Haven in 1919 with the dew of his confirmation still on him, he was introduced by Tink, an ardent High Churchman, to the rector of Tink's church, and was encouraged to "receive instruction" from him with a view to becoming an Anglican Catholic. The instruction seemed pretty Papist to Lefty, but he told himself he mustn't be narrow-minded. The core of it was "the validity of orders," which Presbyterians lacked. Father whatever-his-name-was couldn't leave Presbyterians alone. "I don't mind people going over to Rome," he confessed, "but how anyone can become a *Presbyterian* . . . !" Although "Low" Episcopalians might lack the true afflatus, at least they were in The Church. All this did not seem very important to Lefty, nor, indeed, very Christian, and he continued going to Trinity Church on the Green, which offered his brand of Episcopalianism.

At Farmington there was no question which was The Church. It was the White Church, the Congregational Church, whose exquisite spire dominated the landscape. The Episcopal Church was a late nineteenth-century structure built of cobblestones; the few parishioners were served by an aging Englishman to whom Farmington was inferior to any village in England, where "nonconformists" met in "chapels" and were looked down upon by the gentry. It wasn't that way at all in Farmington where Episcopalians were the dissenters. The Congregational Church in Connecticut had been in the beginning as authoritarian as a state church; the Farmington ministers extended back in an honored line to 1652 when its first Meeting House was built. Four of them had been Fellows of Yale College, as their memorial tablets on the walls of the present (1771) Meeting House attested. Lefty would go to this beautiful church with Mrs. Barney on his Farmington weekends from Yale. She sat just off the center aisle on the right, the third pew from the west door, a pew that offered ready egress if egress should be necessary. It never was necessary, just as the "restoratives" (smelling salts and brandy) that she carried in a large black leather bag were never needed, but it was well to be prepared for emergencies. The service had the classic simplicity of the Meeting House itself. Lefty found it more ethical than religious in character: the Old Testament God that sent two she-bears out of the wood to tear the forty-two children who mocked Elisha still lurked in the background. There was no cross; the pews were so narrow you could not kneel in them; crosses and kneeling were for Episcopalians and Roman Catholics. When you prayed you looked severely at your lap unless you were an ex-Episcopalian; then you tipped forward and closed your eyes. The former choirboy missed the processional and recessional; the Farmington choir, girls from Miss Porter's School, merely wandered in and out. All was bright and cheerful. Light pouring through the many windows comported with the standards of morality and conduct that were upheld in the sermon and "made-up" prayers. The value of worshipping together in public was stressed: members of the congregation toiling, rejoicing, sorrowing, should give to and receive from their neighbors help and kindness and understanding. Mrs. Barney lent the weight of her support to the minister, his wife, and his principles.

When Lefty moved to Farmington he played golf or tennis Sunday mornings; none of his friends went to Church except Mrs. Barney. Annie Burr brought him back, part way, to it. As a girl she was taken by her family to the Madison Avenue Presbyterian Church in New York during the winter, to Trinity at Newport during the summer, and to the Congregational Church at Fairfield in the spring and fall. While at Miss Porter's School she went to the Congregational Church, and so it was easy for her to join it after she was married. She did so because she loved the church itself, because she liked feeling part of the community, and because going "did her good." She had no theological worries, such a question as the Incarnation bothered her not at all. "What difference does it make?" she would reply to her husband who thought it did matter, but they didn't go on about it.

Shortly after Lefty's return to Farmington from the hospital in 1947 he was called on by Harold King, the new Congregational minister. When Harold came to Farmington on graduating from the Harvard Divinity School Lefty went to Church quite regularly with Annie Burr and admired the young man's earnestness as it showed through his evangelical sermons. After Lefty's religious ebb time set in again Harold was disappointed, but Christians turn the other cheek and he called on Lefty while he was convalescent from his detached retina. Lefty, encouraged to do so, told him what it was like to be sightless and concluded by saying that he had gained something from the experience that he would not give up. Harold observed, "*Now* you may amount to something." This was not mere tactlessness but the authentic Puritan voice, and Lefty liked it.

With each reappearance of a physical symptom and resultant recourse to his notebooks Lefty wished more and more for the support that an active faith in Christianity provides. His detached retina and return to Holy Writ made him receptive to two recent books by English laymen, *Mere Christianity* by C. S. Lewis and *The Recovery of Belief* by C. E. M. Joad. The former was a professor of English literature who had been an atheist; the latter, a philosopher who had been a militant agnostic. C. S. Lewis was clear on the two views of the universe, the materialist and the religious. Lefty joined him eagerly in espousing the religious view. He liked the idea of a Supreme Being, "Old Whiskers," as Holmes called Him, and had no difficulty in believing that He produced the universe and ordained its laws from the orbits of the outermost stars to the life cycle of the amoeba. As to the problem of evil—why if God is a good God did he create rattlesnakes, permit Belsen, and allow drunken teen-agers to run over old ladies?—Joad's explanation satisfied Lefty: "God did not wish to create a race of virtuous automata." He gave human beings free will, a chance to go wrong as well as a chance to go right. He filled the world with danger as well as beauty to make the human passage through it more interesting and difficult. This is rough on the victims of Belsen and teen-agers, but Lefty, unlike Milton, would not try to justify the ways of God to man. He believed that God knows best, even if He should decide to let man, "too clever by half," blow himself up and so conclude the human experiment.

Lefty liked Joad on the soul. "The soul," Joad said, "is the source of genius and the medium of inspiration," the place where God influences man when man lets him do so. Through trial and suffering, Joad said, man may in the end achieve salvation, "conceived as a condition of timeless blessedness in communion with God. The world, then, is a school for the improving and strengthening of our moral characters." Life as God's school on earth suited the Congregational Church, but the supernatural element in Christianity made it uncomfortable. It had to say from time to time that Christ was the Son of God, otherwise it would be the Unitarian Church, but it did not have to go into particulars. Lefty decided to join it and had the candidate's ritual session with the minister in which his faith was confessed. The talk went smoothly even when Lefty brought up the Virgin Birth and was told that it was "nothing to worry about." Lefty had been startled many years earlier when the mother of one of his friends, a dedicated Episcopalian, observed casually, "We say every Sunday we believe things we don't believe"; that is, the members of the congregation while repeating the Creed in unison make private reservations and deletions as they go along. The Farmington Congregationalists got round this awkwardness by not saying the Creed at all. "For what it may be worth," Lefty told Harold King, "I can say the Creed and believe every word of it with a little help from St. Paul on the resurrection of the body." He felt like Wordsworth's pagan "suckled in a creed outworn." Harold was surprised, but there could be no question that Lefty was ready to join the Church.

He stood before the congregation a few Sundays later to be received into it with one other new member, a youth of sixteen.

Lefty had nostalgic twinges about Christ Church, Alameda; "apostate" is what one Episcopalian friend did call him: but he felt that at last he really "belonged" to Farmington, a feeling that was strengthened when he became a deacon two years later. The deacons are in theory the lay shepherds of the flock, a responsibility that is symbolized by their passing the elements at Communion. Deacon Lewis's chief contribution during his four-year term was to persuade his colleagues that Harold King and his wife should have a trip to the Holy Land. They had had virtually no vacation during their seventeen years at Farmington, and Harold was showing signs of battle fatigue. One or two of the brethren wondered why he needed a vacation—he worked only on Sundays, didn't he? a question that indicated unfamiliarity with the sixteen-hour day that a parish minister puts in seven days a week.

During the ten weeks that the Kings were away Deacon Lewis was in charge of the services, which may be conducted by laymen in the Congregational Church, and "supplied the pulpit" with lay preachers. He was then able to satisfy two lifelong wishes, to read the Lessons and to preach a sermon. For the First Lesson he frequently chose a passage from the Apocrypha, an act of protest against its rejection by the "free churches." If he came to a word or passage he did not understand or that he feared the congregation would not understand he substituted silently the translation in the Revised Version, but he tried to do so without destroying the beauty of the King James Version. When in the Wisdom of Solomon it is asked, "What hath pride profited us? or What good hath riches brought us? All those things are passed away like a shadow, and as a post that hasteth by" he changed "post" to "messenger" and so removed the image of a telephone pole. One Sunday Archie MacLeish preached the sermon in which were the rudiments of his *J.B.* Lefty seized his chance to preach. His sermon was on "Doubting Thomas." On rereading it I find that he tried to say too much in his twenty minutes. He approached the subject as he had approached Albany in *Lear* by putting himself in Thomas' place and seeing Jesus through his eyes. That was all right, but he would have done better to have stuck to the resolution of Thomas' doubt and not to go on to point out, as Deacon Lewis did, that the incident happened only nineteen hundred years ago, five hundred years after Socrates, whose existence no one questions. Lefty's attempt to show that Christ was the Son of God was praiseworthy but confused. He learned that it is easier to criticize a sermon than to write one.

The Kings' trip abroad was such a success that they added to their family and Harold was called to another church at nearly twice his Farmington salary. They left just before Annie Burr's last illness. Harold's successor did the best he could and wrote Lefty when she died a feeling and understanding letter. He promised to call often and Lefty who needed and wanted the comforts of religion encouraged him to do so, but warned him, "I am not going to church for a while. This doesn't mean I've taken my hand from the plough, only that the music, especially the hymns, is too upsetting." The minister dropped him abruptly and Lefty hasn't yet returned to the beautiful church whose east wall Annie Burr helped to restore shortly before she died. His conscience troubles him a little; he should have risen above this disappointment. He would like to go to church to touch base, but only to a church that is beautiful, that uses the King James Version and the Book of Common Prayer, and that has a clergyman who can read and who can preach a reasonably good sermon without irritating mannerisms or unctuousness. Annie Burr used to say that he would never find such a church, but Battell Chapel was one when Sidney Lovett was Chaplain of Yale. Its ugliness was mitigated for Lefty by agreeable memories, the music was superb, the tempo of the service spirited, the visiting preachers the best in the country, and the congregation was permitted to hear the King James Version of the Bible, the most beautiful book in our language. Sid Lovett, a Congregationalist, also used the Prayer Book. Lefty got to Battell only three or four times during his chaplainship, but the recollection of those visits remains with him.

XXVIII

SPEAKING AND LECTURING

His detached retina was another watershed in Lefty's life, physically as well as spiritually. Tennis he had already given up; golf, which Annie Burr made him play, he reduced to nine holes; croquet became the only exercise he enjoyed. His doctors and Annie Burr encouraged him to make fewer speeches.

He liked speaking, but it took time and energy. His father had told him he should learn how to "make a talk," that people who could do it had a great advantage over those who couldn't. Speakers were soloists, the center of attention, which Wilmarth was quite prepared to be. As he grew older he noticed why speakers succeeded and failed and identified himself with the successful. When sitting in an audience where there was no possibility of his being called on he would think what he would say if he were. He would imagine himself in fantastic situations. In one he was at a convention of rubber planters in Singapore. The Chairman announced, "We cannot adjourn without hearing from one who is sitting modestly in the gallery. I call on the Friend of Rubber, Mr. Wilmarth Lewis!" I remember how Mr. Lewis was rushed to the platform amid tumultuous applause, but not what he said.

Horace Walpole, collecting, libraries, and Yale were his

usual subjects in real life. He read his talks only on solemn occasions or when they were going to be printed. A prepared text reduces the stress and strain of the occasion, but he learned as a small boy when his mother took him to hear Charles R. Brown preach in Oakland that if you really want to impress people you must speak without notes. When he did so the speech he gave was never the same as the one he made to himself in preparation; he added bits that occurred to him on the spur of the moment and forgot other bits that he meant to give. He would wake up in the night afterwards and think of the things he wished he had said until he repeated an "extemporaneous" speech, used the forgotten bits, and forgot what went well the first time. The result was not a success, and after that he did not agonize over his omissions.

The only speech he ever tried to memorize was the one at Thacher on the Iron Maiden of Nuremberg. That a memorized speech is unsatisfactory even when the reciter gets through it was demonstrated to the Lewises by a well-known actress at no less a place than the White House. She had memorized and rehearsed her remarks. They were twinkling and darting and she twinkled and darted as she recited them in the voice and with the manner she had selected as appropriate. The Roosevelts donned the high smiles that go with high office, but the rest of her audience stared at their empty coffee cups. With or without a written text the final minutes before a speech—the rendezvous with the introducer, the quiet words of greeting, the silent march to the lecture hall—were like, Lefty thought, being wheeled from your bedroom in the hospital to the operating table: for better or worse he was in the hands of God. On the platform waiting to be introduced, he would gaze amiably at the audience thinking what delightful, intelligent, and friendly people they were and how much he liked every one of them, an attitude rewarded by the reflection of reciprocal sentiments on their faces when he greeted them confidently, "Ladies and Gentlemen."

He developed a sense of audience and watched the expressions and attitudes of the three or four people—on the left, in the middle, on the right—that a speaker notices specifically. He learned that listeners are more susceptible to manner than to matter, that fluency, timing, and confidence, are more than half the battle (*possunt quia posse videntur*), and that it is better to stop too soon than too late. Whenever he could he tested the amplifying system beforehand. No lecturer can surmount a loudspeaker that hisses, mocks, or lets out sudden roars. He also went to see what was wrong with the lectern. Perfect lecterns are rare. Ordinary lecterns are too high or too low, their light fixtures wobble or swivel, they do not conceal the typescript from the audience and so permit it to watch the discarded pages rise and the unread pages sink. A narrow lectern was a horror to Lewis who slid the pages to the left as he read them because it is a mistake to remind the audience constantly that one is reading a lecture by lifting up the pages and turning them over. A narrow lectern meant that he had to worry about keeping his left hand on the rising pile of discarded pages to prevent them falling off or encroaching upon the page being read. The worst of all lecterns is a narrow one out of doors—in a wind. When he could, and there was no danger of it blowing away or being snatched up and carried off by a preceding speaker, Lewis had his typescript placed on the lectern by someone else to spare his audience the sight of the speaker clutching what appears to their alarmed imaginations as an interminable address. To help them forget that his speech was written he went over it until he could deliver it by glances. He rehearsed with a stopwatch—it took him five seconds to read a line, one and a half minutes to read a page (which was triple-spaced). He remembered that when he went to a lecture braced for an hour he was grateful for a reprieve of eight or ten minutes.

A dozen of Lewis's written speeches were printed. One was a Harvard Phi Beta Kappa Oration on "The Trustees of the Privately Endowed University," at which time the orator was made a member of the Harvard Chapter of the Society (thirty-five years after he failed of election to the Yale Chapter by a very wide miss). He couldn't make a preliminary visit to the hall where he was to speak and when he got to it, in a procession that followed a fife and drum across the Yard, the promised lectern was not there. Emissaries, dispatched to find one, returned with a music rack while the orator was in the middle of his oration, its pages nakedly exposed in his hand. The music rack looked strong enough to support no more than one note for the flute. The orator waved it away. When he finished an elderly woman with her own ideas of dress came up. He adjusted his features to receive the felicitations all speakers expect after their performance. "Are you a member of the Class of '90?" she asked abruptly. "Well, no . . ." "Are you the man who gave the Oration there?" and she pointed to where the orator had stood. "Yes." "That man," she said, "*was* a member of '90, and I *know* it!" and walked off.

At the Smith College "Rally Day" in 1954 Lewis spoke on "The Difficult Art of Biography." Rally Day begins with a procession of the faculty in academic dress to John M. Greene Hall where awaiting it is the entire undergraduate body also in academic dress. Such a procession does a lot for the speaker. It produces an atmosphere that raises him to the foothills of sacerdotal significance. The procession wends along, perhaps to the accompaniment of a band, the speaker on the arm, so to say, of the President. In John M. Greene Hall the audience is in front, beside, and behind the speaker, each member of it is aware that she looks well in her cap and gown. The speaker may be excused if he succumbs to the enchantment of his situation. Particularly pleasant it is when at the end he must turn round to acknowledge the applause of the audience behind him, bowing and smiling, but he must remember not to bow over too often or too far. After lunch on Rally Day there was a basketball game during which Dr. Lewis in the presidential box was serenaded to the tune of "Pop Goes the Weasel" by singers who were hard pressed to find rhymes for "Lewis" and "Lefty."

As Senior Fellow of the Yale Corporation he made the induction address at the inauguration of President Kingman Brewster in 1963. It took him five months to write it and nine minutes forty seconds to deliver it. Owing to something amiss with the loudspeakers his colleagues on the platform, whom he had much in mind, heard not one word. The high point of the day for him was standing at the head of the Corporation on the steps of the Cross Campus while the delegates from the sister universities marched slowly down from the Library with Oxford and Paris at their head. It was a sparkling April day that set off the European visitors in their scarlet and green gowns and exotic hats. At a discreet distance, not too near, not too far, a band played Brahms's Academic Festival Overture. The delegates moved on, the Corporation closed ranks behind them, the new young President walked down from the Library and he and the Senior Fellow, preceded by a marshal bearing the University's mace, followed into Woolsey Hall. The audience of 2700 rose on their entrance. Fanfare. Trumpets. Wilmarth Lewis standing in the bathtub at Alameda commanding listening senates did not envisage anything so splendid.

He gave three courses of lectures that were published, the Colver Lectures at Brown in 1941, the Sandars Lectures at

Cambridge University in 1957, and the Andrew W. Mellon Lectures at the National Gallery, Washington, in 1960.

Endowed lectureships abound in universities. The famous ones confer on their holders academic distinction as well as cash: W. S. Lewis received £79.10.0 for his three Sandars Lectures, $10,000 for the six Mellon. Lectureships are usually in a specified field—the law, medicine, theology, the fine arts. The most honored of them are those that publish the lectures. Publication "puts the bee" on the lecturer; he cannot afford to do less than his best. Instead of his remarks evaporating when his audience leaves the hall they are embalmed in a book that becomes part of his bibliography and will be read critically by reviewers and colleagues whose judgments will affect his reputation. Printed lectures give the speaker two audiences, the one that comes to hear him and the later one that reads him. Publication may work to the disadvantage of the first audience if the lecturer sacrifices his listeners to his readers and writes for the eye rather than the ear. Some lecturers try to spare their listeners a script written for readers by putting their texts aside and "talking" to their first audience, a solution that can be as trying as a monotonous reading. Other lecturers when they come to publication remove all traces of the auditorium, converting the lectures into chapters and adding new material. A third course was followed by W. S. Lewis who tried to write for both those who heard him and those who he hoped would read him; instead of decontaminating his text of all traces of the platform he left them in to remind his readers that his book was delivered before a particular audience.

When in 1940 he was asked to give the Colver Lectures at Brown he knew at once what he would talk about (the subject was left to him): three imaginary trips to eighteenth-century London. He used to wish that he and Annie Burr could take a train at the Grand Central and go there. If they left in 1940 at six in the afternoon and traveled at the rate of ten years an hour they would reach 1800 at breakfast and get to London in 1760 around noon. They would step into the eighteenth century and what would they find? However long and conscientiously they had prepared themselves for this journey by reading, poring over prints, and visiting museums they would find the filth and noise and brutishness of the place almost overwhelming. They would get to their lodgings in St. James's Street somehow—by hackney coach?—thankful for the glass that shielded them from the stench and the small, pocked, and frightening people in the streets. They would be greeted by their hostess but—and we do not know the answer to this—could they understand her? On arrival in eighteenth-century London twentieth-century tourists should take it easy for a day or two, just as Dr. Johnson should if he were set down at Piccadilly Circus today. Lefty wrote his three lectures in six months with Annie Burr's help. They relied heavily on the journals and letters of foreign visitors; Boswell, Walpole, and Hogarth were major sources. Lefty chose three years arbitrarily for their visits, 1748, 1776, 1797, confessing that he was more interested in the theater than in the Royal Exchange and pointing out that tourists are not expected to see everything.

The lectures were given in the evenings a week apart. The Hill in Providence is one of the few places in this country where one may still sense the eighteenth century. Its streets bear names that appear in Lefty's genealogy on his mother's side and give him a sense of kinship with the community. The lecturer kept his text to forty-five minutes, explaining at the beginning of each talk that the lights would be turned off towards the end to show slides for five minutes, that they would be turned on again, and he would conclude. (Nothing is more perilous than a lecture in the dark after dinner.) This worked well except for a few who sat under a balcony which provided an accoustical eccentricity that left them undisturbed except for the lights going off and on. Carl Rollins designed an attractive little book for *Three Tours Through London, in the Years 1748, 1776, 1797* with fifteen illustrations. It was the only one of Lewis's books to reach more than one edition.

In 1957 he became the Sandars Reader in Bibliography at Cambridge, the second American to be elected to the Readership since its establishment in 1895. A liberal interpretation of "bibliography" was necessary to make him eligible, but he felt safe in his subject, "Horace Walpole's Library." The Reader spent six months on each of the three lectures, which were given on successive days at five following tea, the ideal hour for lectures in England when the audience is cheered but not inebriated. He asked H. R. Creswick, the University Librarian and his correspondent in the matter, about how many he might expect in his audience, reminding him of the visiting lecturer at Cambridge who had an audience of one. The lecturer went gallantly forward. At the end of an hour he paused and asked his auditor if he might take ten more minutes of his time? "Take all the time you want," the man called back with an encouraging wave of his hand, "I'm your taxi waiting to take you to the station." "I know," Lewis said, "I'll have more than one. There will be my wife and *you,* the S. C. Robertses and the Geoffrey Keyneses, Tim Munby, John Oates, and Jack Plumb. That's ten. Will there be anyone else?" "Oh, yes," Creswick replied promptly and paused, "at least for the first lecture." In the event, several of the Biblios came down from London and the audience got to nearly sixty each day; very good, the Reader was told, for a Sandars Lecture.

There were no undergraduates, but there was a boy in the middle of the third row wearing a school blazer, his cap over one knee. Lewis could not imagine an American boy going to such a lecture. He was in the same seat the second day, leaning forward eagerly. Lewis asked Creswick later who he was and learned that his name was John Thorpe, that he was an ardent book collector who did the best he could on his allowance of a shilling a week, and that his father was at Cambridge on sabbatical leave from Princeton. After the third lecture John walked with the Lewises to a sherry party given for them by the Vice-Chancellor in the Old Library. Creswick kindly pushed his bike along the King's Parade so that he could talk about his collection to Mr. Lewis. At the party the latter learned what it is like to be proud of a thirteen-year old compatriot. John was exactly right, not embarrassed, not precocious. He had a question for Annie Burr. "Mrs. Lewis, do you mind Mr. Lewis collecting books?" "No, John, I don't. Do you think it would make any difference if I did?" "No, ma'am, I do not."

Lefty learned that he should not write home fantastic stories. Ray and Maude Atherton sent him a cable of cheer and encouragement before his first lecture and followed it up with a letter asking to hear all about how things went. "It is not for me to say," he replied, "but after the last lecture I *was* carried through the streets of Cambridge on the shoulders of the audience while they shouted 'We forgive Foster Dulles!' " (It was not long after Suez.) The Athertons generously believed him and dined out in Washington on the story, moving a Republican Senator from the Plains to observe wistfully, "I had no idea the English felt so strongly about Foster."

The lectures were on the books and their arrangement at Strawberry Hill, the use Walpole made of them in his works and letters, their dispersal in 1842 and partial recovery since then. The Cambridge University Press brought out *Horace Walpole's Library* with ten illustrations in an edition of 750 copies, which went rapidly out of print owing to the large number given away by the author. He wrote: "The library is a projection of the man. We learn more about him from it than from Rosalba, Reynolds, or Ramsay. We get a picture of Horace Walpole by merely reading the titles of the books that he bought. Discovery of when he got them and where he kept them brings him a step closer. When we handle the books themselves and read what he wrote in them we approach intimacy. In his library we see his interests and prejudices, his egotism and altruism, his fears and loyalties, his visions, and his concern for posthumous fame." The last sentence shows how a writer, or at least how W. S. Lewis, can work and work over his text and fail to see something that is obscure and untrue. Walpole's library and marginalia do not show his altruism, fears and vision; *they* appear only in his letters. Such a statement is a blemish, and to see it too late is exasperating.

Shortly after he became Director of our National Gallery, John Walker asked Lefty to give the Mellon Lectures there. "I want you to be the first American to give them," he said. Lefty of course was honored and flattered, but he did not know enough about the subject proposed, the political and personal satires of the English eighteenth century, and regretfully declined. A year later Johnny asked him again, this time suggesting the taste of the period with special reference to its collecting. The subject was closer to what Lefty thought he might do, but after a year of reflection and note-making he knew that it would be unwise to try and follow in the wake of Jacques Maritain, Kenneth Clark, Herbert Read, and Étienne Gilson in a subject that called for far greater knowledge of esthetics than he had. He declined a second time when the Walkers were staying with the Lewises over the graduation of their daughter from Miss Porter's School. Johnny's disappointment was the more flattering because it was tinged with annoyance. "Do you know what you would talk about?" "Oh, yes, but it falls outside the specifications of the lectures. Horace Walpole." "Then, we'll change the rules." "I'll have to talk it over with AB tonight," Lefty said. She had just got through the Sandars Lectures and it was only fair to consult her before embarking on another session of blood, sweat, and tears. "Oh, dear," she said when they were alone. "But of course you must." He spent the next three years on the six lectures. Annie Burr lived to read four of them. The fifth was written in the intervals of her illness when, in the mocking way of cancer, she seemed better; the sixth was written after her death.

The lectures were given in February and March of 1960 on six successive Sunday afternoons at four in the auditorium of the Gallery. Lefty would fly down a day ahead and stay with friends. Before the first lecture he inspected the speaking arrangements. Since he was not going to use slides the reading desk (it was too solid to be called a lectern) was moved from far to the side to the front center of the stage. The desk, amplifying system, and accoustics were flawless; the 350 seats were comfortable and did not squeak when their occupants moved. On arrival at the Gallery Sunday afternoon the lecturer would go to Johnny Walker's office where a young man would appear to take his typescript and place it on the reading desk. A second young man escorted him across the entrance hall and down a long passage to an unobtrusive door. It led to an angle of the stage that was concealed from the audience by a thin curtain. The lecturer groped about in the dark until he found a chair and crouched on it. Sonatas were raging on a mighty machine in the auditorium playing Mozart, Vivaldi, Haydn. The music stopped and the lecturer wondered, *Was* that the last movement? He parted the curtain, stepped out into a blaze of light, and walked across the wide stage to the reading desk amid the sound of welcoming applause. The stage seemed very high. Down below the first six rows were reserved for friends. I see them now: Felix, very bright and expectant in the center of the third row with the Achesons and Joe Alsop beside him; the Auchinclosses were there and the Bayne-Joneses, Caccias, Finleys, Sammy Hood, Macgill Jameses, Lippmanns, Charlie Stones, and Walkers. Week after week they came; Ellic Lamont and Nin Ryan made special trips from New York and the Knollenbergs and John Parsonses from Connecticut. They came, Lefty knew, as much for Annie Burr as for him.

He was pleased by the faithful strangers, the nuns from Catholic University, the Negroes from Howard, and wondered what they wrote so busily in their notebooks. In the first three seats of the front row on the left-hand side were always two women and a man who greeted him with the pleasantest of smiles and then after a while went decorously to sleep. Five minutes after he began a gray-haired, wind-blown woman would weave down the right-hand aisle to the front row with the expression of the blandly intoxicated. Tacking cautiously into a seat she would gaze affectionately up in the general direction of the lecturer, and then she, too, dozed off.

The six lectures were on Walpole's Family, Friends, Politics, Strawberry Hill, Lord Orford's *Works,* the Letters. The lecturer mentioned the difficulty of choosing from the many subjects that Walpole offered. "Should it be Walpole the historian of his age or the arbiter of taste, the literary artist or the antiquary?" he asked. "Should it be Walpole as one of the germinating forces of the eighteenth century whose long shadow reaches us today? Six lectures could be given on each of these subjects, but the one I have chosen is more interesting to me than any of them. It is the man himself. . . . It is my hope that when we have Walpole's weaknesses and strength in perspective and his lifework is seen in the light of the obstacles that he had to overcome to carry it out, he will be less baffling." The lecturer also hoped to discover what Virginia Woolf called "the connecting word"—love, ambition, religion, or whatever—that "once found there is no biography without its form, no figure without its force." In his last lecture he disclosed that he believed the connecting word in Walpole's life was "fame."

The most difficult lecture for Lewis to write was the third one, on Walpole's political career and his *Memoirs,* in which for forty years Walpole recorded, secretly, parliamentary history. This lecture was difficult for Lewis because he knew less (and cared less) about eighteenth-century politics than about Walpole's other major activities and because the *Memoirs* are, except for their "characters" less well written; they also cause their author's friends to grieve because they show him at his worst. The lecturer had to break through thirty-five years of partisanship and do his best to portray his subject's defects.

"Although," he wrote, "faction and the kaleidoscopic politics of the midcentury with its guerilla warfare suited [Walpole's] temperament, he was too volatile to maintain power, even in the only role he aspired to, which was that of prompter. When he converted a situation into a cause, he became extremely active, writing pamphlets and scurrying about collecting, reporting, analyzing news and anticipating the enemy's next move. There was always an enemy: Pulteney, Hardwicke, Bute, George Grenville; and there were always buffoons, among whom the Duke of Newcastle was first. Not that many of these characters remained fixed. Enemies could become allies, allies enemies. . . . Although Walpole's political friends—both long-term and temporary—respected his ability to discover what was in the wind and frequently sought and acted on his advice, they regarded him with uneasiness. Moderation and temperate action in the heat of battle and concentration on routine business were beyond him. His inner uncertainties shimmered out and disconcerted his associates. His exhortations and flutterings exhausted their patience. His tastes, his celibacy, his independence, set him apart from ordinary men; his talk about disinterestedness implied that he considered himself superior to them. He made people feel that he was quicker and more discerning than they were; they were afraid of his tongue, as they might well have been. He was no respecter of persons, but spoke up caustically to anyone, and repeated what he said in conversation and in his letters. His friends knew that he was passionately attached to them while they agreed with him, but that a divergence of opinion convicted them in his eyes of irresolution and disloyalty to principle. He himself said that he always leaned most to a man in Opposition, and was on the side of the rebellious. It is not remarkable that when his friends distributed the plums of victory his name was not even mentioned."

The writing of this lecture changed for the better Lefty's relation to Walpole, and, oddly, Wilmarth Lewis discovered that in writing it he had, somehow, swept away the last lingering hold his mother had on him.

XXIX

LESSONS OF THE FIFTIES, I

As I look back on Lefty's education in his fifties (the prime of life), the first lesson I think of has been described, his detached retina. A second lesson was *Collector's Progress*.

Wilmarth's determination to be a writer did not keep pace with his determination to be a speaker, but he had not forgotten it, and when in 1944 Blanche Knopf made a trip to Washington to urge him to write a book on his collecting he started right in on it. The title of the first draft was *The Education of a Collector*. Since he had left the O.S.S. he had plenty of free time and dashed it off in a few months. Wilson Follett, who was again the reader, began his report, "There is a lot of legitimate light entertainment scattered through these twenty-four chapters. 'Scattered' is the word, for the book is conspicuously short of anything that would be called form or structure. . . . Frankly, it is nothing like so good a book as we were entitled to expect from W.S.L., or as I did expect, or as the devotees of his Yale Walpole must be expecting," and so on for three closely worded pages every word of which the author, with sinking heart, knew to be just. "The Education of a Collector," Wilson pointed out, "is a title that implies, if not a systematic book, at the very least an orderly one. It points to the record of a steady and logical growth—a history of someone acquiring year by year a surer and surer grasp of his subject, generalizing from his experience and his mis-adventures, mastering a subject the hard way, and becoming in 1937 fully abreast of considerations of which he was hardly aware in 1935." Instead of making his story coherent W.S.L. had "tumbled the raw matter of his experience together into a rather shapeless heap and invited you and me to sort it out to suit ourselves."

It took W.S.L. a year to recover, which he did with the assistance of Ted Weeks of the *Atlantic Monthly* who, on the suggestion of Alexander Woollcott, asked him to write as many essays as he pleased on his collecting. This was a welcome invitation from the editor of the magazine to which W.S.L. in the twenties had submitted unsuccessful sketches. The eight essays that Lefty contributed from 1945 to 1950 became the basis for his rewritten *Collector's Progress*. Its second draft was better than the first (the second reader was John Winterich, whose criticism was also invaluable), but Alfred Knopf patiently pointed out that still more must be done; as in Mrs. Blood's class, Wilmarth had to write his exercise a third time. The book appeared in 1951, seven years after W.S.L. made his ill-planned start. It begins with Wilmarth's collection of houseflies and ends with his best wishes to anyone who might be encouraged by it to collect seriously "—provided, of course, that what is collected is anything under the sun except the works and possessions of Horace Walpole."

Two presentation copies of the English edition (which Michael Sadleir took for Constable's) have come back to the author. The first was the one that Lefty gave to Queen Mary when word was conveyed to him that she would be pleased to receive a copy. Her thanks for it were sent to Farmington by her lady-in-waiting, Lady Constance Milnes Gaskell:

MARLBOROUGH HOUSE
Sept. 27 52

Dear Mr. Wilmarth Lewis,

I am commanded by Queen Mary to thank you very much for the copy of the book Collector's Progress. Her Majesty read it with great interest and enjoyment, being such a keen collector herself the story you tell delighted Her Majesty.

May I add that I read your book too and as my husband sold the Milnes Gaskell Library (to my sorrow!) after his Father's death, I was immensely interested to read your references to it and I am glad to think that some of the books are at Farmington. . . .

Constance Milnes Gaskell.

Queen Mary gave her copy to Owen Morshead as he noted on a flyleaf when he sent it to Farmington the Christmas after Annie Burr's death, adding, "and I now, after some thirty years of affectionate collaboration, give it to W.S.L."

The second copy was the one W.S.L. sent to Max Beerbohm following the Lewises' lunch with him at Rapallo in 1954. It was sold in Max's sale after his death and now contains his thank-you letter:

VILLINO CHIARO RAPALLO
24th May 1954

Dear Wilmarth Lewis,

I have just finished reading "Collector's Progress"—reading it with deep delight and admiration. With envy, too. To have a consuming and overwhelming passion and to be able to write about it so lightly and well is surely a most enviable state. If Orestes with the Furies ever at his heels had been, in his headlong flight, able all the while to be talking charmingly and wittily about them he would have a modern counterpart in yourself. Accept my congratulations. How many people must wish they were you!

Elisabeth Jungman and I constantly talk about the delight we had in the company of you and Mrs Wilmarth. I do hope Fate may bring you again to these shores.

Yours very sincerely,
Max Beerbohm.

A year after *Collector's Progress* was published Lefty put together *A Layman and Libraries,* a collection of articles and speeches, and sent it to Alfred Knopf. His reply was as kind and disappointed as John Berdan's had been in 1919 when he told Lefty the truth about *Cushioned Campaigns.* "I took your manuscript home," Alfred wrote, "and read it with great interest. But, Lefty, this time I am absolutely certain: this is no book for me or any other trade publisher. You could reprint your various talks with brief introductions, explanatory paragraphs and publish it suitably privately. . . . The mixture of the two which you have concocted simply doesn't jell." Lefty had not yet learned that a book must be planned and worked over and not just dashed off.

A lesson in publicity was given him in 1944 when *Life* ran an article, "*Life* Visits the Greatest Walpole Collection in the World." There it was, the ignorant boast made to Azro twenty years earlier, announced to the world as accomplished. Lefty had a stand-in who sat on sofas or stood before a shelf or filing cabinet. After the scene was composed and the lights adjusted Mr. Lewis would be asked deferentially to sit or stand just so. This went on for three days. The climax came with a picture that took an hour to arrange. Mr. Lewis was placed on a sofa, Fidèle beside him. Five people held flash bulbs aloft: Miss Nina Lien, the director of the enterprise, her assistant, the stand-in,

Ross, Bruno. Mr. Lewis adjusted his features. The gallop of tiny paws was heard racing down the long hall. Mr. Lewis said "cheese" and the bulbs flashed just as Fred, the dachshund, arrived in the center of the picture and lifted his leg on a chair. Six pages of pictures finally appeared and taught Lefty that national publicity does not invariably engulf one in correspondence. He heard from only three strangers: The Director of the Oriental Institute at Luxor who reported Walpole's set of *Archaeologia,* 12 volumes, 1770–96, and expedited its passage to Farmington, a war-mother in Bridgeport who told him to sell his library and give the money to the War Effort, and an Indian in Madras who asked Mr. Lewis to forward ten thousand dollars so that he and his wife and six children could move to Farmington and live with the Lewises the rest of their days.

Beside the *Atlantic* essays and *Life*'s visit there were earlier newspaper reports of W.S.L.'s library and the Yale Walpole, notably an interview with a columnist of a London evening paper. The American confessed his uneasiness to the columnist, he shrank from publicity, but when he was assured that the interview would certainly produce Walpole letters he threw discretion to the winds. The result was a piece with the headline, "Dark Eyes Dancing" and the opening sentence: "With the enthusiasm of a schoolboy starting off on his holidays tall Mr. Wilmarth Sheldon Lewis, an American scholar, is preparing a book that may run to fifty volumes." The interview produced nothing but embarrassment. Accordingly, when Geoffrey Hellman went to Farmington to talk about a Profile in *The New Yorker* Lefty was on his guard.

That others agree on what we are like is shown by the game "analogies" where one person goes out of the room and the rest choose a man or woman whose identity the absent player guesses on his return by asking such questions as "What animal is he?" "What month?" "What article of clothing?" etc. The company agrees on "hog," "November," "shorts," thus showing the personality that we, all unsuspecting, present to the world. Lefty would wonder uneasily what bird or vegetable he was. Geoffrey Hellman, one of the most keen-eyed satirists in the business, would show him and so would the artist who drew the caricatures that headed the two parts. Lefty was right to tremble before the latter because the caricatures were so repellent that he could not face the text on the pages where they appeared. Geoffrey spent eight months on the Profile, "The Steward of Strawberry Hill," interviewing many others as well. He listened so quietly, took notes so unobtrusively, asked such good questions, that in no time his subject was again talking without reserve, lured on by the promise that much of what was wanted was merely "for background," that he would see the draft of the text, and could delete anything that he objected to—a promise that was kept except for one anecdote that Lefty feared, unnecessarily, would cost an old friendship. The Profile had appreciative glimpses of Annie Burr and Ross, quotations from reviews, and extracts from *Tutors' Lane,* Lewis's articles in the *Atlantic,* and *The Yale Collections.* Geoffrey prefaced his quotation of the epitaph on Othniel Marsh's gravestone from the last named book: "To Yale he gave his collections, his services, and his estate," with the remark that it might "someday conceivably apply to [Lewis] himself." On rereading "Farmington Revisited," a sequel to "The Steward of Strawberry Hill," which was written in 1959 a few months after Annie Burr died, I have been struck again by Geoffrey's mastery of a form of writing he has made his own. Under the casualness appropriate to a satirical magazine he has concealed his artistry, his industry in research, skill in selection and arrangement of facts, but I am struck even more by the affection he showed to a friend then deeply troubled.

Shortly after the second part of the Profile appeared the

editor of the Yale Walpole was reading proof of the correspondence with Samuel Lysons. He had come to a letter of February 14, 1787, which was first printed in *Bentley's Miscellany,* 1850, but had not been seen since. The letter has a reference to a pack of fifteenth-century playing cards that belonged to a man called Putet in *Bentley's* text. The Yale editors gave their reasons for changing his name to Tutet in a footnote. While the editor was admiring it Ross entered with the morning's mail. In it was a letter from Conger Goodyear saying how much he had enjoyed the Profile and that he owned a Walpole letter. When it arrived (he generously gave it), it was the letter to Lysons of February 14, 1787. The questioned name was Tutet.

Such coincidences are familiar to collectors who also have a sixth sense that leads them to objects that they wish to find. When it happens witnesses fall silent with wonder. Lefty demonstrated this useful faculty in a country house in Ireland. The owner's late father had reported a book from Walpole's library, but his son couldn't find it. At tea Annie Burr spoke of her husband's ability to find missing Walpoliana, calling it his "geiger counter." Everyone wanted to see it work, but its possessor explained that it refuses to do so if people stare at him expectantly. So after tea the Lewises set off alone with their host to find the missing book. As soon as he entered the library on the ground floor Lefty knew it was not there and the trio left at once for a second library on the floor above. Half way up the long flight Lefty announced rashly, "The geiger counter is beginning to work." As he walked to the end of the upper library the geiger counter slowed down; when he started back it picked up and ticked madly in the left-hand corner of the room. He hesitated and then took a book off the shelf with Walpole's bookplate and the Strawberry Hill pressmarks, E.2.22. It was not the book that they were looking for, but another of Walpole's books that the owner did not know he had. (The book they were looking for hasn't yet turned up.) When the discovery was reported to the group waiting below they made noises of startled incredulity while regarding the discoverer with puzzled awe, the sort of look that Faust must have had to get used to.

These stories could be multiplied. I like to tell them, but it could be objected that they have little to do with education. One more I will tell to show this strange power working in another and to suggest that Walpole's possessions may have an especially strong attraction for it. On finishing the chapter about the Strawberry Hill library in *Collector's Progress* an Englishwoman wondered if there wasn't a book from it in her brother's vast library. She went into it, but viewed the shelves with dismay. How could she possibly find a Walpole book even if it was there? After a minute or two she walked across the room and picked one off the shelves. When science gets around to explaining this corner of extrasensory perception a new avenue of education will have been opened up.

The magic of the geiger counter should not be confused with Serendipity, the word that has introduced more people to Horace Walpole than all his letters and books put together. His definition of it appears in a letter to Mann: "I once read a silly fairy tale, called *The Three Princes of Serendip;* as their Highnesses travelled, they were always making discoveries, by accidents and sagacity, of things which they were not in quest of." Such discoveries he called Serendipity. The word acquired its present vogue after it was used to describe the discovery of penicillin. The "Serendipity" folder at Farmington contains notices of many shops in England and this country that have adopted the word and inquiries about its origin. One of them came from a Chicago surgeon who telephoned during an operation in which he apparently found something interesting he was not looking for. That the word is wandering from its original meaning is suggested by an advertisement of "Serendipity the Serene Pussy Cat. He comes with every serene pillow you buy." Lewis received a cable from Tim Munby and others on January 28, 1954, who were dining at Emmanuel College, Cambridge: "Greetings on bicentenary introduction into English language word Serendipity from Founders Association for its pursuit." Lewis, pressed for a bright reply, sent congratulations to the new Society "from hemisphere discovered by Serendipity."

The Lewises resumed their English visits in 1948, going every other year only. "You are now biennials," Chapman said. In 1954, an off year, they went to Sicily where Lefty had never been. Sicily seemed to him the most rewarding of all countries for a mere tourist, but he had lost interest in sightseeing—art galleries apart—unless Walpole was somehow concerned. In Palermo after they had done the churches he wondered if there just might not be a Walpole letter or a book from Strawberry Hill in the University Library? You never could tell.

The Library proved to be up two flights of stairs at the top of which was a guard. Annie Burr, who had a little, a very little, Italian asked Lefty, "What do I say to him?"

"Tell him we want to see the Librarian."

The guard carried them to the office of the Assistant Librarian who sprang up wildly on their entrance.

"What do I say now?" AB asked alarmed.

"Tell him we want to pay our respects to the Librarian."

"But I can't think what 'respects' is."

"Well, then, try something about Horazio Walpole."

She began, taking deep breaths and smiling desperately. Her husband, she explained, was the editor of Horazio Walpole's correspondence and she said something about Yale. The Assistant Librarian had not heard of either.

"Say I'd like to see their catalogue," Lefty muttered.

"Ah!" The Assistant Librarian beamed understanding and, all eagerness, produced a book in English on Euclid. No, AB said, that was not what she and her husband had in mind. The Librarian had an inspiration, disappeared, and returned with a volume of the *Encyclopaedia Britannica.* No, that wasn't it, either.

"Try 'catalogue' again, louder."

"Cataloghi!" AB's voice was raised and her smile more determined. Their host led them enthusiastically to the catalogue. As Signor Lewis fumbled to the W's he was interrupted by the arrival of a newcomer whose presence had been privately solicited by their host. One of AB's statements, her husband learned later, a statement he had apparently confirmed by vigorous nodding, led the librarian to believe that the American gentleman was a professor of French. The newcomer confessed with much deprecatory bowing that he spoke the language "très peu." This was also Professor Lewis's case, but the new man had acknowledged defeat and Professor Lewis launched forth bravely, only to waver to a dead stop while the others stared expecting him to go on. *"Please* help me," he begged his wife. Then the Assistant Librarian said something that made her gasp.

"What was *that?"* Lefty asked.

"He says he will take us to the Librarian."

"We must get out of here!" Professor Lewis seized the Assistant Librarian's hand, *"Many* thanks, signor! I am most grateful to you." He seized the newcomer's hand, "Au revoir, monsieur. Merci bien!" Annie Burr followed him, thanking and saying good-bye in both languages as they hurried down the stairs.

The accessions book at Farmington shows no falling off in the collector's progress during his fifties. The decade came to a climax with the sales at Christie's in 1954 and 1955 of books and manuscripts from Lord Derby's house, Knowsley Hall, near Liverpool. The 13th earl was the largest private buyer of the Strawberry Hill books in 1842, but he bought through a dealer and the books were not all identified at Knowsley. Fortunately, Chapman was called in to advise the new Lord Derby about what should be sold and what kept. No one in England knew the books at Farmington better than Chapman and no one was more eager to fill the gaps in Walpole's library there. Lefty was able to guide him and the Knowsley librarian, Miss Dorothy Povey, from afar. They found many books with the Strawberry Hill pressmarks; they also found copies of books that Walpole owned without the pressmarks or Walpole's bookplate because the books had been rebacked or rebound with new endpapers. What, they wanted to know, were they to do about *them?* Lewis said to send them to Christie's and that he'd take a chance on their being "right."

The compiler of Christie's catalogue was Kenneth Maggs, Lewis's agent "in the rooms." He and Lewis discussed the nice point that this relationship raised: Walpole's ownership of a book increased its value—not nearly as much then as now—but somewhat; should Maggs use Lewis's knowledge of Walpole's possible ownership of the books that bore no signs of it? He would not have known that they might be Walpole's if Lewis had not told him and if he used this information in the catalogue he would be making Lewis pay for his special knowledge. It was clear to Maggs that he should not do so. At the sales he bought all the Walpole letters and manuscripts for Lewis and all the books from Strawberry Hill but one, a book that the Deputy Keeper of the Queen's Pictures wanted for the Royal Library at St. James's Palace. Chapman and Miss Povey sat together at the first portion of the sale. Kenneth Maggs told Chapman that younger booksellers had said to him, "Don't let Lewis get his books too cheap"; Chapman tried to spot the opposition, but was unsuccessful. However, it was brisk only on a few lots and Maggs got what Lewis wanted very reasonably. When the 106 volumes (which included 172 titles, seven volumes of manuscripts, and seven of drawings), reached Farmington Lefty had the nineteenth-century endpapers of the rebacked books removed. The Strawberry pressmarks were on all but two of them, a demonstration of the value of "provenance" that would have pleased Seymour de Ricci.

During the months of exploration at Knowsley Lefty kept urging his co-adjutors to find Prior's *Poems on Several Occasions,* 1718, a large folio with the pressmarks L.1.1. Since Boone had bought it and the three other books in the same lot were found at Knowsley, the Prior should be there. Where was it? It was hard to believe that a guest would absent-mindedly go off with so large and heavy a book. Miss Povey found another copy of it that was certainly not Walpole's, but the last sale came and went and L.1.1. failed to appear. A few months afterwards Lewis got a letter from a stranger in Maryland who owned a book that had belonged to Walpole's mother. Would Mr. Lewis like to see it? It proved to be a copy of Prior's *Poems on Several Occasions,* 1718. The front cover was loose, but it had been miraculously preserved. A small bookplate had been removed and above where it had been was "L.1.1." The 13th earl entered the Knowsley location inadvertently on a back fly-leaf. The Maryland owner wrote that Lewis would have to send him a set of the *Encyclopaedia Britannica* in exchange if he wished to keep the book. After this was done he told how he found it. He was a collector of firearms and a frequenter of junkshops. While stationed near Phenix City, Alabama, during the last war he saw a brace of flintlock pistols there that he wanted. In the subsequent discussion of price the junkman offered to throw in "an old book," which was L.1.1. How had it got to Alabama? One can only guess, but it seems possible that Lord Derby, with a fine copy of the book already and embarrassed by his having entered the Knowsley shelf-marks upside down in Walpole's copy, told his librarian to get rid of it in nearby Liverpool. Liverpool, cotton; Alabama, cotton: the heavy book sailed away as ballast before the Civil War?

The chapter of Walpole's books at Knowsley was not yet finished. A few years after the final sale at Christie's one of them turned up in the Library of the University of Liverpool, having eluded even Miss Povey's vigilance. But the University Librarian was Mr. K. Povey, Miss Povey's brother, who sent the truant volume to Farmington with the Library Committee's resolution that it be "presented unconditionally to Mr. Lewis, in recognition of his eminent services to literature, and that the Librarian be instructed to replace it at the University's expense."

In his review of *Collector's Progress* John Carter wrote:

Perhaps his [Mr. Lewis's] most impressive achievement in the purely technical sphere can hardly be appreciated by the layman. . . . It is that, in spite of being . . . known as the keenest Horace Walpole collector in the world, he has managed to avoid putting prices up against himself. To be a magnet is very well: to be a target can be expensive. There must have been many occasions when more than one bookseller reckoned that here was something Mr. Lewis had simply got to have, and resolved to outbid his neighbor for the privilege of selling it to him. There may even have been times when a dealer not favored with a commission from Farmington sought to teach Mr. Lewis and his agent a lesson. Only a combination of resolution and finesse with the power to attract and retain the trade's good-will could have kept the tortuous course between the Scylla of an extortionate price and the Charybdis of a missed opportunity. Mr. Lewis, with a studiously degagé *hand on the tiller and his cap at the jauntiest of angles, has made such a course seem like a straight line. . . .*

Part of Mr. Lewis' increasing immunity from competition has been due, of course, to the forbearance of other collectors, most of whom have by now tacitly accepted the proposition that anything remotely Walpolian belongs by right at Farmington. Even if bibliophiles as a class are not as curmudgonly as their critics sometimes suppose, it is still eloquent testimony to Mr. Lewis' international reputation that his natural rivals, instead of swooping on some enviable piece and thus winning a trick from the maestro, tend rather to withdraw in his favor—and even to keep a spare eye open in his interest.

For thirty-odd years Mr. Lewis was able to keep his hand on the tiller. This was easy in 1924 because, as I have said, no one else was collecting Walpole and the trade was indulgent to the young man over-excited by an inexpensive author. Its interest in him grew with his collection, but Walpole they began to think, was going too cheap. One by one the bigger booksellers "tried it on"; that is, they asked an exorbitant price for something they assumed Lewis had to have. He told each of them to sell it to someone else, but since there was no one else, he eventually got what he wanted at about his own price. The gold standard was abandoned in both countries, inflation darted upward, yet Walpoliana remained relative to the general rise of all prices where they had been in 1924. Lewis avoided "Scylla's" extortions. As for the few missed opportunities swallowed up by Charybdis, most of them were regurgitated and reached Farmington, some by purchase, some by gift (notably from Arthur Houghton and Victor Rothschild). Lefty's practice at auctions had been prudent and commonsensical. He gave his bids to Maggs in London, and in New York to Byrne Hackett as long as he lived, David Randall until he retired from Scribners, and finally to Michael Papantonio, who combines knowledge, integrity, and tireless concern for his customers' interests to a degree that makes bookselling a learned profession. Lewis put a general limit on his bids. "I am ready to pay more than anyone else," he would say, "but not much more," a puzzling remark now that I think of it. Whatever it meant, it worked until prudence yielded finally to incaution and then to recklessness. "Please get lot" such-and-such, he would write not adding, "But don't go through the roof." Scylla put on her six pairs of spectacles (one for each head) and waited as the veteran, his hand off the tiller, his course no longer a straight line, careened towards her. He got within range in October 1959. Kenneth Maggs, the conscientious and judicious, had died. His inexperienced successor paid thirty times the average price of a Walpole letter. Scylla had pounced.

Since auction prices are a matter of public record, Lewis's folly was public knowledge: he had gone over the falls, he would pay anything for Walpole, the time that John Carter feared when he would be shut up in a padded library was at hand. He no longer haunted bookshops; a new generation of dealers had risen up that knew not Joseph except as a target, together with a new generation of collectors and librarians who saw no reason why they shouldn't buy Walpole if they wanted to. The encounter with Scylla was painful. Lewis told himself that although she had his jaunty cap, she did not have the rest of him. Sadly he watched three letters go elsewhere. A small university library paid for a Class E note a sum that would have bought seven Class A letters before the war. The entries in the Farmington accessions book dwindled away, but in time the wounds inflicted by Scylla were dressed by Dudley Massey in London and Michael Papantonio in New York and Walpoliana, the swelling greatly reduced, are again reaching Farmington. Lewis wishes that the three letters were there, he thinks the scholarly world would be better served in the long run if they were, but one day they may be. Meanwhile, he acknowledges that his punishment was just, the penalty meted out sooner or later to hubris, folly, and delusions of grandeur.

XXX

LESSONS OF THE FIFTIES, II

Lewis's membership on educational boards other than the Yale Corporation has been noticed in these pages. The long table, the pads and pencils, the agenda, the budgets, the reports of standing and ad hoc committees became familiar features of his life. He learned that superficially they are constant for the boards of all privately endowed institutions—school, university, library, or museum—but that each board differs from every other board (like the stars in their glory), that they change as their members change, and that no matter how much they differ one from another, whether they are a "good" board or a "bad" board, a happy or unhappy board, green or seasoned, they are all affected by the interplay of personalities, the character and ability of the president, headmaster, or director, and the strengths and weaknesses of the chairman and individual trustees. His reflections on the duties and functions of trustees, their powers and limitations, their relationships to the administration, faculty, and graduates, led him to choose "The Trustees of the Privately Endowed University" as the subject of his Phi Beta Kappa Oration at Harvard in 1952. At the time he could find only two comments on trustees, both by presidents who detested them. His talk was printed in part in the *Harvard Alumni Bulletin* and *The New York Times* and in full by *The*

American Scholar and in *Man Thinking: Representative Phi Beta Kappa Orations, 1915–1959.* The Presidents of Chicago, Oberlin, Princeton, Smith, and Yale sent it to their trustees; references were made to it in "The Role of the Trustees of Columbia University" and by Harold Taylor, who was then President of Sarah Lawrence, in his *On Education and Freedom.* The subject is now always included in symposiums on university management.

Lewis's experience on boards of trustees has made a major contribution to his education. They are, he was to learn, very different from what they are imagined to be by those who haven't served on one. This misunderstanding does not seem to be owing entirely to the bad example set from time to time by the trustees of state universities. Even so informed and friendly a student of this country as Harold Laski wrote in his *American Democracy,* 1948, that the trustees of our colleges and universities (and he meant private ones) "are chosen because they are successful alumni or eminent, that is to say wealthy, men or women from whom direct help for the university may be expected, either from their own resources or from those it is thought they may be able to influence. . . . They are, all things considered, the most powerful influence in settling the terms of academic appointments and, very often, the choice of important professors, and the general direction within which academic policy must be framed. . . . They want, above everything, to safeguard the university from straying, through the habits of its teachers, into paths that may lead to inconvenient discussion in general or to be regarded as 'unsafe' by powerful economic interests on matters which those interests believe to be vital to social stability. And they expect the normal American university president to be their executive agent, among other things, in carrying out this policy." This is the stock picture of trustees at its most farcical. The joke, "successful alumni or eminent, that is to say wealthy," misses fire when I think of my many fellow trustees who though "successful" and "eminent" (and what is so terrible about that?) were not "wealthy."

Lewis's experience as a trustee has been limited to privately endowed institutions. He has never encountered the ignorance that harms state universities, and on the boards of which he has been a member it is completely untrue that trustees are "the most powerful influence in settling the terms of academic appointments and very often the choice of important professors." What actually takes place is that the appointments come to the trustees after months of deliberation by the faculty and are passed by the trustees as routine business. The absurdity of any other course is plain when the candidate teaches Sanskrit; it is less plain when he teaches economics or law or some subject in which individual trustees may have or believe they have professional competence. The Clerical Bloc on the Yale Corporation set a good example in this respect as in so many others. They not only kept in quiet touch with the Divinity School, but voted for the Dean's appointments even when they wondered if better ones might not have been made. In thirty years of service as a trustee, during which Lewis voted on thousands of appointments, there were only three occasions, all during the McCarthy era, when an appointment was challenged by a trustee on ideological grounds and on all three occasions (two of them were not at Yale), the challenger was conspicuously unsuccessful.

The belief that the trustees of privately endowed universities and colleges have a "policy" of "safe guarding" the economic establishment and that they "expect" the president to carry it out conforms to the naive image of them. Even Santayana accepted it. In *Persons and Places* he reports a talk with his old friend President Garfield of Williams: "When I mentioned Bentley Warren, Garfield said, 'Oh yes. He is one of the Trustees of our College.' From this I gathered two things: that Warren had been 'successful' and was now rich. . . . I expressed surprise that in their Faculty Room they had no portrait of his [Garfield's] father—an old member of the College and a President of the United States: and he said it was not for him to suggest that. . . . But why didn't his Trustees or whoever governed behind him—for Presidents of Colleges are secondary powers . . . attend to something so obviously proper?" We don't know why, but Santayana's belief that such Presidents as Mark Hopkins of Williams, Wayland of Brown, and Cary Thomas of Bryn Mawr—to name the first college presidents that come to mind—were "secondary powers," shows that even the greatest academicians may not understand university management.

Lefty soon saw that a member of the learned professions has an initial advantage over those whose formal education ended in college. Lawyers, doctors, clergymen, have had first-hand experience of a graduate school; they have found out how to use a library and have discovered that it is the core of the university; but every new trustee has much to learn, no matter how faithfully he has read the alumni magazine and gone to alumni dinners and talked to his undergraduate sons. He sits through his first meetings in a haze of bewilderment. What are all these new schools and institutes and centers? Friendship was the great thing in his day. A businessman unfamiliar with academic boards who has a strong sense of "management" may have a lot to unlearn. He must get over the idea that members of the administration and faculty are employees who can be hired and fired as in industry. He must learn about "tenure" and the conduct of academic business. It may be hard for him to divest himself of the awe or dislike he has of teachers as a genus, older people to whom as a boy he recited and by whom he was punished, praised, and judged and to respect members of a profession that accept a standard of living that industry scorns. He should get some idea of a teacher's professional obligations outside the classroom, the burden of committee work, what "research" means and its ardors and exactions, and the need for a teacher to establish himself in his profession.

He learns that the president is required by law to bring to the trustees much routine business and that they should not feel inconsequential when they approve it. The absurdity of their passing on the professional merit of a professor of Sanskrit is plain; it is equally absurd to think that they can make a thorough study of the budget with its figures and schedules and exhibits that have been prepared by dozens of experts during the past months when it is presented to them for their approval. During most of Lewis's twenty-six years on the Yale Corporation it was told grimly, "Next year we really *are* going to have a deficit." These dolorous predictions moved Lewis after a number of years to describe the treasurer "in a winding sheet" making the board's flesh creep annually; everyone knew that manna—extra dividends, gifts—would avert the promised disaster. As I think of this speech now it seems to me rather flip—one should never be facetious about a promised deficit—but at the time it delighted the Clerical Bloc and thereafter the budget was presented in a different way. After he became a veteran Lewis turned the pages of the budget silently and murmured "Aye" when the question of its adoption was finally reached; like Coriolanus, he had "put on the napless vestment of humility"; but he was humble about the budget long before he became a veteran. When the treasurer pointed out its special significances he was seldom at the right page; if he was at the right page he could not find the significant figures; when he was at the right page and found the significant figures he did not understand their significance. One morning page, figures, and significance seemed to be clear in a matter of special concern to him, all too clear: the special concern was being diddled out of its just due. Greatly daring, he asked a question. The answer, after the briefest of startled pauses, was given in the tone of one determined to be reasonable with a troublesome child: "That is only bookkeeping." From novitiate to veteranhood Lewis murmured "Aye" to the budget with relief as well as with humility. Perhaps one day there will be a series of fearful deficits, one right after another. What would emerge after the shambles had forced pruning of dead and decayed courses and activities might, I think, be a better university.

Lefty also discovered that a trustee's education on a private school board, library, or museum is fundamentally the same. The trustee of a school has to learn that it is not proper for him to intercede for the admission of a friend's child, no matter how eager the friend may be to get the child out of the house (before he or she reached the teens he and his wife couldn't bear the thought of separation), but if the trustee knows the child he may say so to the headmaster, who will be grateful for a report. Similarly, he may call the attention of a librarian or museum director to an object that he thinks they may want to know about, but again he must not exert any pressure for its acquisition even if he is ready to pay for it himself.

The more Lefty saw of academic societies the more they reminded him of the Mastick War, except that there are three entrenched armies, not two, struggling on the darkling plain. The armies represent the Estates of the academic realm, the trustees, administration, and faculty, and protect the prerogatives that each Estate possesses. Only extremists challenge these prerogatives: the right of the trustees to choose the head of the institution and supervise its property, the right of the president to represent it and conduct its affairs, the right of the faculty to choose its members who teach what and how they please. Between these well-defined frontiers is the No-Man's Land where the battles are fought. They do not occur all the time or even frequently, but each army is on guard against any invasion of its sovereign territory. In a university the greatest turbulence is in the Third Estate, the Faculty, where there are always a few burning and suspicious spirits who sense threatening encroachments upon their rights and privileges and who know that they could run things better than they are being run. W. S. Gilbert has shown one of them in Lady Blanche, Professor of Abstract Science, in the university presided over by Princess Ida under whose sneers Lady Blanche writhed for years although a born Plantagenet. Her daughter, Melissa, asks:

Now wouldn't you like to rule the roast,
And guide this University?

BLANCHE. *I must agree*
'Twould pleasant be.
(Sing hey a Proper Pride!)

MEL. *And wouldn't you like to clear the coast*
Of malice and perversity?

BLA. *Without a doubt*
I'll bundle 'em out,
(Sing hey, when I preside!)

The Old Guard on the Faculty looks askance at its Lady Blanches and they are seldom chosen for administrative tasks. When they are they find them harder than they look from a safe and irresponsible distance. Although each of the Estates may have civil wars the most sanguinary of them are waged in the faculty between factions and individuals who provide examples of what Heidegger called "the strong animosity of the parties one against the other; and a sort of itch of some people's minds, which is fed with contest as the chameleon is with air." An extreme instance of this was furnished by the chemist who disposed of a colleague first in a learned journal and then in an incinerator. The groves of academe are not free from violence.

The Fourth Estate in the university realm is the alumni. It is a comparative newcomer. When in the middle of the last century Yale graduates began meeting President Woolsey warned his faculty, "Mark my prediction—if our alumni meet together year after year, with nothing to do but talk, and time enough for that, they will be trying to govern us. You must stop their mouths with long addresses," and it was not until 1890 that alumni help was permitted. In that year the Corporation voted "to establish a fund to be known as an Alumni University Fund, applied to any use of the University." It turned out all right, for graduates now subscribe over four million dollars to it annually, the largest fund of the kind in the country. After the University began counting on this annual gift to balance its budget the Fourth Estate had arrived. In 1906 the Alumni Board was founded to enable other devoted graduates to engage in University affairs, primarily to interview candidates for regional scholarships. Lewis attended its meetings regularly when he was chairman of the Library Associates. The Chairman of the Board at that time was Marshall Holcombe, a fellow Farmingtonian who was as distressed as Lefty by the administration's lingering fear of the alumni, which was strengthened by the letters of its lunatic fringe. Yet throughout the country responsible and busy people, proud of being Yale men, were giving time and energy to do anything they could to help the University. It seemed unwise to hold them suspiciously at arm's length. Among the newcomers on the Corporation who agreed were Edwin F. Blair and Irving S. Olds. The result was the creation of an advisory group, the University Council that was made up of twenty-five outstanding graduates from all parts of the country. Some serve as members-at-large; others as chairmen of special committees on the chief segments of the University, each of which has a "visiting committee" of five members, not necessarily Yale graduates, who are experts on its subject. The Council has proved to be all that its proponents hoped that it would be. Under Reginald G. Coombe the Committee on the Medical School recommended changes that wiped out its staggering annual deficit; under Edward R. Wardwell, the Committee on the Music School brought about a marked improvement in its standing. Without the administration's cooperation these results would not have been accomplished. Several of the Council's members have been elected to the Corporation.

From the emerging Fifth Estate, the students, the trustees are protected by ranks of deans. Few undergraduates at Yale fifty years ago apart from the editors of the *News* ever heard of the Corporation, and Lefty did not get the usual muddled impression of its exaggerated powers until the twenties when Monty Woolley led a crusade to have himself given the rank of "assimilated Assistant Professor" in the English Department, a modest goal for one so successful. "The Woolley Affair" was a confused Mastick War that involved undergraduates, the English Department, the President, and one member of the Corporation. It was an unprecedented uprising against academic authority at Yale and it went on for years with bad judgment on all sides. G. W. Pierson in *Yale: The University College, 1921–1937,* called Wilmarth S. Lewis one of the "impassioned alumni" who petitioned President Angell to appoint Monty. The truth is that Lewis refused to sign the petition until its much too high-pitched language, which would have put the petitioners hopelessly in the wrong, was modified. When trustees get involved in student agitations they become ridiculous. Even if they do not approve of sexual promiscuity and marijuana they should leave these matters to the deans whose business it is to deal with them.

A meeting place for trustee, administration, faculty, and alumni may be the committee on honorary degrees. The members enjoy a special sense of importance. They are going to confer honors greatly coveted and they have all the world to choose from: the President of the United States, Nobel Prize winners, the great and good everywhere. Lewis in the course of his twenty-five years on the Yale committee was impressed by how large a part luck plays in the choices—at least two ardent supporters are usually needed to put over a candidate—and the part played by personal prejudice and predilection. The LL.D.'s, which tend to promote the most discussion, have the largest number of awards that would later be withheld. These are the statesmen who appear to their sponsors in December as shining knights in armor, but who by June have said or done something that has been disillusioning. It is advisable, Lewis learned, to have the selections proceed with reasonable speed. Since only a dozen of the candidates will be chosen, nothing is gained by spending time on those who, however admirable, will obviously not be on the completed list. If the meetings go on too long members of the Committee are apt to identify themselves with individual candidates and to become emotionally involved in their success. When the list is settled the committee always feels that it has done well, an opinion that is challenged after Commencement by those who loathe one of their choices or who protest that the list is dull.

The fiercest struggle of all in a board room—or out of it, for that matter—is the one that takes place in an individual, the never-ending conflict between the vices and virtues. The forces most actively engaged are Pride, Wrath, and Sloth on the one side and Prudence, Temperance, and Charity on the other. In the long run the latter, rather battered, usually win out. Another feature of the board room is the pecking-order that always exists there—it begins forming at the first meeting of a new board. Diotrephes "who loveth to have the preeminence among them" must earn his place. Those at the top combine knowledge, judgment, and the readiness of the conference table; those at the bottom are the cowed, the brisk seconders of motions, and the trustee-hounds whose vanity is titillated by joining many boards the meetings of which they are too busy to attend. When those at the top have inherent friendliness things go more smoothly and people enjoy themselves. Companionability is a quality that is often overlooked when choosing a new trustee; it weakens dislike of "the boys in the back room"; it makes those not on the executive committee feel that they are not just rubber-stamping actions already decreed even when they are.

In due course Lewis discovered that the tone of a board is affected by apparently trivial details such as whether the dates of its meetings are set a year ahead and conscientiously kept. Boards whose dates are shifted are less valued by their members and have more absentees. The tone and atmosphere of the meetings are also affected by the degree of formality that is maintained, whether first names are eschewed, and whether the chair is addressed punctiliously. The meeting place influences the proceedings. Somebody's office or a private dining room in a club lack a sense of intimate and elevated connection with the institution; a room in which the accoustics muffle the low-spoken and muddle the audible is irritating and exhausting even for those who do not have to cup their ears to hear.

Lewis became increasingly aware that a board through its collective wisdom, inherited sense of continuity, and objectivity, may serve as a temperate balance and guide: not all of the president's or director's proposals are necessarily good ones. The trustees may nudge a sluggish chief executive forward;

they may restrain, gently, a prancer-and-dancer. From the beginning of his experience on boards Lewis believed that the trustees' most important function is not to elect the head of the institution and oversee its finances, but to carry out the duty specified in the original Yale charter "to improve and encourage." Since encouragement can be expensive and expense is what "practical" men want to avoid some trustees habitually exercise their right to discourage. It seemed to Lewis that those serve the institution better who urge that it be first-class in whatever it does. He saw that the power of the trustees is and should be limited: they do not and cannot run the place, but as its nominal custodians they should press for an impossible perfection.

I enjoy board meetings so much that I wish they might go on longer to permit the trustees to know the institution really well. I wish that there could be leisurely talk about it, thinking out loud without worrying whether Flight 922 is going to be cancelled and what will you do if it is? Such talks could be stimulating and rewarding if the trustees were articulate, imaginative, and sensible. They would perhaps not suit the officers of the institution, who are naturally eager to get the trustees out of town as quickly and smoothly as possible, but I think that the institution would gain by them. This, alas, is a dream impossible of realization because life is too hurried and the engagement books of the trustees are too full.

The longer I serve on boards the more aware I am of Paul's attributes of charity—not being puffed up, for example, and not being easily provoked—but the one that seems to me most helpful for presidents, trustees, and faculty alike is "seeketh not his own," a precept that echoes the earlier writer who said, "Consider that I labored not for myself only, but for all them that seek learning."

XXXI

THE SENIOR TRUSTEE

President Seymour told the Yale Corporation in April 1949 that he would retire at Commencement in 1950. The Corporation then entered upon its most conspicuous function, the choosing of a new president, and did so with the dedication trustees show when their great hour strikes.

The retiring president recommended an innovation, a "Survey Committee," that should act as a clearing-house for candidates and report them to the Corporation. This committee became Bishop Sherrill, Irving Olds, and W. S. Lewis. Its first move was to consult about fifty representative members of the Yale faculty. Three quarters of the list were on the administrative side, deans, masters of colleges, heads of departments; a normal allotment. No prima donnas and ballerinas were on it, nor were the Olympians who dwell in cloud-capped towers. Such people are essential to the welfare of a university, but they are not looked to for help in times of administrative crisis. The committee divided up the list and called, singly, on the selected few in their offices. Two questions were asked: "Have you any views on the presidency—how it could be made less 'impossible' "? and "Have you a candidate?" The faculty was pleased to be consulted, after 250 years, on the choice of the new president.

The committee's visits were disappointing. None of those consulted had thought about the nature of the presidency. They were equally unhelpful about specific candidates: they understood that President A of B College was a good man, and there was what's-his-name at C in the West who was highly spoken of. The only thing that everyone agreed upon was that there was no one on the Yale faculty who was up to the job: the Corporation would have to look elsewhere. The non-Yale B.A.'s believed that the new president should have been an undergraduate at Yale; the Yale B.A.'s said that it didn't matter where he had gone to college, so long as he was "the best man." Nearly all agreed that the newcomer should be a member of the teaching profession and that it would be disastrous if a general or "a man of affairs" were chosen, a tendency strong at the time. Among the few advocates of a man of affairs was A. Whitney Griswold, who had just been made a full professor in the history department. The committee turned next to the leaders of alumni activities and other representative graduates and to university presidents and foundation directors. This wide and conscientious survey went on for ten months, but was conducted with such discretion that when it ended with the election of Whit Griswold everyone was surprised including Whit himself. The new president had been found on the Yale faculty, after all, and soon the entire community was praising the Corporation for its discernment.

A month before the Corporation's decision Lefty was asked by his classmates to talk at their annual dinner in New York, if he would, about the forthcoming election. Certainly, he would give them the specifications for the job and describe the leading candidate. "The Yale President," he said, "must be a Yale man. He must be a person of character with religious convictions. He

The Garden, 1958

The Garden, 1958

S. C. Roberts and WSL on the Cam, 1953

The North Library, 1966

Strawberry Hill by ABL. It was copied from a watercolor drawing and was the first needlepoint ABL did.

ABL and WSL at Strawberry Hill with the Rev. K. Cronin, Principal of St. Mary's College, 1951

President Kennedy, Felix Frankfurter, and WSL, 1963

Fred and Fidèle, 1944, in the guestbook at Farmington

such a badge at the top of their own arms; This discovery I made by a
talisman, which Mr Chute calls the sortes Walpolianæ, by which I find
every thing I want à pointe nommée wherever I dip for it. This discovery
indeed is almost of that kind which I call Serendipity, a very expressive
word, which as I have nothing better to tell you, I shall endeavour to explain
to you: you will understand it better by the derivation than by the definition.
I once read a silly fairy tale, called the three Princes of Serendip: as their
Highnesses travelled, they were always making discoveries, by accidents &
sagacity, of things which they were not in quest of: for instance, one of
them discovered that a mule blind of the right eye had travelled the same road
lately, because the grass was eaten only on the left side, where it was worse
than on the right — now do you understand Serendipity? one of the most
remarkable instances of this accidental sagacity (for you must observe that
no discovery of a thing you are looking for, comes under this description)
was of my lord Shaftsbury, who happening to dine at Lord Chancellor Claren:
=don's, found out the marriage of the Duke of York & Mrs Hyde by the res:
=pect with which her Mother treated her at table. I will send you the
inscription in my next letter; you see I endeavour to grace your present
as it deserves.
Your Brother would have me say something of my opinion

The First Appearance of "Serendipity"

Lord George Gordon in Prison

Eighteenth-century Conference at Smith, 1947.
Reading from left to right: F. W. Hilles, C. B. Tinker, D. Nichol Smith, President Herbert Davis of Smith, and WSL. They are looking at the picture by Thomas Patch described on page 453, which was lent by WSL to the exhibition of eighteenth-century English pictures held at the Conference.

The Colonies Reduced

ABL, Christmas 1958

The Print Room, 1966

The East Library, 1966

View from the Garden, 1966

The Yale Corporation, 1964.

Front row, left to right: John Hay Whitney, Juan Trippe, WSL, President Kingman Brewster, Jr., Edwin F. Blair, Gardiner M. Day, B. Brewster Jennings; back row: Caryl Haskins, William McC. Martin, Jr., Amos N. Wilder, Herbert F. Sturdy, J. Richardson Dilworth, J. Irwin Miller, Harold Howe 2d, T. Keith Glennan, William P. Bundy, Frank O. H. Williams.

The Castle

The Castle

WSL and Columbia, 1966

must be a scholar of international reputation with deep respect for science if he is a humanist and who loves the arts if he is a scientist. He must be a man of the present with knowledge of the past and a clear vision of the future. He must not be too far to the right, too far to the left, or a middle-of-the-roader. Poised, clear-eyed, informed, he must be ready to give the ultimate word on every subject under the sun from how to handle the Russians to why undergraduates riot in the spring. As a speaker he must be profound with a wit that bubbles up and brims over in a cascade of brilliance; his writing must be lucid and cogent, his style both Augustan and contemporary. He must be young enough to have 'dynamic ideas,' but old enough to be sensible about them; courageous, but not foolhardy. He must be 'a great personality,' by which is meant one who commands respect, who soothes the ruffled and charms the sentimental, an Olympian who is one of the boys without affectation or jocularity. He must have intimate knowledge of all the University's colleges, schools, departments, institutes, libraries, museums, and special projects, and know how to administer them efficiently and economically, delegating authority while keeping his finger on every pulse and in every pie. He must be a man with a heart who will share the private joys and sorrows of his faculty. Above all, he must be a leader, leading of course in the right direction, which is to money. Morning, noon, and night he must get money; money for salaries, money for buildings, money for scholarships, money for new projects that will prove he is dynamic. Since his job takes eighteen hours a day seven days a week eleven months a year, his health must be good—no colds, no ulcers, no slipped discs. Finally, his wife must be a combination of Queen Victoria, Florence Nightingale, and the Eest-Dressed Woman of the Year. As I have been talking you have guessed who the leading candidate is, but there is a question about Him: *Is* God a Yale Man?" Instead of running this in the class notes at the back of the *Yale Alumni Magazine* the editor brought it forward where it was seen by Charles Poore and reprinted by him in *The New York Times* whence it spread far and wide across the land, and only yesterday was quoted (inaccurately) from a New York pulpit.

As I look back on the election I think particularly of Irving Olds. Owing to illness, Henry Sherrill (the best chairman I have ever served under) was unfortunately away for three of the final months and so Olds and Lewis had to go alone on their visits to prospective candidates and officials of the educational world. Irving had the "big" lawyer's ability to assemble facts and present them in an orderly and clear way and the gift of almost total recall of conversations, which he reported without unconscious editing to the Corporation. He suggested to Lefty that they should not discuss the candidates when alone but weigh them independently, a course that I believe was also followed by all their colleagues with the result that there were no cliques and conspiracies working in the interest of any candidate. Irving was, I think, a model trustee, informed, correct, dedicated. One morning when the pair was crossing a distant campus, a trip arranged on short notice, Lefty asked him where he would be if he were not there. He thought a moment. "In Pittsburgh, talking to Phil Murray," the union leader who was conducting a strike against the U. S. Steel Company of which Irving was Chairman. "Do you wish you were there?" "Oh, no!" Irving was rather shocked. "Oh, no! This is far more important."

The Griswolds and Lewises were close friends, but it was not until Whit helped with the organization of the University Council in 1947 that Lefty realized he had what is rare in the teaching profession, an awareness of the University as a whole, the Forestry School as well as the History Department. When he was elected president Lefty told him of Mrs. Hadley's comment on the enmities that may spring up between sponsors and sponsored. Lefty did not want this to happen between Whit and himself. He would not embarrass and annoy Whit by hovering over him possessively. He could be found in Walpoleshire, whenever he was needed. Whit, who was a Do-It-Yourself, Don't-Fence-Me-In president, accomplished the great amount that he accomplished because the Corporation gave him a free hand. Had he not been given it he and Yale would have suffered. When a president is as independent as he was the trustees may rebel or lose interest, but the Corporation's delight in his gaiety merged with its admiration of his vision and drive and Yale was the gainer by its compliance.

Lefty learned how similar independence was exercised by another president when in the spring of 1940 the Signet Society of Harvard invited the Elizabethan Club to join it in celebrating the seventy-fifth anniversary of the Signet's founding. Lefty as President of the Elizabethan Club led the New Haven visitors to Cambridge and was placed next to ex-President Lowell at dinner. Their conversation got off to a confused start because Mr. Lowell was under the impression that Mr. Lewis was a professor of government, which Mr. Lowell had himself been before becoming President of Harvard. His manner and attitude changed when he learned that Mr. Lewis was a member of the Yale Corporation; the world famous scholar being nice to a junior disappeared and the affable man of the world arrived. Then, unfortunately, Lewis brought up the subject of the relations between a president and his board. "Oh," Mr. Lowell waved it impatiently aside, "I just ran the place." It can be done, but not by all presidents.

The situation that faced the Corporation in 1963 after Whit's tragically early death was entirely different from the situation in 1949. In 1963 there was a candidate with overwhelming support from the faculty and within the Corporation itself, Kingman Brewster, who had proved his ability as Provost and while acting as President during Whit's final illness and after his death. In the absence of a president the Senior Fellow, W. S. Lewis, presided. The search was even more thorough than it had been in 1949–50, but was concluded in five months amid universal applause.

Following both elections Lewis got letters asking for advice from trustees of other universities who were looking for new presidents. He wasn't able to be very helpful because an outsider seldom knows what a university needs most at a given time. If a period of consolidation after one of rapid growth is indicated, it probably should have someone with a gift for maintaining an even keel; if it is desirable to heave the university out of a period of stagnation an "activist" is no doubt desirable; but everyone tends to exaggerate the consequences of the decision. The university runs itself to a great extent; thanks to the able men on its faculties it may flourish under an indifferent head. Whatever the general need of the moment may be it will not do badly with a member of a learned profession who prefers administration to research and teaching, who knows how to get on with people, and who in the words of the Preface to the Book of Common Prayer, can find "the happy mean between too much stiffness in refusing and too much easiness in admitting variations in things once advisedly established." Such a view does not conform to the fine-sounding "We should have a great scholar," yet if the new president's first love is research he will probably be among those who resign before their time with impaired health and disposition. Amid the frustrations and harassments of office he will think wistfully of the books he planned to write and now will never write, of the developments in his field that he is not keeping up with, even of the annual meetings of his former colleagues when they herd together to read papers to each other and to look over candidates from other universities for posts in their own. He has moved from the Senate to the White House and is now the generalissimo of an opposing Estate; he has abandoned his professional career as a teacher and a scholar for presidential power and prestige.

This is a great and seductive lure. University presidents are our protestant cardinals enthroned in the present-day seats of salvation. They are the spiritual as well as the temporal lords of the mystery called "Education," which is the panacea for society's ills and the key to success. It is no wonder that they are highly regarded. They descend from the American folk figure of Prexy, who was clerical, learned, austere. When the undergraduates met Prexy on the campus they took off their hats and bowed. He was a father image and the personification of the beloved institution. He was Alma Mater's husband. Although his horse and buggy carried him away years ago, his grim portrait looks down on his successors today and contributes to the mystique that separates him from other men. The mantle of Elijah has fallen on Elisha.

After the president has been chosen the trustees enjoy a season of euphoria; the long ordeal is over, they accomplished what they set out to do, they got the best man, the millennium is at hand, but fear of the Lord goeth before the obtaining of authority. The deference accorded to the president morning, noon, and night may turn his head. In any event he, being human, will make mistakes and after his first one each of his close friends on the board has a problem. Will the trustee talk to him privately, offering advice and caution? Or will he say nothing and hope that the mistake will not be repeated? Whether he speaks or remains silent his relations with the president are altered slightly. As time goes on the trustee who voted for the new man because he had the virtues that his predecessor lacked may begin to think of the predecessor's virtues that the new man lacks.

When the honeymoon of a new administration is over criticism of the president begins. The things he does well are taken for granted; people, alas, prefer to talk about his mistakes. At the first hint of a presidential manner the faculty Cassiuses, who are congenitally against authority, will ask, "On what meat does this our Caesar feed that he is grown so great?" They will murmur that he is "only an administrator" who got his job by discreet but assiduous cultivation of the right people; they will criticize him for something he said or didn't say, for doing too little or too much, for acting too quickly or too slowly, for being cold-hearted or playing favorites. These whispers will filter back to the president and if he has a thin carapace he will feel as he lies awake that he hasn't a friend in the world.

If he is tough and the habit of command becomes confirmed in him he can handle his academic critics, assuming that he is himself a member of their profession, but the alumni and trustees are another matter and his latent hostility to the latter may emerge. This is not remarkable: he owes his elevation to the trustees (indebtedness breeds dislike), and even if he presides at their meetings he still belongs to a different Estate; the trustees are the only people whose formal approval of his actions he must secure, an irksome and time-consuming ritual. Presidents are

like favorites
Made proud by princes, that advance their pride
Against that power that bred it.

They become increasingly aware of the faults of individual trustees: the stupidity of A, the arrogance of B, the hostility of C. If he is wise the president will cultivate his trustees individually and engage their interest in whatever aspect of the university they are particularly qualified to help—the portfolio, perhaps, or the medical school, or art gallery. If, instead, the president's constraint leads to demonstrations of impatience he may be hurrying on to resignation. Impatience begets impatience and the trustees who also have the habit of command may remind themselves that the statutes of the institution assign to them "the oversight full and complete, right, liberty and privilege to furnish, direct, manage, order, improve and encourage" the university and to appoint its president, officers, and faculty. When either the president or trustees get above themselves warfare breaks out. Since everyone is hurt in these encounters the sagacious try to avoid them.

The Annual Report of the Carnegie Foundation for the Advancement of Teaching for 1961–2 addressed itself to "the relationship between trustees and president." It pointed out that this relationship "not only varies from one institution to the next, but from one president to the next in the same institution. It depends on the president's strengths and weaknesses, on dominant personalities in the board, and on the problems facing the institution at a given time," a statement that could not be bettered. However, it goes on to say that "the relationship is best described in terms of the familiar distinction between policy and operations. The board limits itself to broad considerations of policy. The president is the operating head of the institution." He is this, certainly, but if he is the dynamic leader that the trustees hoped for when they elected him he will not be a mere operative under their direction. "George, be King," the leader tells himself and also, "I shall be master in my own house." He will make the policy or he will quit (if he begins talking about quitting things have reached a pretty pass). When he became president he assured his friends that it was "a great opportunity." To do what? Not only to correct existing weaknesses, but to launch out into new and exciting projects, that is, to determine policy. The trustees can always fall back to their last trench, "We can't afford to do this," but when the president raises the money for it who has determined the university's policy?

The Carnegie Report also says, "The most important responsibility of the board is to select a president, to back him when he is doing a good job, and to remove him when he is not." Everyone assents to the first two responsibilities, but to justify removing the president the trustees must have something stronger to go on than his failure "to do a good job." What, precisely, does that mean, and how many boards are qualified to judge whether or not he is doing a good job? The academic community would take the side of the dismissed president against the trustees in any situation short of treason or spectacular sin because the trustees are still identified in the academic mind with reaction, a view kept alive by trustees of state universities. The shoulders of the trustees are broad, they could stand the attack that would be made on them, but removal of a president who was merely not doing a good job would hurt the institution so much that the trustees should have the courage to appear cowardly and carry on as well as they can until time, inexorably, brings relief.

In addition to running the university, a president has the unremitting problem of raising money. He is helped by a new organization on the campus whose real purpose is not concealed under the euphemism, "The Development Office." Yale's successful solicitation of money today is an advance on Lefty's one attempt at it. That was in 1921 when he was attending a booksellers' convention in Chicago for the Yale Press. It occurred to him that it would be nice if he got some money for the Press while he was there. George Day and Nig Donaldson and everyone in New Haven would be so surprised and pleased.

He called on two of Chicago's leading Keys graduates, John V. Farwell, who besides being an eminent merchant was a member of the Yale Corporation, and Robert McCormick, owner of the Chicago *Tribune*. Both saw Lefty at once and both were rather taken aback. Lefty had no "program," nothing specific to ask for, just the bright idea that it would be a good thing if the Press had more money. When Lefty reported his unsuccessful visits to George Day he was praised for his initiative, but cautioned against using it again.

This well-intentioned fiasco was in Lefty's mind twenty-five years later while the establishment of the Development Office was being discussed. At that time the graduates were complaining of the excessive number of Yale appeals that rained down upon them not only from the Alumni Fund, but from individual sharpshooters like Lefty in 1921. These last were controlled, the University's begging letters were greatly curtailed, an order of priorities was established. The technique of "handling" big potential donors is now the same everywhere: light massage, deep massage, and high irrigation administered by the president. The coup de grâce becomes increasingly distasteful to sensitive presidents.

It is not remarkable that two hundred presidencies of privately endowed American universities and colleges fall vacant annually, the great majority through resignation. When President Ezra Stiles of Yale wrote nearly two hundred years ago that "The diadem of Yale is a crown of thorns," he was speaking for all presidents then and now. The trustees are the ones who can make the crown more wearable. In his talk to the American Law Institute in 1963 Lewis proposed electing the president for a term long enough for him to accomplish what he most wanted to do and short enough to save him from deification. A president usually makes his chief contribution early; as time goes on his administration tends to become a holding operation against the assaults upon it. He may escape into illness; he may resign. With more and more presidents resigning before they have to it has become evident that something is wrong with the traditional view of the presidency. I think one trouble is the length of the term which may be twenty-five years and even longer; a limit of four years seems to me desirable with the trustees having the option to renew it for a second four years. The hardest question to answer in talking about a radical curtailment of the term is What becomes of the president after he finishes it? Lewis's plan provides for him to go back to where he came from, to being a dean and a member of an Academic Senate composed of the university deans and the librarian. The trustees would choose the president from the Senate, which would be the training ground for the university's chief executive. The status of the Senate's members would be enhanced; they would become familiar with the entire university through its weekly meetings and would acquire a sense of responsibility for the university as a whole. When a member's turn came to be president he would know far more about the place than most newcomers do. On resuming his decanal duties at the end of his term the university would be strengthened by the knowledge of its over-all problems that he would have gained while he was president. He would be offered presidencies by other universities and colleges, but having been a president he might prefer to remain a dean. Although the trustees applauded the plan in Washington it is so revolutionary that many more presidents will have to resign before it or something like it is accepted.

Which among the seven cardinal virtues is the one that the academic Estates should try to cultivate: Faith, Hope, and Charity; Prudence, Justice, Temperance, or Fortitude? The claims of each are strong, yet after years of reflection I would vote for Prudence. This formerly noble word has come down in the world; it has acquired overtones of politic behavior; timidity has crept into it; but I understand that these qualities were not the meaning of Prudentia. Rather was it sound judgment and discernment in practical affairs. In Prudence are subsumed all the other virtues: she led her sisters at the ball in the Earthly Paradise. Her third eye is a little disconcerting, but one can admire it when one learns that it is wisdom.

XXXII

THE PRINT ROOM

Lefty prudently gave up playing squash in 1936 after Dunham Barney almost beat him. This he had never done and Lefty did not want him ever to do it. In his bath afterwards, gasping, black specks, racing pulse, he realized that if he had one more such game (a) he would die and (b), worse, Dunham would beat him. The squash court passed out of his life for seventeen years until one evening when he told Annie Burr how he thought the Yale Walpole could be improved. She was again at rather loose ends having just catalogued all the houses in Farmington down to 1830, photographed them, written their histories from the records in the town clerk's office, and given the whole thing to the Village Library. What would she do next? Although she could organize and run large affairs, she preferred a job that called for close attention to detail as well as knowledge and imagination. Her husband had thought of an answer, but he had learned after twenty-five years not to be precipitate. "I've been thinking how the Edition could be improved," he began cautiously on the fateful evening. "We've nearly doubled the number of letters, identified just about everybody and explained just about everything, we've poured on unpublished pertinent material, but we've done virtually nothing with pictures—portraits and caricatures. We have to depend on the British Museum's *Catalogue of Political and Personal Satires* and its *Engraved British Portraits.* They're invaluable, but they aren't equal to the caricatures and prints themselves and they are not complete." The attentiveness of his audience encouraged him to go on. "Museum print rooms want the masters—Dürer, Rembrandt, Goya, and so on—not eighteenth-century prints, which they look down on; librarians don't want them because they don't know how to handle them; scholars haven't got on to them yet and collectors neglect the caricatures because they're unpleasant. When Chapman first saw our watercolor drawing of Lord George Gordon and his friends dining in Newgate he looked at it with disgust. 'Why did you get *that* thing?' I got it because Lord George Gordon is a major minor figure and because it makes the eighteenth century come alive. We ought to have a collection of prints and caricatures and a print room. The squash court could be made into one easily. The trouble is none of us knows enough about caricatures—I don't know who does in this country—and we haven't the time to learn. We need a new full-time person." Two nights later Annie Burr asked shyly, "Left, do you think I could help in the print room?"

The Lewises were introduced to the study of portraits before the war when Lefty asked Henry Hake, the Director of the National Portrait Gallery in London, why he thought a Nathaniel Hone there labeled, "Horace Walpole, Earl of Orford. Historian of English Painting and Author of a Considerable Correspondence," really was Horace Walpole? Hake was startled. "Good God! Don't you think so?" Lefty said he didn't, but when asked who he thought it was he could only say, "A nasty little man with a bad cold." Hake looked grave. "We must have an Inquest," he said.

It was held in the Gallery. The jury were Hake, Kingsley

Adams, the Assistant Keeper of the Gallery, and Lewis. The latter was seated in a cinquecento chair before a screen round which curious visitors peered from time to time. On the screen hung the questioned picture flanked by Eccardt's and George Dance's portraits of Walpole, both indubitably "right." Hake, very magisterial in his wing collar and black tie, presided. When had the picture come to the Gallery and from whom? In 1861 by purchase at auction from the collection, so it was said, of Lord James Stuart. This intelligence was not helpful. When was the picture painted? Not before 1760, Hake and Adams agreed, because the subject was wearing a coat with a rolled collar, a style that came in then. How old was the sitter? Not over thirty. If the picture could not have been painted before 1760 and the sitter was not over thirty, he could not be Horace Walpole the letter-writer who was born in 1717. Further evidence was assembled. When, Lewis was asked, was the Eccardt before them painted? In the background of it appears the east front of Strawberry Hill with the two rooms added in 1754. So Lewis guessed, "1754 or 1755, but if you look on the back I think you'll find Walpole dated it," and so he had:

Horace Walpole
youngest son of Sir R. Walpole
by Eckardt
1754.

Lewis wondered if the sitter was not Walpole's cousin, Horace Walpole of Wolterton, who at the end of his life also became Earl of Orford. Before the Inquest was over Adams produced a mezzotint of him in old age by Henry Walton which satisfied him and Hake that the two portraits were of the same man. The Hone was sent to the Gallery's lower regions; the postcards of it were removed from public sale. Everything was cleared up except the whereabouts of the original Walton of Walpole's cousin. Ten years later the Lewises found it in the dining room of the American Embassy at Canberra, Australia. Like the Hone in the National Gallery, it was labeled, "Horace Walpole, Earl of Orford," which was correct so far as it went. When the Ambassador learned that the sitter was not the letter-writer he let the picture recross the Pacific to Farmington.

Shortly after the Inquest Hake invited Lewis to join him and Adams in making an iconography of Walpole. When Lewis pointed out that he knew nothing about iconography that, in fact, he was not entirely clear what the word meant, he was reassured. "We'll take care of all the technical business," Hake said, "but we can't do Horace Walpole without you." So Lewis accepted without further demurring. The trio would identify Walpole's portraits and their artists, say when they were painted, give as much of their history (provenance) as they could recover, record when and where they had been sold and resold to whom and for how much and where and when and by whom they had been exhibited, state whether they had been engraved, and who were their present owners.

Lewis asked to see some of the iconographies that the Gallery had done. Hake was embarrassed. "This will be our first."

"But there must be some model I can look at?"

Hake brightened up. "There is. Your George Washington by a man named John Hill Morgan."

"Who lives," said Lewis, "a quarter of a mile from us in Farmington and is next door to us at Brown's now." Iconography was a small world, after all.

Hake, Adams, and Lewis divided Walpole's portraits into four groups: (a) those that are rightly named; (b) the possible, but unproved; (c) the wrongly named that have been called Walpole publicly; (d) the wrongly named that have been identified as other persons. There have been two grievous interruptions, the war and Hake's untimely death in 1951, but now, thanks to Adams's and Lewis's renewed assault upon the book it is nearing completion. Several new portraits have been found; several accepted portraits have been rejected. To reject a portrait long believed by its owners to be a famous ancestor puts a strain on the rejector's relations with the family. The iconography of Walpole will show the fallibility of family tradition, the credulity of purchasers, and the value of provenance.

In 1951 Annie Burr, who as a Vice Regent of Mount Vernon had run into dubious portraits there, was also able to change a label at the National Portrait Gallery in London. It was on an authentic portrait of Bishop Berkeley and said that the background was of Bermuda. "But," Annie Burr pointed out, "Bishop Berkeley never got to Bermuda. He stayed in Newport and that background is Paradise Rock there." Later in the summer she took a photograph of it from the same angle and sent it to Hake who was grateful for the correction. When Lefty talked to her about the importance of iconography he was talking to the converted.

This cannot yet be said of many except art historians. You are "in" English or History or Economics, and if you wander outside your subject you run the risk of being thought superficial. Tinker was one of the first to stray when in the twenties he made studies of the Boswell and Johnson portraits and considered pictures in relation to eighteenth- and early nineteenth-century poetry. After Lefty became a trustee of the Institute for Advanced Study at Princeton he could talk with Erwin Panofsky as well as read his books on iconography, which he defined as "that branch of the history of art which concerns itself with the subject matter or meaning of the history of works of art, as opposed to their form." The interpretation of iconography he called "iconology—the correct analysis of images, stories and allegories," and he pointed out that "it is in the search for intrinsic meanings or content that the various humanistic disciplines meet on a common plane instead of serving as handmaidens to each other." Lefty was dazzled by the richness and splendor of the new world that Pan introduced him to and by his casual erudition that sweeps from the ancients to the present in demonstrations of affinities between the Middle Ages and antiquity such as "when the figure of Orpheus was employed for the representation of David, or when the type of Hercules dragging Cerberus out of Hades was used to depict Christ pulling Adam out of Limbo," or when he and his wife traced the history of Cupid, blind and sighted, from Theocritus to the Counterrevolution. While writing *Three Tours* Lefty was struck by the vestigial remnants from earlier centuries of habits, forms and ceremonies, and traditional points of view that lingered on into the eighteenth century, and he became aware that discrimination of these inherited manners and ideas must be made before the century can be fully understood. They are even harder to spot than the tacit assumptions of everyday life—when and how people dined, how they lighted their houses and streets, how often they washed "all over," etc. Prints are documents, Lefty reminded AB the evening he opened the subject of a print room at Farmington and are a primary source for investigation of everyday living, especially the neglected caricatures and satirical prints because their artists showed streets, vehicles, rooms, and costume as they were.

In 1953 Dick Kimball divided the squash court by a floor, thus making two rooms, one below grade for stacks to house 10,000 books and an upper room for 2000 books, cabinets for 35,000 prints, files for 100,000 cards and four desks. The former squash court gallery subsequently acquired a sink and a thymol cabinet made by the Yale Art Gallery in which prints and books are placed to kill the acids that cause mildew. The

Curator of Prints in the Lewis Walpole Library (whose appointment was the only one in Yale's history known to have been made by a standing vote of the Corporation) entered into her new dominion. This consisted at the outset of Walpole's collection of W. H. Bunbury and the folio, "splendidly bound in red morocco," in which Walpole himself pasted "Prints engraved by Various Persons of Quality." Hogarth was well represented, and scattered about in extra-illustrated books that had been bought because they contain Walpole letters or prints annotated by him were many miscellaneous prints. These now came into their own, not only the caricatures, but the portraits and views of country houses and London.

Since Lewis no longer had the time, energy, or memory to pick up prints singly he asked George Suckling of London to act for him. Mr. Suckling did it effectively for two or three years, but before long Lewis was buying from any and all dealers who had prints that he lacked. However, he doubled his collection before Scylla quadrupled the prices. Hughdie Auchincloss gave to Yale his great collection of 3000 English caricatures for the new print room and recently another superb gift of 1500 caricatures has been given Yale for the Farmington print room by Augustus P. Loring of Boston. It is the major portion of the collection formed by his grandfather, Alfred Bowditch, who was one of the first in this country to see the value of political prints. Gus Loring, a loyal Harvard man and member of the Walpole Society, gave the collection to Yale for Farmington because he believed that it would be more useful to scholars there than elsewhere. He emphasized that the new owners were free to sell or trade any of the prints to strengthen the collection, an enlightened license not always accorded by donors. The blessing of Walpole on this gift was conferred by the discovery among the prints of four annotated by Walpole himself.

Yale has also transferred to Farmington, with the enthusiastic approval of the donor, the collection of many thousand prints of portraits, country houses, and views of London, given to the University by Joseph Verner Reed. The portraits solve problems raised by a political print that is not in the British Museum *Catalogue of Political and Personal Satires.* One gets to recognize quickly the leading politicians of any era, but since eighteenth-century artists did not label their figures the lesser known ones may offer some difficulty. The first place to turn to for help with them is Horace Walpole, who not only mentioned in his letters and memoirs the political incident being caricatured, but often described the print, figure by figure. The collection of portraits confirms his identifications.

Lefty's knowledge of eighteenth-century satire had been increased in 1938 when the first portion of the William Randolph Hearst collection was offered for sale by Parish-Watson in New York. They had no idea whether there was anything from Strawberry Hill, only a minute portion of the vast collection was on view in 57th Street, but Mr. Lewis was invited to look around. He wandered through rooms filled with Spanish choir stalls, Etruscan vases, and porphyry urns, but the geiger counter did not stir until he reached the top floor. There, leaning against the wall among Frederick Remington cowboys and Meissonier battle scenes, was a large eighteenth-century conversation piece labeled "Hogarth." Two lordly men are being shown trinkets by dealers; a third has turned to read a letter of introduction presented by a toothy young man who has entered from the right and is smiling expectantly in the doorway. The reader of the letter is clearly the host. He is sitting in a chair with the royal British crown on the top of it; the unicorn supports it on the right, the lion can be imagined on the left behind the sitter who Lefty was certain was Sir Horace Mann although the only formal portrait of him that he knew was the one by John Astley, which Mann had painted for Walpole. The host in the picture before him was older, more rugose, but with the same broken nose and air of a capable esthete. Lefty was equally confident that the artist was not Hogarth but Thomas Patch, who went to Rome in the 1750s with Reynolds and who never returned to England. He moved to Florence where he painted groups of visiting Englishmen in conversation pieces that were buried in English country houses until the descendants of the sitters began selling them in recent years. Mr. Lewis got permission to send a photograph of the picture to Francis Watson at the Wallace Collection in London who confirmed that Patch was the artist and that Mann was the figure reading the letter. The Hogarth label was removed, the price was reduced 97.6 per cent, and the picture hangs now in the long hall at Farmington opposite a later acquisition, Astley's portrait of Mann with Walpole's identification of the subject and artist on the stretcher.

Four other Patches have come to Farmington. All the figures in them, except Patch himself, are painted in profile, a view that aids the satirist. Although Patch is called a caricaturist, the features of only a few of his people are exaggerated. He is a candid camera, frequently unflattering, showing people as they were, which was quite different from the conversation pieces of Zoffany and Devis in whose elegant compositions the figures sit and stand and stare, but do not converse. With Patch all is animation and noise: men make elaborate entrances, servants carry trays and pour drinks, dogs skulk or lie about obscurely; everybody is talking or listening and is doing so in his own peculiar way. Mannerisms were Patch's forte: a special way of taking snuff, a swishing walk, an effeminate wave of the hand. Even the pictures on the walls contribute to the babble, for they were invented by Patch to heighten the jokes hidden in his scenes and to raise the laughs that died away two hundred years ago. Patch, like Walpole, made Lefty feel he was in the eighteenth century and did it by the same witty reading of character.

The print room was the closest the Lewises could come to the train that would take them to London in the eighteenth century and they embarked on it in that spirit. They learned how to store, catalogue, and index their material from Lawrence Wroth who had devised a system that brings order out of chaos and opens up the collection from many approaches. They took it over gratefully. Some prints have a dozen cards in various categories. Gradually the subject file emerged as the most rewarding. The curator became more and more skilled; her knowledge of what to look for, her imagination in anticipating what the users of the index might be seeking produced an aid to research that does not, so far as I know, exist elsewhere. The subject file goes from Abolition of the Slave Trade to Zebra. Panofsky's influence is shown in such entries as "Mythology" and "Personification" (Fame, Folly, Fortune, etc.). The subject file settled a point that was raised when Lefty was asked whether he thought curtains in colonial America came down to the floor in heaps and piles and mounds of silk as they do in many American Wings. Lefty was no expert on curtains; he did not think they came down to the floor in eighteenth-century England, and if they did not there they did not in this country, which followed English fashions, but AB's index answered the question in two minutes. Thirty-eight prints between 1712 and 1800 showed that curtains were higher and lower during the century, that they had pelmets of varying elaborateness and man-eating tassels at one point, but that they never touched the floor.

The hidden thoughts of the time are classified when they have been discerned, such as "Dismemberment of the Empire." This was stumbled on one day when Lefty got his copy of the

Proceedings of the American Philosophical Society that marks the 250th anniversary of Benjamin Franklin's birth. An article in it by Edwin Wolf 2d shows that the print, "Magna Britannia her Colonies Reduc'd," was instigated by Franklin to encourage the repeal of the Stamp Act. In the print Britannia is leaning against a globe of the world. Beside her lie her spear and shield, which are no longer useful to her because her arms and legs labeled "Virginia," "Pennsylvania," "New York," "New England," have been chopped off. Her expression is understandably wan. The British navy is beached in the distance; the British oak in the foreground has been reduced to a leafless trunk. Over the globe and Britannia is draped a ribbon on which is printed "DATE OBOLUM BELISARIO." A lengthy EXPLANATION points out that the valiant Belisarius who saved Rome under Justinian was mutilated by that ungrateful Emperor and forced to beg for alms, "Give Belisarius a penny." The Explanation is followed by a MORAL that leaves nothing to the imagination. When Lefty took this to the print room, a 1749 version of the dismembered Britannia just happened to be lying on a table. In it Britannia's arms labeled "Cape Breton" and "Gibraltar" are lying on the floor and she is being disemboweled for good measure. AB found another print in 1756 in which the British lion has lost a paw, "Minorca," and is about to lose two others, "Nova Scotia" and "Oswego." Franklin's print attacking the Stamp Act by showing Britannia dismembered was not original with him, after all: he was preying on the fear that Englishmen had of losing their Empire by using a symbol familiar to them.

In the four years that Annie Burr had to work on her index she made upwards of 12,000 cards, working whenever she could right up to the end. She used to wonder wistfully whether anyone would ever use her cards, but visitors are doing so now and are finding material they have not found elsewhere on subjects ranging from Queen Charlotte to wallpaper. Annie Burr built a six-lane highway straight across "the vast and relatively unexplored continent" that will be traveled as long as the Lewis Walpole Library exists. After her death a neighbor, Elizabeth Creamer, who had been with her as a volunteer from the first, carried on gallantly alone, but a full-time curator was needed. Where was he or she to be found? Lefty's friends in libraries and museums had no idea. What was needed was someone who was meticulous and imaginative and not intimidated by unfamiliar country. Mrs. Richard Butterfield, a neighbor only two doors away in Farmington, proved to be the person. With her arrival the work went vigorously forward again. She is kept busy by the influx of new prints and photostats of prints not yet at Farmington. My guess is that by the year 2000 the print room will have been greatly expanded (there is plenty of room to the south). It has now the largest collection of English caricatures to 1801 (including photostats) and I think it will become the most active part of the library in time.

Hogarth looms larger and larger as the work progresses and I think of him now as a second subcontinent in the eighteenth century. Walpole called him "that great and original genius" who caught "the manners and follies of an age living as they rise. . . . The very furniture of his rooms describe the characters of the persons to whom they belong. . . . The rake's levee-room, the nobleman's dining-room, the alderman's parlor, the poet's bedchamber, and many others, are the history of the manners of the age." He and Hogarth were fellow historians of the eighteenth century and Walpole accordingly made what he believed was the most complete set of the artist's prints in existence. Lefty's collection of them was acquired mostly *en bloc* as occasion offered. Annie Burr gave him Hogarth's first sketch in oil of "The Beggar's Opera" because it had belonged to Walpole; he had a few of Hogarth's prints that Walpole owned, Walpole's copies of Hogarth's *Analysis of Beauty* and Nichols's life of him, a respectable start that took a long stride forward after AB's death with the acquisition of George Steevens's collection of 705 prints, which was apparently second only to Walpole's in the eighteenth century. Steevens, like Walpole, knew Hogarth who discriminated for him the various issues of his earliest and rarer pieces—the tradesmen's cards, coats of arms, and exhibition tickets. This hit-or-miss collecting has resulted in what Ronald Paulson, the compiler of *Hogarth's Graphic Works,* which established the canon of the artist's prints, has called "a major break-through in Hogarth studies." He and Walpole can now be "read" at Farmington.

XXXIII

ANNIE BURR'S DEATH

In late October 1958 Annie Burr went as usual to the annual Council of the Mount Vernon Ladies Association of the Union. Lefty met her in Washington at the Athertons' where the Lewises were to stay before flying with them to New Orleans for a meeting of the National Trust, of which AB was a director. When she got to the Athertons' from Mount Vernon she was very tired. Since everybody is tired after the ten days of "Council" this was not remarkable; but the following day she was even more so, and Felix, who had dined with the Lewises at the Athertons', agreed that Lefty should take her back to Farmington instead of pressing on to another exhausting four days. This he fortunately did. Two weeks later Walls Bunnell, the Lewises' beloved Farmington physician, alarmed by her getting steadily worse took her to the Hartford Hospital. At eleven on Wednesday the 13th of November in his office he told Lefty that Annie Burr had cancer.

Such a revelation crashes through the crust of one's existence. You move about in a nightmare from which you cannot wake.

Lefty told Annie Burr the truth at once. There can be no rule about telling a cancer patient the truth, but if he has the courage to face it everyone gains by his being told, the doctors and nurses, his family and friends, and, above all, the patient himself. Lies do not have to be invented—lies that fool nobody. An atmosphere of honesty and support is created instead of one that breeds suspicion, fear, and gossip. How can you fight a deadly enemy if you are afraid to look at him? The power of cancer is increased by the fear of it, which is so strong that some cannot bring themselves to utter the word. It would be well to abandon "cancer" for "carcinoma," a professional name without sinister connotations, as "consumption" was abandoned for "tuberculosis" and then "TB." The Lewises did not avoid the name or the fact. Annie Burr had feared cancer for years, had annual examinations with it particularly in view, and knew enough about its treatment to have made deception impossible. She and Lefty had always discussed their fears and doubts and often knew each other's thoughts without speaking them. It was out of the question for them not to share this last dreadful test. Annie Burr would have felt that Lefty had abandoned her when she needed him most. They would have missed the journey hand in hand through the valley of the shadow of death.

On that first day at the hospital Lefty was able to reach his Yale classmate, Reggie Coombe, who was then President of Memorial Hospital, the great New York cancer hospital, and Reggie arranged for its head, Dr. Henry Randall, to see Annie Burr the following day, a deeply appreciated visit. Dr. Randall said that her case was "inoperable." The Lewises were told that the cancer had spread from its primary source, but they did not realize that "metastasis" meant that Annie Burr's case was almost certainly hopeless. This ignorance made her last six months easier than they would have been had they known that she was probably doomed. Since the state of the patient's mind affects his body and the spreading or retarding of the disease, his chances of recovery are not improved by discouragement. In cancer no one can be certain of how a case will go: patients have been sent home to die who, instead, have got well. These recoveries are called "miracles." Walls Bunnell believed in holding out hope based on whatever favorable signs he could discern. Night after night he came to see Annie Burr and she and Lefty slept better for his visits. Lefty sent telegrams at once to Father Leonard and to others around the world who he knew would pray for Annie Burr's recovery; "the prayer squad," he called it. She was particularly pleased that he had called Father Leonard. "I feel their prayers are more professional," she said. On his return from the hospital late in the afternoon he would go to Lu and Babs Robinson, who were temporarily in the Root house, a 1786 house on the Lewises' property, and tell them of AB's progress, and that was a great comfort. In a month she was so much better that she came home from the hospital to a quite normal Christmas with the figure of George Washington in the garden as a pleasant surprise on Christmas morning. She was inclined to agree with her husband that the nightmare was over, but in January it returned and on May 9, 1959, she died. She faced death with such dignity and poise that when it came she seemed to have triumphed over it.

The Congregational Church in Farmington was filled with old friends for the funeral, many of whom came long distances on short notice. Henry Sherrill and Palfrey Perkins, the minister of King's Chapel, Boston, another longtime friend, assisted the Farmington minister: an Episcopalian, Unitarian, and Congregationalist. The Lewises had agreed on the service years before. It was the Order for the Burial of the Dead in the Prayer Book except for a special prayer, which Palfrey gave.

Carl Rollins printed the Lewises' service, which Lefty sent to those whose letters were so moving that he could not do justice to them at the time. Such letters are written from the springs of feeling that we tend to hide except in time of grief.

Two English friends wrote to the London *Times,* following the warmhearted English practice. The first was from John Carter:

The many friends of Mr and Mrs Wilmarth Lewis and Walpolians all over the world (who almost invariably graduated to that estate) will learn with sorrow of Mrs Lewis's death last Saturday, after a cruel illness borne with the serenity which graced her life.

She was Annie Burr Auchincloss, and the stamp of that aristocratic lineage was as plainly visible in her handsome presence as it was subtly perceptible beneath the charm and friendliness of manner which endeared her not merely to her own wide acquaintance but to hundreds of scholars, students and connoisseurs whom her husband's dedicated passion for Strawberry Hill and its master continually drew into the Farmington orbit.

Mrs Lewis's natural abilities were fully extended during the war, in a high post in the American Red Cross, and for a number of years she had been "Madame Connecticut" among those august priestesses, the Ladies of Mount Vernon. But she will be best remembered by her English friends as the perfect, resposeful complement to an unabashed enthusiast: whether on their many visits to this country (immemorially based on Brown's Hotel) or, for the luckier of us in the comfortable library at Farmington, smilingly attentive at once to her embroidery and to the latest fantastic chapter of the great Walpolian saga.

The second letter was from S. C. Roberts:

There will be many on this side of the Atlantic who will be deeply grieved by the news of the death of Annie Burr, wife of Wilmarth Sheldon ("Lefty") Lewis, the eminent collector and editor of Walpoliana.

Lefty and Annie Burr Auchincloss were married in 1928 and nothing gave them greater pleasure than to entertain their friends, American and English, at their delectable eighteenth-century house in Farmington, Connecticut.

Lefty would delight to show you his incomparable collection and enrich his narrative with lively anecdotes; but the key to the lovely serenity of a sojourn at Farmington was the calm and gracious personality of Annie Burr.

She was the happy colloraborator in all of Lefty's pilgrimages and when, some years ago, his eyes failed him she read aloud to him the whole of the Bibliography of Horace Walpole *in proof. When, more recently, Lefty converted his squash court into a print room it was Annie Burr who, with unpretentious efficiency, undertook the duties of curator.*

A doer of good by stealth, she was active in innumerable good causes and it is with wistful melancholy that her friends now contemplate a Farmington bereft of her quiet and queenly radiance.

Lefty saved the thousand and more letters he received during Annie Burr's illness and after her death. The way she struck the young is shown in a letter from the daughter of a school friend of Annie Burr's who wrote to say how she remembered "Aunt Annie Burr as I last saw her when mother and I stopped in in the middle of the winter. Her presence, her company, was such a delight that day. I had known her for twenty-one years, but had never felt so keenly her individual loveliness. She showed us the print room and then stood by the library window with us, remarking on the statues, asking me about New York. . . . I best like to remember her laughing by the window. I'm so grateful for that day; I could have spent hours with her in the print room. There she was, completely herself."

It is noteworthy that the plight of old widowers is not portrayed in the Bible or Shakespeare. Ezekiel was told by the Lord, "I take away from thee the desire of thine eyes with a stroke: yet neither shalt thou mourn nor weep, neither shall thy tears run down"; and Ezekiel records, "at even my wife died; and I did in the morning as I was commanded." We are left to imagine him stifling his grief in purposeful activity. Shakespeare does not provide even that much of a glimpse. There are old widowers in Shakespeare, but none of them gives a thought to his dead wife. Companionship in marriage with the wife admitted at last to full partnership seems to be a modern enlargement of experience. When a wife of many years dies and half of her husband's life is sheared away he may be pathetic, but he is not tragic because he has had his day. As his infirmities increase and his reason for being declines he is usually more lost than an old widow who has her housekeeping and domestic life to continue and who tends to be more adaptable and self-sufficient; after a while she has what the French call "le réveil de la veuve" and accepts her new life with resignation and cheerfulness, but it is hard for an old widower not to become engulfed in loneliness.

Lefty's return to a single life was made as easy as it could be by his household. When the Rosses went back to Scotland in 1954 they were succeeded by Anna Brogan and Janet Sharp; Agnes ("Carrie") Carlos, who had arrived five years earlier, stayed on. These three continue to look after Mr. Lewis and his friends in whom they take a personal interest with a care, concern, and skill that is reminiscent of an earlier day. Bill Day comes in from the garden to deal with problems that do not require the attention of a professional plumber, carpenter, painter, or electrician. He brings the cut flowers for Carrie to fix and places the plants himself. The dogs are adored by all. Their daily pattern is as fixed as the progression of the hours. Its high points are their excursions into the garden and tireless searches for a mouse, any mouse. They are big, affectionate, disciplined, and are the best protection there is against marauders.

Annie Burr's arrival at Farmington after one of her infrequent absences from it without her husband would be announced by the dogs barking furiously. They would rush ahead of Ross or Carrie or Janet to greet her, their master bringing up the rear. When later she was going through the mail by "her" sofa he would tell her what happened while she was away. Since her death he has thought of these home-comings and what he would have to show her that was new—pictures in the halls, the addition of the East Library, changes in the Print Room. She would be struck by a piece of furniture in the library, the armchair her husband had at the Yale Corporation. This was the gift of Ted Blair, who with characteristic thoughtfulness and generosity has given their chairs to the retiring members. It is a daily reminder of its donor whose knowledge, imagination, and courage make him a model trustee and friend.

The garden has been kept as closely as possible to the way it was in Annie Burr's time and has become more beautiful every year. Although beetles have destroyed a dozen elms the two most conspicuous gaps have been filled through the kind offices of Ben Holden with maples from the Yale nursery; Dillon Ripley when he was Director of the Peabody Museum gave a metasequoia grown from the seeds of the tree (millions of years old) that was discovered in China in the 1940s. Its offspring has shot up prodigiously and will be several hundred feet tall in another million years.

Down at what was the Lewises' tennis court before it became a small nursery there is a sculpture in lead by Mary Knollenberg. It is a young woman looking up at her year-old boy that she holds on her left shoulder. His outstretched arms make a cross. The pedestal is of many-colored Westerly granite; on its face is incised, "To A.B.L. from W.S.L.," not too deeply, because W.S.L. wished to avoid any hint of the mortuary. There is a birch tree a little to one side behind it and a semicircular path bordered with myrtle and laurel. In the early spring there are daffodils in the unmown grass beyond it; the laurel and dogwood flower later and the dogwood turns scarlet in the fall. Annie Burr and Lefty used to walk to the nursery in the late morning during the last month of her illness.

Her grave is marked by a slate stone with her name and dates lettered and cut by John E. Benson. It is in the Riverside Cemetery at Farmington, the "new" cemetery there, which was opened in the mid-1800s. Halfway from the road to the river is the Civil War monument, a brownstone shaft with the names of twenty "Volunteer Soldiers from this Village," and, at the top, the battles in which they died: Fort Wagner, Winchester, Antietam, Gettysburg. Annie Burr's grave overlooks the river. It is next to a monument to the Tunxis Indians on which are inscribed Mrs. Sigourney's verses, "Chieftains of a Vanish'd Race." Ada MacLeish's parents and the MacLeish's little boy are on the other side of the monument and there Archie and Ada will also be one day. Nearby are Lefty's early Farmington friends, Mrs. Barney, Mrs. Cowles, Winchell Smith, and many more.

Lefty visits this beautiful place to confer, as it were, with Annie Burr and to seek her help when he has a problem that disturbs him. He knows what she would have said and he acts accordingly. A hundred feet below her grave the Farmington River turns abruptly north in the meandering way of rivers to join the Connecticut ten miles distant. Westward the meadows appear to stretch to the Burlington Hills. Lefty thinks of the first river that he saw, the stripling Sacramento, and the river of life that rose for him in Alameda and carried him away to such different scenes. He acknowledges his congenital deficiencies and the gaps in his education and is thankful that they did not prevent him from having as full a life as he has had. He counts his present blessings: his friends and his household who look after them and him with such devoted and expert care, his health, independence, and work. He thinks of Annie Burr and his thirty-one years with her that passed, it seems now, in a flash. As he stands by her grave he hopes for "the glory which shall be revealed in us" in a future life and he contemplates without longing or dread the time when his mortal remains will lie by hers above the lovely river flowing in its circuitous way to the sea.

XXXIV

THE FUTURE USE OF YALE IN FARMINGTON

From the moment he began collecting Walpole Lefty thought of his books as going eventually to Yale. This was the result of Tinker's plea to the graduates in 1924 to fill conspicuous gaps in the Yale Library, but as manuscripts, pictures, drawings, and prints supplemented the books and the house at Farmington grew, Lefty inclined more and more to keeping his library there. Furthermore, the Lewises wanted to preserve and protect the early part of their house. The whole place if given to Yale and endowed could become a center for eighteenth-century studies under pleasant circumstances, but this solution alarmed Mr. Keogh and his associate, Charles Rush, who one day in Mr. Keogh's office told Lefty solemnly that his library would be more useful and easier to control if it were moved to Yale where they would find a room to house the highlights in it; the rest would be shelved according to the Library's classification system; the duplicates would be disposed of. Lewis was aware that Messrs. Keogh and Rush were paying the highest compliment to his library by offering a room for some of its books, but he believed that scholars would gain more by living with all of them for a term or two under the conditions that would be provided for them at Farmington. That he was right in thinking work on Walpole could be done quicker there than in New Haven has been proved in recent summers by Dayle Wallace who can edit Walpole's letters about three times faster at Farmington than at Yale. Instead of having to go all the way down from the Walpole Room there to the catalogue, put in a slip, and wait for the book to arrive (if it is not out), he can be certain of finding it in a few minutes at Farmington. A weekly visit to Yale is usually necessary to answer questions that cannot be answered at Farmington, such as, for example, a row among journalists at Parma in 1741 or details of how Pietro Torrigiano starved himself to death at Seville in 1522, but most of the eighteenth-century books he needs are there. So the collection and the house will become Yale in Farmington. University counsel has studied the clauses of the Lewises' wills that concern Yale and is satisfied with them. Besides maintaining the house and grounds the endowment will provide a director and staff to run thc place for the resident scholars there.

The testators have not laid their hands heavily upon the future, but the Director of the Library must be a full professor on the Yale faculty living and teaching in New Haven (he may be brought from the outside) because the Lewises wanted to keep the library in the main stream of the University to prevent it from becoming an elegant asylum for some agreeable older person without academic eminence. The Director's salary will supplement the one he receives from the University. He will be Chairman of a Board of Control composed of the University Librarian (or a surrogate for him), the Director of the Art Gallery (or a surrogate), the Director of the Peabody Museum, the Director of the Yale University Press, and the Secretary of the University. The Lewises have stressed the importance of adding to the collections because libraries and museums become static and mouldy unless they are reinvigorated by new accessions.

"Maintenance" includes physical care of the books and pictures as well as of the house and grounds, repairing bindings, making slipcases, doing what may be needful to the pictures and furniture. It was discovered recently that the framed drawings and prints were nearly all suffering from conditions that in time would have ruined them: they had been framed touching the glass and on paper and with glue that engendered acid. Mr. Francis Dolloff of the Boston Museum of Fine Arts removed, cleaned, and remounted them on rag paper away from the glass and they are now safe. The danger of fire has been reduced by every sort of device, including one that detects smoke. This last is connected with the town Fire Department where there is a panel that indicates the room in the Lewises' house that has the smoke. The alarm goes off with a terrifying bell, the detector in the afflicted room flashes a light, and the town siren summons the members of the Volunteer Fire Department from whatever they may be doing. The system worked the morning it was installed when Mr. Lewis's toast popped up smoking slightly. It has been calmed down, but still goes off if guests light tobacco directly under a detector: the bell sounds, the lights flash and flash, the siren alerts the countryside, the dogs bark wildly, the faithful and remarkably quick firemen appear in their helmets prepared for the worst. The system paid for itself—and the false alarms—when it was set off by a short circuit in the air-conditioning unit that could have progressed to a serious fire.

Comfortable accommodation, as small resort hotels advertise, will be provided for half a dozen married couples and a single man or two. They will live in the main house and the late-eighteenth-century Root house. Additional desks and files have been supplied by the new East Library (very functional), which makes Yale in Farmington a professional institution without sacrificing its amenity. The endowment will publish the books written by the members at Farmington. Publication is rarely underwritten by foundations, which tend to take care of the man while he is working on his book, but not to take care of the book after it is written. To get it published the author has often to contribute part of his savings and he is lucky if he gets them back. Yale in Farmington will relieve its members of this uncertainty. They will pay for their food, but not for their lodging. They will come on their own—partly with their sabbatical leave salary, partly, perhaps, with foundation grants—for a term or two on invitation of the Board of Control.

Who will the members be? Senior people of proved achievement and juniors of outstanding promise who can move beyond the fixed boundaries of humanistic studies into unexplored territory. Farmington will give them a chance to write their books and free them temporarily from the exactions of teaching and committees. It will offer opportunities for fresh enterprises and speculation, a place where the members will live, it is to be hoped in amity, exchanging views with and learning from each other. The humanities are suffering from a sense of inferiority to the sciences whose spectacular triumphs make their studies seem sterile. The cure is not a pseudo-scientific jargon, but fresh insight. Lewis hopes that it may be found at Farmington since "the wisdom of a learned man cometh by opportunity of leisure."

The ideal Director of the Library will be preeminent in his own right as a scholar. It will make no difference what his field is, whether English, history, the arts, economics, so long as he has what Whitehead called "the imaginative consideration of learning" and knows that students of the eighteenth century need many "disciplines" to master their subject. This broadening is sometimes called "cross-fertilization," but I prefer "ecumenical" in its general, universal, sense. Horace Walpole and Hogarth furnish endless opportunity for exercise of the ecumenical spirit and together cover the life of the eighteenth century. The ideal Director will be an ecumenicist. He will also understand something about the techniques of collecting (which can be learned only by experience) and will believe that their skilful use is vital to the health of the Library.

His job will not be a sinecure. In addition to choosing the members and overseeing their physical and academic needs he will have a considerable correspondence. Lewis has discovered why Mr. Keogh used to speak of amateur genealogists with dread. When a letter begins, "I am tracing the line of," he can see the tracer: purposeful, undeflectible, driven by obscure but irresistible forces to rescue a fact, any fact, in the life of some dim and distant relation. A folder at Farmington labeled "Nuisances" has letters from the deranged and exotic such as the man in Hyderabad who sought help with the Philosopher's Stone and Elixir of Life. A Texan urged Mr. Lewis to persuade President Eisenhower to declare a National Correspondence Week to further "the promotion of mutual understanding between acquaintances and help preserve the memories of associations"; he suggested "the month of September containing 16th," his birthday, which "is also a national holiday observed in Mexico." Not all correspondents are so altruistic. A woman in Co. Kerry wrote to Mrs. Sheldon Lewis for assistance in sending her "little girl aged 9 who is very clever" to Loreto Convent, Killarney, where she would "get a chance of developing her genius." Mrs. Sheldon Lewis's reward would be "the prayers and blessings of an Irish mother." Mr. Sheldon Lewis recalled how impressed he was by such prayers and blessings in 1909 when the *Saxonia,* bound for Boston, called at Queenstown. Irish mothers swarmed aboard to sell objects made of blackthorn. Mr. Sheldon Lewis, then plain Wilmarth Lewis, bought a pig with a shamrock carved on it and was given a blessing that launched him into the future with greatly enhanced prospects of success.

Less exotic applicants range from the experienced and courteous to the green and peremptory. The Director will work out a formula for handling them. Lewis has usually resisted the temptation to ignore the strangers who want exclusive use of unpublished material and want it promptly; instead, he writes to say that it has already been promised to another scholar, a formula that eliminates the undesirable without tears. The sooner unpublished material gets into print the better for everybody, but a manuscript botched in publication loses its bloom forever; better the rage of the rejected. Lewis's attitude towards applicants is influenced by their original letters. Years ago a manufacturer of "quality" paper used to quote Emerson in his advertisements: "What you are speaks so loud I cannot hear what you say." The applicant reveals himself in many ways besides his stationery. Lewis is predisposed in his favor if he states his case clearly, briefly, and modestly. He must not sprinkle the sugar of flattery too generously; he must not be jocular; he must not give the impression that he has a "right" to the material that he wants to use; he must not ask that his work be done for him; he will do well to show his awareness of the trouble to which compliance with his request would put the owner; he must not conclude, "Looking forward to hearing from you at your early convenience"; he must not enclose stamps for the early reply, but he should say that he will pay for the reproductions. The English are masters of letter writing, even the English without pretence to literary skill. In so far as Americans have neglected this art, and most of them have, they are at a disadvantage with British owners. The American professor who wrote to the Duke of Richmond for help and addressed him after a conscientious study of Debrett as "Messrs

Richmond and Gordon, Dear Sirs," was disappointed. Instruction in how to write letters should be given in our graduate schools, but there are not too many who could give it.

As the library became better known more and more strangers wrote to ask to see it. Lefty, like Walpole before him, was flattered for a while by this celebrity and then got tired of it. Speaking of Shenstone Walpole said, "Poor man! he wanted to have all the world talk of him for the pretty place he had made. . . . The first time a company came to see my house I felt his joy. I am now so tired of it, that I shudder when the bell rings at the gate." Annie Burr also got tired of so many visitors to the library and asked one day if Lefty did not think they were having a good many of them? He counted up nearly 300 between Labor Day and Thanksgiving of that year. From then on the Lewises were less hospitable. Today when large groups come they are subdivided and guided through eight rooms by Miss Martin, Mesdames Day, Butterfield, Creamer, and Mr. Lewis. If the visitors are *very* keen they are shown the stacks in the office and squash court, but only the very keen enjoy stacks. On these tours no one sees much, but they get a general impression of the whole.

After the Yale Edition of Horace Walpole's Correspondence is completed, a second multivolume undertaking should be started, a new edition of Walpole's *Memoirs,* all of them, from 1746 to 1791, a work of some three million words. The text has been misread and tinkered with by editors and mutilated by owners. Until the *Memoirs* are printed as Walpole wrote them with all the resources of modern editing the most extended memoirs dealing with the Parliamentary history of those years will not have been made available to scholars as they should be and as they now can be from the originals or photostats of them. A large undertaking will, I trust, be a volume, possibly two volumes, of additions and corrections to the British Museum's

Catalogue of Political and Personal Satires down to 1801. The corrections will be comparatively few, especially in Mrs. M. D. George's part of it, but the additions will be many, some 2000 of the "new" prints at Farmington and in the Pierpont Morgan Library, with which the Lewis Walpole Library has an ideal working arrangement. All this will take many years, but it has a definite terminus. What has no limit are the books that may be written from the materials at Farmington. I hope the users of them will not employ what Chapman called "the spade of unenlightened industry."

The name "Lewis Walpole Library" has become a misnomer; Lawrence Wroth and Edgar Richardson have called it "universal" in its range. It has a precedent on a much bigger scale in the Folger Shakespeare Library, which, under Louis Wright's direction, has spread so imaginatively and so fruitfully beyond Shakespeare. Walpole's reputation will rise and fall, as all reputations do, but Yale in Farmington will be able to support serious studies in any aspect of his time.

One day in 1958 Annie Burr and Lefty were walking down the garden when Bill Day appeared with a cigar box full of arrowheads, "all found on the place." The Lewises, to their shame, showed only polite interest and nothing further might have been done about the arrowheads had not Lee Stone after AB's death given Lefty a copy of a map made by Louis Alexandre Berthier when he was with Rochambeau on his march from Newport to Yorktown in 1781. Napoleon's future chief of staff made maps of the places where Rochambeau's force camped. The map Lee gave Lefty shows that the French site in Farmington was on the Lewises' place. Lefty hurried out with it to Bill Day. Had he found any coins or soldiers' buttons? Yes, a few and lots of flints and broken clay pipes. He cleared out a tool house for hundreds of stone objects that he and his family had picked up in the Lewises' field after the spring thaws and when the field was ploughed, a display that convinced the owner that they deserved a better home than cigar boxes. Lefty consulted with Walls Bunnell, who had rescued eighteenth-century houses in the neighborhood and moved them to his property where he converted them into the most attractive shopping center in Connecticut. Did he know of an old house that Lefty might buy and move to store the Indian relics? "I not only know of one, but own it and I'll give it to you if you will move it." The house was built about 1750 by the Congregational Church for one of the Tunxis Indians, a tribe so mild that its members ended up singing in the choir. The house was moved and the Day Collection installed in it. The interest aroused in "The Museum" gave Lefty pause: if it were opened to the public there would have to be a caretaker, tickets, etc.; the visitors would wander into the garden leaving the gates open and letting the dogs out. He did nothing further about it for some years until, troubled by conscience, he asked Irving Rouse of the Peabody Museum at Yale to come up and tell him what he should do, pointing out, "This will one day be your responsibility." The visitor was agreeably surprised: the objects in the cases that Bill Day built and that overflowed neatly onto the floor cover a period of five thousand years, a span longer than had been found elsewhere in one New England site. Yale in Farmington turned out to have an unexpected facet. Could, Rouse asked, Yale use it as a dig? It would be much handier than Florida or Venezuela where he had been working. The results might fill the present gap between the Archaic period (3000 B.C.) and the late Woodland (A.D. 1000) in the paleo-Indian New England culture, periods new to W. S. Lewis. It would be hard to imagine anything more foreign to Horace Walpole or that would have interested him less, but Lewis welcomed these antediluvian predecessors who were dropping "projectile points," drills, knives, scrapers, gouges, and hatchets on his land two thousand years before David chose five smooth stones out of the brook and slew Goliath of Gath. Trenches will be dug as soon as possible, cataloguing the hundreds of artifacts and potsherds already discovered has begun, and the Peabody Museum will join with the Yale Library and Art Gallery in exploring the resources of Yale in Farmington.

The transition of the Lewis Walpole Library to Yale will be effected smoothly, so close is the tie now established. The present officials at Yale are relatively young. They have allayed Lefty's earlier fears of what may happen to his library on his death for should that occur tonight Yale in Farmington would be in the hands of understanding and sympathetic friends for years to come.

XXXV

CONCLUSION

Senior Year in God's School on earth has turned out to be very different from what I thought it would be. I was misled by the poets who I supposed knew everything. Wordsworth wrote, "I see by glimpses now. When age comes on may scarcely see at all," and Matthew Arnold said that in old age there is "no emotion—none." Both were making pronouncements upon a subject that they had not yet experienced. Although I am still seeing by glimpses I believe I am seeing more. As for emotion, my problem is not having none but too much. Like Goneril, the elderly have to be on their guard against "the unruly waywardness that infirm and choleric years bring with them." Choler keeps emotion alive and so does fear, fear of losing one's mind and money and health, fear of falls—those treacherous little steps in the dark. Society's beleaguered state today heightens the fear of violence and vandals; old people are natural prey for the underworld as Lewis discovered a few years ago when on entering the Hartford train in Grand Central Station he was set upon by three pickpockets in the murk of the vestibule. He frustrated them before they got his wallet, a satisfaction, but he found the incident disturbing.

Although the sages assure us that adaptability is the key to a successful life, it isn't easy for one nursed on Lewis Carroll and *St. Nicholas* to accept the modern playwright who presents youths smearing a baby with its excrement before stoning it to death. No generation has ever had more to adapt to than the one born at the close of the last century. We have seen the dissolution of the empires that covered much of the globe, the rise to world power of the U.S.A., the emancipation of women and youth, the miracles of science and technology. As we view the rubble of what we were brought up to respect and cultivate we are tempted to be thankful that we do not have much time left to adapt to, but acceptance of accomplished facts seems to be essential to a good performance in the home stretch. It eases settling into retirement; it checks a tendency to prattle of outlived importance; it helps adjustment to the built-in obsolescence with which we are all born. The advance of decrepitude is noted by one's contemporaries: "Poor Mary is blind as a bat," "George shakes so he can no longer hold a glass." After I passed sixty, younger acquaintances began identifying themselves distinctly when we met. I didn't know how to take this kindness then; now I am grateful to them. The deaths of old friends may make one think of the men clinging to the *Titanic*'s life rafts in the icy water during the long night and dropping off one by one, but Aunt Annie Jennings, George Dudley Seymour, and Carl Rollins had no morbid fantasies in their later years. Aunt Annie kept up her unflagging pursuit of the activities she believed in, unobtrusive concern for the welfare of her family and friends, and interdiction of talk about ill-health and old age; George Dudley Seymour, chairbound and speechless, finished his life of Nathan Hale by pointing at letters; Carl Rollins went on designing books after he was blind. Karl Menninger in *Vital Balance* observes that withdrawal, giving up, is penultimate death. In Senior Year you must try to keep your name in the book of life.

Annie Burr would find the pattern of her husband's day not much changed except for the Yale Corporation. As his time drew near to retire from it he kept recalling the final exit of the Senior Fellow in June 1938. No one else saw him go out the door with a brave little smile, his quarter century of devoted attendance finished. Lefty was haunted by that exit, but when his own time came to leave it was quite different. Ted Blair made a speech and then the whole Corporation stood up. Lefty's emotions going down the stairs afterwards were very different from those he had going up to his first meeting twenty-six years earlier—twilight and evening bell instead of rising sun and reveille—but how fortunate he was to have had so long an association with such friends and such a university. The Yale Walpole and Lewis Walpole Library are stronger links with it than those held by most emeriti—football tickets in Portal 16 (which Lewis has not entered since 1940) and seats on the Commencement platform, neither of them, naturally, as far forward as formerly.

Annie Burr would share her husband's regret that he is no longer on the board of Miss Porter's School, which has the same sensible retirement rule, but his other extracurricular employments protect him from the bitterness that may infect the last years of those who have nothing to retire to by taking him out into the world and giving him a sense of participation in it. Annie Burr, who was the Americanist in the family, would be amused to find that four of her husband's remaining boards, the John Carter Brown Library, the National Portrait Gallery, the Henry Francis duPont Museum, and the Heritage Foundation at Deerfield, Mass., are concerned primarily with American culture about which she knew his knowledge was small. No matter, one doesn't have to be an expert to see that they promote American studies. She would be touched to learn that her beloved colleagues at Mount Vernon have elected him to its Advisory Committee.

Winterthur and Deerfield are examples of creative collecting on a noble scale. They are, properly, meccas for tourists, but their special appeal to Lewis, apart from his regard and affection for their creators, Harry duPont and the Henry Flynts, is for what they could be giving to higher education. At them the early American culture can be studied, to use the academic phrase, "at the highest level"; yet they are still viewed askance by the teaching profession, owing in part to their founders being rich "amateurs" (by which is meant that they have no Ph.D.), in part by instructors who, not having been taught how to use museums in graduate school, assume that museums have nothing to teach them. If Winterthur and Deerfield were solely repositories of manuscripts they would be besieged, for "documents" are now canonized. That artifacts, even beautiful ones, are also documents has yet to be grasped by the generality of educators. Both Winterthur and Deerfield are eager to be used; their skilled and generous creators have "nothing in mind but the good of mankind." Lewis is doing what little he can to encourage students of American history and culture to mine these Golcondas that have been placed at their disposal and this would please Annie Burr, who became increasingly interested in the preservation and care of American antiquities.

The Redwood Library at Newport, to which Lefty escaped in 1929 for light on the Duke of Albany, is his sole connection with the life of that community. He became a director of it in 1947 after Annie Burr took over the Castle at Hammersmith Farm. The oldest part of The Castle (a nursery joke of the Auchincloss children) is about 1680, the main part, 1710. First the British and then the French used it during the Revolution as a hospital; in the middle of the next century Harriet Beecher Stowe wrote *The Minister's Wooing* there. Annie Burr got Dick Kimball to renovate it and it is the most darling small house to be seen anywhere. Newport has the perfect summer climate, not too hot, not too cool, just enough fog and rain to keep things fresh; at the Castle there is usually a southerly breeze blowing from the sea across the golf course. Lewis works all day (these words are being written there at 6 a.m.)—outdoors if the dogs insist on it. The work goes better than it did forty years ago when Lefty carried his pad and pencils to an upper bedroom in the big house and looked discontentedly out the windows. Dick Bates, a retired Rear Admiral and historian of the war in the Pacific, comes to lunch and he and Wilmarth talk about Alameda where Dick, too, was born and went to Mastick and sang in the Christ Church choir sixty years ago. The only party given at the Castle is for the neighboring children. Caroline Kennedy presides at their supper, which they eat decorously at a table planned with imagination and affection by the household. Supper over, the guests rush out to the orchard, run around, scream, and throw apples at each other until the first long wail indicates a direct hit. Then they are hastily gathered up by their nannies and led away and Uncle Lefty's Newport season is over for the year.

At Farmington he has a wider circle. The guest book records over 2500 visitors for one or more nights since 1926. Lewis has indexed it and keeps the cards in a box that John McDonnell had made for them by Sangorski in London. Friends come for lunch, his classmate Mac Baldrige from Washington, Conn., Harold Hugo from the Meriden Gravure Company to talk a little business and much about the book world, Corinne Alsop Cole to talk about anything and everything as she and Lefty have done for over forty years. After lunch he has a nap to comply with his regimen:

Early to bed; late to rise;
A nap after lunch, and no exercise.

He goes faithfully to the Monday Evening Club of Hartford, which has been meeting six times a year for nearly a century. The members dine in each other's houses and listen after dinner to a twenty-minute paper written with much thought and anxiety, an evening that perpetuates the older New England tradition of improving one's mind by literary composition submitted to the critical discussion of one's peers. Mark Twain made fun of the Club in his day, but no one is inclined to do that now. Lefty also goes to the meetings of the Walpole Society, which was founded in 1910 by the group of collectors who did so much to stimulate the preservation and study of the earlier American decorative arts. They took Walpole's name because he was the pioneer historian of painting in England and the enthusiastic champion of his country's architecture. Since Lewis is not a collector of Americana his membership in the Society is still another debt he owes to its patron. The meetings are held twice a year anywhere from Maine to Georgia, the local custodians, private and public, open their treasures to the visitors, and at the end of the weekend Lewis can no longer tell the difference between a table and a chair. Shortly before he died Irving Olds told Lefty that of all his clubs the Walpole Society meant more to him than any other, and this I think would also be said by most of its members.

Lewis has to force himself to leave Farmington where he is so comfortable and has everything so exactly as he likes it. He knows that a change of scene helps combat the "easy and capricious valetudinarianism" that Dr. Johnson warned is a temptation of old age, but he finds it more and more of an effort to move. He was shown recently how stick-in-the-mud he has become by one of his very few acquaintances in the Jet Set. The following colloquy took place:

ACQUAINTANCE: I'm going to Portugal tomorrow. Come along with me.

W.S.L. (*staggered*) : I've guests coming here.

ACQUAINTANCE (*after incredulous stare*) : What difference does that make?

Despite his increasing inertia Lewis does get out to San Francisco and the Ojai Valley every year or so. A memorable trip was in December 1963 when he was given a lunch by his Mastick Grammar School class in Alameda. Thirty-two came, including some from neighboring classes, the first reunion of the Class since it graduated fifty-five years earlier. Wilmarth had seen none of its members in the interval and found the occasion like a scene in Barrie in which the characters meet, all at their best, on a magic island. Mastick itself he discovered has been torn down and in its place is a modern building on the walls of which are cut "Truth, Culture, Wisdom"; "Health, Character, Citizenship," and "The Foundation of Every State is the Education of its Youth." What, he wondered, would Mrs. Blood make of that? The Christ Church that he knew was also gone, burnt down one foggy night by a woman who liked to set fires. 1625 Central Avenue has become a rooming house. As he gazed at it Lewis thought, rather pleased with himself, "Let the dead past bury its dead," but it isn't as easy as that. I see Wilmarth clattering down the front steps on his way to school, hunting for the money Ralph scattered on the lawn, climbing into the car beside his mother bound for the Sunday picnic. The past lives on, furtive, malign, beneficent, and won't stay buried.

Traveling alone without Annie Burr is a melancholy business for Lewis especially going to New York, which is now harder for him to get to than Washington. In New York he is increasingly conscious of the inane horn-blowing of taxis, the despairing whistles of doormen, the fire engines and ambulances wailing wildly in the night. Since it is impossible to get a cab at the Yale Club in the early evening he takes the Madison Avenue bus when he dines uptown. It is not crowded at that hour. As it grinds northward it acquires passengers bound for Harlem, nice-looking people who gaze at him and his dinner jacket politely but speculatively. He is, they conclude, headed for his dance orchestra and since he has no instrument he must be the pianist, possibly even the conductor. Safely at dinner on time, he enjoys himself very much and gets back to the Yale Club in a taxi, which at that hour and locality is always at hand. He hires a magic carpet for flights not made by commercial planes, but dreads airports with their vast distances and labyrinthine passages streaming with purposeful people pressing on to Gate 15 in the North Annex. He has learned how obliging the airlines can be when the airport he is flying to is closed by fog and the pilot announces that he is flying elsewhere. Lewis puts on the light over his seat, the stewardess comes, and he says, "Please ask the pilot to put me down at"—Santa Barbara, Wilmington, or whatever place is nearest to his destination—and the pilot does so if the airport is open. Although he has yet to fly to the wrong city, he came close to it recently in Washington when on climbing into the cabin and announcing "I am going to Hartford," the stewardess answered sweetly "An' *we're* goin' to Atl*an*ta."

Collecting preserves interest in living; Walpole's letters and books are received at Farmington as eagerly as ever. After forty-three years he continues to reveal new light on the eighteenth century and on himself, a man of infinite variety, entertainment, and instruction. These qualities are obvious to any reader; what is less obvious is his desire to make the world a better place to live in; although he was what today is called a liberal, anti-establishmentarians have always been blind to his merits because, as Byron explained, he was rich and highly placed. I am struck by passages that show discrimination and respect for character. The other night after reflecting on the virtue of moderation I read Walpole's eulogy of his father: "He could forever wage war with knaves and malice and preserve his temper; could know men, and yet feel for them; could smile when opposed, and be gentle after triumph. He was steady without being eager, and successful without being vain. He forgot the faults of others and his own merits; and was as incapable of fear as of doing wrong." If the bombs fall the Lewis Walpole Library will be destroyed (it is fatally near Hartford), but sets of the Edition will survive somehow in less vulnerable portions of the earth and will preserve the record of Walpole's life and of his time. The day this book is published, in the fall of 1967, will be the 250th anniversary of his birth (by the old-style calendar). There will be celebrations throughout Walpoleshire—bonfires and dancing on the green—and a *Festschrift* of essays on him will be presented to W. S. Lewis by his English and American friends. Walpole would be pleased, embarrassed, and not at all surprised by these tributes to his memory.

The Lewis Walpole Library and the Yale Edition of Horace Walpole's Correspondence are a satisfaction to me and I am glad to see various projects flourish at Yale and elsewhere that I started. I rejoice in the successes of the younger men whom I backed for positions of responsibility. To atone for this self-indulgence I think of my mistakes and merited disappointments, of why I had them, and of how I can perhaps avoid them in the future. For the past dozen years I have spent all my free time on *Horace Walpole's Library, Horace Walpole,* and the present book. Wilmarth's resolve to be a writer is in my mind now and I believe that my welfare in the rest of Senior Year depends on my adding another book or two to my slender bibliography.

I enjoy good writing more and more, no matter what its subject is, but I now have to mark passages that strike me and make an index to them on the flyleaves because I forget them. New (to me) upstairs authors keep appearing such as the New Testament Apocrypha, an ideal bedside book. It reveals the minds and passions of the early Christians about whom I had known nothing at all. The child Jesus' reproof of his teacher in the Gospel according to St. Thomas, "Thou that knowest not the Alpha, how canst thou teach the Beta?" shows the need for better teacher-training then as now. The Shepherd of Hermas offers a striking instance of courageous behavior in alarming circumstances. Hermas is counseled by a lady in "a great white chair of white wool," "Be manful, Hermas," and also, "Doubt nothing." This advice saved Hermas from a sea monster one hundred feet long with fiery locusts streaming from its mouth. Hermas advanced boldly upon the beast, which lay down and merely stuck out its tongue as he passed.

The Church Fathers furnish wonderful passages such as Tertullian's excursus on the resurrection of the dead: "Day dies into night and is everywhere buried in darkness. . . . And yet again it revives, with its own beauty, its own dowry, its own sun, the same as before, whole and unimpaired: slaying its own slayer, death, tearing open its own sepulchre, darkness, reappearing as heir to itself, until night also comes to life again, it too accompanied by its own retinue. For the rays of the stars which had been quenched by the light of morning are rekindled; the absent constellations, which time had removed from sight, are brought back to view; the mirrors of the moon, worn away by her monthly course, are restored to fullness. Winters and summers, springs and autumns, come back again, with their strength, their characteristics, their fruits. . . . All creation is in a state of renewal. Whatever you meet has existed before; whatever you have lost will return again. Everything comes a second time, all things begin when they have passed away, nothing perishes but that it may be recovered. All this revolving order of things is evidence of the resurrection of the dead." This is very beautiful, but surely there is something more, a postgraduate school in which one may advance to sublimities inconceivable on earth. I find belief in such a school more sustaining than the mawkish talk of "eternal rest," "peace at the last," and "little life rounded with a sleep," which endorses the total extinction accepted by atheists.

A man's education on earth, it seems to be agreed, is concerned primarily with his search for "the good life." It is easier to see the good life working in people than to say what it is. Those who have it are guided unassumingly by the copybook virtues of moderation, kindliness, and charity. They face tragic situations with dignity and courage; they are realistic, adaptable, and outgoing, by which I mean that they wish well to others and help when they can without parade or fuss. They give more than they receive, but don't worry about it. They haven't a trace of goody-goodiness; they usually have humor. They are the healthy who live by love.

We are more aware of the unhealthy because every day we read that the world is sick and that we are swirling faster and faster to catastrophe: there are too many people living thickly together in distrust and fear. Perhaps we are nearing the day when the heavens shall pass away with a great noise and the elements shall melt with fervent heat, but we are not there yet. Individuals can cure themselves of much sickness by a great effort and society in the mass is made up of individuals. If my education has taught me anything it is that while fear unchecked produces what it fears a man may overcome it when he will and invokes a strength beyond his own.

INDEX

INDEX

INDEX

INDEX

INDEX

INDEX

INDEX

INDEX

INDEX

INDEX

INDEX

INDEX

INDEX

A NOTE ON THE TYPE

The text of this book was set on the Linotype in a type face called Baskerville. The face is a facsimile reproduction of types cast from molds made for John Baskerville (1706–75) from his designs. The punches for the revised Linotype Baskerville were cut under the supervision of the English printer George W. Jones.

John Baskerville's original face was one of the forerunners of the type style known as "modern face" to printers—a "modern" of the period A.D. *1800.*

The book was composed, printed, and bound by Kingsport Press, Inc., Kingsport, Tennessee. The illustrations were printed by The Meriden Gravure Company, Meriden, Connecticut. Typography and binding design by Betty Anderson.

As the title of his book indicates, Wilmarth Sheldon Lewis regards education as a lifelong process. Although his formal education at school and at Yale during the years immediately surrounding the First World War had a decisive role in determining the course of his career, he has, as his autobiography reveals, acquired his most essential knowledge of the world from his encounters with people and from the introspective reflections these encounters often occasioned.

Mr. Lewis is perhaps best known to the scholarly world as the editor of Horace Walpole's correspondence and as the man who over the course of forty years has brought together, and handsomely installed in his home in Farmington, Connecticut, a unique collection of books and manuscripts relating to Walpole and his times—a collection of inestimable value to students of eighteenth-century literature and history. Naturally, the story of the origins and growth of this collection plays a prominent part in Mr. Lewis's own story. His travels in search of Walpole material have led him throughout England, across Europe, and as far afield as Australia; they have sent him from stately homes to dusty bookshops; and they have brought him into contact with a rich variety of people, about whom he writes with candor, wit, and perception.

Although it is inevitable that Mr. Lewis's name should be permanently linked with Walpole's, it will, with equal tenacity, be associated with Yale's. This association began during his undergraduate days (which he describes in affectionate and evocative detail) and has grown in depth over the years, during which he has served the university as a lecturer, trustee, and benefactor. His participation in the transformation of Yale has prompted his reflections on the needs and uses of university education, and these reflections are intimately related to his personal narrative.

One Man's Education is the autobiography of a very busy man, whose multifarious activities have enriched his inner life, while contributing to the cultural heritage of the scholarly world.

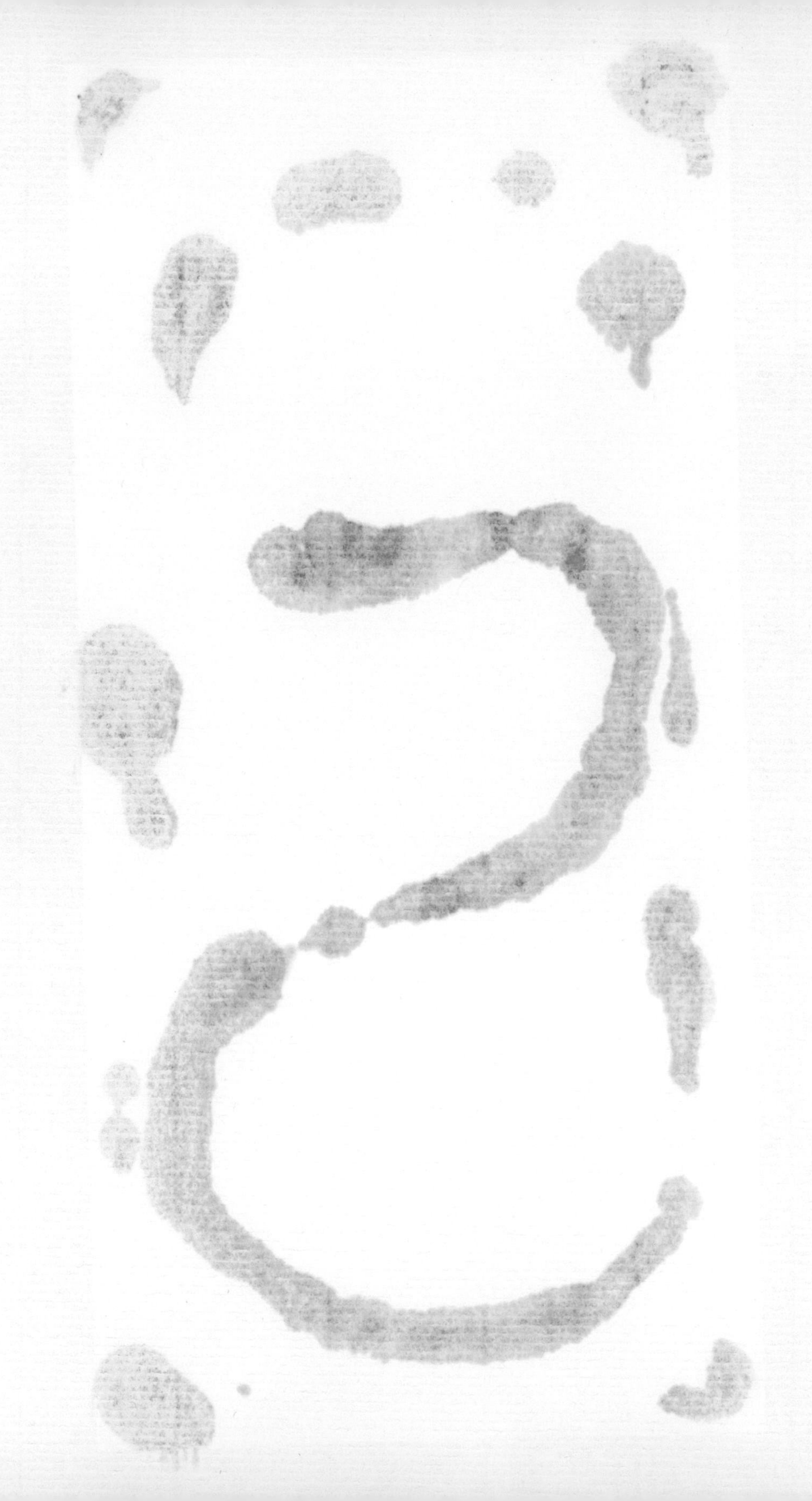

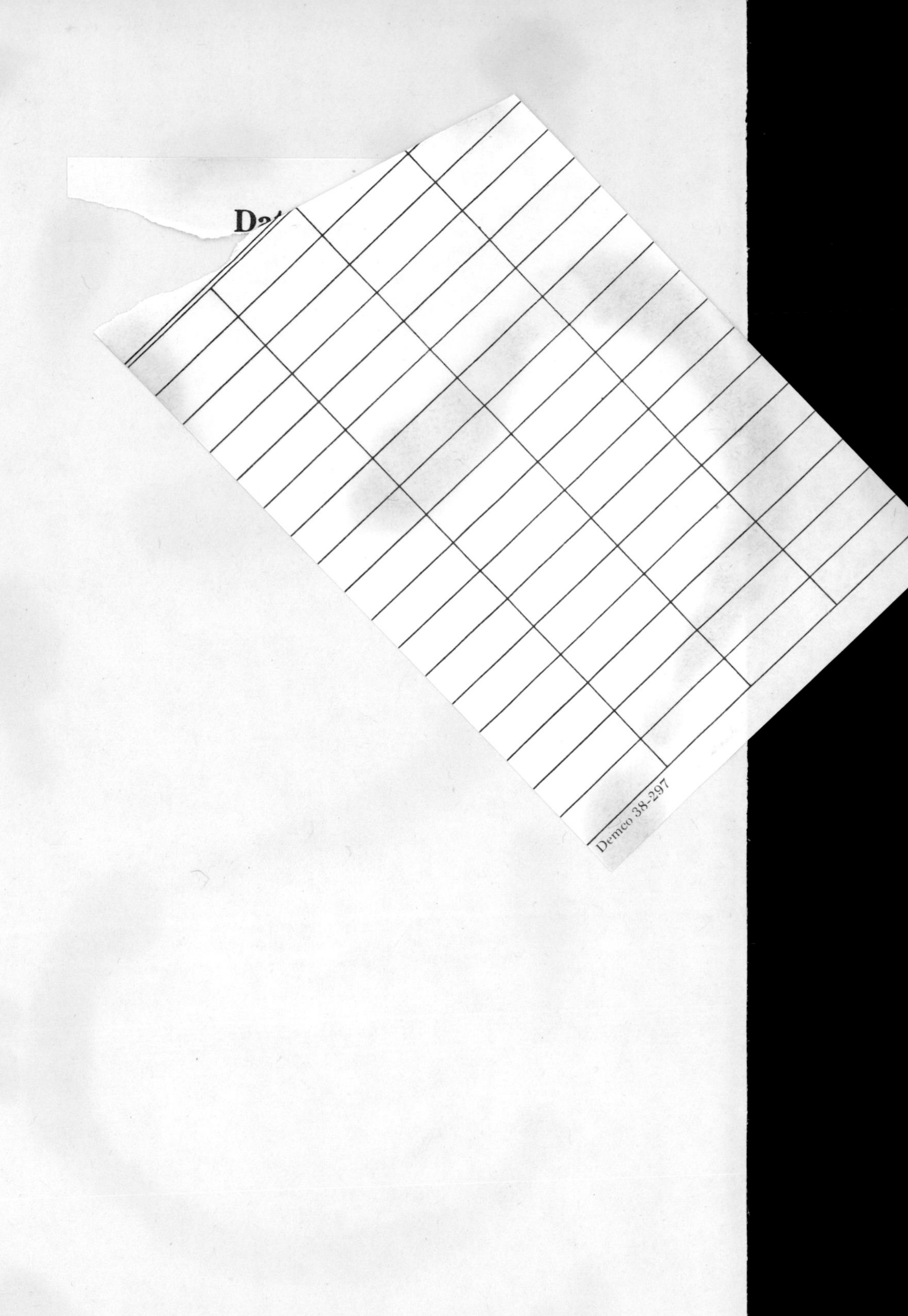
Demco 38-297